BLACK

TRANS

FEMINISM

BLACK OUTDOORS

INNOVATIONS IN THE

POETICS OF STUDY

A series edited by

J. Kameron Carter and

Sarah Jane Cervenak

BLACK TRANS FEMINISM

MARQUIS BEY

DUKE UNIVERSITY PRESS   *Durham and London*   2022

Project editor: Lisa Lawley
Designed by Matthew Tauch
Typeset in Arno Pro and Saira SemiCondensed by
Westchester Publishing Services

Library of Congress Cataloging-in-Publication Data
Names: Bey, Marquis, author.
Title: Black trans feminism / Marquis Bey.
Other titles: Black outdoors.
Description: Durham : Duke University Press, 2022. | Series: Black
outdoors: innovations in the poetics of study | Includes bibliographical
references and index.
Identifiers: LCCN 2021015695 (print)
LCCN 2021015696 (ebook)
ISBN 9781478015178 (hardcover)
ISBN 9781478017813 (paperback)
ISBN 9781478022428 (ebook)
Subjects: LCSH: Feminism—United States. | Blacks—Race identity. |
Gender identity. | African American feminists—History. | Queer
theory. | BISAC: SOCIAL SCIENCE / LGBTQ Studies / Transgender
Studies | SOCIAL SCIENCE / Feminism & Feminist Theory
Classification: LCC HQ1410 .B49 2022 (print) | LCC HQ1410 (ebook) |
DDC 305.4201—dc23
LC record available at https://lccn.loc.gov/2021015695
LC ebook record available at https://lccn.loc.gov/2021015696

Cover art: Morel Doucet, *Red Hot (Under the Sun Black Girl's
Dreams)*, 2020. Acrylic on paper, mylar, aerosol paint, and
indigenous flora and fauna. 22 × 30 in. Image courtesy of the
artist and Galerie Myrtis.

For those we don't know yet

Contents

Acknowledgments

If I were being honest, I wouldn't call this section the "Acknowledgments." The word seems to imply a kind of nod from the person who did most of the heavy lifting; it implies, on one reading, that I did the bulk of the work, whereas all these other folks were peripheral and "minor characters." But this isn't entirely true, as some of the people I will mention did an inordinate amount of work for this book, for my thinking, for my very ability to write it. So, instead I might call this section an account of my collaborators, my coproducers, my coconspirators, my accomplices.

The late and nothing less than great Toni Morrison, to whom I must express an immense gratitude for her sheer intellectual force, made a crucial distinction by which I, no pun intended, live. She noted that "there's a difference between writing for a living and writing for life." The former is a profession, a thing one does in order to reap financial rewards or notable symbols of status. This is a distinction, not a dis, to be sure. The latter is what one does in order, quite simply, to ensure the maintenance and proliferation of life and livability. To write for life is what you must pen so that the things you've been thinking have a place to rattle around and make inroads outside of your head; to write for life is what you must get out so that those like you or unlike you or not even considered "those" yet might be able to engage the world on terms not of this world, terms that would be, finally, ethical. This book, *Black Trans Feminism*, is what I have written—along with my collaborators—for life.

I thank, then, all those who conspired with me in these thoughts, all those who contributed to the life force, as it were, of this book.

I must thank those who have thought alongside me, pressing and critiquing me, being pressed on and critiqued by me in turn. Danny, my beloved Sisyphean comrade, sharing in imaginative and concerted happiness with me since 2010 Concepts of Mathematics, front row of class, eye-rolling the professor: you, my friend, have been invaluable, truly. I need you to know that our dialogues are fundamental to how I move in this world, how I move among things. I hear your voice coaxing me at times to think more expansively, more broadly, more honestly and lovingly, more rigorously. We have traveled different yet strikingly similar paths, and with you I am always emboldened to—as this entire book is birthed through, essentially—think devilishly.

I need to thank Jess Goldberg, too. We met before I even got to Cornell, your email response to my timid and inquisitive senior-undergrad-just-accepted-into-Cornell's-PhD-program request was my very first experience of the department. And now look at us, editing special issues of journals together, thinking aloud on panels together, discussing the finer points of anime. You have long been a friend and a comrade and an intellectual sparring partner, and for that I am unyieldingly grateful. It is a rare friendship, one predicated on love and understanding and the encouragement of radicality and, too, accountability. I remember telling you that it feels like we don't even need to say anything to each other half the time because the knowledge is already known between us. I still feel that. And it is an interpersonal gift for which I am so thankful.

I need to thank, too, Biko Mandela Gray, whose Heideggerian and religiophilosophical mind has given me chills; Dagmawi Woubshet, who spent hours reading the progression and deepening of my thought, always encouraging me to read more deeply and sustainedly; C. Riley Snorton, who, my god, has gifted me with the wisdom to take thoughts as deeply as they'll go, to engage ideas as seriously as I can, to have in my mind always a soundtrack of sorts that I might open myself up to adding lines and verses to based on unexpected experiences, and to dwell in black and trans thought; La Marr Jurelle Bruce, whose hours-long phone conversations over the years have been so rich with tea, rigorous thought, and grace that I don't know how I managed to finish grad school without our dialogues; Eula Biss and our lovely writerly conversations, our genuinely touching and deep thinkings-together about how we might use language to engender the world we wish to see; Treva Ellison and their impeccable mind and radical black and trans politicality; Josh Chambers-Letson, who has been so kind to me with his time, so generous to me with his candor about the profession and students and scholarship; and Sophie Lewis and her stunning intellect, fierce radicality and commitment to abolition, and all-around generously biting and bitingly generous spirit.

And also Sarah, who may be relatively new to my life but has had such a dynamic impact, the kind of impact only an inveterate and sustained love of infusing a radical queerness into life can have. The thoughts herein were exercised and exorcised with you, over three thousand miles of outstretched roads through the Midwest and Pacific Northwest, over breakfast at our dining room table, in bed when we were unable to sleep, on walks with that banana-loving, snarfy monster of a dog. Sarah, you have my thanks because you listen yet you push me, you care and proffer invaluable knowledge and wisdom, not to mention fearlessly cultivate space to be wrong, to be gloriously right, to be not-quite-there-yet. And we, both of us, revel in that space, loving intensely in it and forging something epic within it. Not to mention you sat and listened, patiently and lovingly, to me read the long-ass footnote, and I'd known you, what, like a week and a half? Now that's love, and I am, truly, thankful.

I must thank my current and former colleagues, too, for they, in so many unique and vital ways, have cared for me. They have cared for my mind and academic work, for sure, but also, no less important, they have cared for my physical well-being, my understanding of departmental and environmental histories and exigencies, my comfort, my time. So, thank you immensely, Martha Biondi, Nitasha Sharma, E. Patrick Johnson, Alex Weheliye, Tracy Vaugh-Manley, Nikki Spigner, Sherwin Bryant, John D. Marquez, Barnor Hesse, Celeste Watkins-Hayes, Lauren Michele Jackson, Justin Mann, Kelly Wisecup, Nick Davis, Chris Harris, Tristram Wolff, kihana miraya ross, Mary Pattillo, Michelle Huang, Julia Stern, and Jennifer Nash (Jen, you have no idea how meaningful your very aura has been to me, how deeply cared for and held I feel when we talk). And no doubt I can't forget in this Seth Bernstein and Suzette Denose, both of whose tireless efforts, meticulous institutional knowledge, and generosity make academic life quite pleasant.

My Cornellians! Or at least those of you whom I met at and may still, at the time of this publication, be at Cornell. So many thanks to my "Bey Club" (not the name I chose; the credit for that belongs to Cat): Raven, Cat, Lexi, Barr, Matija, Emmy, Emma, Aaliyah, Kyra, and Valery. Many thanks also to those grad students who chatted and vented and shared space with me during those complexly rich five years: Ama Bemma Adwetewa-Badu, Mint Damrongpiwat, Stephen Kim, Becky Lu, Zach Price, Alec Pollak, Maddie

Reynolds, Jessica Rodriguez, Kevin Quinn, Amaris Brown, Gabriella Friedman, Gary Slack, Chris Berardino, Brianna Thompson, Matt Kilbane, Kristen Angierski, Mariana Alarcon, Liz Alexander. And I could never forget those who came into my life via unexpected and impromptu means: Andrew Cutrone, one of the brightest and most passionate young minds I've encountered in a while; Josh Bennett, who has been a peer and friend since way back in my senior year of undergrad, our initial meeting and conversation about Richard Wright and Basquiat morphing into phone conversations about black life as I drive from Chicago to NY; Tyrone Palmer, our friendship flourishing over that long weekend at my apartment during the Spillers symposium, a friendship that endures genuinely even with our disagreements on the ontological state of blackness; Marcella, so graceful and kind and compassionate, my dear friend and French tutor, whose intellect is one wrapped in a kind of eclectic inconspicuousness; and Jelliott, Jelliott, Jelliott, who is, as I and Sarah realized, pretty much the same person as I am, though we should be dramatically different people—you, Jelliott, you're a good one, a smart one, one who has not yet realized the level of your radicality (but you will, I will make sure of it). I really, truly look forward to a lifetime of vibing together, making obscure *South Park* and *Half Baked* and *Trailer Park Boys* references (Randy!), and shaping, with love and care and probably hundreds of dollars, our decks for *Magic: The Gathering*.

All of my students deserve thanks as well. In and outside of class, you all push my thinking and make me engage ideas in more honest ways. I want to express special thanks to Leilani and Jack, for without you two being open to sharing your thoughts on my thoughts, and your thoughts on the various ideas swirling around there, I could not have written what I have written in the same way. And, to Mustafa, I swear I wrote the things in this book before our independent study, where you expressed, like, 90 percent of the things written here. You may not know this, but you've also taught me, which sounds super clichéd, I know. But your willingness to take radicality seriously, to really, deeply commit to insurgent trans thought, has in fact allowed me to feel more confident about this book. And that means something to me.

And how could I not thank this book's series editors, J. Kameron Carter and Sarah Jane Cervenak, not only for the dope platform of the Black Outdoors series but also for their amazing scholarship, both solo and collaborative. Your work, Jay and Sarah, continues to inspire and challenge and excite me. Both of your spirits are life-giving. Jay, I remember when we first met, way back in late 2013, and I thought you were the coolest academic around (and still think that). Your intellectual acumen shone radiantly both via video chat with the Race and Religion class and your mic-dropping talk the subsequent semester. And Sarah, your attention to the quotidian and interstices of life always compel me to tinker with thought in the world. And your Twitter presence and scenic photos are so, so refreshing.

And I also feel absolutely compelled to thank the anonymous readers at Duke University Press. After my editor, the always-amazing Ken Wissoker, sent me the reviewers' comments late one evening, I chose not to read them right then because I knew they would likely affect my sleep that night. The following morning, before reading the email containing the reviews, I was fearful—what if they want me to change things I really like, or what if they don't think it's very good, or maybe I'm going to have to rewrite it in a way that I ultimately won't like? But reading their comments made me feel so loved and so seen. I am an anxious person, socially and intellectually, so I feared that kind of visibility. But the readers cared for my writing and my thoughts like no one ever has; they loved my writing by praising it and gently, compassionately pushing it to be better. I lie to you not, I started crying when I got halfway through. It was just so magnificent to finally have someone read the entirety of my thinking and not only not run for the hills but actually say, as one reviewer said, that it's exciting and "is achingly needed in the fields it addresses." With as much gratitude as possible, I say thank you.

This book has also benefited from key research grants for which I am incredibly thankful—namely, the Ford Foundation Dissertation Fellowship, Cornell's Truman Capote PhD Writer's Award, and Northwestern University's Provost Faculty Grant for Research in Humanities, Social Sciences, and the Arts.

Thank you to the interlocutors of the ideas in this book that were presented at conferences and keynotes and symposia. Those who engaged this work, in whatever way—be it via questions or silent meditation or written engagement in private or public or not-yet-public work—at the following occasions are, too, part of the collaborative effort: the 2018 TRANS(form)ing Queer: Queer Studies Symposium and National Women's Studies Association: (Il)Legible Bodies and (Im)Possible Transitions to a Fuller Trans Politic panel; the 2019 American Studies Association: Sex and Gender as Racial Projects Roundtable on Feminist, Queer, and Trans Theories, Berea College's day-long invitational talk and class sit-ins courtesy of the always-brilliant black feminist thinker M. Shadee Malaklou; the Salon and Social attendees at Northwestern University, courtesy of the efforts of kihana miraya ross; and the American Philosophical Association's political theology conference panel attendees and interlocutors (thanks to the kind organizing efforts of Roberto Sirvent, who is a phenomenal friend and the greatest academic hype person ever), the UC Berkeley guest symposium speaker series on Keywords in Trans Methods, courtesy of the amazing Grace Lavery.

It seems that there are always others who need to be thanked, even if at times they don't believe they should be. But their "minimal" contributions are still, nonetheless, contributions I wish to note. So for those contributions that span a brief phone conversation or a passing phrase or an unrelated chat, I have to thank my uncle Junior, whose twenty-plus-year incarceration has affected me in indelible ways, ways that have seeped into this manuscript; my mom and grandma and brother and sister, for they all, in their own ways, sustain me; Tommy, my goon brother, over there in Auburn "~~Correctional~~" (because prisons ain't correcting nothing) putting in work and expanding his thinking with respect to blackness and especially feminism and transness; and Jeremiah Barker, Jordan Mulkey, Candice Merritt, and Jared Rodriguez for their insightful intellects.

Lastly, I ask you, reader, to consider the bibliography of this book a list of everyone else who has been integral to my thinking. That bibliography holds those whose work has spoken to me so much that I had to engage it in some way in this text, the piece of writing that means the most to me to date. I thank each and every one of those people, too, whether I love everything they have to say or think they need to go sit down somewhere.

Abolition, Gender Radicality

GUIDE QUOTES (AFTER SYLVIA WYNTER)

While, as Fanon asserts, there is an imposition onto the figure of the black that would signify the confluence of racial identity and racial inferiority, there is also, in a way that is prior to the regulative force of that imposition and calls it into question, a resource working through the epidermalization of afantasmatic inferiority as the anti-epidermalization of the radical alternative, to which the peoples who are called black have a kind of (under)privileged relation in and as the very history of that imposition. One might speak, then, of the blackening of the common, which would imply neither that any and every person who is called black claims or defends the sociopoetic force of that fantasy nor that persons who are not called black are disqualified from making such claims and enacting such defense.

FRED MOTEN, *The Universal Machine*

If feminism is, at its core, about combating the dangerously unfair ways that power and oppression, recognition and repudiation, are distributed to individuals based on how their bodies are categorized, trans concerns lie at the heart of feminism.

LAURA HORAK, "Trans Studies"

The black feminist position as trouble. . . . It refuses to disappear into the general categories of otherness or objecthood, that is, blackness and womanhood, and refuses to comply with the formulations of racial and gender-sexual emancipatory projects these categories guide.

DENISE FERREIRA DA SILVA, "Hacking the Subject: Black Feminism and Refusal Beyond the Limits of Critique"

Feminism will be trans-feminist or not at all.

THE WHOREDYKEBLACKTRANSFEMINIST NETWORK, "Manifesto for the Trans-Feminist Insurrection"

The future(s) of blackness move(s) us to name the ways in which refusal to sequester, to quarantine black from black, is inherent to blackness itself.

AMEY VICTORIA ADKINS-JONES, "Black/Feminist Futures: Reading Beauvoir in *Black Skin, White Masks*"

But I need to make a distinction between black women, black women as the subject of feminism, and black feminism as a critical disposition. . . . I should like to think that black feminism, as a repertoire of concepts, practices, and alignments, is progressive in outlook and dedicated to the view that sustainable life systems must be available to everyone.

HORTENSE SPILLERS, "The Scholarly Journey of Hortense Spillers"

From the Combahee River Collective (a collective of Black feminists meeting since 1974) and its critique of biological essentialism as a "dangerous and reactionary basis upon which to build a politic" to trans genealogies of Black feminism—*Black feminism* [*i*]*s always already trans.*

CHE GOSSETT, "Žižek's Trans/gender Trouble"

Transgender is the gender trouble that feminism has been talking about all along.

JACK HALBERSTAM, "Why We Need Transfeminism"

Black. Trans. Feminism. Or black (trans feminism), (black) trans (feminism), and (black trans) feminism. Where blackness is concerned, there is the refusal of sequestration, which is to say both a refusal to be set aside and isolated, as it is itself a sociality that demands relations of myriad natures; and, too, a refusal to limit this work to epidermalized demographics, dispersing its penchant for politicized subversion to all of those taking up the task. As mutinous relation to imposed ontology, blackness enables and conditions the inhabited spirit of subjective abolition. Transness, always shadowed by its echolalic blackness, as this book will demonstrate, unfixes gender from essentialist moorings and posits itself precisely as that unfixation, as a departure-from without the presumption of a stable destination, or indeed a departure that itself destabilizes destinational desires. This transness is endemic to a genealogy that has at its foundation the fundamental critique of the capaciousness of "man" (or "Man") and "woman," and as such the critique of the regulative regime of normative gender and categorization. Feminism, which is to say trans feminism—which is, more, to say black feminism—is an agential and intentional undoing of regulative gender norms and, further, the creative deconstructing of ontological racial and gender assault; a kind of gendered deconstruction, an unraveling that unstitches governant means of subjectivation; feminism as the reiterative un/gendered quotidian process of how not to be governed and given from without.[1] That is, feminism marks here the vitiation of imposed racial and gender ontologies that then demands an abolitionist modality of encountering the racialized gendered world.

What you hold in your hands is not another treatise on how we might righteously rail against harms done to an already-known "us"; it is not a meditation on the violences done to black or trans or femme "bodies," nor is it one concerned, in the main, with flipping the valuation of maligned identities (e.g., the practice of lambasting white folks as the pinnacle of loving and doing black radical work, or the extent to which one points out the oversights of white [feminist] cis women as the extent to which one is a hardcore black feminist). I am quite uninterested in talking solely about bodies and about what we already (think we) know. Indeed, our bodies cannot and must not be coveted in the final instance. For sure, it has come to be the site that suffers oppressive forces because that is precisely how oppressive forces wish to construct our subjectivities—to form to them and understand themselves as formed, in toto, by them. What we have come to name our bodies, though, is not the only way we can or should think ourselves possible in the world. Our subjectivity—my preferred, though still imperfect, term—indexes the amalgam of the various ways that we engage sociality, an engagement that is not determined wholly by or confined to the surface of corporeality. And if aspects of the body have come to be that which are formed by violent forces, it is necessary to find liberation in the aspects that are not confined to the body; it is necessary to find liberation in the aspects of subjectivity that exceed and ooze out of the body. And this ooze, this uncaught-ness, is variously inflected and named, at least in part, by the black, the trans, and the feminist.

Additionally, this facilitates the dissolution of the things we may have come to regard as quite dear—namely, our given, and even reclaimed, identities. It has come to a point, it seems to me, where many of us have crafted as virtuous the mere fact of holding steadfast to the historically maligned identities we hold. Many of us have come to doubling down on racial identification, or gender identification and expression, on the grounds that such identities have historically (and contemporarily) been expunged from the province of positive valuation. There is little efficacy in clutching the purported fact (which is not a fact, unmediated and transparent) that one is right or righteous or unceasingly wise because they do not hold in contempt their racialized blackness or their cis womanhood, for instance, categories that have been and are marginalized. That is not what this all is about. These identities are at base hegemonic bestowals and will thus have diminished liberatory import in the final analysis; indeed, we cannot get to the final analysis—which I offer as an abolitionist analysis—with these identities if such an abolitionist terrain is given definition by way of the instantiation of the impossibility of violence and captivity. Black trans feminism cannot abide such classificatory violences, so it urges us also to abolish the categories we may love, even if they have not always been received well. If the aim of the radical project of black trans feminism is abolition and gender radicality, which is the case I will be making, it is imperative to grapple with what that actually means. We cannot half-ass abolition, holding on to some of the things we didn't think we would be called to task for giving up. If we want freedom, we need to free ourselves, too, of the things with which we capture ourselves. The project at hand is interested in a thoroughgoing conception of freeness, and it seems like black trans feminism, to call on Saidiya Hartman, "makes everyone freer than they actually want to be."[2] When the white woman or the black trans person or the queer-identified person comes at such a project with their indignation about me, us, black trans feminism, trying to take away the very things that they've worked so hard to achieve, we are surely to meet them with a certain level of kindness as an ethical attentiveness to how such trauma has been felt and the joys of mitigating, in whatever way, those traumas. But, and I mean this, we are not to capitulate to a sort-of abolished world because some people who may look like us or the people who have been forged in oppression are pleading to us. We still, even when Grandma doesn't (think she) want(s) it, work to abolish the world. That is what black trans feminism, as an orientation toward radical freedom, commits to. And that will not be easy, nor will it feel good in the ways we expect.

All of this converges into what will concern this text: black trans feminism. Black trans feminism names this convergence and grapples with the tense and conflicting legacies that inhere in its nominative permutations of black trans, black feminism, and trans feminism. The aim, then, is to mine each of these for how they contribute to the culmination of black trans feminism as a modality of worldly inhabitation, an agential and performative posture in and after this world. In this way, black trans feminism theorizes power, and, more important, the subversion of it, in excess of wholesale notions of immediately discernible "identities." Maintained, then, is how commitment to nonnormativity—where normativity is understood necessarily as "the *terror* of the normative," of which black (trans) feminism is disruptive and interrogative—is also concerned with an impossible desire for being held.[3] While captivity connotes violent grips confining our flourishing, perhaps in thinking of a movement away from captivity that is not toward but facilitated in its movement by an embrace—perhaps an impossible embrace without arms, an embrace without being bounded, a bear hug by arms that never close—we gain a different understanding of that toward which we aspire. The work of black trans feminism is always an aim for the *creative* dimension of abolition and the worlds that arise because of the undermined hegemonic categories. Indeed, we are various shades of brokenness and lack, and I wish not to venerate this plight. We need to be healed and do not wish to remain writhing in our broken pieces. We need, in other words, to be held. But what I wish for, what black trans feminism might wish for, is the reconfiguration of how we hold each other without stopping, without *with*holding, all while we are on the run.

I want to wager that this holding and being held without withholding is how one might be able to find footing on what is ultimately no ground. We cannot import some of the violent things into the world we are trying to create and cultivate in the rubble of the old, in the same form, for we would belie the world we are creating. The urge to do that comes from wanting desperately to have a place; it comes from a desire promoted by a fear of loss. But, as Claudia Tate has put it, "while desire is constitutive of a loss, desire also generates by-products even as it makes that deficiency conspicuous."[4] Desire makes things, it makes something else, it *invents*. There is thus a different image of the world after the world I wish to posit because I wish to take the scariness seriously. So, abolition urges for the eradication of every and all violent holdovers. It is possible, though, that, even on groundlessness, even in a wholly other world, we can be held insofar as we are embraced by that which does not know us and, in this unknowing, truly loves and caresses us. Think: we might become anything at all, something wildly other than what we are, and in order to give in to that we need to be encountered by a world that really, actually, truly holds and loves us by never, ever presuming to know what shape we will take, what we will want, before we show up. We need to feel held, and we will be held when we are not known from the start—the world we inhabit after and amid abolition and gender radicality doesn't know a damn thing about us, and it smiles at such a fact, because when it finds out, it will know that we emerged from no coercion and no violence, no impositions. And then we can begin another kind of living.

There is, thus, a fundamental commitment to life and livability, and to modes of life that will not look like "Life" precisely because of their dazzlingly abolitionist dwelling in the generative rubble after the oft-mentioned end of the world. As such, black trans feminism is given over as a loving but appositional shimmying away from the constantly repeated rhetorical move "Violence against women, *especially trans women*; violence against trans women, *especially trans women of color* or *especially black trans women*." The move is understandable, and, please, keep making that gesture when it is appropriate as a way to highlight the populations onto which violation is disproportionately imposed—because we know transantagonism is very much about the targeting of poor black trans women and trans women of color. I proffer a caution, though, in service of an attempted refutation of the assumption embedded in the italicized subclauses, an assumption that the subclause *is* black trans feminism, that one's black trans feminism is encapsulated by a pointing to the violated lives (and deaths) of black trans women. This to me troublingly only allows (black) trans femme subjectivity to emerge through violence. Black trans feminism as articulated in this book is a love letter, a box of chocolates, a warm hug, a place to sleep after a hot meal, a "They got problems with you, you come get me" for those who live in excess of that purportedly unlivable nexus and those hailed by those analytic nominatives—and, further, for those whose subjectivities are such that the world cannot yet accommodate them.

Black Trans Feminism's overall intent is to intervene in two primary discourses: first, a general identitarian discourse—which, to be sure, is not to be haphazardly denigrated as an unthinking "mob" mentality—that considers blackness, transness, and feminism to be possessed identities from which politics emerge (i.e., "I *am* black," "I *am* trans," "I *am* a feminist"). My aim is to think about how we might rally around subversive politics, which then serve as one's identity as such—Cathy Cohen's political identities, or what Judith Butler calls thinking in alliance. I wish to deem the corporeal surface as only one node of blackness, transness, and womanness, and the taking of such theorizations seriously will necessitate radically undoing what we have come to hold very dear. A subjectless critique, the broader argument of this book refuses to posit *a* or *the* subject of black trans feminism, rejecting a "proper" object of both study and knowledge production in service of an "eccentricity," to take language from Teresa de Lauretis. It is a black trans feminism that does not coincide with the amalgam of black and/or trans and/or women subjects, assuming that the being of these historicized demographics intends a certain relation to power and normativity and worldly inhabitation, but, instead, a black trans feminism that "arises as a force of displacement, as a practice for the transformation of subjectivity," a methodology in conversational politicality with Nahum Chandler's desedimentary, originary displacement and paraontological Negro problematic that is also, I would argue (and have argued), a gender problematic.[5]

The second discourse in which I am intervening is that which surrounds intersectionalist feminisms, or social justice work done through an intersectionalist frame. Oftentimes this discourse takes the identities that make up the various titular intersections to be givens, needing no critique or, even more treacherously, abandonment. While it is certainly a valiant and useful type of political work to reckon with how one's race *and* gender, for example, bear on their situatedness in relation to institutions, history, and discourses, there is much to be wanted that black trans feminism seeks to examine. I maintain, in alignment with another loving critic of aspects of how intersectionality is deployed, that "intersectional identities are the byproducts of attempts to still and quell the perpetual motion of assemblages, to capture and reduce them, to harness their threatening mobility," a mobility to which I wish to give primacy as the constituent force of black trans feminism.[6] In other words, what could be missing in intersectional feminisms is an attention to what is happening on the sidewalks along the road, the sewers underground, the skyscrapers up above; or what it sounds like out there, how hot it is outside, what snoozed alarm made the person late for work and in need of going fifteen miles per hour over the speed limit in the first place. Black trans feminism desires an attention to these things as well, and ultimately the possibilities for reconfiguring what streets can look like, what kind of vehicles we use, and how the traffic patterns move in tandem with the pulse of the city.

Inevitably, in all of this, one wonders about the role and status of the body. While blackness, transness, and feminism are not entirely extricated from the body—it remains that the processes of materialization known as race and gender shape how we experience (what we come to understand as) our bodies—there is still an insistence here, first, on their fundamental distinction from being confined to corporeality. On this score, *Black Trans Feminism* makes a twofold argument: first, that matter and materiality are not to be equated with mere being, a transparent and unmediated facticity of "the body." I am critical of an understanding of the material body as an unmitigated bearer and disseminator of truth, as if matter cannot be and has not been touched, as it were. The matter that makes up black and transgender and women's subjectivities is in fact a regulatory ideal that has been made to congeal into a certain look, a look that inevitably excludes other looks for what might validly be considered black or transgender or woman. We come to know what a "proper" one of these subjects looks like by way, unbeknownst (or willfully ignored, when it gets down to it) to many, of highly regulated parameters that I am in the business of deconstructing. It is precisely those regimes of regulation that, while they give us the shape and feel of marginalized identities held dear, are the culprits of various normativities inherent to which are violent hegemonies. Regulatory norms create the obviousness of the "fact" of such and such a body as black or transgender or woman through a forcible, which is to say coerced, reiteration of tenets of what is said to be possible for one to be. Because black trans feminism seeks to destroy such coercion, violences, normativities, and hubristic assumptions, it is necessary to express a critical eye toward a simplistic formulation of materiality that fails to consider its highly regulated grounding. It is thus my contention that if such grounding were dutifully critiqued it would yield the necessity for an abandonment of how "matter" and materiality are commonly understood in favor of a joyous disposition toward the tinkering and playing with how materialization has and can occur differently. There is an ongoing agency to materiality, thus processes of materialization, what we come to understand as matter, are glimpsed in the transness and transing of matter.

The second component of the twofold argument is that "race" and "gender" are necessarily different from this book's constitutive terms, which cannot be located on or in, strictly speaking, the body. That is, the constituent terms of this book's title cannot be said to be "simply" names for race and gender (or a disposition gotten to by a specific gender identification [e.g., "woman"]), nor can they be "found" on or in the body in some legible and transparent way. So, while we indeed feel various oppressions in a visceral way, I want to make the claim that it is not because of our immediate access to a material body that is acted upon by external forces, subsequently translating those feelings to a "self" that has perfect communication with that body. The body, too, or what we have come to understand as our body, is subject to epistemic scrutiny; it is not privy to unmediated knowledge or our unproblematic possession. We feel oppressions by virtue of those oppressions giving to us a subjective shape that houses that oppression, is formed in the image of that oppression. The various ways we come to be confined and disciplined, which is to say the form and texture of our bodies, does not preexist ontologizing forces—whether benign or malevolent—but is coeval with them.

In short, the construction that is "the body," which is never as simple as the definite article implies, since other identificatory vectors always complicate its definitiveness, *becomes* largely through hegemonic structures that trek along on axes of epistemology, ontology, ocularcentrism, and neuronormativity, all of which is to shorthand what we might recognize as the project of Western civilization. These are territorializing projects—colonial and imperialist projects, if you will—that must be subverted even if they are the visceral bases of our comfort. Indeed, black women and femmes along the jagged orbit that meanders around cis and trans have long taken their imposed corporealized ontologies as indicative of a system with instabilities and fractures that they were made to bear the weight of and thus are poised to deploy those fracturative forces against the system itself.[7]

I want to commit to the argument that neither blackness nor transness, nor the implicit "woman" as the subject of feminism, is tied to a specific kind of body or identity. They are, to me, inflections of mutinous subjectivities that have been captured and consolidated into bodily legibilities. With this, however, it is ethically necessary for me to say something about the lives of those who live life as black and/or trans and/or women and to dwell on something perhaps idiosyncratic about these identities *as* identities (ethically necessary because of my own identificatory positionality, which reads a certain way but is, I wholeheartedly submit, inaccurate [curious minds will want to read this endnote]).[8] Thus, I choose not to recapitulate the worn discourse of "lived experience" that I speak to a bit more in chapter 2 but to advance the much more complex and rich notion of "opacity." Given its most fleshed-out articulation by Édouard Glissant, opacity denotes a departure from the Western imperative of transparency, inherent to which is a reduction. In other words, to be transparent and thus legible to the predominating schema of intelligibility one must always have the breadth of their subjectivity reduced, distilled. One's differences that may fall outside of scripts of possibility (e.g., gender nonbinariness) must be captured by the norm, linked to it in some way, which deprives the difference of something "essential" to it. Glissant offers opacity to combat this "enclosure within an impenetrable autarchy."[9] Opacity refuses reduction and perfunctory transparency and preserves the singularity of those who are so often coerced into making themselves digestible. Opacity also allows for a kind of quiet (or loud) claim to something unable and unwilling to be given to others. Such a privacy is ethically important because of its potential for something like solace amid regimes of violence. I am conceding the fact of opacity for those who live through the identificatory markers of blackness, transness, and womanness because it may very well be one of the few things keeping them alive. And I am committed to nothing if I am not committed to life.

But there is more to be said of opacity as it relates to my concerns. Opacity is more robustly a tactical evasion that eludes medicalized, biometric, and regulatory frameworks of "knowing" a subject. Marginalized and oppressed subjects like those indexed by the titular terms of this book can retain the specificities of their positions as differentially subject to the aforementioned regulatory regimes. And this is what I must hold on to, though the "unfixation" I delineate in a later section of this introduction must still be foregrounded. To do this, I urge readers to understand opacity as a vehicle precisely for the eradication of those differentiations that are, at base, violences structured and created by forces of hegemony. To be understood as categorically black or trans or woman is, fundamentally, an identity imposed—a "given ontology"—that, ultimately, in the world after the end of the world, must be discarded because of its link to being forged in the cauldron of an originary violence.[10] Opacity in my usage argues that one's situatedness is important in that it provides access to the mechanisms of power that have created the conditions for ontologized accidents (e.g., epidermal blackness, nonnormative gendered physicality) to be denigrated and expunged from the province of social validity. There is a way that being forced to hold this denigration on what gets consolidated as a kind of body that approximates but does not measure up to the human ideal in some way is crucial to note, as bearing the viscera is a different kind of knowledge that some do not have access to. *But opacity does not end here*, and certainly not in the way that proponents of an unceasing and uncritical valorization of lived experience as the pinnacle of epistemic argumentation put forward. Opacity concedes this experiential specificity as radically inclusive, which is to say that it is specific to certain kinds of bodies but it provides knowledge and world-making onto-epistemic forces that can be mobilized by any and every body and nonbody. Immediately following Glissant's mention of the impenetrable autarchy, he goes on to say that "opacities can coexist and converge, weaving fabrics." This is to say, one's experiential blackness or transgender identity is and can be opaque to nonblack and nontrans people, indeed; it says, simultaneously, however, that the knowledge and itch for otherwise ways of living gleaned from being positioned as such is not parochial and is in fact weavable, convergent, coexistent with everyone else.

Furthermore, this is to say that opacity is not static. One is not simply to be black or trans or woman, being opaque to those who are not black/trans/women, which is then the end of the story. Opacities shift and move depending on how various identities get positioned in a given context and also, perhaps more importantly, how identities get deployed in order to create opaque pockets that become impenetrable to power (or, if penetrated, how that probe may enter but not come out, to creatively remix Zora Neale Hurston).[11] We come to understand that opacities are *created*, not simply given or possessed ontologically, so the shifting of opacity is predicated ultimately on how we create zones of opacities. And that is what I mean by political identities.

UNFIXATION

I maintain as axiomatic that, as Nat Raha has clearly argued, a radical feminism must center the needs, experiences, and material concerns of trans women, trans femmes, and nonbinary femmes. Any black/trans/feminist worldview is undeserving of the name if it is not grounded by the various epistemic forms proffered by the aforementioned demographics. Too, though, I want to maintain this while simultaneously maintaining the unfixation of transness—and blackness and feminism, and their factorial proliferations—from the sole terrain and ownership, and thus burden of responsibility for liberation, of those who are said to (and/or say of themselves) embody the numerous imbrications of these identities. The black trans feminism I want to begin to theorize, nonexhaustively so, is one that, again, as Raha notes, "is not simply about the inclusion of trans bodies or transfeminine people into feminism," and also one that is not simply about assuming that one's embodied marginalized identity is sufficient for proffering a radical politics.[12] To do black and/or trans and/or feminist work is not done solely or monolithically by those whom historico-sociality has deemed black or trans or women, or all three. Indeed, if the project of radical trans feminism, and most certainly black radicalism, is characterized as a "heterogeneous, decolonising anti-capitalist feminist project," then black trans feminism here wishes to think itself and its adherents as those who commit to engendering themselves through these performative enactments.[13]

To inhabit the world as unfixed requires one to let go profoundly. But this profound letting go is with respect to a profound gaining of something else that might allow us to do things differently. The present conditions must undergo an immense detachment; we must detach, unfix, from such conditions if we are to engender something other than this. It is untenable to stick with what we have now, what exists now, if we heed that a radical end of the world requires a radical *end* of *this* world and its signatories. The other world that is here and now, an other world that harbors otherwise states of becoming and a "you beyond you," to borrow from Alexis Pauline Gumbs (whose work will be discussed in chapter 4), necessitates the serious rethinking of who we are and what we know. It is a fundamentally radicalized onto-epistemic vitiation in service of finding another way to live with one another.

Black trans feminism is nothing other than radicalism and is a departure from typical definitions of "radical"—the etymological going back to the roots—toward, well, a more radical definition: radical as an imaginative will to engage life unbounded. The radicality discussed in these pages is an adjectival mobilization toward what has not (yet) been realized or conceptualized, an imaginative speculation about how we might be, where we might end up, what might exist, and what might be possible. "Radical" and "radicality" denote a way of being unbeholden to normative constraints for legibility, politics, subjectivity, knowledge, and relationality. Blackness's radicality functions in a transitive manner because it is inflected with respect to but not confined by sedimented notions of racial quanta.

It staves off certainty, invites troubled orientations, ill-abides taxonomy, keeps at a distance existence ahead of itself; it is an unfolding of the fold that demands a different subjectivity. Transness's radicality functions differently than, but not to the exclusion of, "transgender." Specifically, it "functions as a way to think about how things come together and how they work with, on, and in one another." About movement and change, transness asks us to meditate on the manifold ways a thing can present itself differently and, as Kai M. Green states, "allows us to let go of the stability."[14] Black feminism's radicality, that perpetual refusal of institutionalization, manifests as an attunement to the regimes of ontological genders and works those regulative traps by unsuturing them and fracturing gender's impositions. Black feminism and its underpinning trans feminism mutate the state's attempt and function to render things immobile, a function Michel Foucault has noted, and names that which cannot be kept in place or moored to the normative ledgers of history. Taken together, these understandings of blackness, transness, and feminism undergird the start of the hieroglyphic theorization that will come to be understood as black trans feminism, an abolitionist gender radicality.

An ontological blackness and ontological gender are anathema to those abetting the proliferation of black trans feminism, as these ontologies tend toward a reification by which race and gender in particular become treated as if they exist objectively and independent of historical contingency or subjective intentions. Resultant is a categorically essential racial and gender consciousness unable to hold difference and hostile when met with critique, leading to a nebulously and inconsistently exhaustive principle of Racial and Gender Identity, their "thoroughgoing index" entrapping more than liberating.[15] Indeed, "the terms homosexual/heterosexual and transsexual as well as other markers like man/woman, masculine/feminine, whiteness/blackness/brownness," Jack Halberstam writes, "are all historically variable terms, untethered in fixed or for that matter natural or inevitable ways to bodies and populations."[16] The contingency, though merely a speculation of what might have been, is precisely the space in which I dwell here, as what might have been is what we are after, since it is in contradistinction to the violence of what has been and is. Rather than seeing contingency as a bygone thought, it is read here as the seeds of the possible ways we might unfix ourselves from the violence of what has been and is. If what might have been, that historical contingency, is fundamentally not what has been and is—which is the battleground on which we do all this radical work—then it serves as a potent and rich dossier of rethinking ourselves differently, of unfixing ourselves, and unfixation is an extricative transitive relationship to power's grasp and its ability to coerce meaning onto us. What might have been can be what will soon be.

Readers may have begun to notice something that could be seen as troubling—namely, the seeming overlooking of structural barriers. A structural, and indeed terrestrially, sociohistorically ontological *antiblackness, sexism, and transantagonism* is an onus not elided in an anti- and antecategorical blackness/transness/feminism. No, no, do not mistake me. What I offer is a celebratory and radically liberatory analysis of these modalities instead of a rehashing-type account of how their identificatory corporeal signifiers are hemmed and maligned by hegemonic forces. And this, I assure you, is in service of the absolute eradication of the forces compelling the hegemon. Antiblackness, transantagonism, sexism, and the (hierarchized) gender binary are all structures that disallow such freedom of choice and movement that I have implied thus far, one might think. And, to be sure, one thinks this on justifiable grounds, as one cannot merely opt out of the plight of antiblackness, say, by willing oneself in excess of those structural fetters. But the radicality of self-determination, for example—to claim and fashion one's own subjectivity even in the "objective" face of historical, material, and social structures—is a bedrock of any subversion of the very ills that foundation oppressive structures. An outside to the structures must be imagined if there is any chance in negating their sovereignty. Their utter undermining in the form of gender self-determination might be one of those outsides. And there are others. Inasmuch as perinatally designated sex and gender, or white supremacist epidermalization of value, or cis male supremacist subordination and invalidation of those who are not cis men are structural regimes, their cessation requires an irreverence toward their organizing logics and all of their claims about the world. The politicality of blackness, transness, and feminism allows this to occur, as they are not tied to the structures that attempt to "know" subjects on grounds that precede them. Blackness, thus, will outlast "race"; transness will outlast "gender"; feminism will outlast "women." They outlast the identities often sutured to them because, as engendering fugitive forces, they precede and exceed their capture in these identities, and further, they referentially index one another as different literal and proverbial hues of one another—blackness, transness, and feminism are radical and fugitive rhymes for one another.

> The moment "Ain't I a woman?" had to be addressed by Sojourner Truth, the moment she had to bare her breasts to prove that she was the woman, was already a queer, a trans moment. So that rather than seeing ourselves as outside blackness, as outside the dialogue of queerness and trans, I think that we need to place ourselves as black females at the core of the dialogue.
>
> **BELL HOOKS**, "Are You Still a Slave? Liberating the Black Female Body"

Black trans feminism indexes a thing that has been simmering for a while now, bubbling up in the most and least incendiary of places. It is instructive to excavate the historical archive for the way it has tried to manifest blackness through the vector of fugitivity, though imperfectly, as all manifestations of fugitivity are happy to be. And it is fugitivity that I want to use here, for now, as an indexation of the paraontological distinction between blackness and people deemed black, which will then open up transness and black feminism to similar distinctions. So, into the archive.

Approved and signed into law by George Washington on February 12, 1793, the Fugitive Slave Act of 1793 articulates a preoccupation with stateliness and territory. In the burgeoning formation of a nation, boundedness in more ways than one—national, corporeal, intellectual—became prioritized. Fugitive slaves, then, were broadly conceived of as those who transgressed imposed boundaries: breached the geographic confines of the plantations that they did not and could not call home; undermined the perceptual boundaries of the limits of slave, or Negro, capacity; escaped the grasp of whips, horses, dogs, laws, and desires demanding their confinement; and demonstrated the capacity to autonomously steal that which was deemed property—themselves. Fleeing the "State or Territory" was effectively an escape to life-in-freedom, as the fugitive's status as slave, being bounded by the state or specific location from which they fled, dissolved on the run. Of note, too, in Section 6 of the amended Fugitive Slave Act of 1850 is that "in no trial or hearing under this act shall the testimony of such alleged fugitive be admitted in evidence," an extension of imposed incapacity onto the very ontology of the slave, in this era (and, arguably, into the contemporary moment) synonymous with blackness. But in all of this, the law cannot hold. The two laws were inadequate, as they could not ensure the fugitive's capture. On some accounts, in fact, it became even more difficult to recapture fugitives as they became more adept at eluding power's grasp. Mr. Mason of Virginia, he who introduced the 1850 law because the previous one lacked sufficient severity, tellingly notes that under the 1793 Fugitive Slave Law "you may as well go down into the sea and endeavor to recover from his [*sic*] native element a fish which has escaped from you, as expect to recover such a fugitive."[17] The runaway, the subject engendering another iteration of themselves, transing themselves, quintessentializes the tenor of fugitivity: a perpetual, fishy, escapeful slitheriness that power's hands cannot contain. The law attempts to enact sovereignty on an insovereign nonentity.

In both laws fugitivity extends to those who do the work of aiding and abetting a fugitive and, more notably, impeding the capture of fugitives. Fugitive slave law enlisted everyone, claimed everyone, to make a dire choice: choose the proliferation of captivity or the proliferation of escape. With the historical mobilization of fugitivity through blackness, I want to gesture toward their interrelatedness. I want to gesture toward, because of this historical proximity, blackness being given the capacity I intend for it through fugitive slave law. As the 1793 law states in its second section, "If any person or persons shall, by force, set at liberty, or rescue the fugitive from such agent while transporting . . . the person or persons so offending shall, on conviction, be fined . . . and be imprisoned"; and as the 1850 law says in its seventh section, those assisting runaways "after notice or knowledge of the fact that such person was a fugitive from service or labor as aforesaid, shall, for either of said offences, be subject to a fine . . . and imprisonment."[18] I am thoroughly aware that, say, white abolitionists helping usher fugitive slaves to the North do not occupy the same historical and ontologically abjected position as the runaways themselves, and I do not wish to conflate the two. My assertion, in part, is that these white abolitionists engendered themselves and their world through and in proximity to a paraontological blackness; they, as I expound upon later in this book in a slightly different context, "became-black" and subjectivated themselves politically via a deployment of fugitive blackness. Blackness becomes nonproprietary in a radical and serious, a seriously radical, sense. On this front there is this to say:

> This [paraontological] movement . . . refuses to give definition or essence to purportedly extant historical figures precisely because, via the desedimentary, deconstructive, *différantial* workings of thinking these subjects, there is to be found no definition or last essential analysis.

The deconstructive work of desedimentation, its paraontological sinews and ligaments, is, if you'll allow me this neologism, nondefinessential. Because of this, we cannot and can never distinguish between who or what is within or without the ostensible boundaries of the very thing we mark as possessing a transparent definition or essence. Hence, the criteria for inclusion and exclusion dissolve into nothingness, thus making the work of paraontology the recognition of this dissolution and, from there, joyfully conceding that there are no criteria for subjective verification, no ontological ground on which to stand in order to be viable, and indeed a no-groundedness that invites subjects into it as a place to stand, para- and non- and nega-ontologically. . . .

Blackness, in its paraontology and the taking seriously of that paraontology, can and must be mobilized by any and all who commit to radicality and ontological desedimentation named in that insurrectionary radicality.[19]

My assertion, in an additional part, is also that neither do two different fugitive slaves occupy the "same position," that positions are ever-shifting and dependent upon myriad vectors of subjectivity, so the matter of deeming only those who have and are subjected due to what was called then "Negroid" phenotype is moot. One is indeed placed, as it were, in a box by virtue of racialized blackness. That box, however, does not imply a closed input-output loop allowing us to predict the outcome every time (or, one might say, as a gesture toward radical transfiguration, *any* time). Being put in a box says little about how one occupies that box and how others relate to that box. A slave in this era may, if you will, be sitting in the bottom right corner of the box; another might be standing in the center of the box; one more might have tunneled out the bottom unbeknownst to anyone else; and still another might be running around the box without clothes, taunting the box's edges, finding seams in its walls to stick a toe into or peer out of. All of these textured ways of inhabiting the box matter more than given credit, and it is the way we move and live, or not, in the box, and what others understand about the box—do they call it a box or a cube or square? Do they like boxes or not? Do they know how the boxes were made and do they plan to do something about the presence or shape or internal temperature of the box? Do they tell others about those in certain kinds of boxes, and do they do things to eradicate boxes or exploit the seams in those boxes to create more air flow?—that matters quite substantively. It is not sufficient to say, as I *know* some of y'all are thinking, that "they're still in a box" precisely because one is not known and one does not live only via the vector of imposition. "We" are not in our entirety "box people" because we, too, interact with the box, forging who "we" are in that relation, so much so, perhaps, that "boxed" says less and less about our circumstances and mode of inhabitation than other, *as important* stitches of how we show up in this and other worlds.

My interest lies in the thing, or nonthing, that is being punished—fugitivity—as the site of proximity to blackness, which then serves as blackness as such. It is blackness that is the "criminality that brings the law online," a lawless force that, though named blackness, "must be understood in its ontological difference from black people." Important, too, is Fred Moten and Stefano Harney's claim that while this "anoriginary drive" they deem blackness—an *an*origin that is the surplus of an always unlocatable origin, a displacement of origins and desires for origins—is distinct from people called black, those deemed black "are, nevertheless, (under) privileged insofar as they are given (to) an understanding of it."[20] The opaque beings that index and allude to the open onto-epistemic trove. That trove is the "understanding" to which the (under)privileged are given, but the understanding is open to being understood by any and every one and non-one.

But, in the spirit of this introduction, indeed this entire book, there is the immense need to examine the *gendered* components of this fugitivity. What if to argue for blackness's fugitivity and fugitivity's blackness is already to argue in and through the volatility of gender, gendering, and ungender(ing)? To illustrate this in a historical sense, we can fruitfully turn to a variety of laws and social decrees that derogated gender expression not "befitting" one's "true" gender. Setting a biblical precedence is Deuteronomy ("second law") 22:5, which notates that "a man's item shall not be on a woman, and a man shall not wear a woman's garment; whoever does such a thing is an abhorrence unto Adonai [or, Jehovah or God]." To don dress, which is potent with an implicit and expected revelation of gendered veracity, that does not align with one's gendered assignation is a divine abhorrence. To trans one's gender through the sartorial in this case is a transgression of the sovereign force of God, biblically speaking. Briefly, then, we see how transness and blackness converge, where a trans expression is a rebuking of purported divine sovereign decree, and blackness's radicalism is found in "the critique of political theology and thus of 'God' as governor or world manager," blackness as indexical, according to J. Kameron Carter, of "sacrality without property and without sovereignty."[21]

If we can conclude preliminarily that laws and customs prohibiting certain modes of dress served to curtail people from inhabiting social space in ways not part of the legibility of sociality as dictated by discursive and sociohistorical power, there is a crucial connection to be made.

Even before explicit laws prohibiting people from appearing "in a dress not becoming his or her sex," there are glimpses of regulation in the United States as far back as the early eighteenth century. Using South Carolina as a case study, Act No. 586 of its "Act for the Better Ordering and Governing Negroes and Other Slaves" (ratified on March 29, 1735) dictated which textiles enslaved people were permitted to wear, sedimenting maximum measurements for "nigger cloth," which emboldened white citizens to seize any and all clothing deemed too extravagant or refined for the enslaved. The language of the law reads,

> And whereas, many of the slaves in this Province wear clothes much above the condition of slaves, for the procuring whereof they use sinister and evil methods; for the preventing, therefore, of such practices for the future. Be it enacted by the authority aforesaid. That no owner or proprietor of any negro slave or other slave whatsoever, (except livery men or boys,) shall permit or suffer such negro or other slave to have or wear any sort of apparel whatsoever, finer, other, or of greater value, than negro cloth.

Further, in 1795 a "regulation" was adopted to prohibit both the enslaved as well as free persons of color from wearing anything that might disguise themselves. What these prohibitions do is highlight "the anxiety felt by the [white] ruling class about people appearing or pretending to be something other than that which local customs and laws permitted them to be. In short, the laws of early South Carolina in general and Charleston in particular were very much concerned with physical appearances in the public realm and their role in constructing and maintaining a traditional social hierarchy."[22] Pervasive throughout this era was the forbidding of disguise—that is, dressing in manners associated with a different class status or profession, and donning apparel that made white people appear as indigenous (as was often the case during populist protests like the Boston Tea Party) or black people appear as white.

The laws became gender-specific beginning in 1848, when an ordinance in Columbus, Ohio, declared that it was forbidden for someone to appear "in a dress not belonging to his or her sex." Picking up steam in March 1868, an anonymous member of the City Council introduced "A Bill to Prevent and Punish Indecent Exposure or Improper Conduct, and For Other Purposes," which was subsequently printed in the local newspaper. The bill reads, in part, as follows:

> Be it ordained by the Mayor and Aldermen, That if any person shall appear in a public place in a state of nudity, or in a dress not becoming his or her sex, or shall make any indecent exposure of his or her person, or be guilty of any lewd or indecent act or behavior, or shall print, engrave, make, exhibit, sell, or offer to sell, any indecent or lewd book, picture, or any other thing, shall be subject to a fine of not less than twenty dollars, nor exceeding one hundred dollars, or imprisonment not exceeding one month.[23]

The decree conflates indecent exposure (e.g., nudity) with dressing in a manner not becoming of one's sex, and gender nonconforming dress is seen as on par with a criminalized offense ("guilty") of lewd or indecent behavior of one's person or of material like books and pictures. In other words, gender transgression is akin to, and punishable on par with, legal transgressions of indecency. This instantiates the gender binary and cis genders as natural law, deviation from which is likened to deviation from the pristine tenets of lawfulness.

Such a deviation, though, was and is necessary for some, indeed life-sustaining and -creating. There are myriad instances of the enslaved using, in the words of C. Riley Snorton, "gender fungibility as a contrivance for freedom," including Harriet Tubman's wearing of pants and disguising a black man in a bonnet to facilitate their escape, and Eliza of *Uncle Tom's Cabin* cutting her hair and disguising herself as a boy (and her son as a girl) to facilitate her final flight to Canada to Harriet Jacobs's assumption of masculine garb ("a suit of sailor's clothes, jacket, trowsers [sic], and tarpaulin hat"), among others that may have escaped the historical ledger. Enslaved black life utilized the fissures in normative gender as a means of escape, which is to say that black life and blackness enable their freedom—their ability to live—precisely through fissured gender, making blackness and black life given not only to fissuring gender but, indeed, to being and becoming *through* fissured gender, blackness as itself always and already proximal to, indexical of, and given to an understanding of transness. This is what is being made clear in the above epigraph in which bell hooks draws a queer, trans, and black feminist lesson from Sojourner Truth's need to negotiate her racialized (non)womanhood. As allegorized through Truth, there is a way that the nexus of black and woman, instead of being an untroubled additive gesture, asserts that "rather than accepting the existing assumptions about what a woman is and then trying to prove that she fit the standards, Truth challenged the very standards themselves. Her actions demonstrate the process of deconstruction—namely, exposing a concept as ideological or culturally constructed rather than as natural or a simple reflection of reality." What occurs at point zero of the convergence of black and woman is, Patricia Hill Collins concludes, "deconstructing the concept *woman*."[24]

Blackness, as I have asserted and will continue to expound upon, is a force of transfiguration, of being and becoming otherwise-than, a modality facilitating mutability and paracategorization. Inasmuch as black skin has been made to index (albeit imperfectly, as with any categorization and taxonomy) this modality, and inasmuch as it is often presumed that such a physiognomy is an immutable bodily characteristic, other ways of adorning oneself as a mechanism for identification took on a potency that needed to be made as immutable and categorical as physiognomy. Thus, the various ways that one expressed oneself via dress, which was rife with class and gender significatory power, needed to be curtailed. To mutate one's dress as a method for expressing a gender "not becoming of" one's sex was taken as needing to be fixed, sedimented, like physical blackness was presumed to be. And this is substantiated explicitly in the twentieth century, when medico-juridical practitioners invented medicalized notions of gender *as* a form of race, as a phenotype.[25] There is thus a generative convergence between blackness and gender nonnormativity. Historically, there is often a connection made between blackness and nonnormative gender—or, rather, transness—through the thread of the possibility of insurrection or abolitionist sentiments. As an example, in 1859 Caroline Wilson was arrested by the chief of police after "circumstances transpired which led to the belief that he [*sic*] was not what he [*sic*] seemed." (Because of the inauspicious and non-self-determined nature of the "outing," it seems to me that I can neither assume "he" pronouns [or "she" pronouns, for that matter] nor a certain identificatory grounding for Wilson.) Wilson confessed that Wilson "had regularly appeared in woman's apparel since he [*sic*] was ten years old," though "confessed" is much closer, in my view, to coerced. Too, surviving reports indicate no charge for the arrest, the arrest having come from, in effect, no identifiable wrongdoing on Wilson's part—or, at least, no de jure laws were transgressed. The point of noteworthiness here is what was said in the local press: "It is suspected that this disguise has been assumed for some ulterior purpose," it said, "as he [*sic*] has been seen frequently in close conversation with negros [*sic*], a suspicion has been raised in the minds of some that he [*sic*] is an Abolition emissary."[26] Gender transgression is made to be close kin with a proximity to blackness, indeed, to abolitionist sentiments. Wilson's transing of Wilson's gender evoked nefarious plots to upend the conditions that subtend pervasive captivity. It might be argued that Wilson indexed and mobilized anticaptivity, dramatizing the interarticulatory nature of blackness and transness as abolitionist gender radicality. Gender transgression was made legible *through* blackness and abolition; in other words, gender transness cannot help but evoke blackness, for both are radical insurrectionary postures enacted through the sociopolitical sites of race and gender. And such is the very aim of *Black Trans Feminism*: to excavate and delineate the nebulous and generative texture of abolitionist gender radicality.

ABOLITION AND GENDER RADICALITY

The organizing framework of this text's conception of black trans feminism is what I will be understanding as abolitionist gender radicality. Surely not to the exclusion of other possible ways of organizing black trans feminism, I understand abolitionist gender radicality as a prime analytic for clarifying the effects and implications, as well as structure (if such a term is even apt), of black trans feminism.

Abolition, as articulated here, is broader than just prison abolition, both in that it is concerned with systems of oppression and captivity that are things other than prisons, and in that the "prison" is to be understood much more capaciously than just the institutions that incarcerate people behind bars. Abolition can be succinctly defined as a modality and orientation to life and livability that is not reactive against "bad" prisons but a way to make forms of carcerality impossible. Abolition is not one spectacularized event but a quotidian working toward eradicating carceral logics as predicates for sociality and relationality. Like what Sarah Lamble terms "everyday abolition," I offer abolition as "changing the ways we interact with others on an ongoing basis and changing harmful patterns in our daily lives," questioning punitive impulses and relations of captivity.[27] This book urges abolition in a broad sense: the making impossible—and creation of a sociality indexed to the impossibility—of carcerality, any form of captivity, which can include categorical taxonomies, agential circumscription, and the like. We create abolition and do abolition in each moment we move toward the alleviation of subtle ways of curtailing the ability of anyone to become liberated. It is fundamental to an ethics of nonviolence, which is to say the commitment to refusing the proliferation of the originary violence of ontology. Abolition, in doing away with the very violence that has orchestrated our very sense of ourselves and the world, an orchestration that has dictated who we have been permitted to be and who we permit others to be, is a quotidian effort of mitigating violation.

I understand and proffer abolition as putting pressure even on terms such as revolution. A prominent understanding of revolution is akin to a Marxist seizure of the means of production; it manifests in taking (back) the government or capturing the office of the CEO. Underlying this, however, is the assumption of an inevitable and natural government and office. Uncritiqued and simply taken for granted is the shape of power itself, which is implied to inevitably look like the state—by which I mean not simply "government" but a horizon of stanched possibility and set of practices predicated on circumscription, order, law, and discipline; the state, that is, as a relation inflected through punitivity, transaction, capitalist investment, and hegemony—and, furthermore, there is the assumption that the state and its limbs are recuperable rather than, definitionally, progenitors of violence. On one reading, revolution seeks to equally distribute the violence embedded in the state. Abolition, on the other hand, is a doing away with the state. And since the state is a relation rather than a mere establishment, the state-relationality takes myriad forms, racial taxonomization and gender binaristic impositions and hierarchical sex classification among them. More than just resistance, abolition as made here to engender black trans feminism is committed to moving "*beyond* the state in the service of collective liberation," making a founding coalitional drive constitutive of it. It is also a call for something other than epistemic mastery over where we should go from here; it is "a provocation to *care* more than we can *know*, to extend our analyses past the ruins of the world (and the discipline) as we know it."[28] We do not need to know for certain the parameters of what comes after this hell. And perhaps we cannot know, if we are truly to get to a place not beholden to extant modes of conceptualization. What is primary is that we care for and about one another's livelihoods. We then cultivate the conditions that can lovingly accommodate such livelihoods.

Black trans feminism is also committed to gender self-determination in a way that slightly departs from the term's popular conception. Typically, gender self-determination is believed to simply be the acceptance of everyone's right to choose whatever gender they want. I say my gender is *x*, which means you must respect that, and if you do not you are impinging on my right to determine my own gender. This is sensible and not entirely off the mark. But the gender self-determination argued for here, nuancing the popular conception, disallows the building of hierarchies for genders. It disallows battles between genders based on proximity to a mythical realness or authenticity. Gender self-determination is much more than "any person, any gender," for such a conception of gender self-determination, the one that seems to be in place now, bears traces of neoliberal individuation presuming that the process of gender is extricated from sociality and nevertheless evaluates the contours of that gender through a marketplace economy of its use-value, legibility, and ability to still be productive. The gender self-determination affixed to black trans feminism is a social dance, but a sociality not really here; black trans feminist gender self-determination avows a subjective cultivation of ways to do illegible genders, genders that abolish the bestowal of gender, genders that allow us all to be and become expansively outside of the very desire to have to bestow onto ourselves gender. This means that when we advocate for gender self-determination from this purview we do not say "Yes" to any and all genders one chooses; it means we advocate for the ethical requisite to say "No"—or better, to decline to state—with regard to the imposition of gender.

How, then, does a wide-reaching abolition that includes the abolition of the ontologics of racialization and gender hold with it gender self-determination? It is maintained that gender self-determination, as argued by Queer (In)Justice, "require[s] that we reach toward abolition, *not just of prisons*, and for some of us, police, but of the systems that produce them, and which replicate systems of policing and punishment beyond prison walls."[29] The systems spoken of are not discrete entities that we can do away with while leaving the general landscape intact; they are the ontological order that has bestowed a fundamental sense of being onto anything that can be said to properly exist. In order to self-determine one's own gender it must be the case that, first, there is an unviolated self, which is to say the abolition of self toward something like another self; and, second, what is determined by that self must be noncoercive and noncompulsory, which may, again, be to say abolition of gender as we know it. Gender self-determination is both a theoretical/philosophical practice (like part 1 of *Black Trans Feminism*) as well as a discursively enfleshed practice (like part 2 of *Black Trans Feminism*) that utilizes a coalitional desire to create a space in which gender might be fashioned radically noncompulsorily and nonviolently, or without imposition and immutability onto oneself and others. Thus, gender-self-determination is a movement toward dissolving given gender ontologies;

self-determination is a kind of desedimentation or paraontology inasmuch as it is not given from without.

In short, the commingling of abolition and gender self-determination is actually reciprocally facilitated by each since one cannot emerge through what I would deem genders that might have arisen but for Gender if the latter has not been abolished. If abolition must be a project not only of closing violent doors (Gender) but the cultivation and proliferation of nourishing and transformational things (genders that might have arisen but for . . .), abolition cannot occur without gender self-determination as Gender is one of the chief forms through which coercive, compulsory violence and captivity are carried out, and gender self-determination cannot be actualized without widespread abolition. Indeed, "sex," rooted in the gender binary, hands over gender assignation to someone outside of oneself, someone buttressed by the medical and juridical institutions that bestow the validity of gender. One's inaugurative possibility is quite literally deprived from them and instantiated in another. This is far from self-determination; this is another's literal determination of oneself and one's self. So gender as well as sex abolition enable gender self-determination. Sex and gender assignment can be read as a perinatal ontological foreclosure in service of maintaining the established ontological ground, a primordial violence seeking to quell the mutiny of black anoriginal lawlessness or unruly transitivity.

And, lastly, all of this—abolition and gender self-determination, or a gender radicality, which I will discuss below—is in service of a radically open claimability and indiscriminate demand. They require that we all get touched by abolition and gender radicality, as it were, forcing us all to become woven into it, for we cannot stand on the outside if we are seeking to abolish such ontologized distinctions; we cannot simply be "in support" of abolition without sullying ourselves and dissolving, abolishing, the very things abolition stands in contrast to, meaning that we, too, *become* through abolishing the ways we ourselves have been formed. Put differently, "if we really take the queer, trans, gender-non-conforming political *position* seriously," writes Che Gossett, "we have to understand that to undertake the work of gender self-determination and gender liberation, we don't simply 'stand alongside/behind' our queer/trans peers; we inhabit a position *with* them in absolute political intimacy."[30] Abolition and gender self-determination, fueled by and fueling black trans feminism, means that when we do these things we inhabit the space with and through them; when we take on the work of abolition and gender self-determination we take on the work of black trans feminism, which is to say we, and I mean this, take on, in and as ourselves, the black, the trans, and the feminist.

In turn, gender radicality is radical insofar as it is presented as the *undoing* of roots (not a going back to the roots), indeed rootedness itself; radicality is an extirpation, not a tending. Radicality refuses to reduce its aim to static templates of what is only possible in the current discourse. Thinking of radicality as a departure rather than a return shifts the line of thought toward a fundamental dismantling of the current order of things. To be radical is not to wish to go back; to be radical is not to want to go back to a prelapsarian image of perfection, but rather to seek that which can be possible—or maybe even to seek that which is *im*possible. Gender radicality yearns for genders that might have been but for the normative binary regime of gender. They are otherwise genders that imagine what might be possible and impossible; they are imperfect and molten genders that subjectivate us differently.

Gender radicality, as the underlying tenor of black trans feminism, indexes what Amey Victoria Adkins-Jones calls a black/feminist future, a black feminism that is notably imbricated with the transness of black fugitive study that Jack Halberstam designates as an "unregulated wildness."[31] Drawing on Beauvoir and Fanon, Adkins stakes her black feminism in a radical liberatory "perigendered, periracial world" that insists on pursuing freedom, that space of abolition, "within an ethics of community that questions the assumptions of the aesthetics and politics of difference and that acknowledges the abilities of 'the other' to move across various social categories as a beginning to enact independence."[32] A gender radicality, notably not a radical gender, is fundamentally perigendered and periracial, ante and prior to the forces of gendering and racialization—gendering's and racialization's discontented alternative modality of subjectivation, I'd argue— and as such builds community on the interrogation and undermining of race and gender insofar as they are predicated upon notions of purity. If the politics of difference rest on normative logics that have cordoned off where racial and gender categories begin and end and have themselves instantiated categorization as the means by which one enters into valid (read: normative) subjectivity, questioning those assumptions is the grounds for advancing a future of gender radicality. The Other as a proxy for those who move away from normative confinement can and must move across categorization because it is the becoming that works before, after, and outside of static being that is originary. In short, Adkins concludes, blackness moves in excess of race since race "is inflected by a desire for purity and fidelity," and imagines that "the future(s) of blackness move(s) us to name the ways in which refusal to sequester, to quarantine black from black, is inherent to blackness itself."[33]

What intrigues me and powers this articulation of black trans feminism is a deviant echo of a mellifluous chiming by Jasbir Puar on Brian Massumi's work: How might we degrid the cartographical maps that have been imposed not simply on but *as* our bodies? How do we, salvifically, refuse positioning ourselves retroactively into a gridlocked self—which is to say, definitionally, Identity—for something that we are forbidden from becoming: unrecognizable, unbounded, unself, all of which are to say, in different ways, an abolition of the strictures of having to *be* some*thing*? How can we, as Eliza Steinbock says of trans studies, remain in an indeterminate, non-fixed space and suspend the desire for retroactive installment of ourselves and others into the paradigmatic (racialized, gendered) grid?[34]

It is to the end of abolitionist gender radicality that each chapter serves. I've broken the book up into two distinct parts. The purpose of this organization is to facilitate a discretion in service of a collaboration, by which I mean I want to fracture and break toward the end of bringing together and communing. I am, admittedly, attempting in my own way to actualize Alexis Pauline Gumbs's instantiation of black women who "make and break narrative" by, here, breaking the narrative components of this text apart in order to make something not able to be made were it not for the breaking. Surely *Black Trans Feminism* could have been a straightforward theoretical meditation thinking philosophically about how the three titular terms speak to and through one another; and surely too it could have been a literary meditation, taking up the 1980s and 1990s black feminist tradition of close reading novels and poetry and racialized and gendered literary language; or it could have attempted, as indeed is done in the conclusion, to think about black trans feminism strictly as a certain kind of legible praxis via activism and protestation and livability. Yet the project this text sets out on is a promiscuous one, needing all of these different approaches. It is also a project that wishes to think about the dissolution of genre (especially considering black trans feminism's gender abolitionist project and the etymological link of "genre" to "gender")—a kind of allusion toward gender abolition through, as it were, genre abolition. Thus, the literariness of part 2 moseys into the theoreticality of part 1, and the theory of part 1 skirts into the literariness of part 2, which is also to say that the theory of part 1 is concerned with nothing but how to think about life and livability on a broad, philosophical scale, and the literature—poetry, essays, tweets, blog posts—of part 2 is written and disseminated oftentimes literally to sustain one's life.

Part 1, then, ought to be understood as a philosophical articulation of black trans feminism, where philosophy is a sustained practice of thought toward neither knowledge acquisition nor epistemic mastery but, rather, a way of conceptualizing meaningfulness in excess of the semiotic regimes currently in place. Part 1 theorizes black trans feminism from different angles that cultivate the altered understandings underlying it, grappling with the philosophical concerns implied in such a sociopolitical and epistemic shift. To that end, chapter 1, "Black, Trans, Feminism," aims to think the three terms of my title in relation to one another. What is meant, and what is illuminated, by thinking black and trans together? Black and feminist? Trans and feminist? Though necessarily incomplete and a bit disingenuous insofar as the omitted term always creeps into my discussion—and insofar as the discussed terms are already embedded within one another—I use this chapter as an occasion to mine in detail the nexus of black/trans, black/feminist, and trans/feminist with the hope that the three terms' constitutivity becomes even more apparent. The chapter makes the case for the nonidentitarian ethos of blackness, transness, and feminism, which is to say the politically identificatory queerness of the terms in the vein of Cathy Cohen, and furthermore excavates black studies, black feminist theorizing, and transgender studies for their recalibration of identity through a subjectless predication on abolitionist gender radicality. The case is made for a blackness and transness and feminism that understand themselves as radically open claimable postures that place a visceral and rigorous demand to do the ethical work of approximating the "poverty-in-spirit" inflected in variegated ways by way of history's contingency.

Chapter 2, "Fugitivity, Un/gendered," theorizes how inhabitation of a fugitive spirit, as it were, must incite an un/gendered subjectivity. To that end, I meld the theorizations of Hortense Spillers's "flesh" and Kai M. Green's and Treva Ellison's "tranifest" to create what I call "traniflesh." If Spillers understands flesh as a distinct liberated subject position that stands in contrast to the body, flesh refuses gestures of cohesiveness and foreclosure. Green and Ellison articulate tranifest—to transformatively manifest—as an operative comportment that runs exceedingly across and to the side of normativizing racial, sexual, and gendered gestures. Such a conceptualization is used in this chapter to think subjectivity—a subjectless and unsubjugated subjectivity—outside of cohesive logics of power through traniflesh, or a haptic and tactile (the *hac[k]tile*) grammatical refusal through fissure and dehiscence. Conversant with L. H. Stallings's "illusive flesh" and C. Riley Snorton's "appositional flesh," traniflesh is a move to un/gender, to feel "somewhere elseone," to be on the run from gender in gender's undercommons.

"Trans/figurative, Blackness," as the subsequent chapter, advances Spillers's claim that blackness—or, in her words, "black culture"—is "no longer predicated on 'race'" and instead names insurgent "vantages" from which one un/relates to the hegemon. Such a move unfixes it from the terrain of corporeality and gives blackness over to a trans analytic, a trans/figured promiscuous assemblage that mobilizes instability. Drawing on the biblical "Transfiguration" of Jesus as a changing of form, my use of the slash to, well, transfigure transfiguration refuses the inherent valuative hierarchy of the biblical precedent and (un)settles on trans/figuration's work as a destabilizing becoming otherwise. This, I argue, is the work of blackness and its inherent transness, a trans/figuration that refuses dichotomy and finds its ethos in excess. It is a "de-personed" modality of presentability (not representability), a metamorphosis-in-black, a boundless movement outside the tendrils of History that cannot be anticipated. In short, it is the means by which we might disorder the world otherwise.

Part 2 of this book articulates black trans feminism literarily and textually, specifically *poetically,* providing readings of both well-known radical black feminist writers (Gumbs) and lesser-known black trans poets and essayists (dodd, Selenite, Edidi). Poetry has emerged as the genre of insight in this text because it seems to be the genre, the discursive avenue, through which many black and trans and femme people have chosen to write. Those who find themselves living and agitating at the nexus of black and trans and femme have not really used the form of the novel to express the kind of black trans feminist work to which this book is attesting, nor have they utilized short stories or other kinds of long-form fiction. They have, as has been illustrated by people like Shaadi Devereaux and Monica Roberts and Raquel Willis and Kat Blaque and a few others, utilized the form of the essay—or, more precisely, the online think piece—to illuminative effect. There is, however, more of a *journalistic* utility to many of these writings, a conveyance of information rather than primarily a meditation on black trans feminist life. This is not to diminish the journalistic essay; it is, though, to assert a different tenor and texture to what that genre is doing. Poetry seems to be, at the present time, the genre that harbors the weight of black trans feminist *thinking*. Indeed, novels and short stories and essays are sites of thinking as well, but the poetry of the writings in this text are doing *black trans feminist thinking* in a sustained, intentional, affective, intellectual, and committed way. It is not for simply informative ends, as in the journalistic essay, nor is it a fictionalized account used to illustrate what it's like to be black and/or trans and/or femme. Poetry appears to be, as will hopefully be made clear in part 2, black trans feminist writing; it is the literary form that black trans feminism takes. And I don't know entirely why. But, I hope, that's okay.

In light of this, there is something crucial to be gained by not simply drawing on the work of established black women or black femme writers whose books have been published by academic presses but focusing also on black and trans women who have self-published their books or published with small, lesser-known, independent presses, focusing on the black trans women—a nexus, in this instance, simultaneously identificatory and not, as this book will make quite clear—who have needed to create Patreon accounts to make financial ends meet and who need to ask for donations via Twitter in order to pay rent. This is a different, though no less or more important, avenue into understanding black trans feminism. Part 2 provides readings of texts and discourses by these thinkers to give discursive and literary flesh to the theorizations in part 1. Chapter 4, "Feminist, Fugitivity," examines Alexis Pauline Gumbs's poetic triptych: the books *Spill: Scenes of Black Feminist Fugitivity*, M *Archive: After the End of the World*, and *Dub: Finding Ceremony*. The chapter reads these three texts through a lens of excavating their radical recalibration of blackness and gender. *Spill* showcases people who, as Gumbs says, are fugitive from patriarchal definitions of masculine and feminine, which indexes the black and trans feminist underpinnings of the text. M *Archive*, in turn, is the assessment and evaluation of the end of the world by a black feminist metaphysician. As *Spill* thinks racialized gendered subjectivity outside of given ontologies and as "fugitive from patriarchy," so, too, does M *Archive* assert a different analytic evaluative frame for what happens when the current regime is abolished. *Dub*, lastly, is an interspecies communion that attempts to go beyond taxonomic structures, beyond taxonomizing gestures, and find the kinship between those entities said to in no way be kin. *Dub*'s interspecies, nontaxonomic betrayal of the regime of Man, with Man's constitutive whiteness and cisness, advances a coalitional movement defiant of the hubris of phrases like "We the people" or, even more fundamentally, "people" as an automatic kinship.

The fifth chapter, "Questioned, Gendered," concerns black trans femme writer and poet jayy dodd's work. dodd's corpus puts under scrutiny, and examines the potentialities of, racialized gender, conveying radical ways of thinking alongside blackness and gender nonnormativity. The chapter proceeds by meditating on what to dodd it means to be "blxck," her own idiosyncratic spelling for "black," which I argue is for her a mode of inscribing, or making graphemetically apparent, blackness's gender trouble, its indexation of the departure from normative gender symbolics; to be trans, a transness that is always already what she calls a "peak blackness"; to be feminist, or a fraught feminism that resides in the radical praxis of illegibly inscribing otherwise modalities of subjectivity; and to be someplace not here, which I theorize through a close reading of two poems in dodd's 2019 poetry collection *The Black Condition ft. Narcissus*.

Chapter 6, "Trigger, Rebel," reads Venus Di'Khadija Selenite's essays and poems in conjunction with Dane Figueroa Edidi's poetry and interviews. Selenite and Edidi, both black trans women, imagine other ways of living. From Selenite's refusal to work a traditional nine-to-five job as a way to opt out of capitalist logics and the violence of the sphere of professionalism, among other things, to Edidi's understanding of herself as a goddess who has existed before herself and in numerous locations, this chapter mines their essayistic and poetic acumen for imaginative politics. Indeed, Selenite and Edidi imagine how things might operate differently through the blackness and transness and womanness of their lives. They express self-determinative black trans feminism unbounded by normative discourse or intelligible notions of history and time. Their black feminist theorizations, James Bliss might say, are "out of place," as they definitionally mark themselves as outside of institutionalizability. Black trans womanhood becomes, for them, a force of gender defiance, genealogical fracture, spiritual interstitiality, and triggering without warning.

The conclusion is an attempt to showcase what it will look like to live through black trans feminism. Black trans feminism requires a substantial kind of hope, which propels one's in- and exhabitation of the world. It is a stalwart defense of hopefulness that does not capitulate to rosy imagery of things getting better but to what I term "fugitive hope." The conclusion, which I've titled "Hope, Fugitive," essentially gives the theorizations in the previous chapters a way to live. How, the chapter asks and tentatively answers, does one live in the world black trans feministically? Often is it argued that the abjected and marginalized must and should leave the world, must go to outer space, in order to exist. But I want to posit that black trans feminism and all those who take up its demand can claim the world; black trans feminism, too, has a place here, can stay here blacking it up, transing and feministing it up. In claiming the world, the world is overturned and disallowed from simply spinning as it has done; taking hold of the world through the dictates of black trans feminism, in effect, ends the world in order to claim the world, a world emerging in the rubble of this world, anew, in order for something that used to be us to live. It is a chapter and ultimately a theorization of life. Death, though pervasive in academic, material, and social discourses, will not enter here. This chapter is wholeheartedly and tearfully about life. We move, we find joy, we continue to live, we are "still fucking here," as Miss Major would say. And that is all life. We are "won't die things," we refuse death. We, in a word—or, two—hope fugitively.

As I write this, I know that I am on lovingly embattled terrain. I know, for example, that there will be black trans women out there who vehemently disagree with things I say herein. And I am pained, truly, by this fact, for I often feel so strongly that the work I write and think within, the people who have gifted me this knowledge, are trying to inscribe in some faint way a liberatory path precisely for, among many, many others, black trans women. But I have come to realize, via some tough and challenging conversations, that black trans feminism is not *about* black trans women. The radical politics that black trans feminism names are not beholden to "being" a presumed type of subject because it is denoted here as a politics that knows full well that, as micha cárdenas argues, "there is no longer a link that can be assumed between transgender experience and radical politics, if there ever was one"; that identifying as and being identified as black is not a proxy for political radicality; that deeming oneself female or feminist does not do the necessary *werq* feminism, in this radicalized iteration, demands.[35] It is not the aim to think of black trans women as a monolith or automatically, by identificatory virtue, right about what black trans feminism is or might be. Even as I understand myself as part of the project of black trans feminism I must remain cognizant of its heterogeneity, that some under its heading will approach it differently, will feel differently about it. Thus, what I am engaging in these pages is the tradition of immanent critique, wherein I hope to provide a critical and alternative vocabulary—and an excavation of vocabulary that has long been here but has been obscured and forgotten—for the very fields I find myself a part. (I am also engaging "intramural critique," as Spillers would call it, which is surprisingly hard to come by in certain pockets of my fields and social spaces; it is a mode of critique that many have been less concerned with than they perhaps should. So, I am concerning myself with it.) There is the risk that while I aim to write something that will ultimately be liberatory for us at a radically fundamental level (i.e., the level of ontology) I may still be read as hostile to the very people and legacies that have birthed me. My hope is for the former.

Black Trans Feminism is in many ways a plea that tries to invite into its vicinity all those who wish to oppose, undermine, counter, appose, destroy, abolish, or refuse the hegemonic constraints of power. It wants, indeed needs, us all because it is the only way we can save ourselves; it knows, like Malcolm X did in his later, wiser years, that "the only way we'll get freedom for ourselves is to identify ourselves with every oppressed people in the world."[36] Every oppressed people *in the world*. While this particular iteration of black trans feminism takes many of its sources and discourses from Americanist texts and histories, it is with the aim of a borderless and thus geographically dissolutionary world. A specificity in service of an unspecificity; it is, and can be and should be, "about" unbounded sociality, portable outside of the specific U.S. context. I have little interest in anchoring this project, because anchorage is much too close to the conceit of origins; because genealogies are always fraught and unable to account for the links in the lineage that needed to be forgotten in order for the genealogy to maintain its cohesion; because kinship and affinities are promiscuous and irreverent, temporary and dis/located from legible coordinates; because geologics, even if of a darker hue, are logics I ultimately seek to dislodge, for what is place and space at the quantum level? In other words, I am in the business of dissolving borders and boundaries. As I note in my discussion in chapter 5 on jayy dodd, when she discusses being-but-not-being in the United States, much of what I argue is an attempt to write the unbounded and thus is in search of something that also defies national boundaries. Like dodd, while I occupy and draw citations from the place called the United States—which may no doubt circumscribe my audience, a consequence I accept—I am writing with those citations toward and in service of someplace not here, nor there, strictly speaking.

We are still searching for our mothers' gardens. This book is an homage to those who imagined and lived imaginatively in otherworlds while still being here, yet refusing to concede to here's violence. If our mothers and grandmothers, our many-gendered othermothers, moved "to music not yet written. And they waited," as Alice Walker says, what I've penned here is an attempt to write the music to end their waiting.[37]

PART 1

Black, Trans, Feminism

Blackness is an approach, a way of taking in the world.
AUDRE LORDE, "Above the Wind: An Interview with Audre Lorde"

. . . trying to mangle the "truth" of gender and identity
without giving people too many easy answers.
GEO WYETH, "Representation and Its Limits"

In the vein of Cathy Cohen's recalibration of queerness in her land-
mark essay "Punks, Bulldaggers, and Welfare Queens," the kind of nonnormativity expressive of black trans feminism urges for rethought modes of
inhabitation. Cohen argues that queerness, instead of being a possessed
sexual identity ascribed to lesbian, gay, or bisexual people, should be understood as an existential orientation, as a relation to power, which broadens
the ambit through which queerness is interacted. Put another way, this shift
toward the primacy of politicality indexes Angela Davis's feminist posture,
wherein such feminist formations reside "in the possibility of politicizing
this identity—basing the identity on politics rather than the politics on
identity."[1] The desire to radically reconfigure what "identity" means is motivated by "identity" being understood, here, as a normative ideal. The typical
conception of blackness or transness or womanness as an identity, as something that is possessed on the body, is to be rigorously interrogated. Identity
rests upon an assumptive coherence, knowability, and nonporousness, all
of which are regulated, normative regimes of legibility and stability.

But what's wrong with the normative? Do we not want and need a normative, some standard toward which to strive or by which we evaluate our process? Is it not a good thing to instantiate a normative ideal so that we can point to it and say, Look, this is what you need to reach in order for us to become freer? And is not this very meditation an attempt to create a normative apparatus for black trans feminism by which others who wish to do this work can measure their own and others' political commitments?

I respond to the question of the normative with an understanding of it as necessarily violent. Normativity is not merely an innocuous criterion, nor is it simply what is typical or numerically, statistically "normal." Within normative ascriptions—as it is indeed always an ascription, always prescriptive, always an imposition and a coerced rubric to measure against, punitive consequences betiding those who do not measure up—is a demand to meet the evaluative metrics of normativity. It is a *mundane, quotidian* kind of violence. Normativity is defined as that which pertains to norms that govern a given realm of ontology. It is an ontological requisite for one's very ontology; it is a coercive mechanism for livability by only certain means, falling outside of those means relegating one to a nonlivable life. Whiteness and cis genders, for instance, are normative endeavors not because they are purely descriptive of most people in a given environment but because they determine who and what counts as valid, ideal, normal, and representable; bestow consequences on those who do not live up to, adhere to, or who deviate from their rubrics; and cast as imperfect, unfinished, nonideal, or deserving of fewer life chances those who are not proximal to, or who do not appear through, or who stray from, whiteness and cis genders. But the normative also "pertains to ethical justification, how it is established, and what concrete consequences proceed therefrom."[2] Where and how we locate racialized gender is always and already woven into normative operations that dictate such intelligibilities, and what is considered subversive is always and already subject to the ways that the imposition is occurring, when and where it is occurring, to whom it is occurring.

To clarify this meditation's understanding of the normative as it relates to the subversive, I reference Judith Butler: "I am not interested in delivering judgments on what distinguishes the subversive from the unsubversive. Not only do I believe that such judgments cannot be made out of context, but that they cannot be made in ways that endure through time ('contexts' are themselves posited unities that undergo temporal change and expose their essential disunity)."[3] They (that is, Butler)[4] go on to say, "Subversive performances always run the risk of becoming deadening cliches through their repetition and, most importantly, through their repetition within commodity culture where 'subversion' carries market value. The effort to name the criterion for subversiveness will always fail, and ought to. So what is at stake in using the term at all?"[5] It is not a matter of a violence that is somehow spectacularly normative but the very violence of norms (and these norms shift over time and space), a violence that supervenes less along the ways that, say, normative gender expectations do violence to those who do not measure up; it is for me, instead, both about how the normative is necessarily coercive and nonconsensual—the normative only permits you to "be" on its terms, negating your ability to determine your inhabitation of sociality before you even show up precisely because you can only show up if you adhere to its systematicity—as well as how the normative forecloses other realms of intelligibility, making impossible alternative modes of life. The question for me is not what kind of violent things the normative is doing to us; rather, the violence inheres most substantively in the question, What is the normative literally making impossible for us to do, to be, to aspire toward? We cannot begin to parse what is merely descriptive or statistically extant from what is imposed and deemed acceptable because the field of power, normativity, has already dictated what appears as racialized gender and how it exists as intelligible to be considered in the first place. The assessment is rigged from the start.

My commitment to the nonnormative is thus a commitment to what has not been permitted to appear on the scene. The nonnormative must be carefully distinguished from the "counter" or the "oppositional" inasmuch as these, to me, express a reaction to what has been established. To counter or oppose, which is not without meaning and efficacy, is simply insufficient in the final instance as an abolitionist gesture because it maintains the logics imputed by that which is countered or opposed, logics that have orchestrated the very framework sought to be done away with. The nonnormative, thus, does not accept or *decline*—it doesn't "cline" at all; the nonnormative is an operation on other grounds and by other means not predicated on legibilizing identities, knowledges, or sense-making apparatuses already in place. It is also, crucially, about a way of relating and unrelating, or nonrelating, giving it the tenor of politics massively uninterested in the presumptions that inhere in certain configurations of somatics. Nonnormativity is here distinguished as a multifaceted and polyvocal interruption of ontological tenets, doing the work of interruption on various registers that may even be more substantive than the somatic; nonnormativity is here distinguished as the way that politicality engenders what we subsequently might mean and how we might literally matter or show up in the world, a *potentia* that morphs into, or that is always already, a *kinesthesia* that is not an identity nor possession—it is a modality, a disposition, a deployment, a subjective plenum we move through and amidst as an indexation of what else might be possible for us to become unbeholden to the violences that have purportedly forged all we can be.

All of this also might go under the heading of a commitment to what has been deemed the otherwise, or Denise Ferreira da Silva's articulation of an interrogative inclination to ask "other"-wise, as the otherwise elaborates an alternative that by necessity critiques the given and the normative, critiques the normative in service of something, anything, other than what has been mentioned and given and touted as that which is all we have.[6] Irrespective of the efficacy of what is already deemed legible, it stands that what is already here has coexisted with the violences of the world. Black trans feminism commits to the nonnormative because nonnormativity references the world of abolition. It is not a reference necessarily to gender nonconformity or what are deemed nonnormative sexual practices; the nonnormativity of black trans feminism may well inflect and have these things as its partial archive, but when I use the term in these pages I am talking about the stuff that has been expunged from the field of power, the stuff that might be the sinewy anarchitecture of the world in the midst of abolition's onset, for nonnormativity is meant to reference nonviolated existence and indeed existence that gains its definitional heft by virtue of its expulsion of ontological violation. Gender nonnormativity, then, for example, will be what gender might be and become were it not for Gender, what we emerge into when we are not nonconsensually given an ontology of gender—that is, not simply binary gender but the very structure of or imposition necessary for legible subjectivity that we have come to call Gender—and that is the nonnormativity about which I speak here.

So, how one subjectivates oneself nonnormatively references more a *political* identity, three of which go by the irreducible names of black, trans, and feminist, which name sites of coalitional conspiracy and furnish fluid mechanisms by which to cultivate what it means, politically, to live among others on more ethical grounds, across and within differentiations.[7] I maintain that insofar as corporeality situates one in literal and symbolic space, the simple fact of one's occupying such a space with others says little about the affective and political substance, or even the fact of membership, of the space's inhabitants. To belong with and in this space with others is not simply, or primarily, to end at the corporeal surface; to belong with and in this space with others is more specifically a way of relating to spatiality, politicality, history, and subjectivity in a way that cannot be physically assumed. Of importance is affiliation and commitment to insurgent forms of life, rather than an exclusionary limning of boundary, because it concerns itself with how we interact with one another via an open critical posture. I wish to emphasize a sociality-in-differentiation, one that is not possessed natally and ad infinitum; a "sociality without exclusion," as J. Kameron Carter and Sarah Jane Cervenak would have it.[8] This is the fashioning of subjectivities formed through a desire, as noted in the introduction, to be held, but such a holding is an encompassing openness that eases but does not contain. I want to express some kind of subjectivity that allows for us to be loved and embraced without, and as a rejection of, fixing us, limiting or knowing us in totality, without stalling movement as a means to manufacture commonality and legibility. The holding, which is always a facilitator of rather than impediment to our movement, in fact lets us *come* together instead of being *brought* together.

The forthcoming breakdowns are necessarily misguided, but it is in the service of illumination that I am misguiding myself and readers. To say, as I do subsequently, "black and trans," "black and feminist," and "trans and feminist" is incomplete and half-truthful because they cannot be so easily parsed, as any intersectionalist could explain, though I myself care much less for that terminology than others. But extending intersectionalist critiques, the impossibility of parsing "black" and "trans" and "feminist" from one another is because of their inflections of one another, their intrareverberations. "Black" and "trans" will, or at least ought to, inflect feminism; "black" and "feminist" will, or at least ought to, inflect transness; "trans" and "feminist" will, or at least ought to, inflect blackness.

BLACK AND TRANS

Emphasizing the conversation, the rap session, that blackness and transness have long been having is to emphasize their capacity for deploying mutability in service of exceeding modes of regulatory captivity. So, first, let's think blackness. Blackness might be glimpsed in the flesh, which I will discuss more at length in the following chapter. Flesh is "ante- and antimatter," which uncouples it from the materiality and purported objectivity of the visual surface.[9] And matter, we know, does things, is not merely lying in wait to be acted upon; matter is a performative metaphysics that is not a latent thing but an agential doing, a performativity that rebels underneath and to the side of, not against, preexistence and moves with the force of desedimentation. Blackness's adherence to flesh rather than bodies delinks it from taxonomic racial classifications, which are the province of bodies, and opens it up to the fleshy subjectivity of all who dare to claim it. If we are to live in and through the flesh, if flesh is the different modality of existence engendered when fully inhabited, if the flesh is the onset of the abolition of (overrepresented) "Man" (making it not only a "racial" critique of Western civilization but, too, a "gendered" critique, which too many fail to make explicit even if blackness is, as so many often use as absolution, "ungendered"), blackness must be unhinged from the terrain of encroachable racialized bodies and dis/located elsewhere, in the uncapturable. Such work becomes unusual politics, an unrecognizable "transgender politics" that Aren Aizura maintains "invests not in an identity category but in disrupting the litany of injustices that comprise twenty-first-century capitalism. . . . If race, gender, and sexuality determine the norms of intimate and public social relations, those of democracy, nation, prison, property, labor, and (settler) colonialism, a trans politics aimed at disrupting those institutions may not read as politics at all"—it may read as radicality or abolitionist work, which, for my purposes, is to say black trans feminist work.[10] When we divest from the categories created by the state, we might then be able to inhabit the flesh. Mere reversal of the valuative hierarchy between the hegemonic and the subordinated reifies its logic, fails to interrogate the texture of hegemonic identities, and keeps in place the identities modernity has created. In short, such a move, as J. Kameron Carter has argued, is "not radical enough," and we must instead commit to "nonracial flesh," unracial and ungendered flesh, trans/gendered flesh.[11] But I'm getting ahead of myself; more on this explicitly in the following chapter.

This is the bind in which I want to dwell: the fact of a visual field coded through racial optics that fixes bodies deemed black into static racial templates deserving of fatal policing, and the more substantive *doing* of blackness, the iconoclastic doing of one's subjectivity in refusal and subversion of governmentality. Though a solidarity on the basis of historically epidermalized pathology is significant to the extent that a common oppression allows for a unique insight into how one traverses the world, it is a troublesome thought to fix solidarity in blackness to a primordial moment of violence, terror, and pathology. Blackness is not to be reduced to its epidermally formative moment of violence, as it constitutes blackness solely in and through violence and horror. Understanding blackness only or primarily through violence constructs blackness only insofar as it has the intensified capacity to be terrorized. Blackness becomes, simply, that thing that can get you killed, which, to me, greatly flattens what blackness has been and can and will be. I am black, this argument goes, because—and mostly only because—they are coming to get me.

No.

Blackness on my account of black trans feminism is linked to opening and unfixing, which promotes its capacity for life, though lived in ways that may not look like life to current evaluative tools. If there is to be any relation between black and trans it comes from the mobilizing torque that makes the static, imposed, and assumed lose these essential properties. I am not interested in adjudicating the final definition of blackness as an identifiable entity but in allowing blackness to, simply, do work that initiates nonnormative, insurgent effects that trouble and ultimately dissolve what we have been given. The work comes from rendering the status quo, hegemony, normativity—pick your terminology for that which engenders violence and circumscription—unrecognizable and thus able to be gotten away from. The given terms diminish subjective possibility, so blackness might describe the process by which, illegible as it may be, different modes of being and becoming are glimpses of life lived unfettered by normative violence moving through us by way of white and cis male supremacy (etc.). These different modes of being, designated as black modes of being, inasmuch as blackness engenders the possibility of mutability, require a loosening of the things that purport to allow us to exist. It is maintained that these things that call themselves identities do not actually allow us to exist as we wish; they limit our capacity to be otherwise, which is, I want to argue, what subjectivity, what a self-determined self, is par excellence: the ability to be other than what we are. It is in that that self-determination rests, and it is in that that blackness gains its peak transness (to rework jayy dodd, about whom I speak later in part 2 of this book). Blackness, because of its inherent feminism (on which I elaborate momentarily), is fundamentally "an anticaptivity project," so in opposing captivity we must oppose the various ways in which we are not only captured (enslavement, racially coded optics, etc.) but capture ourselves in logics and frameworks that could never encompass our breadth.[12] This is a tapping into blackness's queerness, drawing from it the queer counternarrative, or perhaps even nega-narrative (how closely this prefix rubs against the epithetic), of relational identificatory engendering; this is blackness's otherwise identification, located in the interstices, frictional relations, and rebellious communing with those we are not supposed to commune with, befriending the misfits and being/becoming in excess of what has been permitted. In other words, blackness, reconceptualized in this way, is a queer relationality, a "blackqueer aesthesis," that "otherwise mode of relationality not predicated upon blood quantum nor juridical declarations of law and land."[13] Blackness names one of the many ways we affectively recompose subjectivities in the name of liberation, flight from the nonbecoming hegemon of Man. It is a trans blackness that is an ante-anti-category, a preceding and subverting predilection for opposing cohesive categorization.

Okay, now let's think transness. The transness integral to an understanding of blackness bears an intimate link to it by way of transness's disruption of bodily coherence. If transness is distinguished from being transgender, and if transness marks primarily a *movement* away from an imposed starting point to an undisclosed (non)destination, then this emblematizes abolitionist gender radicality: the fixedness and presumed immutability of bodily bestowal is dissolved through a departure toward something else through the vector of gender—or, more precisely, through a generative warping of gender toward something else. Since a paraontological blackness expresses the inadequacy of a "given ontology," transness, too, bears a referential relationship with blackness because of both's refusal of enclosed coherence, rejection of imposed racialized gendered ontologies, and movement away from captivity. The colonial record does not have the last word on who we can be. Transness's propinquity to blackness, their kinship, develops different kinships for us all, a kind of "trans*kinship" that acts "across, through, between, among, those with whom we identify, to whom we are attached, that is not simply a question of blood, or even of archive, but rather, and more suggestively, of proximity and affinity, touch, breath, dream." This kinship demands that we ask, "What if we breathe together as queerly connected, as trans*historical kin," or, how might we "imagine otherly" ways, per LaVelle Ridley, to aspirate not beholden to epistemic, ontological, or necropolitical constraints?[14] And we know, at least since July 17, 2014, in Staten Island, but also so much longer before that, that breathing is of vital importance. How can we breathe together, find ways to inhale oxygen as well as, say, water, smoke, blood, any readily available material to sustain ourselves? How can those with an abundance of breath give that breath to those whose reserves are nearly depleted? Breathing gifts us with an attention to wonder, which then alerts us to mutability and alteration, culminating in a realization—a critical interrogative (black) trans feminist realization—that "challenges assumptions about 'proper' scientific or political objects." This wondrous breathing, Magdalena Górska has written, connects us to others across imposed differentiations.[15] We come to a breathing oddly together, looking for different breath, impossible breath, airless air to saturate our lungs, as the pursuit that puts us in sync with one another.

The black and trans, if there is to be a fundamental and convergent link between them—as I vehemently argue there is—must be thought not through strict identificatory means, which nearly always manifest in exclusionary, border-delimiting criteria, but through a radically insurrectionary mode. Such a conception allows for jettisoning stilted discourses surrounding authenticity and "realness" that only work to limit the number of accomplices we might otherwise have to combat violent regimes. Too, a blackness and transness given over to us conceptually via abolition makes for a clearer and more capacious assemblage of politicized subjects capable of inhabiting a sociality after abolition *lived now*, which acts in subversion of the normative frame that so broadly structures the current necropolitical, circumscriptive one. The insurrection at the heart of these two analytics, which do not simply analyze but operate from a subjective and material reality that provides epistemic access to a radically inclusive analytic trove, refutes the misguided and (often unintentionally) violent presupposition of the dominance of the purportedly biological. If there is a description of blackness that follows thusly—

> concern over the supposedly stultifying force of authenticity exerted by supposedly restrictive and narrow conceptions of blackness, worry over the supposed intranational dominance of blackness broadly and unrigorously conceived (in ways that presuppose its strict biological limitation within an unlimited minoritarian field), or anxiety over the putatively intradiasporic hegemony of a certain mode of blackness (which presumes national as well as biological determinations that are continually over- and underdetermined) indexes some other trouble that we would do well to investigate[16]

—then it becomes clear that in this refutation of a biological determinism in which there is no validity given to the imposition of an ontology onto putatively biologically immutable "facts," blackness is a trans matter inasmuch as transness can be understood through an insurrection of the axiologically dominant valorization of "sex" (the location[s] of which is/are often never settled or defined in any systematic way) as determinative of "gender." To continually root blackness in a somatic endowment that gains its substantiveness by way of a belief in its immutability, its presumed ethical need to delimit it, its nationalistic and biological definitiveness, and its territorial need to secure and defend is a disservice and, I might wager, a misreading of how we ought to understand blackness in order to create a way of relating to others on more just, coalitional, abolitionist, radical, loving, and hopeful grounds. Getting to this requires a relinquishing of the predominance of the biological, so often deployed in violent and exclusionary ways, which elaborates blackness through an investigative disposition skeptical of the biological, the territorial, and the immutable. Blackness, in other words, is a trans matter; transness is a fundamentally black praxis. This black and trans matter is the "other trouble" that we are correctly urged to investigate. What is in your hands now is that very investigation.

The cohabitation of blackness and transness creates space for the unknowable to emerge. Kai M. Green sees the nexus of these two forces, in part, as asking us "to develop new optics, a new way of seeing that is less reliant upon categorical delineation" and more reliant on escape from categorization, escape from normative conceptions of who we are permitted to be.[17] Blackness and transness trouble narratives like being "trapped in the wrong body" and urge for existence in transition. The wrong body narrative sees transition as a frustrating means to an end, buttressing two distinct poles of a binary, the end of which is untroubled situatedness in an identifiable norm. But a blackened transness, so to speak, unproduces this narrative and thinks about the multifaceted ways we can be, as Green concludes, "unpredetermined movement."[18]

The black and trans attune us to how radically comporting to the world via nonracial and nongendered, or unracial and ungendered, subjectivity emergent through black trans radicalism begets a politicized subjectivity fueled by an abolitionist posture. The underground politics and furtive insurgency are what matter here, not to the exclusion but in *excess* of other things that might (have been said to) matter. My hesitance to affix the politicality and fugitivity of the black and trans to the physiognomic stems from the fact that their corporeality implies little about how one does their work. There is, in Sylvia Wynter's words, "no guarantee that even if you experience yourself in self-alienating terms," which might be to say you occupy the racialized or gendered position of blackness/womanness/transness, "you will not push that out of the mind; it shows that there is no guarantee that you cannot be assimilated into seeing yourself in normative terms."[19] Put crassly, you can be racialized black, identified and identify as a woman or transgender (or both [or all three]) and still do some fucked-up shit, still hold steadfast to violent norms. Thus, the weightiness of the things formerly known as identities must shift to the ways one deploys oneself in subversion of power, and in alternative relationality. I want to lovingly, painstakingly move toward black and trans, in this instance, naming those alternative relationalities. Inextricable are blackness and transness under racial capitalistic regimes, black and trans life generatively folding into one another referentially and speaking a transient, transductive, and transformative "werqing" of social categories. Black and trans people, then, put in werq— and it is my contention that "black" and "trans" are names for that werqing— the deformation and denaturation of racial, gender, and sexual categories that grip our ontologies. Werqing, indexical of the paraontological force of blackness and transness, is the destabilization of the purported homes of race, gender, and sexuality, the excessive fissures of the project of Man.[20]

BLACK AND FEMINIST

It is 1983. Alice Walker, in *In Search of Our Mothers' Gardens*, gives her now-famous and off-the-cuff quotable definitions of "womanist." Her second entry of the definition, emphasizing love for women, concludes with a telling conversation between a child and mother. "'Mama,'" the child asks, "'why are we brown, pink, and yellow, and our cousins are white, beige and black?'" The mother answers, "'Well, you know the colored race is just like a flower garden, with every color flower represented.'" In the wake of the Black Power era's more prominent strains of monolithized blackness, Walker presents a radical disruption of such thinking, and the thinking of what constitutes "the colored race," read "black." What does it say that the "colored race" can be, in a word, any color? What does it say that one's colored—black—family can be not only brown, black, or "high yella" but also pink and white? Walker seems to be unfixing blackness and familial affiliation with it from set epidermal measurements and locating blackness, coloredness, somewhere else. Walker, in this anecdote that one can hear in the voice of their own mama, advances a blackness that pervades various shades, a blackness echoing an artistic axiom presented by conceptual and performance artist Lina Iris Viktor: "Every color in the spectrum is contained in black"; and echoing, in a scholarly vein, Tavia Nyong'o, who writes in *Afro-Fabulations* of a "uchromatic" blackness (following François Laruelle), "a blackness which is not the absence or opposite of color, but the possibility of any color whatsoever. Blackness not as the end, but as the one: the anorigin of minoritarian anarchaeology."[21] It is a commitment to the polychromacticity of blackness that allows one to enter into black-ness from a variety of positions, giving blackness a radical openness unanticipated by logics of hegemony; it is Denise Ferreira da Silva's "un-moored" black feminist blackness, which moves "in excess of the objects and subjects it creates," resisting definitive racialized bodies said to be black; it is CeCe McDonald's—Honee Bea's—request for us to use every color imaginable to fashion who we are, self-determinedly, as every color can and does constitute the texture of our blackness and transness when we, rejecting ontologics that masquerade as unmediated and natural, "go beyond our natural selves."[22] Blackness's openness, its ability to claim vari-ous unanticipated subjects, makes it a cunning beast.

Walker's deployment of blackness as capacious and multivalent is also affixed to an ethics. Blackness denotes "paying the cost," claiming deviance and dwelling with normativity's subversion. That is to say, a deployable, paraontological blackness marks "a kind of *ethical* gesture to claim this dispossession . . . this radical poverty-in-spirit."[23] Surely it is understood here that a history of the way particular characteristics, and thus particu-lar positionings, have been made to attach to skin color makes it sensible to see kinship in those who, too, have been subjected to similar racialized plights as oneself. My critique is that a substantive solidarity rests not in how one has been treated—which almost exclusively gets tied to histori-cal terror and trauma as opposed to, for example, racialized instances of joy—but with how one approaches world-changing, politicality, and thus radical politics to beget a more habitable world. "We are the African and the trader," Walker notes. "We are the Indian and the settler. We are oppressor and oppressed. . . . We are the mestizos of North America. We are black, yes, but we are 'white,' too, and we are red."[24] We are fugitives to purported immutable and imposed identities. Or we are trans to racial categorization. Unification, or coalitional subjectivity in blackness and feminism, is assem-blic; "we" can live in this undercommon space because it is open, but only if you dare.

Also, Walker's remixed and extensive blackness is saturated with and in her black feminist, her womanist, vernacular theorizations, and this is where I wish to dwell for the moment. In short, this remixed blackness is necessarily womanist. (I am aware, of course, of the analogical relation-ship between womanism and [black] feminism. I am timidly conflating them here because Walker notes one of the definitions of womanist as "a black feminist," and I am ultimately utilizing womanism's close proximity to black feminism in order to reveal how we might extend a paraontological distinction and emphasis on politicality to black feminism.) Indeed, her definitions of womanism concern less mere natal corporeal or cultural happenstance and more with proclivity, with preference, with politics. Womanism is to *act* grown, to act audacious, outrageous, to exert *"willful behavior"*; to *commit* to survival; to love in the struggle. Tying a pervasive, almost rhizomatic blackness to a deeply black feminist politic inflects it in a way that refuses being hemmed by hegemonic seductions from white *or* cis male supremacy. It refuses as well your run-of-the-Negro-mill shallowly deployed blackness by, largely, black (cis[?]) men who take on a narrow nationalistic blackness that "merely call[s] on Black people to love Black, live Black and buy Black," which Alicia Garza and numerous other black queer feminists have critiqued time and again.[25] Black feminism is and must be, for Walker, integral to a capacious, multivalent understanding of blackness. A blackness that is constituted by black feminism forces one to lose stable ground to the end of self-threatening—rendering one's own hegemonic destruction—and opening sociality until we can become-black together differently, excessively. Black feminism is in fact constitutive of such an understanding of blackness, and thus it is sensible to argue that blackness as capacious willful subversion *is* what we mean by black feminism.

It bears making explicit that feminism, that darling of white women who clutch dearly their claim to being oppressed and never oppressor, does not belong to whiteness. If feminism is that which perpetually must trouble its own ground and assumptions, that must work to a constant posture of destabilizing violent normativities (or, as the Combahee River Collective notes, "we are committed to a continual examination of our politics as they develop through criticism and self-criticism as an essential aspect of our practice"); if feminism is the commitment to vitiating gendered hierarchies, (cis) male supremacy, and heteropatriarchy, which necessitates that *gender* itself must be the aim of that committed vitiation; and if feminism might be said to actualize its radicality by those who subtend its most vocal aspects—if it is fueled most by "the forgotten women who 'fell down the well' (as Carolyn Heilbrun puts it) in subsequent rewritings of Women's Liberation as exclusively white"—then feminism *can only be* black trans feminism.[26] Black feminist study is everywhere, beholden to no strictly delimited demographic, bearing no strict criteria for entrance, always expressive of a "radical inclusivity" because, in "mak[ing] possible new worlds for Black life forms," it becomes the most capacious analytic for making possible *new life*.[27] Black trans feminism is the feminism black feminism has been talking about, the feminism trans feminism has been talking about. What

I assert, then, is that the inextricability of the terms in black trans feminism stem from their convergence and concatenation with one another as analytics for differently inflected modes of subversion and transformation. Blackness converges with feminism inasmuch as there is a history of black women and femmes pointing out the inseparability of race and gender as well as a history of blackness radicalizing feminist social justice aims. Additionally, "Black feminist theory [i]s essential to Black trans theory and to transgender studies [because] Black feminist thought, labor, and commitment have been essential to the de/construction of gender and sexuality," as the guest editors of the "Issue of Blackness" volume of *Transgender Studies Quarterly* note.[28] Transness forces feminism to heed its radical commitment to inclusivity, which, as it were, is propelled by the radically inclusive blackness of black feminism.

Black feminism, or the feminism of blackness and the blackness of feminism—and this way of breaking down the common term denotes how feminism, to be feminist, must always be generated by blackness's insurrectionary relation to gender and blackness must always, in order to do what blackness does, vitiate the gender binary with the paradoxical aim of gender expansiveness and abolition—is misunderstood if it is understood as parochial and about establishing epistemological property. So very often black feminism is misattributed as a minority form of knowledge that pertains strictly to an identitarian demographic and relevant only to the denizens of that demographic when it is, in fact, like Audre Lorde's understanding of blackness articulated in the epigraph above, an approach, and a radical abolitionist one at that.[29] We do not comfortably inhabit this black feminism but operate via an exhabitation; we enact political aims by way of deploying ourselves from black feminism since it is something that commands us to do rather than deems that we are. We are all of us entangled and intra-acting, and diffusive in that entanglement—infectiously spreading while coming together in unforeseen ways—which displaces being for becoming. So, the perhaps expected distinction underlying my claims is that between black feminism and black women. Black feminism is not the sole province of black women; black feminism is a commitment to inhabiting, disseminating, becoming, and choosing a disruptive and excessive posture of critique, one that has (to be frank, arbitrarily) been historically, but contingently, rooted in those subjects deemed black women. (I will take this question up further in chapter 2's discussion of "becoming-black-woman" as well as in chapter 4's meditation on Alexis Pauline Gumbs's work.) To reinsert in a more expanded version a quote by Hortense Spillers noted in the introduction,

Black feminism also seeks a degree of critical independence in relationship to the social order so that *its posture is the critical posture*. But I need to make a distinction between black women, black women as the subject of feminism, and black feminism as a critical disposition; all three of these distinctions might well overlap and show relationship to each other, but they also define distinct positionalities that we tend to occlude; for example, *not all black women are feminists, or the subjects of feminism, not even black feminism*, and insisting on the difference allows us to capture nuance, and enough nuance spells the difference between night and day, hot and cold, etc. . . . I should like to think that *black feminisms, as a repertoire of concepts, practices, and alignments*, is progressive in outlook and dedicated to the view that sustainable life systems must be available to everyone.[30]

Though black women think and act in ways that reveal their "distinct angle of vision" of the social world, black feminism is not reducible to an amalgamation of the ideologies, thoughts, political leanings, proclivities, etc. of black women, a line of reasoning that concludes that only black women can do and create black feminism. Rather, black feminism is an epistemology, "knowledging" the world-as-world and becoming imbricated, habituated corporeally and discursively, in the production of renegade knowledge, that historically indexes black women but is not reducible to them. Because I also bring the trans to bear on all subjectivities, it is necessary to trouble where, how, and when we "know" a black *woman* appears, as often the assumption that black feminism is about, simply, black women leads to troubling implications of only talking about "cis" black women, with the oft-mentioned discourse of the "black maternal" (which sometimes instantiates black women as, definitionally, maternal figures), the elision of incarcerated black trans women and the specific violences they face, or the shallow gesture toward trans inclusion in literal parentheticals yet continuing to make implicit and explicit arguments predicated on the gender binary and anatomical essentialism. The trans, in other words, significantly throws loving but necessary shade on the monolith of The Black Woman, querying, in a fashion that has been offered by 1970s black women throwing shade on white feminists: What do you mean "we," black (cis) woman? And, indeed, too, black feminism stages an entrée into onto-epistemic sociality, exculpating black women as bearers of the onus of representation and responsibility. A trans/feminist understanding of this might be to reconfigure black feminism as an approach, or as a mangling of the "truth" of race and gender, as Geo Wyeth says in the second chapter epigraph, which follows Lorde.

It is precisely the goal of black feminism to decouple anatomical medicalized markers of gender (e.g., genitalia) from sociogenically gendered subjects (or black feminism as a refutation of mainstream, white "marketplace feminism," which implies that simply being female [transantagonistically reduced to having a vagina] is effusively celebratory and the extent of the work of feminism), *and*, I would argue, from epidermalized markers of blackness.[31] It does not abide implicit assumptions about its biological grounding in either race or gender; instead it operates on the understanding that it, black feminism, is a theorizing first and foremost, one that suspends assumptions of race, gender, and sex because they must be approached with the posture of interrogation and destabilization. C. Riley Snorton makes a similarly cogent argument in his critique of black male feminism's uncritical self-reflexivity, noting that it, and by extension black feminism, must include "studies of masculinity along a range of bodies—never diminishing its critique of patriarchy—but refocusing its critique on processes of socialization that do not rely on particular (mis)readings of anatomy." Black feminism is thus "a radical destabilization of" racialized and gendered subjects—their transfiguration, as Snorton would say—and about which I will say more in chapter 3.[32] If somatic readings are inadequate to racial and gender designations, it is perhaps an illegible anteoriginal force motivating the consolidation of bodies into categories that index such forces. Hence, my interest lies in the excavation of the texture of that force, a force that black feminism cites in its racial and gendered inflections of abolition. Therefore, black feminism is not merely a history of black women critiquing white men, white women, and black men, but a citation of the fissuring besidedness of that primordial mutiny that renders the troubling of the historical indexations of the attempt to mitigate that mutinous force (e.g., whiteness and cis masculinity).

What if black feminism remixed, then, is less a matter (or nonmatter, ante- and antimatter) of who is black and woman and more a kind of subaltern nonlocation that "necessarily resides outside the grasps of hegemony"? Thus, black feminism becomes, here, what Eric A. Stanley calls the dream of an "insurgent trans study that refuses its own complicity in the brutality of exclusion," its radical inclusivity motivated by the unfixing of immutable "identities" from what we are said to be able to do and become.[33] Black feminism is open to anyone who takes up the work of black feminism, its black and trans insurrectionary work. Black feminism is a praxis, a performative process of engagement and subversion that "rests" nowhere but is instead incited to continue living, hard and always with intention, in the moments when it is committed to. It has always been such, and, as being such, it bends biomythographically, offering "vast possibilities for rethinking 'questions of identity' in its ability to formally dissemble identities' 'static limitations.'"[34] And in this sense, too, it becomes clear that what people like Che Gossett, Tourmaline, AJ Lewis, and Nat Raha have argued is decidedly true: "Black feminism has always been trans."[35]

TRANS AND FEMINIST

In a very real sense, feminism and transness need one another. To the extent that transness—or transgender identity, or transgender studies—is persistently routed through a liberal individualism that assumes a singular, internally autonomous subject, feminism contributes to this a coalitional politics and recognition of power's productivity (i.e., how power produces the very options, or nonoptions, at our disposal; how power acts on and through us in ways that orchestrate, to some effect, what we understand as our and others' gender). And, insofar as feminism has a deeply embedded history of trans-exclusion and discursive, political, and personal violence toward gender-binaristic deviation—indeed, feminism's history of, with white and cis male supremacy, instantiating and buttressing the purported inviolability of the gender binary—feminism needs transness/trans studies in order to deliver on its claim of radical inclusivity.

What has come to be called trans feminism was initially understood as something like looking at feminism through a transgender lens, or bringing transgender women into the folds of feminism. Instead of a focus on patriarchy understood through a rigid male oppression of women, trans feminists took aim at the gender binary as a more fundamental and robust bedrock for the gendered ills that plague us. Instead of addressing symptoms like that of the power and value imbued into those who identified or were identified as men to the inverse siphoning of power and value from those who identified and were identified as women, trans feminism aims, historically and contemporarily, to address the *genre* of this phenomenon—namely, the hierarchized binary itself. Trans feminism is an assault on the genre of the binary, that ontological caste that universalizes itself and structures how we are made possible.

Many accounts describe trans feminism as an iteration of intersectional feminism detailing how sexism and transphobia intersect and mutually reinforce one another. On this account, trans feminism was first articulated in Spain (as *transfeminismo*) in the late 1980s in order to call for the inclusion of trans women in feminist politics. Thankfully, subsequent to this origin trans feminism became part of a broader feminist politic that aimed to resist capitalism, bring antiracist and postcolonial critiques to state policies, and act in anti-institutional and radically democratic ways. So while trans feminism has sometimes meant merely the inclusion of trans women in feminist politics, it now describes "an epistemology—a theory of knowledge and power—that guides a diverse array of transfeminist activist political practices" with four pillars of influence that Sayak Valencia, a Mexican trans feminist scholar, delineates as U.S. women of color feminists, postporn and anticapitalist subcultures, movements to disarticulate trans identity from medical governance and the clinic, and acts to aid the life chances of migrants.[36]

The transness of feminism is indebted to those of transgender experiences—the violences that betide those who are transgender, violences that can prove fatal upon being "found out" during or after sex acts and then retroactively blamed by way of "trans panic" laws; embodied experiences across, beyond, and between gendered categories; distinct angles of insight into the gender binaristic interstices in professional, medical, and carceral realms. The transness of feminism, too, seeks to inflect the disorienting work of those whose bodies are positioned in antagonistic ways with respect to the gender binary and understand transness through this disorientation, this rebellious and abolitionist spirit, rather than placing the onus of gender disruption onto the bodies of those who position themselves and are positioned as transgender. In excess of the set criteria for gender (non)comportment (criteria still open for debate), I am articulating transness in a way that two trans lesbians and their allies in Le Zoo (a French queer group, founded in 1996) articulate it: "We identify as trans because we are doing politics, not because of our transsexualism."[37] Transness becomes a way of doing oneself as nonnormatively related to a coercive gender binary that saturates the world, a deployment of oneself as ill-fitting with the tenets of this world, escaping the circumscriptive reach of hegemony. Transness, as what Cameron Awkward-Rich describes as "a project of undoing (gender, disciplines, selves), a project that . . . never tries to build a house," finds generative circulation within feminism as its radical circuitry, inasmuch as feminism and its attending blackness—radical feminism as a necessary black feminism—is a persistent vigilance as to how it must undo and un-incorporate its own foundation.[38] Ungrounded and opposed to any notion of a "proper" object of study, the conjoining of trans and feminism inducts all who wish to bring about world transformation. Transness and feminism place a demand on all of us who wish to bring about an abolished world, forcing us to put our proclivities and ourselves in service of gendered disruption irrespective of corporeal positionality. We as feminists are not off the hook.

"Transfeminism" has been most sustainedly theorized by Emi Koyama in her "Transfeminist Manifesto." Koyama notes that trans feminism, like numerous other iterations of feminism, was first thought to be a "distraction" that fractured a movement that sought to maintain a cohesion and undifferentiation. (I can sympathize here, as my articulation of black trans feminism has been deemed an unnecessary extension of black feminism by none other than Patricia Hill Collins herself, implying that "black trans feminism" is an unneeded term and thus a distraction from the work of black feminist thought.[39]) Trans feminism, though, forced a response from feminism, since it made "other feminists . . . rethink their idea of whom they represent and what they stand for," and subsequently it critiques the capaciousness of their efforts. Trans women, for Koyama, "further [expand] the scope of the movement." Trans feminism has at its core trans women but—in a nonidentitarian fashion, which Koyama finds to be more libera-tory as well as consilient with trans feminism's ultimate aim—escapes defi-nitional constriction by remaining open to anyone who claims a coalitional solidarity with trans women because they believe "their alliance with trans women to be essential for their own liberation."[40] Fundamental to trans feminism is self-determination, the choosing of one's own subjectivity and the expectation that this chosen subjectivity will be the means by which they and those who encounter them engage sociality. This is in primary service of the eradication of violence, of which normative impositions are prime culprits. Too, there is a recognition of subjective complexity and nonteleological subjectivity—that one is not required to be "born" some-thing in order to become something else, nor does one's differing natal identity with one's current identity disqualify or negate either identifica-tion. Any external or coerced impositions of sex or gender undermine the aims of trans feminism, which advocates for "a social arrangement where one is free to assign her or his own sex (or non-sex, for that matter)." Important as well is a resistance to the temptation of "wrong body" nar-ratives that operate on the assumption of essentialist, biologized origins of gender identity and expression. The implications of such narratives, for

Koyama and her theorization of trans feminism, skew troublesomely into the realm of female and male souls or minds, bifurcating dualistic genders in axiomatic ways, which then ultimately harms women and transgender people, essentializes gender identity, and disallows self-determination. The argument made by trans feminism is that we want to "dismantl[e] the essentialist assumption of the normativity of the sex/gender congruence."[41] And with this comes a necessary penchant toward abolition, not as a seizure of the means by which we have come into subjectivity, expanding the criteria for sex and sanctioning the validity of "misaligned" criteria or adding valid genders to the options for our social media profiles. Not revolution, but abolition: we are not playing the game anymore, not altering the rules—we are leaving the field, throwing away our equipment, depriving funding from restoration efforts, and joyfully watching the stadium crumble not because we smashed it to bits but simply because we left and refused to come back.

Bringing trans and feminist together, making them hold hands, as it were, is a quest to radicalize them both. If transness has a strain of history that rejects feminism (Virginia Prince, Caitlyn Jenner), and if feminism has a strain of its history that is transantagonistic (Janice Raymond, Michele Wallace, Sheila Jeffreys), how might bringing them together refuse those histories and make them each find an identity not solely in a common history but in their advancement of a political posture of radicality? Transness's and feminism's existence within one another must find life outside of a strict sharing of genealogical trajectories as the basis for relationality and identification and in a rallying around a sociality that can accommodate divergent pathways. These pathways cannot be anticipated, which is precisely what must commence when we dare to actualize the radical world of which we speak. It will be unexpected; it will look different; it will be what we yearned for. And we may be terrified. But we have known terror, have been bred in part by it. And we know how to live amid it, in spite of it. But if we trade in the terror that has long gripped us for the terror of what a life without being suffocated might be like, we then fear only the wild possibilities of life as it can be for us: life un/gendered.

Transness's and feminism's coalition make plain that sex/gender are "absolutely political categor[ies]" since they maintain "an eminently political binary articulation, *the product of oppression, just like racial difference.*"[42] These categories are oppressive bestowals and impositions, at base. Transness and feminism, then, interrogate Western thought and set out to dismantle the foundational tenets on which Man rests. What culminates is a refusal of the categorization of sex and gender, inscribing into (black) trans feminism gender *and* sex abolition *as* gender radicality. A feminism that is immersed in a transitivity is tasked with refusing to be exhausted by exhaustion. Indeed, this open-ended critique and undoing of themselves allows transness and feminism to name as their aim the excess that spills over as the point of departure (and never "arrival") for trans and feminist work. It is what we must constantly, vigilantly, not only commit ourselves to but understand, that the thing to which we commit ourselves—black trans feminism—is operable *through* its own interrogation. "We must always be willing to interrupt ourselves," Kai Lumumba Barrow suggests, "even when we think we've got it 'right.'"[43] I might say, further, that what I am trying to describe is precisely that interruption of ourselves, a politics comprised of those moments where we interrupt our coherence as a self and the normative logics upon which we base our political valences. Necessary is the risk of deviant multiplicity, vitiation of borders—our borders are that of the unbordered, and we politicize and find politicality in this refusal to be bordered. Unbordered politicality makes us fracture ourselves, uncongeal ourselves, unbecome ourselves and deviate our identities from nation-state and hegemonically imposed modes of subjectivity.

Transness and feminism, when sutured, or when focusing on their constitutive suturing, assert Outrans's declaration that "transfeminism is a major opportunity to build a politics of resistance and alliance," which is to say that those who do trans feminism become trans feminists on the grounds that they work to build this politics of resistance and, by virtue of this, become allied together in trans feminism and as trans feminists. The politics stemming from transness is and must be "a feminist one," Outrans continues, that sees itself as already a part of black feminism, "third-wave feminism, queer feminism, and postidentity feminism."[44] Transness and feminism encourage us to think anew because they sit uncomfortably in the current order of things, so much so that they require a new world *dis*order. They make untenable old forms of relation and organizing, old forms of identity and understanding. Indeed, the "birth of transfeminism" has shown that

> we cannot count on old forms of political organization based on identities alone. Maybe the best alliances are those of and for people of different backgrounds who are eventually compelled to understand and fight for one another. These new arrangements are an effort to *do* intersectionality, to put into practice new forms of political organization that do not premise themselves solely on the politics of identity marginalization

or on the belief that an identity category is sufficient for describing the kinds of oppression experienced by all members of that category.[45]

Intersectionality here means that alliances and political cohabitation can and must occur with those of varied backgrounds, side-stepping expected political formations, to create subjectivities in excess of backgrounds. *Doing* intersectionality is read as the doing of black feminism, which is not a conflation but a nod to black feminism's birthing—or perhaps midwifing (or both)—of the concepts that comprise intersectional thinking but ultimately exceed intersectional feminism. It is no coincidence that so many iterations of trans feminism make note of intersectionality or black feminism. In addition to the above, Susan Stryker and Talia Bettcher note the "tremendous worldwide effect" intersectionality has had on trans feminism and go on to cite the Combahee River Collective's refutation of biological determinism as an adequate basis on which to fashion a politics. Also, Jack Halberstam remarks that changes to support trans women or advance trans justice will ultimately benefit everyone, echoing again the Combahee River Collective's dictum that "if Black women were free, it would mean that everyone else would have to be free." In short, because of its questioning of sexual and gender difference in a way that did not take the sexual and gender binary as a given, critiquing the utility of "woman," and having an analysis of race always foregrounded, Stryker and Bettcher assert that "this intersectional version of feminism laid the foundation for transfeminist theories and practices in the 1990s and subsequently."[46]

Yet there is a noted elision in the accounts of trans feminism's indebtedness to intersectionality—namely, the couching of the radical edges of blackness into "intersectional." But, first, simply by dint of how its definition has been carried out, I part with intersectionality on some of its grounds for their insufficiency and what appears as a disingenuousness. That is, before even speaking to the obfuscation of blackness in the term, on its own terms, to me and others like Jasbir Puar, Mark Rifkin, and most notably Jennifer Nash, it often conflates black women with the wholly oppressed and thus evacuates them of the possibility of privilege and the ability to do harm (generating, as Nash terms it, "the monolithism of 'black womanhood'"); it proves at times unable, with its overwhelming focus on the multiply (and assumedly entirely) marginalized, to think the efficacy of attending to the confluence of identities of, say, a white trans disabled man; and it uncritically invests in identities that become consistently reified and presumed natural, in need of no critique, dissolution, or, indeed, abolishing.[47]

But, even more, intersectional feminism, while surely capacious, nevertheless dilutes the blackness of the black feminism that propelled and that haunts it. If it is accurate to say that intersectionality is the product of black feminist theorizing, then to make intersectionality the quintessence of radical feminism fails to truly grapple with the blackness inherent to intersectionality. Blackness on my account is not one descriptor among others, nor is it a description only of the people who do the feminism to which it is attached. It, in fact, has a capacity that intersectionality may not have, and the linking of trans feminism to "intersectional feminism" rather than, explicitly, black feminism does a disservice. Thus, my goal is to highlight this and bring to the fore trans feminism's decided blackness. First, in having the Combahee River Collective speak as the key text that clarifies trans feminism's intersectionality, there is an unstated but forceful black feminism. The collective's text is not "An Intersectional Feminist Statement"; it is a *black* feminist statement, and their commitment is to blackness and its specificity, or opacity, which is precisely that which enables the freedom for all. In other words, the specificity of black women as a synecdoche for black feminism, or even the specificity of trans women as a synecdoche for trans feminism, is the very thing that will allow us to bring about freedom for all. It is because black feminism and trans feminism are coalitional epistemologies, are coalitionally inclusive and interrogative of normative grounds, that they can and should be spoken of in the same breath. Intersectional feminism has the potential to always reify the limits of the still-discrete identities that converge; intersectional feminism maintains that only the crash that happened is the accident, the building and mapping of the streets and curbs and road lines needing no interrogation, assuming them to be innocuous mainstays in the landscape. Trans feminism and black feminism critique the very streets that form the intersection, work to both look elsewhere and in excess of the streets and roads for the totality of one's subjectivity as well as refuse to let the city planner have the last word on the definition of streets. They do not permit gender to remain what it is, remapping it outside of determination, a commitment that requires a quotidian intention— because some of y'all, a lot of y'all, say y'all want the undetermined, the non–biologically determined, the ungendered, yet do not take that to its end of abolition and gender radicality. Trans feminism and black feminism give affirmative consent for gender abolition. And they mean it: *gender abolition*. Trans feminism and black feminism want different streets, or want dirt roads, or want waterways and sewers, or want open meadows, just something other than the congealed, solidified rigidity of concrete and tar.

Both transness and feminism challenge the givenness of gendered on-tologies. Transness and feminism are always in the interest of becoming, and an already given ontology that nonconsensually and coercively claims one's subjectivity cannot hold the openness of an ontological becoming. Abolition and gender radicality, unlike the appropriative grasp of ontology, serve as forms of self-*expropriation*. There is a deep urgency in this mode of living because gender and sexual normativity are destabilized, creating a crisis that becomes an opportunity to enact new forms of assemblages, coalitions, collectivities, affinities, and life. We are told that we must be the men, the women, the white people we have been forced to be. But we do not have to be them; we can become something different, in excess of our-selves, in service of something else. We want, we need, something else. And "transfeminism is that 'something else.'"[48]

BLACK AND TRANS AND FEMINIST

> ... other ways to be trans ... with which blacks in the
> New World had much practice.
> C. RILEY SNORTON, *Black on Both Sides*

> Imagine other ways of being and feeling black feminist.
> JENNIFER NASH, *Black Feminism Reimagined*

Dora Silva Santana, in "Mais Viva! Reassembling Transness, Blackness, and Feminism," dwells at length on trans feminism as imbricated with blackness. She begins by querying how the experiential knowledges of black Brazilian trans women could introduce a radical epistemic shift in the terrain. How could centering black trans women alter what qualifies as knowledge, or what is deemed "the world"? This is a query into the politi-cal stakes of knowledge production, and a movement toward the radical possibility of black trans women naming, unnaming, or leaving beautifully unknown the contours of the world. Santana goes on to inquire as to how black trans *life* might be thought about and focused on as black trans women resist death. So often the subjectivities of black trans women are mentioned only when they no longer live—when they've been murdered, met with antiblack and transantagonistic violence, often deadnamed and misgendered in headlines (if given headlines at all)—so Santana yearns for care of black trans women while they still live and, indeed, care that allows for the continuation of that life. Methodologically, Santana employs *papo-de-mana*, or "sista talk," a foregrounding of the conversations black women have with one another as the primary site of black (trans) feminist knowledge production. In conjunction with the Trans Revolução (Trans Revolution) support group comprised of trans women, trans men, transsexual people, and nonbinary people, Santana alludes to her own gendered and racialized transition and asserts that transition is "a nonlinear, undirected, dislocated, and localized movement."[49] Black trans women, and black trans feminism more broadly, fashion subjectivities around the pursuit of "unsubordinated living," undirected and unsubjugated life begotten by the subjective embodiment of the primordial, insurrectionary force of black trans feminism.

Her focus is on black trans women *in movement*. She distinguishes between black women, be they understood as "trans" or "cis," in feminist movements and black women in motion, doing actions, organizing in coalitions, a distinction that to me articulates black (trans) feminism through the ways subjects mobilize different kinds of subversive work that breaches the very confines that structure the marginalization of the people for whom black trans feminism is in service. It is less about joining groups based on who one is; it is about coming together by way of how work is put in. Santana's black trans feminism constitutes a politics for liberation from racialized gendered oppression and a transing of fugitive spaces (what she identifies in the text as *quilombo*). Resistance against racialized gendered violence that assaults nonnormative subjectivities "is where trans feminism and black feminism meet," she writes, and this nexus is a fugitive one, where "fugitivity is a refusal of systems that keep us captive to situations that oppress us."[50] The sista talk of the black trans women Santana spoke with generates black trans feminism. It is talk and knowledge, collectivity and politics, that assert the continued life of black trans women. And in this is a politics for the alteration and even destruction of the world as it is known. For Santana, "to do black trans feminist work is to bring in the fugitivity of blackness, that unspecified movement of transness and the gendered and ungendering racialization of bodies pointed out by black feminism."[51] It is an apparatus electrified in its circuitry by fugitive blackness, or blackness as a mutiny of racializing categorizations; by transness as unpredetermined and wayward, a deregulated movement through and beyond gender toward its recalibration and destruction; and by black feminism, an epistemological stratagem that fractures hegemonic fetters of racialized gender in ways that limit ontological breadth.

Following Santana, black trans feminism is no provincial project. Inasmuch as one radical stance one could take in the social milieu is one in which black women, trans women, and black trans women are kept alive, are indeed those whose lives foundation our calls that social justice is predicated on the mattering of the lives of the most marginalized, black trans feminism becomes *a name* for radical politics. It would then be a misnomer to say that one is radically politically oriented if blackness, transness, and feminism do not hold notable interest in one's political purview. And these are references not to quintessential bodies that look a certain way, but to modalities of subjectivation hinting at alternative socialities. That is, black trans feminism has a certain archive from which it draws, yes—and that archive, too, is one of many, a multiplicity of nonhierarchized archives that do black trans feminist work even if the archive is not "about" or "composed of" those who ostensibly "are" black or trans or women. I have named this treatise and political penchant "black trans feminism" for indexical reasons, by which I mean they name things other than what they've come to mean in this particular sociohistorical concoction, and those things—which are characterized by unnamable forces of mutiny, desedimentation, paraontology, categorical displacement, and many others—are always entangled with the various ways they might be named by other means. Black trans feminism might be said to erupt from the convergence of the "other ways" to be and do nonnormative, trans genders with which blackness is well practiced, as Snorton notes in this section's first epigraph, with the contention in the Nash epigraph that we must imagine "other ways" to do and be and feel and enact black feminism. Black trans feminism names the "other way" suturing the trans, the black, and the black feminist. This expansively specific project might be complemented by another project under a different heading—say, that of decolonial radical socialisms, or indigenous anarchist insurgencies, or what have you. Black trans feminism neither supersedes nor rejects these; they are all in coalition, working angles and avenues in service of another way to be that does not stand for the ills that plague us. That other way has come under the banner, here, of abolition and gender radicality. Because I am not talking about identificatory possessions but, rather, politics and forces, modalities and relations, it is able to be maintained that such a project called black trans feminism does not work over and against other radical projects in a supersessionist sense. What I've collected black trans feminism as under the banner of unfixation permits a generative promiscuity that is flexible and nonterritorial—that is uninterested in territorial gestures and allows for other projects of radicality to serve not as competitors but goons and accomplices in the struggle together.

Put simply, and clearly, I want to affix blackness, transness, and (black) feminism to an abolitionist and radical posturing. This is not to reduce these historically and phenomenologically specific modalities to a homogenous understanding of one another. In other words, no, blackness, transness, and (black) feminism are not all the same under this helm; they are names that index escape and theft of life in and through the nonnormative, the subversion of hegemony, unbecoming, breach. They are names for unmeaning, particularly nonparticular unmeanings that take these names because of how history has consolidated the anoriginal fugitive force into various corporeal and behavioral postures deemed deviant or unsettling. I am making a similar claim as I make elsewhere about blackness and transness:

> This is not to collapse blackness and trans*-ness, diluting their uniqueness and utility as analytics for different, though related, disciplinary fields. They are, rather, nodes of one another, inflections that, though originary and names for the nothingness upon which distinction rests, flash in different hues because of subjects' interpretive historical entrenchment. That is to say, they are differently inflected names for an anoriginal lawlessness that marks an escape from confinement and a besidedness to ontology. Manifesting in the modern world differently as race and gender fugitivity, black and trans*, though pointed at by bodies that identify as black and/or trans*, precede and provide the foundational condition for those fugitive identificatory demarcations.[52]

Because I am interested in how fugitivity has arisen from black studies and is thus tied to the name "blackness," and because blackness, for me, is not tied to any specific racialized body, the gendered kin of and in this blackness usefully bear the names "transness" and "feminism" because these, too, are fugitive flights that inflect strongly the contemporary world. This book is adamant about blackness, transness, and feminism because they are, to my mind, metonymic instances and poetic flashes of a critical disposition. The radical criticality herein names itself as always prepared for a necessary self-critique. It is open to its own undoing because critique signals more than mere externalized criticism; it seeks to negate—to make unexistent—the hegemon as well as build otherworlds, or create in this world the conditions of possibility for otherworlds to proliferate in unanticipated ways. Black trans feminism might be called a general theory (always in hieroglyphic form) that, *in what it theorizes*, instantiates the impossibility of a general theory insofar as a general theory rests on universalism—antithetical to the subversive sociality yearned for by the blackness of black trans feminism, the transness of black trans feminism, the feminism of black trans feminism.

The claim made here, and that a black trans feminism attempts to make clear, is that the external and supposedly obvious is at best an ostensibility, at worst a phantasm (with no set criteria to discern which). That which appears simply there and an unadulterated mainstay of, say, the body is not in fact such. These external things subject to the senses are, as Denise Ferreira da Silva puts it in the context of problematic Enlightenment reason and rationality, "already an effect of regulating reason"—that is, already mediated and tainted, as it were, by the white and cis and masculine genre of being a valid subject. We are already touched by violence and supremacist discourses even when we wish to claim that which has been pathologized on and in us, making even the gesture to say "I am black/I am a woman, and that's okay" understandable but not the final resting place of our political endeavors. It is because one's categorical race and gender, despite its feeling of deep inherency and self-fashioning, is an "exterior thing"; racial and gender *identity*, da Silva would conclude, "constitute but effects of the interior tools of 'pure reason.'" It is pure reason, which is mired in white supremacist, cisnormative, masculine conceptions of the subject, that has authored the very idea of identity, racial, gender, or otherwise, and thus the abolitionist and radical forces indexed in black trans feminism act as a negation, a "radical gesture" toward not merely their reclothing; no, black trans feminism, to take da Silva's call seriously, insofar as racial and gender identity are "exterior things," serves as "the declaration of the ontoepistemological *inexistence* of exterior things."[53] This is a radically abolitionist project, a project that, in the grand scheme of things, is a black and trans and feminist project.

Black trans feminism is an analytic praxis inflected in various ways due to historical contingencies but is nevertheless excessive of historical instantiations and identitarian subjectivities. This is not to elide materiality—abstractions do not abandon, and in fact often have as their primary aim of redress, social, material, and cultural meanings. Black trans feminism is the devastation of violences, whatever form they may take. Perhaps the blackness, the transness, and the feminism of it all, their promiscuous coalitional affiliations and insurgent politicality, are indexed in the defiant togetherness of an unlawful assemblage, an unregulated and prohibited way of getting together and going together. Ideally, sought after would be a raucous liveliness in the exquisite shadows that illuminate those things that promise something beyond our catastrophic situation, things that exceed what their context dictates of them and nevertheless desire something not this. We don't know what will arise if we realize this thoroughgoing dream I've been spouting, nor should we. To claim to know in advance would belie the aim, as we would only entrench what might be into the current logics we have at our disposal. We don't know, and that is okay. We just want something else, a something we do not know yet.

2 Fugitivity, Un/gendered

Get it? Gender is a country, a field of signifying roses you can walk
through, or wear tucked behind your ear.

Eventually the flower wilts & you can pick another, or burn the
field, or turn & run back across the tracks.

CAMERON AWKWARD-RICH, "Essay on the Theory of Motion"

TRANIFLESH

The work blackness's proximity to trans/gender does is to foreground
how blackness and transness are, in the first instance, "political move[s],
strategic or tactical move[s] . . . *movement itself*, a displacement between
established plateaus."[1] Blackness and transness reference movement and
cultivate space to live, to become-as-being, in this movement. It becomes
necessary that we retool the language of approaching gender and its abolition, an abolition that is concerned much more with the creation and cultivation of a new way to exist than with incessantly referencing the purportedly bad iterations of gender (e.g., "toxic" masculinity). Abolition means
just that, and black trans feminism stands here for gender abolition even
in the face of those who would, as they say, feel some type of way about
gender abolition after they've worked so tirelessly to gain recognition or
validity in their own (often historically marginalized) gender. Black trans
feminism must respond to the expected question "Even *my* gender? Even
progressive masculinities and *innocent* femininities?" with an understanding

but assured "Yup." And it is in service of gender radicality because (gender) abolition gratuitously expands the ambit through which subjects might become subjects in ways that do not carry with them the normativities of worlds and histories past, which then means we will have the possibility to become something or somethings that have never been permitted to arise. And we could not have gotten to those things if we did not unequivocally, searingly refuse the coerced regime of gender we had no choice but to exist as. When we refuse this, we make possible the very things the regime sought to preemptively, and post hoc, quell. This might be a fugitive un/gendering.

"Ungendering" is of course indebted to Hortense Spillers and is a theorization emergent from an inveterate blackness and feminism. Gender is that which is made to attach to bodies of a domesticized space, predicated on the integrity of an ontology constituted by a white symbolic order. The subjects contained in the "lab" of the ship's hold, as malleable flesh, ungender subjectivity by way of refusing and being refused by the necessary symbolic ontology of gender. In the context of Spillers's other remarks, particularly regarding blackness's unfixation from physiognomy—that blackness is a philosophical skepticism and disobedience available to anyone and any posture; that blackness is a serial critical posture of transformational possibilities that can and must be, and has been, dispersed *across predicates*, across different kinds of bodies and hues to which it is said to be attached—ungendering might be understood usefully as a refusal of an "identity," and furthermore of an ontological grounding.[2] Ungendering's undercurrent of blackness, an abolitionist feminist blackness, is to mobilize the flesh. These two terms—ungendered and flesh—bear much cache in black studies and black feminism, so I wish to make clear that I understand them here as, in Samantha Pinto's words, "a radical differentiation in America's static but quite specifically formed notion of gendering that denotes Whiteness as the base of a normative process" (ungender) and "an opening, a break, an interstice that doesn't so much resist as remake what we think we know about the range and pitch of 'Black women' and Black feminist political possibility" (flesh).[3] I find this description of Spillers's terms quite apt and similar to how I wish to articulate the fundamental project of black trans feminism through abolition and gender radicality. Similar, but not necessarily the same; I may depart from many others' understanding of these concepts—they are, after all, with their pervasiveness, deeply overdetermined and thus subject to many people's steadfast feelings about a "correct" utilization of them—so my intent is to think alongside these conceptualizations, using them as provocations for radical thought rather than with a strict fidelity. Fidelity to a perceived original intended meaning is not my aim, nor what I understand as "careful" reading or theoretical deployment.[4] I seek to amplify the differentiation and the opening interstitial break that does the work of remaking black women and black feminist possibility, for the former inflects the anoriginality I ascribe to blackness's unfixation and propulsion of mutability, while the latter ungrounds racialized gender and posits a trans effort endemic to black feminism toward precisely the undoing of and deviation from naturalized categorization. Thus, I am advancing and caressing Spillers's concepts on these grounds, maneuvering them into a space in fact after the abolition of this world's configuration. It is the entrée into fugitive un/gendering.

A fugitive *un/gendering*, as what I understand a black trans feminism to be given over from, can be consolidated into what I want to call, bringing together Spillers, Kai M. Green, and Treva Ellison, "traniflesh." Because gender via hegemonic logics is predicated on being visible to the mind, being material, being biological, being an immutable substance, traniflesh, in getting outside of those walled enclosures that ultimately signify fallacies and arbitrariness, becomes the un/gendered. It is not gendered, nor strictly speaking ungendered, as the slash in un/gendering marks a necessary slight departure from Spillers by drawing readers' attention to the liberatory, uncapturable otherwise of flesh, of traniflesh. Un/gendering's fleshiness is an overflow that spills over violent categorization and, instead of being generated by whips and frisks, is the unwhippable and unfriskable displacement of normative violence, the levied critique of normativity we hope to move toward as subjective livability. Traniflesh, too, is not specifically tied to gender proper or bodies understood, (im)properly, as nonnormatively gendered or transgender. It is an unspecific generality, that which sparks the onset of a different modality of existence. In this, it is open, insurgent ground on which to tread toward this other modality that is indebted to the racial and gendered opacity that spews an excessive muck we can all get inside and go forth with. Now.

Where Spillers understands flesh as distinct from the body, the body as embedded in captivity and flesh as an antecedent "liberated subject-position," Green and Ellison, in turn, describe "tranifesting"—transformative manifesting—as modalities that "operat[e] across normativizing and violative configurations of race, gender, class, sex, and sexuality," mobilizing across apparatuses of capture designed by the state.[5] The spirit of these two theorizations is what I want to put forth in traniflesh. Quintessential to traniflesh— this unlawful assemblage of illegal black-market parts, where the quintessence is an ecstatic centrifugal and centripetal motility—is an immaterial materiality. In other words, traniflesh mobilizes a kind of subjectivity that does not abide the violative configurations of race and gender, that does not house itself as a body, and that comes to engender us through something like abolished subjectivity. There is an urgent need to conceptualize a mode of living, an alternative and otherwise mode of living, grounded in a radically nonexclusionary sociality that escapes captive and captivating logics of subjectivity. In this sense, what is offered is a way to live oneself differently by way of coalition: to jettison the strictly biological as a criterion on which one relates to oneself or others (what Gayatri Gopinath would call a model of non-blood-based affiliation); to urge the gritty togetherness necessary for nonviolent relationality; and to gather subjectivity coalitionally, leaving open the question of anyone's identity, who they are and who they might become, as an abolitionist gesture. A fugitive un/gendering is this opening, this suspension: it attempts to vitiate gender *through* itself, undoing itself by way of an unyielding, radically opening ungendering. This traniflesh is underbeing, being that refuses being in favor of becoming away from being *as* being. It does not index matter or form but a general sentient sensorium that exceeds corporeal capture and is the inaugurative muck that produces byzantine, rhizomatic relational affinities. Traniflesh is between the haptic and the tactile; traniflesh is hac(k)tile, in all its connotative touch and subversive infiltration, and challenges grammar through dehiscence and suture, always coming apart in service of coming together differently.

What I am suggesting finds collaborative expression in L. H. Stallings's "illusive flesh," drawing from Robert Hayden's poetic phrase.[6] Illusive flesh is Stallings's counterphilosophy to philosophies of embodiment, a mode of subjectivity that escapes the normative hold of the body. She writes that illusive flesh serves as an alternative "to embodiment about what the transaesthetic experience and representation of Otherly human bodies means to forms of life and being that exceed the biological," a stylized transaesthetics that Stallings says "disturb[s] forms, biological and otherwise," a transness that deforms the biological and the sexual, as well as disturbs the "otherwise," the racial, gendered, and physical. Illusive flesh, in conversation with Spillers's flesh—that "ethereal social (after) life of bare existence," inhabitation of which would "lead to a different modality of existence"—is a transed subjectivity, a nonnormative way of living in, or even beside, oneself.[7] Moreover, illusive flesh for Stallings allows black political traditions to opt out of Western interpretations of sex and gender as material: "These discursive practices [of illusive flesh] join Yoruba-influenced spirituality in the United States as black traditions willing to theorize illusive flesh as a form of metaphysical gender, less attached to the notion of a unified body," she writes.[8]

How might we understand illusive flesh as generative for traniflesh, an un/gendered fugitivity? Illusive flesh, Stallings argues, "suggests how we can see black funk's move away from the skin as a styling of self beyond Man that depends upon the haptic aesthetics and sensations felt somewhere other than the skin"; it "provides a different theory of embodiment."[9] And this "different theory of embodiment" may be what engenders the conditions of possibility for new, unknown emergences. This is flesh that precedes the systematicity of bodies, that renders subjects subjugable to the violence of the Law. Illusive flesh is perhaps the tentative name of the unnamed. The flesh, transoriented, denotes a decidedly un/*gendered* antiterrain—it is, after all, "*female* flesh," Spillers notes. It marks the gendered-site-that-is-not-a-gendered-site that welcomes not only those who were exscribed from traditional symbolics of gender, but also, to advance Spillers a bit, those who move toward the ethical and political transgressive posture of fleshiness that engenders a different way of becoming as *that which might have come but for Gender*. The un/gendered blackness occurring here is the black female flesh on the run from gender, on the run from legibility, by way of a kind of stepping out of a lineage, worrying the line, as it were, and tearing being. It is perhaps creating life in becoming-unbecoming. So if "*patriarchilized* female gender," at least "from one point of view, is the *only* female gender there is," perhaps that means that if we eradicate patriarchy—one of the many-headed and -footed limbs of the hegemon—then, extending this line of reasoning, there will not be a liberated female gender, as such a term would lose meaning, but, indeed, something different entirely, a different and otherwise gender that emerges from the abolition of patriarchalized (female) gender: (female) gender *as such*.[10] What emerges in this is not a collapsing universality—that "everyone is female and everyone hates it," per Andrea Long Chu—and not a conception of femaleness, devoid of political efficacy and a stand-in simply for letting another do one's desiring.[11] Rather, what is being posited here is a recognition of "female" being a vehicle for whiteness, patriarchy, and the gender binary, which are violent apparatuses, and thus the abolition of femaleness as such, suggesting something else we might emerge into in its place. Un/gender; traniflesh.

Traniflesh emerges as an impossibly possible space where we know not what will arise because, illegible to us on variegated levels, it does not rely on legibilizing relations to Man and the categorizing hegemon. It is envisioned here as what one's "body" is made of when living in a milieu constituted by abolition and gender radicality. As an emergent force and, like black and trans appositional flesh, "a capacitating structure for alternative modes of being," traniflesh works and becomes in the terrain that skirts captivity where different formations and matterings, different and differing subjectivities, of life can materialize.[12] Traniflesh is an otherwise way of being that exceeds the categorizing logics of race and gender, that exceeds "identities" and (dis)organizes around subversive world-building. It is fluid, excessive, a kind of primordial transitivity that indexes blackness, black feminism, and transness—citing Kimberly Benston's "beginning-as-blackness" and "primordial blackness"; Claire Colebrook's "transitivity"; Kai M. Green's blackness in excess of the category of black; and Spillers's telling femininity that evades definition because of its shadowy ubiquity.[13] I designate traniflesh as the process by which gender is unmoored and unmade *that serves as* an otherwise way to become a subject in excess of gender, or what I've termed "gender radicality." In this radical divergence that one, anyone, moves toward—one disperses themselves outside the constraints of normative (gendered) subjectivity—is the processual space in which gender-that-is-not-gender manifests.

Note, too, the possibility of the resoundingly epithetic if pronouncing the /i/ of traniflesh as a long /ē/. My intent is not for it to be pronounced in the way of the epithet ("tranny-flesh"), but such a pronunciation is latent, simmering beneath the surface of its intended pronunciation (the "trani-" as rhyming with the "mani-" of "manifest"). This presents the ever-present "insurgent ground" of choosing to claim the Spillersian "monstrosity." Traniflesh and the flitting, flickering inhabitation of it—a Steinbockian "shimmer"—is a rigorous commitment to Green and Ellison's "flexible new collectivities" that, on my reading, do not conform to the mechanistic templates we understand as legible identities: race, gender, sex, sexuality. It renames and reconfigures how we become, and continue becoming, subjects that breach hegemonic logics. Traniflesh names that breach, names it as a place to dwell and, more important, to fashion another way of living. Indeed, it fashions a way that too many of us who are not permitted to live simply *can*.[14]

This chapter takes up black trans feminism's underlying abolition and gender radicality via a commitment to something other than representational logics. Thus, identifiable bodies as stand-ins for particular kinds of politics or indexations of liberation are suspect precisely because the aim of black trans feminism is to cultivate ways of living that do not entail reliance on the very taxonomies that promulgated the violence that constitutes our identities. This chapter also wonders cheerfully and boisterously about how transness, when allowed to snuggle up against black feminism, can lead us into some enrapturingly thorny territory like feeling "at home" in homelessness—or, more precisely, the rejection of the stasis of the home on the grounds that it, too, can be a site of violence, immobilization, discipline, and adherence to architectural normativities. The chapter ends on a note of irreverence toward genre: What's the worst that will happen if, when, we forsake the genres we've come to know intimately and form who we are via something else?

BECOMING-BLACK-WOMAN

(Forgive me if this lengthy parenthetical strikes you, reader, as a detraction, but it is imperative that something be made critically clear at the outset before I even begin to say what I cannot help but saying here—that is, the status of "black women." I have on multiple occasions been taken to task on the danger of black women's [which I suspect as being conflated with black female bodies, with its attending perinatal "female" assignation and assumption of a habitable womb and normative anatomy] erasure and the necessity of instantiating the materiality, foregrounding the experiential flesh-and-bloodness, of the figure demographically limned as black and woman. The task-taking is very rightly a warning not to leave black women by the wayside and to heed the very specific contributions of certain kinds of people and, importantly, too, to note the people onto whom the effects of what I am theorizing will be felt acutely. So as not to reiterate what has already been hammered home, I will simply say this before moving on to the ways I want to wiggle within and out of this sentiment: it is not that I do not think black women matter. Black women, historically and contemporarily, academically and nonacademically, politically and socially, have been foundational not only for my thought but, indeed, for thought qua thought. It seems to me, though, that, following Jennifer Nash, my conception of black feminism is a capacious one that strikes some as too capacious. But I cannot not think black feminism in Nash's terms, following Deleuze's terms, as "deterritorialized," as a "move[ment] with figures beyond 'black woman,'" as not an *act* as Nash describes it but a quotidian theoretical practice "of radical anti-territoriality, a refusal of the proprietary relationships that mark" certain bodies as stand-ins for politics or certain given ontologies—which are, however one slices it, violent and hegemonic bestowals—as inherently liberatory or omnipotent. Because I am understanding black feminism in this capacious sense that eschews a posture of propertizing in favor of "a radical embrace of the political potential of intimacy," as Nash goes on to say, I must take that toward a certain conception of radical intimacy that permits the possibility of an intimacy so close that we, whoever we are, become through and in and with and maybe *as* one another.[15]

(This, then, leads me to where I want this treatise on black trans feminism to go. So, allow this thought: in commenting on a conversation between Hortense Spillers and Gail Lewis, Saidiya Hartman elaborates what is termed a "fugitive feminism" through a clarification of ungendering. Ungendering, she says, was not intended to efface the "lived experience of black women," and that black women in particular are not to be erased by ungendering. Rather, Hartman says, it is an interrogative analytic that challenges us to think differentiations across social fields. She goes on to say that with this in mind, the ultimate aim is to "*flee* [*the*] *category of womanhood and also the other categories across the social grid* so we can imagine a liberated future."[16] I submit that discourses like "lived experience," at some point in their offering, run up against a limit unable to be surpassed without significantly diminishing returns, and soon after that in ways that in fact prove ultimately harmful. Related to the discussion in the introduction about the stalwart holding on to historically epithetic identities, to double and triple down on lived experience as an ethically incontestable refutation of what I offer here regarding becoming-black-woman misguidedly takes for granted a presumed transparency and naturalness of the being named black and woman. To do so ultimately reproduces these categories as natural and, indeed, needing no critique or supplanting, in the last instance validating the historical violence that instantiated the difference itself "rather than ... exploring how difference is established, how it operates, how and in what ways it constitutes subjects who see and act in the world," as Joan Scott notes (in addition to so much more than I could gloss here).[17] If our aim is to not only "contest" given ontological and ideological systems, as Scott claims, but to *abolish* them, as black trans feminism calls us to do, we cannot simply reify all things as ever more and more marginalized identities [e.g., black women, poor black women, poor black trans women]. We must think indexical forces, modalities of in- and exhabitation, processes of undoing, and the Spillersian "something wider" [see below] that will not possess *any* of the trappings we know ourselves to be forged by, race and gender—*being* a black woman—among them.

(We must come to know, as Spillers knows, that gender is not to be doubled down on, yet it cannot be flippantly dispensed with; she acknowledges the double bind, and thus the double gesture that must be made. Hence why she remarks in a conversation about her famed 1987 essay, "The refusal of certain gender privileges to black women historically was a part of the problem. At the same time, that you have to sort of see that and get beyond it and get to something else, because you are trying to go through gender to get to something wider."[18] The phenomenological gendered experiences of black "cis" women, or of people of trans experience, is not to be discarded, and other multiply marginalized identities are not to be forgotten. It is not to be forgotten not because I wish to capitulate to those who so badly want to hold on to these remnants—I do not, though I sympathize tremendously—but because there are resources working through the epidermalization and anatomized gendering that will ultimately be in service of the antiepidermalization and antigendering that is the radical alternative: what I would deem abolition and gender radicality. And this is the ultimate goal. So as not to reify the gendered ontology that orchestrates cisnormative and gender binaristic templates routed through whiteness via making other modes of subjectivity impossible, it can be said that blackness and transness and black feminism, with their attending concatenations of and through one another, are prefixal indexations of racial and gender desedimentation. And this is precisely the move of going through nonnormative gendered corporeality's fractures of the binary to get to something wider. Black trans feminism *is* that "something wider."

(I know: some of us, many of us, still want some kind of familiar footing. We still have that desire to be held, somehow. It'll be discarded once we realize that where we're at is luscious and grand, freer than we could have ever imagined, but maybe we need something just to get us past the threshold. Maybe we just need someone there holding our hand, reminding us that we are not going into the angelic belly of the illustriously salvific abolitionary beast alone. I am, truly, tearing up right now, because I know many of us need this holding. But know that you are held by the beckoning into the world after this world, a world that is not far from where you stand. The openness of that world is holding you, in every moment you question the ethics of how you've been treated, in every moment you've wanted to stretch just a bit further, maybe so much that you became afraid but knew that stretching more could present you with something grand. You are held in these pages, I promise, because even the things that might cut deep are there to help us all glimpse what could be if we did not have to defend the violences that have come to be so familiar and thus thought unable to be discarded. You can discard them, you can "let go," as Nash says, as La Marr Jurelle Bruce says, as Alexis Pauline Gumbs says. These categories are very good at frontin', even though they are not treating you the way they should. So, if you wish to know what it is like to truly be held, lovingly, then let them go.

(Okay, now we can begin.)[19]

What if a feeling through another elsewhere is a feeling, which is knowledge, indexical of traniflesh? Even as one might be enclosed by the prohibitions of other grammars, traniflesh acts as the unpunctuated and anagrammatical subjectivity in which we can escape toward another texture of escape. Clarifying the presence of un/gendering in traniflesh is an assessment of black women's subjectivities. That is, black trans feminism heeds the epistemic position of black women for an acute insight into disruption of racialized gender because of an opaque excess, and black women are prime speaking agents on traniflesh because "not properly women, Black women inhabit a trans space."[20] So black women incite the rethinking of un/gendering through a thoroughgoing interrogation—imposed and engendered—of the processual becoming (un)human through the subject placed at the nexus of black and woman. If "the black woman" is, contentiously speaking, an impossible figure, there is a curious kind of becoming-*black*-woman that is not only "read as a twin refusal (of both purity and subjection)," but more pointedly an *evil* twin refusal, a refusal of purification and subjectification.[21] In the first order, "becoming-woman" is an assertion not of a literal reading, which would be a misreading, but an assault on phallogocentric ordering. It is a feminist syntax of sorts—though a few theorists of feminisms past would take great umbrage with such a claim[22]—a feminist syntax that understands radical feminism as a means of escaping power insofar as "what we call 'woman' has always already been the sum of trajectories away from the centres of power."[23] Becoming-woman is the most fundamental becoming, at least for Deleuze and Guattari, the quintessential minoritarian subject (because only the minoritarian, never majoritarian, can *become*; and further, women, regardless of their population size, are always minoritarian, a description of womanness as a relation to normative power rather than a descriptor of an ontological subject [which also suspends the very meaning of that subject]). To become-woman is not the ownership of designated women and also is not something all women already, by virtue of their womanness, do or are. Becoming-woman is open, a *subjectivation* needing to be entered into by all, "women" included, as becoming-woman "affect[s] all of humankind."[24]

There is a "special introductory power" in becoming-woman because of its fundamentality. It is a kind of "sorcery" Deleuze and Guattari say is not reducible to the image of the woman; it may not even result in a being that "looks" like a woman, as it is not about representation but the puncturing of gender's metaphysics. Here we can note an implicit transness to becoming-woman, a radical suspension of attaching to any gender a certain corporeal limit and shape, radical gender self-determination and, ultimately, abolition of the concept of gender adhering to the parameters of a certain kind of body. Becoming-woman can lead to one who "looks" like a "man," a radical trans inclusivity and interrogation of gender.

Importantly, becoming-woman is not mere imitation, though one must take heed not to overlook the import that "behaving as a woman" has on, say, people of trans experience who seek medicalized intervention in the form of gender confirmation surgery and how, because of the medical industrial complex's fixation on normative gender behaviors even as they assist in trans affirmative surgeries, imitation can offer an avenue toward self-determination. "All we are saying," the dynamic philosophical duo write, "is that these indissociable aspects of becoming-woman must first be understood as a function of something else: not imitating or assuming the female form, but emitting particles that enter the relation of movement and rest, or the zone of proximity, of a microfemininity, in other words, that produce in us a molecular woman, create the molecular woman."[25] There is a critique to be made here of how some women are not "feminine" and have in fact been disallowed femininity, as we'll see shortly, but nevertheless what is being offered (and what has been deeply misunderstood in feminist critiques of the notion of becoming-woman) is a way to think about the paraontological primordiality of "woman." "Woman" is indexical of, and thus not reducible to or the sole owner of, the beings historically hailed by the term, indexical of some other thing that serves as what I've deemed abolition and gender radicality, an unbounded torsion that acts in oppositional ways on centralized power. Becoming-woman is the molten flow that cannot abide declarative, uncritiquable statements like "As a woman . . ."—those authoritarian sympathies, as Adorno would have it, with whom I tentatively and temporarily express an affinity—though necessary at times for the reclamation of a history and maybe even integrity. This declaration not only dangerously jettisons internal variation and heterogeneity but also confines the subject of "woman" to a manner of static being rather than a micropolitical subjective and extrasubjective working necessary for all to take up.[26] What follows subsequently is a rummaging through the storage locker of Deleuze and Guattari's old intellectual memorabilia, stealing their valuables because, I feel, they want me to take them, make use of them, because they, too, want me to be "in search of tools and techniques for thinking against representation."[27]

Becoming-*black*-woman would be more than notation of a racial elision in becoming-woman. There is much to glean from becoming-woman, and becoming-black-woman is not meant to reject it. Rather, becoming-black-woman is an intensification. It marks an insurrectionary opacity, a tarrying between abandonment and inclusion, that demands generatively warping the very ontologizing process of gender *through* the irruptive figuration of blackness and womanness or femininity: in short, the going through gender to get to something wider, a width expansively encapsulated by black trans feminism. The argument here circulates, generatively, I think, and in mutual imbrication, with black trans theorizing, with Matt Richardson's claim that "black womanhood" is in fact not something that emerges from being perinatally designated female at birth, *or*, to further Richardson, black at birth. It is something that is forged, something that accumulates. It is in service of desedimenting biologics, or logics of assessing valid subjectivity on biologically essentialist (or, simply, biological) grounds. While Richardson's specific argument concerns that of black trans women and their useful belying of social understandings that equate proper womanhood with a series of bio-teleo-logical signifiers of maturation like breast growth, menstruation, and the like, I wish to extend his inquiry about the fact that one "becomes" a black woman to querying not only the expected (trans)gender site but, too, into thinking about how one "becomes"—which is to say, understands as open and volatile—a *black* woman as well.[28]

Because becoming-woman is not really about "women," becoming-black-woman is likewise not really about "black women." Remember, please, the parenthetical above, and remember, too, that "women" have not always existed. There is indeed a "history" of the notion of "woman," as Denise Riley makes plain; women had to be "invented," in the terms of Oyèrónké Oyéwùmí, as was made apparent to Oyéwùmí by dint of a "realiz[ation] that the fundamental category 'woman' . . . simply did not exist in Yorubá-land prior to its sustained contact with the West."[29] The intensification it is meant to highlight is how the "black" that (un)rests in between becoming and woman precipitates a breakage outward toward not a racially implicitly white woman, much less any kind of "man"; it is a breakage outward toward an enveloping nothingness that exceeds its opacity and results in annihilating the genders that can only be Gender. For becoming-woman to truly move, as Deleuze and Guattari wish, beyond all human normality, it is necessary that we understand the human as normatively white as well, to be sure. It is the nexus of black woman that actualizes Claire Colebrook's assertion that becoming-woman "would abandon the idea of stepping outside man once and for all—but it would also be a refusal of active submission, or the idea that we always already think within a system that we repeat parodically or ironically." This is, in short, *black feminism* because it "refuses to disappear into the general categories of otherness or objecthood"—what Colebrook describes as the "redemptive otherness of woman," and what Denise Ferreira da Silva understands as the intersection of "blackness and womanhood"—"and refuses to comply with the formulations of racial and gender-sexual emancipatory projects these categories guide."[30] Hence, what might be most useful in the formulation of becoming-black-woman is its refusal of a passive reproduction of subaltern or marginalized status, a doubling down on *being* black and woman that maintains the validity of the normative systems that produced such a subject in the first place; it is a figuration that asserts the potential for radical reimaginings and political potencies of alternative, otherwise modalities that configure life and livability in ways not hitherto conceptualized.

This bears being put differently so as to make vanishingly unlikely a misreading. Of interest here, for clarity's sake and likely to the frustration of some, is, once again, not a purported ontological, embodied, entirely known and transparent black (cis?) woman. *That is not the point here.* The project of black trans feminism cares less about people who are black and/or trans and/or women *as the definition of* black trans feminism or black trans feminism's sole progenitors/focus; rather, the project is one that, as Deleuze writes to the "harsh critic" alleged to be his student Michel Cressole, has "nothing to do with the character of this or that exclusive group, it's to do with the transversal relations that ensure that any effects produced in some particular way . . . *can always be produced by other means*"; it is, on Paul Preciado's radical trans countersexual reading of Deleuze, "not so much who can think or talk about what as it is about creating a set of conditions to produce new utterances."[31] I am speaking here of conditions otherwise, ways of being and becoming that are so unenamored of the conceit of this world's supposed correctness that they find solace in how we unbecome, how we un/gender ourselves and others in order to relate to power in illegible and subversive ways. We cannot continue to recap *this* if we purport to want abolition and radicality. If we want radical, if we want the gifts of blackness and transness and black feminism, it is not merely that somethin's gotta give—no, *everything's* gotta give.

The import of becoming-black-woman is made clearer when noting that becoming-woman is predicated on a "microfemininity" that gets mobilized as the thousand tiny sexes that make up the being that is woman, a femininity beyond the rigidity of gendered being. The question that must immediately follow, though, is, What happens when there is a spectrally absent femininity for those beings who "should" be permitted femininity, but aren't? Black women's femininity has historically been stripped; thus the usage of femininity is fraught with femininity's disavowed. What results, then, is a subtraction from the equation "figure of the feminine beyond rigid being" that becomes simply "figure beyond rigid being," so bringing the nexus of black and woman to bear here marks a gendered language without gender. Becoming-black-woman allows for thinking of gender without thinking of, or reifying, gender—gender that might have been but for Gender.

The fundamentality of becoming-woman gets even more fundamental in becoming-black-woman. It is because blackness, too, functions as a radicalization of the minoritarian molecular insurrection of the nonbecoming hegemon of Man. That Man is undoubtedly a genre of a White Man, thinking beyond this particular subjective tendency (to use Deleuze and Guattari's phrase) forces the salvific concession that there are other pulsations of life that escape the definitive logics culminating from and as White Man. Becoming-black-woman is a posture taking on the tendencies, or deploying the onto-epistemic unruliness, of black feminism. The black woman of becoming-black-woman is the being that emerges from the anoriginary, mutinous insurrection that is black feminism, an unyieldingly trans force that delinks radical insurrection from historicized physical characteristics and understands these terms as a differential power or subversiveness. The resulting effect that beings called black women have—that is, unsettling racialized gender and critiquing racial and gender solipsism while also precipitating, because of their exclusion from the racialized category of gender and thus valid human subjectivity, another modality of ontological life—is the force of black feminism, and becoming-black-woman is the repetition of *that*.

Deleuze and Guattari ask, "If becoming-woman is the first quantum, or molecular segment . . . what [is it] all rushing toward?" to which they respond "Without a doubt, toward becoming-imperceptible."[32] With its "anoriginality," blackness necessitates the refusal of a "first." The anoriginary precedes origins and firsts; thus becoming-black-woman is not the first quantum and hence does not rush toward becoming-imperceptible. It is before the first; it is a zero quantum, a null quantum, which is what, exactly? If the quantum level is characterized by being "difficult to categorize" and "peripatetic movement," as "a multidimensional blackness that defies any attempt to make it follow a 'straight line,'" argued by Michelle M. Wright, its zeroness breaks it outside of quantifiability such that it is movement before movement, blackness before blackness.[33] Becoming-black-woman is this very thing, so it rushes toward not an imperceptibility but a fracturing of perception itself. It is slowly becoming popularly known that observation of quantum phenomena, that perceiving quantum phenomena, is insufficient to understanding what happens at that level and speed. One cannot really observe quantum movement. So the anoriginary quantum of becoming-black-woman requires a perception that is not perception; it requires another mode of observation.

Because the gender binary is an "arborescent" sociopolitical orchestration predicated on cisness, whiteness, and categorically disciplinary "rigid segmentarities," becoming-black-woman works to highlight how the subjective intramural always makes tremulous the stultified overdetermination of racialized gender identity. In the hegemonic attempt to instantiate "womanness" or "manness," or even racial whiteness or racial blackness as one's fundamental personhood, down to their very core, becoming-black-woman is the politicized rejoinder that asserts, inasmuch as black womanness is supposedly fixed, "becoming undoes these suppositions. The notion of acting *like* a woman"—or acting like, listening to,[34] perpetually citing black (cis? trans? non-cis/non-trans? cis *and* trans?) women—"has no purchase with reference to becoming—one does, one acts, affects, is affected by, and in these processes one continually produces 'something other than [one]self,' something that destabilizes the holisms that fix and determine that self in hegemonic logics that can only deal with minority identities, not processes of becoming minoritarian."[35] In short, I want to posit the subjective tendency of becoming-black-woman as the production of a certain kind of something-other-than-oneself, as the very production of that something other than the self one is required to be in order to inhabit being. Becoming-black-woman as, in other words, the kind of life possible in abolition *through* a gender radicality.

All the things I am suggesting—traniflesh, the gender radicality of becoming-woman, figuration—are to be found in the nexus that is called "black" and "woman." That nexus, given name by the becoming-black-woman, is a sort of radical performativity that does funky stuff to racialized gender. And this is fundamental to the black radical tradition. According to H. L. T. Quan, the tradition argues that "the rematerialization of the 'ontological totality' of Blackness requires the blending and bending of gender/sex/race structures and meanings."[36] In other words, inextricable from the black radical tradition is crisisizing gender, transgressive and transgressing gender on the run from a body—that is, in un/gendered traniflesh. Becoming-black-woman operates on a trans plane, bringing black feminism into intimate propinquity with trans feminism—becoming-black-woman is in fact a testament to the transness of black feminism and the blackness of trans feminism—by way of its radical detachment from the biologized, racialized genre of what Rachel Anne Williams calls "the cis-normative standard for what a Woman™ is."[37]

To thus inhabit the fugitive spirit of this un/gendering is to incite a radically different way of living. It is a secretive and shadowy force that presents the conditions of possibility for possibility. As possibility for subjectivity, traniflesh holds out for impossible possibilities, shadow possibilities, and thus unanticipated possibilities that do not necessarily rely on normative frameworks for their somethingness. With this, I want to dwell for a period on a well-known philosopher of phenomenology. Allow me, if you will, to quote at length:

> This anonymity innate to Myself . . . we have previously called flesh, and one knows there is no name in traditional philosophy to designate it. The flesh is not matter, in the sense of corpuscles of being which would add up or continue on one another to form beings. Nor is the visible (the things as well as my own body) some "psychic" material that would be—God knows how—brought into being by the things factually existing and acting on my factual body. In general, it is not a fact or a sum of facts "material" or "spiritual." Nor is it a representation for a mind: a mind could not be captured by its own representations; it would rebel against this insertion into the visible which is essential to the seer. The flesh is not matter, is not mind, is not substance. To designate it, we should need

the old term "element," in the sense it was used to speak of water, air, earth, and fire, that is, in the sense of a general thing, midway between the spatiotemporal individual and the idea, a sort of incarnate principle that brings a style of being wherever there is a fragment of being. The flesh is in this sense an "element" of Being. Not a fact or a sum of facts, and yet adherent to location and to the now.[38]

What is called flesh is a sort of anonymity, an opacity to optics and logics external to oneself (though "self" is not the proper term for this thing). The anonymity is foundational and crucial, as its impossibility to be known implies an existence outside. It has no proper name, nor a proper location, and cannot have its identity known, only pointed at indirectly, looked at askance, smelled in the faintest of scents, felt in brushes and stipples. The anonymity is innate to the self that is not quite self but harbors the flesh, that is the improper, inaccurate name for this thing we cannot and must not be able to know quite yet. Traditional philosophy cannot name it, which is to say Western metaphysics cannot name it, for it escapes the knowledge frame that dominates Western civilization. Flesh's anonymity is that black radical critique of Western civilization.

It is not matter, this flesh—and traniflesh, with its indexation of the flesh spoken of here, is not matter either; un/gendered subjectivity cannot (be) matter—but is something else. There is no real "look" of one who inhabits the flesh, as if there is a specific costume or adornment that alerts others to when one is fleshy. This flesh that bears a trans relationship to gender eludes elaborations of what visible existence can be. It looks, in other words, like nothing. This flesh does not simply become matter as we know it, forming beings with muscles and sinew and organs that comprise a "body." It is the fundamental dissolution of these things, as they are fabrications that ultimately have been given, imposed, and coerced into being understood as the only thing we can be, "natural." Neither a fact nor the sum of various facts, flesh knows not what the "biological" is and throws shade on determination from without. What, then, does this mean for gender? To say that flesh, which is *almost* to say traniflesh, exudes a non- or nega-biological penchant and refusal of externalized determination is to say that traniflesh is a kind of opaque excess. The anonymity of the flesh dissembles when trying to be apprehended by the senses generating legibility. Its opacity and unknownness gives an excess that spills over. This spillage can be glimpsed in blackness and the ways its laughter is too much or its politics cannot be contained in the epidermis, in transness when its genitalia does not "align" or its expression cannot fit into binaries or its body cannot be said to be a proper body, in black feminism when its collectivities cannot abide strict criteria of race or gender or its way of knowing the world cannot be found in what we have currently. These are mobilizations of traniflesh because the anonymous and illegible shadows which they generate, and which thus prevent its interiority from being seen by many, are the very things that generate something that all can take up to get at precisely what it can only allude to. The excess comes by way of the anonymous opacity, surging from a specificity into a "claimable" mutiny of all kinds of enclosures.

ON THE RUN FROM GENDER

Che Gossett, in a June 10, 2017, Facebook status update, wrote, "Trans as being on the run from gender . . . trans as gender's undercommons." And my mind set sail. Yes, transness is on the run from gender—gender understood particularly as that material and (white) symbolic regime of binaristic categorization. Insofar as gender is at least one substantive node of legibilizing oneself as a subject, transness as a way of subjectivating oneself "wrongly" articulates a self-effacement inasmuch as one's "self" operates upon a fundamental cohesiveness of which an intact/integral gender is constitutive. Moseying along in the undercommons, transness refuses to be known ahead of itself, slurring subjective embodiment and figuring, in the words of Nathaniel Mackey, "a fugitive tendency towards self-effacement . . . a sigh the elegiac witness to an emergent abscondity not otherwise to be known."[39] The abscondity, the escape, emerges in the open secret of the undercommons, that playground wherein transness emerges *through* its otherwise to be knownness, its escapeful abscondity, its runnin' of its mouf with an untamable wild tongue. Effacing the subject from which it is believed to stem is a move away from subjectivity toward *sub*jectivity, a beneath, an underground, a subversive simmering subterrain where we ain't got no business doin' none of yo' business. I feel you, Nate: I, too, "confess to a weakness for these amphibious, in-between, both/and advances into a realm which defies categorization, this way of trespassing, so to speak, the line which otherwise divides."[40] The intersexual amphibiousness—the goings-on and ontological workings of "crime's offspring," as Foucault has called the hermaphroditic in the first volume of *The History of Sexuality*—a deep historical tie to transness, interstitial and chromosomally/genitally nonclassifiable, defiant of categorization. Where it goes, it trespasses; where it leaves, it tears ever so slightly.

And such a rending disturbance is not an explosive, historically masculine notion of revolution as the toppling of all regimes in one fell swoop, but the transitionality of those "thousands of little gestures of protest and presence" Julian Carter says reach toward "finally achiev[ing] escape velocity from the category you were stuck in all those years ago."[41] Transitioning, which sounds to my ears like the positioning of transness, a trans-positioning that is always askance and askew, is the "escape velocity" from categorization; it's a quotidian act of becoming through openings and refusals. To breach confines of capturability is to position oneself transly, escaping and fleeing gendered captivity: transition, the definition of which those who take on trans's heft in an embodied sense often meet with an "open-ended refusal," because what transness does in one sense is imagine an excessive being; transness invents, and seeks to performatively uptake, what C. Riley Snorton calls "the conditions of emergence of things and beings that may not yet exist," about which I will say more in chapter 3.

Perhaps it might be necessary, with this theorization, to distinguish ever so nimbly traniflesh from Spillers's "hieroglyphic" theorization of flesh. Whereas Spillers gives a spatiotemporal foundation to flesh in that flesh comes before the body, and it might thus be necessary to reclaim a connection to this flesh, I want to understand flesh, traniflesh, as having no accessible preceding point of connection. We cannot go back, if that is the aim. There is no access to an originary connection; what we make is sociality in the cut. The cutting sociality producing unanticipated relations and rhizomatic assemblages to the undermining of normativity is how we must understand traniflesh.

There is, then, too, no home to which we can retreat. With such a long history of "home" as an important site for marginalized subjects, to jettison the notion of home might trouble some of this lineage. Specifically, in black and trans discourses the analytic of home proves vital, connoting comfort and reprieve, per, say, transition narratives that allow one to finally live in and as a gender that confirms their interiority. However, Nael Bhanji, in his essay "Trans/scriptions: Homing Desires, (Trans)sexual Citizenship and Racialized Bodies," takes up the question of "home" as it has been deployed in trans theory and casts it in a more critical diasporic light, colored by his own identity as, on his account, an East Indian/Arab immigrant trans man in Canada who has spent most of his life in Kenya. Finding problematic the production and uncritiqued normalization of whiteness and Anglophone bias in trans theories of home, Bhanji interrogates the very utility, shape, and location of home for trans subjects. To what "home,"

Bhanji asks, does the trajectory of transition lead, particularly for the trans subject who is already diasporic, already in liminality, already (and always) in transgressive motion?

Bhanji's diasporic framework "helps to problematize those unacknowledged 'homing desires' within trans theory." In other words, he argues, "we must pay attention to the different ways in which people (re)imagine and (re)create the edifice of homely belonging; where one's 'real' home can only exist as a romanticized cathedral of constancy."[42] There is a pressure to pass and "arrive" at a destination in trans communities, Bhanji asserts. Often emphasized is not the transition but the destination, the getting to a kind of bodily, gendered "home." In his own words, the pressure to get to one's destination as quickly and seamlessly as possible, to zoom "from transgressive to trans*fixed* results in the transsexual forever rushing onwards to find the space beyond, 'the promise of *home* on the other side.'"[43] Furthermore, Bhanji writes, simmering just beneath this politics of home for trans subjects is the urge for normality and to belong, without complication or trouble, to a normative framework. This urge for normativity is a move away from blackness, from gender radicality, and seeks to subvert transness via its quest for the normative. Trans homecoming, then, is marked for Bhanji as a fantasy; it is the white suburban utopia that Venus Xtravaganza from *Paris Is Burning* so wished for, an embodied "rightness" in which, as Jack Halberstam notes, "'rightness' may [as] easily depend on whiteness or class privilege as it does on being regendered."[44] For Bhanji, "trans" necessarily functions not merely as movement across a particular schism; it also evokes the transgression, transmogrification, and transmutation of norms. Transness by necessity must trouble and destabilize fixed location—or, in other words, it must disarticulate the operative assumptions of fixity in conversations surrounding space and place.

Home is, in fact, a stifled space and maybe even antithetical to how "trans" has been understood throughout this book. Additionally, home can no longer be equated with a sense of unfettered comfort, for there are far too many of us for whom "home" was not only a place where we were fed and loved but, simultaneously, and sometimes primarily, the place where we encountered familial rage and abuse, assault, disappointment, confinement, belittlement, terror. Freeness and solace must not be tethered to feelings of being at home; freeness and solace, liberation and kin, demand another iteration of spatiality not predicated on an architectural site of enclosure. Where we wish to live must be an open and unbounded space. If traniflesh might be a place to live it cannot be our home—indeed, we cannot, perhaps, want a home insofar as home connotes a place where one stays or gets away from it all. Traniflesh, if we are lucky enough to engender ourselves in and through it, cannot be a home in which we are (re)born; it has to be our unhome, our outdoors, because "when home is not where you are born, nothing is predetermined. Anything can be."[45] It is in the spirit of radical openness and coalition that we spurn home. Surely home has been a place of refuge, warmth, and acceptance by many, and it is not this legacy—or any legacy providing a salve for the plights of the marginalized—I wish to disparage. My intent is only to think about the constitutive strictures in our balms, the violences and missteps of our loves in favor of something that, while treacherously terrifying and unknown, might prove to be the last balm we'll ever need.

Out-of-homes is where we might build edifices without walls and roofs. Roofless ceilings are outdoors where we might live in traniflesh. We can begin from the wreckage of the roof, indeed we must. Traniflesh comes in at the crisis point of unsuturing the body and falling outside of subjectivity. Its fugitive, blackened, un/gendered and un/gendering force is indexed in its folds characterized by the "non-sovereign and metapolitical" gender-troubling blackness articulated by Che Gossett, a subjectivity that gains its identificatory heft through its subversive politicality, refusal of dominative calls for sovereign control, and otherwise-politics (politics *un*usual).[46]

All this flesh wants is a chance to live outside of this life in a life that lives. It wants to become on the sly and on the low. Think Toni Morrison's *The Bluest Eye*: "Edging into life from the back door. Becoming," this from a novel that Ann duCille says is "unbound, blackened, feminized, repopulated, and unpunctuated."[47] Unstopped by punctuation, unbounded by limits, populated by denizens unfamiliar so you know things are going to have to change. Traniflesh allows us to *edge* into life, making a verb out of the outskirted, paraontological place of fugitivity, working and werqing that space so it can exude life and livability. It is an unanticipated life because they won't expect us coming in from the back door, the one that they thought was always bolted, not realizing we jimmied the lock. They thought they were the only ones who lived there but didn't know that we, not "were coming," but *be coming*, becoming, vernacular syntactical ontological otherwises that live differently. That's why they couldn't clock us, their grammars too strict and rigid to hold the excess. We, on the other hand, were and always must be unshaken (because always shaking), unbroken (because always breaking).

I want to claim fugitive un/gendering as a means by which we refuse formalized stability and find the shape of subjectivity in the shake of subjectivity. We come into ourselves when we come outside and beyond given ontologies, configuring what "I" means in our dancing, of course, but also in our seeing with things other than eyes, in our feeling through others, in how we cast our voices, an aural torquing into an aural vibration whose sound, as Geo Wyeth says of his beautifully jarring music, emerges from "unknown origins and also places of alienation" as a *kind of irreverence for genre*, which extends to an irreverence for genre's etymological offspring, *gender*.[48]

Even we who commit to fugitive un/gendering still, and will always, have work to do. It is the black and gender radicality at work, placing the incessant demand of black trans feminist liberatory politics. That work necessitates that we move

> to discover the re-routing encoded in the work of art: in the anachoreographic reset of a shoulder, in the quiet extremities that animate a range of social chromaticisms and, especially, in the mutations that drive mute, labored, musicked speech as it moves between an incapacity for reasoned or meaningful self-generated utterance that is, on the one hand, supposed and, on the other hand, imposed, and a critical predisposition to steal (away). In those mutations that are always also a regendering or transgendering (as in Al Green's errant falsetto or Big Maybelle's bass—which is not but nothing other than basic—growl).[49]

Where might we find the rerouted route, or the groove that can't track the rerouting? If traniflesh's un/gendered fugitivity is an uncharted map to somewhere else, a kind of reproduction of cartography so we can make our way there, but a reproduction made by way of a negation or uncovering, all the while being animative, then it becomes an interstitial bop that shakes off the weight of our bodies, themselves fundamentally gendered, making this interstitial bop "a regendering or transgendering." Remix Moten here: it is not neither/nor, nor both/and; traniflesh, its un/gendered and un/gendering fugitivity, is *either/and* this regendering or transgendering. It is mixing up in and with a bad crowd of regendered, transgendered, retransgendered, and transregendered folks, a rageful spitfire of a subjective expression per Susan Stryker's choice words to Vic Frank. I know: traniflesh is the shape of subjectivity that is not made of flesh and bone but of a *growl*.

3   Trans/figurative, Blackness

What would it mean to think about blackness as that which experimentalizes being, that which . . . moves as unfettered ur-matter, unthinkable exorbitance, and deregulated transubstantiation?

J. KAMERON CARTER AND SARAH JANE CERVENAK, "Black Ether"

I think that "trans" is one word for it that is not just one word among others. You know what I'm saying? I have all these shorthand ways of putting shit that I steal from other people, but what I mean is that there are other words that one could use, but none of those words is replaceable. Not only are they not replaceable, they are not substitutable. . . . I'm beginning to think that these things [blackness and transness] converge in an irreducible way. They can't be thought separately from one another, because both manifest themselves in regard to ritual practice. I don't think about blackness as an identity. I think about blackness as a ritual practice, and I feel like I should think this about transness too.

FRED MOTEN, "All Terror, All Beauty"

I want to think of it this way, a way that illuminates the transitional and transfigurative, a way that shows the trans as autochthonous to a certain conception of blackness. If Carter and Cervenak in this chapter's first epigraph denote blackness as being's experimentalization, which makes it that which makes being transform and undergo alteration, transmutation, or transition, or blackness as a deregulated transubstantiation—to change into something else, to transmute—and if blackness comes to mean, then, not a coveted and essential identity but "a disposition toward transition" manifesting as "the realization that transition is the relinquishment of position and location, it is movement on the move that is constantly moving and never arriving," it becomes clearer what I wish to suggest in terms of blackness's transness, as it were.[1] So much discourse surrounding blackness as unable to be captured or pinned down, or given to being other than what has been said to be or designated by the (medico-juridical) powers that be, or refusing that which has been given or bestowed, or ungendered or mutable or outside of white symbolic orders, yet there is less discourse— much less—making explicit the clear, crucial link between blackness and transness. It is my contention in this chapter that blackness is given to an understanding not just of a racialized changing of form or racialized history of mistaken identities; I want to make clear that *blackness is given to an understanding of transness.*

This chapter, in short, brings the trans to bear on blackness. Blackness as transfigured and trans/figured signifies "the reclamation of the critical edge" and recalibrates blackness as "no longer predicated on 'race'" and instead as the naming of insurgent "vantages" from which one unrelates to the hegemon.[2] To this end of vantages, then, this chapter further articulates the unfixation discussed previously and brings it to a head in the specific context of blackness's dovetailing with transness. This chapter will also be less a sequential flow of ideas and readings that crescendo into a transitional bridge to the subsequent chapter, less a typical logical flow of stacked ideas, and will consist more of meditative flashes of trans/figuratively black purviews, vantages, and glimpses.

Blackness trans/figured requires more than seeing it; it requires seeing and touching and feeling and hearing and smelling and engaging and undoing in promiscuous assemblages. The joined sensation of synesthesia uses differences and differentiation as its adhesive. This other sociality, this other sensation from other places, is indexical of radically altered forms, which is to say a fundamental trans/figuration by way of blackness. As this relates to my argument regarding reconfiguring blackness, what I am saying is that "the black's figurative capacity to change form" is less a property of a preexisting entity—"the black"—and more the means by which one comes into blackness, that one's "figurative capacity" is always, as the logic of the clause suggests, a trans/figurative capacity, always a capacity to become other than what one was.[3] And it is this, I submit, that extends across an array of subjects, the enactment of which inaugurates one, over and over, into a kind of blackness. What has come to be understood as black skin is indexical of a preceding threat to modes of circumscription that could all fall under the heading of ontology and that takes on historical weight by virtue of white supremacy designating certain physiognomic surfaces as antithetical to its project of purity. To put it differently, historical black and white people need not have been those who have come to be black and white people; that these are the people—imperfectly and porously deemed as such, mind you—who have come to be known (by whom?) as black and white people is a historically contingent reality. We have come to be deemed black, for example, because within the political agendas of specific geographical coordinates a certain phenotypic trend has been made to harbor all that is transgressive and subversive of the normative project of (racial) purity. And it is that originary transgression with which I am ultimately concerned.

Furthermore, because I am most interested in how we exceed the reigns of history, how we show up uninvited and refuse to comply or go away, I want to offer the possibility of redoing matter—or, more pointedly, how we come to (be) materialize(d). Though the materiality of the body seems inert and transparent, fueling my understanding of blackness is what I see as its penchant to *work* matter. Blackness and its constitutive trans/figuration re- and undoes how/when/where matter matters. A polyvalent feminist and trans blackness "*claim[s] th[e] power—to perform significantion anew, and 'to matter' differently,*" to reroute where materiality happens, what materiality looks like, to possibly foreground the materiality of politicality.[4] I wish to do the work of unstructuring what counts as material to the point where materiality *becomes* through politicality, and blackness names the process of destabilizing. Blackness-as-fugitivity is not, and in fact rejects, categorization. "For the work of blackness," Denise Ferreira da Silva writes, "as *a category* of difference fits the Hegelian movement but *has no emancipatory power* because it functions as a signifier of violence which, when deployed successfully, justifies the otherwise unacceptable, such as the deaths of black persons due to state violence (in the United States and in Europe) and capitalist expropriation (in Africa). That is, *the category of blackness serves the ordered universe of determinacy and the violence and violations it authorizes.*"[5] A *categorical* blackness is blackness as racial classification, blackness as affixed immutably to skin and blood and essence; it serves, ultimately, only to further entrench our politicality in the normative modes of exclusion and violence. Maintaining a categorical blackness, put simply, is not futile but inadequate, necessitating a blackness-as-fugitivity, a paraontological blackness I imbricate constitutively with black trans feminism.

Blackness is not merely subjection to and in those scenes of violence and terror. Indeed, its work is enlivened by a fugitivity, a vitality, a life that tranifleshily exceeds fungibility. Its excess reimagines blackness as unfenceable, which means, again contentiously, that blackness is "unmoored from the axiomatics of (self) possession." Blackness incites "parapossession," to use Carter and Cervenak's term; it incites an interrogation of the way categories like race and gender cannot provide the ground for commonality, as they are not obvious as markers of togetherness or the fact of a common struggle and are, indeed, like the vicissitudes of the weather, not predictable, thus necessitating that "the ultimate connection," so often presumed to be the "analytics of raciality" da Silva details, "must be the need that we find between us"—the ways we manifest subjectivity and work toward abolition and radicality.[6] Displacing ontology qua Ontology, blackness takes up the critical legacy of black feminist critiques of the capaciousness of what we mean when we cast terms over populations, revealing their inadequacies. In its transness, its perturbing acrossedness, blackness gives us an unhomely outdoors—it gives us, to again cite Carter and Cervenak, "an inherently improper unhoming." Such a conceptualization "does something new to the black body—dislodging it as the only source of black knowledge (and therefore liberation)," dislodging blackness from bodyness itself, unhoming subjectivities that enact the practice of escape.[7] This sociality by other and othered means lives outdoors, out of doors, in the wilderness.

TRANS/FIGURATION

I advance the theorizations of C. Riley Snorton here in thinking about "transfiguration" as a site of implosion and continual destruction and recreation and thus thinking of blackness as always unstable. Snorton's interests lay in the space of transition, in which transformational feminist work occurs, and productive reworkings of gendered (and racial) subjectivities can be scrutinized, put forth, and rethought. To transfigure blackness is to move toward, but never settle on, its capacities to undo. It is to change form, and it finds its (non)identity in the very movement of form changing. What I want to theorize as trans/figurative blackness finds itself in the usurpation of form itself, de-forming form, questioning illegally. In short, following Snorton, it is imperative to bring trans subjectivities to bear on blackness.[8]

Though Snorton acknowledges but is uninterested in the theological con-notations of transfiguration, I find them to be fruitful here insofar as trans-figuration's theological uptake is a deeply generative modality through which to proffer my theorizations. The biblical moment of most relevance is Mark 9:2, aptly titled in the Revised Standard Version (RSV) "The Trans-figuration," in which it is written that Jesus was transfigured before Peter, James, and John. Jesus is transformed on the mountain with his apostles before God—a miraculous phenomenon in the eyes of his onlookers. Jesus's transfiguration can serve as a template for the transfigurativity—the transness—of blackness and its mutability. Transfiguration follows, again citing biblical precedent, Romans 12:2's demand to "not be conformed to this world but be transformed," which, by extension, might mean to refuse normative frameworks of legibility, to transform and transfigure them. While transfiguration is etymologically a metamorphosis, and to transfigure is to transform and elevate or idealize/spiritualize ("They saw Jesus transfig-ured in a radiance of glory"), my use of "trans/figuration" is meant to sever the hierarchical connotation of the term. It is deeply useful in its connota-tive becoming otherwise and other than what one was, and it is this sense of the term I wish to retain. The valuative glorification the word connotes, then, is fractured by the slash, negated by the interruption of the word. The menacing slash I insert as a transfigured transfiguration retools the Chris-tian Messiah as a deity that ushers in an otherwise possibility of life in the trans and transed blackness begotten by and in fugitive anoriginality.

Following scholar Cary Howie's meditation "On Transfiguration," in which he understands Jesus's transfiguration as a poetic and theological template for how bodies (particularly transgender bodies) transform, to change form is not to refute the purported "brute facticity" of a given racial (or gendered) world; the world is, however, constantly expanding, being al-tered, opening up to something that has not been present or deemed possi-ble. Ultimately for Howie, transfiguration names the question of the space between facticity and possibility; it names the space of transition. Trans/figurative blackness "refuses to accept the strict dichotomy between what I have been and what I will be," and instead finds volatile solace in the "inter-stitial character of our being-and-becoming-in-the-world."[9] Howie goes on:

> Transfiguration—within the darkness that is both the setting for and the
> very stuff of our changeable flesh—is not something restricted to trans-
> gender bodies; or, rather, it is the sign, the name, for that which, in every
> body (without exception), crosses over, exceeds itself, and thereby

intensifies—instead of relinquishing—what it has been. It is crucial for this argument . . . that the transfigured body be *more* intensely what it has been all along. . . . It is not, in other words, that my body, subjected to the techniques and technologies according to which its gender is apparently reframed, ceases to be what it was as it becomes what it will be, but instead that what I am becoming has been there, nascent, all along. (Which to say that this being-there is unthinkable without its attendant becoming.) My transfiguration, in other words, is my birth to presence.[10]

Howie's transfiguration is a transitive fugitivity. The name for this, of its many names, is blackness, but a general and nonemblematic blackness that remains open. Blackness, in its operational interplay with transfiguration, places a claim upon any and every "body." Trans/figuration when affixed to blackness reveals the work that blackness does by homing in on how we become in excess of what we have been deemed to be. The otherwise that we become is the point of illegibility in which life outside normativity happens. Trans/figurative blackness banks on the unthinkable as a force of deliverance, it doubles down on that which cannot be hemmed as where it wishes to thrive. Trans life and theorizing reveals that to inhabit this space and move within a subjectivity in this space produces social anxiety as well as engenders potential disruption in its visibilizing and vitiation of hierarchies and the constructedness of norms. The between—more specifically, the transgressive site of trans/figuration—becomes a productive site for uncovering the mechanisms mobilizing normativity, so much so that such normativity attempts to vehemently invalidate the existence of the subject occupying the interstitial space.

As a grounding force of black trans feminism, trans/figurative blackness is meant to do (at least) two things: first, to index the futuristic, otherwise becoming that Moten says is a "radical biological indeterminism . . . ineradicable historicality, [and] inveterate transformationality," which I understand as a fundamentally intersexually trans (radical biological indeterminism) self-determination that refuses its prescribed and inscribed embodiment for something else—a something else that does not have dominantly recognized life yet (but is still a life nonetheless).[11] It speaks to the manner in which black and trans, as on the move, always restively and flittingly reject the process of interiorizing and "sticking" race and gender to a biologized body. I understand this, too, as a spectral historicality that is distinct from a historically deterministic influence inasmuch as (and I will say more about this later) the "ineradicable historicality" speaks to the past and cannot be obliterated but says nothing of history's hold over us, which I want to read as history being able to do and be something different while still a presence in the present (and future). It stands that history is in fact open, an openness that is not infinitely revisable but is an unstable oscillation that generates and is generated by change, rupture, eruption, and deconstruction. And, second, trans/figurative blackness forces us to create the perpetual and unceasing attempt for a nonplace where we might, finally, live. It demands that we pursue sociality in other modalities of becoming. And it is this that trans/figurative blackness, and black trans feminism more broadly, sets its sights—or, rather, its various olfactory, gustatory, auditory, and haptic sensoria—on.

TRANS/FIGURE: DE-PERSON

This chapter's theorizations, in the vein of many strains of black and trans feminism, reject the representability of the constitutive forces (black/trans/feminist) of this text as a whole. Representation troublesomely relies on a fundamental tokenization that forces—demands, even—that The One stand in for, exist as, the many; representation fails to capacitate itself for internal irruptions and contradictions, disallowing even the singular to hold differences. Thus, it is necessary to reject representability *as an end in itself* in favor of what I see as trans/figurative blackness's *presentability*. Drawing here on Johanna Hedva's genderqueer-inflected defense of de-personhood, where Hedva maintains that "I am not a representative for a specific kind of experience; I am *presentative* of it," presentability rather than representability insists on a radical unanticipation insofar as presentability lambastes being known before it arrives. The refusal of being limned by anticipatory logics of legibility—what a body can do, what a body can look like, where and when a body can appear, what constitutes a body; dancing on the outskirts of being's Being—is perpetual movement otherwise, a becoming other than what one was, a trans/figurative blackness. This intimacy that presentability shares with blackness's trans/figuration stems from blackness's nonrepresentation, what Tavia Nyong'o—in a reading of Geo Wyeth's performances—calls "the blackness of nonrepresentation," which is to say for my purposes that trans/figurative blackness is not "an enduring positive image of a black transgender identity, but rather . . . a range of unruly residue."[12] It lovingly holds the aporetic, its punctured and puncturing penchant; it chaotically embraces "an affirmation of messiness, a testimony of and to disorder, an honouring of incomplete-ness," Hedva concludes.[13]

To the extent that trans/figurative blackness affirms the aim of de-person-ness there must remain a commitment to what Hedva calls "a radical sociality" which will necessarily be, in all its gorgeously crass profanity, "a big fucking mess." The import this mode of thinking has for trans/figurative blackness in particular, and black trans feminism in general, is its togetherness, a togetherness that is uninterested in the much-too-easy "We're all in this together" and bent on affirming indiscretion. Black trans feminism works for the eradication of hierarchized and imposed-from-without categorization, upon which privilege—the "radical *incapacity* for sociality"—rests, which means that giving up the ghosts of an easy taxonomic identity, be it racial, gendered, or whatever, which all rely on a body that Hedva asserts needs to be eclipsed and nebulized, would immediately have to ensue. Personhood, the subject, a body, and the like are predicated, at base, upon hegemonic "givens" that allow us (indeed, *allow* us—the hubris!) to "be." What trans/figurative blackness provides is the possibility to un-be, to become otherwise—to be "nothing," that irreducibly performative blackness that those smooth 1970s radicals, and Hedva here too, proclaim is beautiful.[14]

When de-personed and trans/figured, subjectivities cannot be "adjudicated by making recourse to the visual," as Snorton argues.[15] Following Snorton, as this chapter sets out to do, along with notable others, it is imperative not to be seduced by what seems sensible, as sensibility is predicated on the likelihood of being embedded in preexistent logics. The dominant logic of identity, one that assumes "race" and "gender" are fixed and knowable, needs not only troubling but interrogative obliteration. There is a transitive property here connoting trans/figuration, and thus also black trans feminism, as a subversive mutability able to pass into different kinds of conditions. That excess that is concerned with but not beholden to the embodied realm is what I want to think through here, because it is the excess that overflows the embodied where bodies that may not be here yet can possibly emerge. In the excess is where becoming occurs, and becoming's inherent nonconformity with being and its sedimented logics act as fertile (demonic) ground for those who might be.[16] Trans/figuration is an ode to those who are not yet permitted to be here but insist on persisting anyway. It attests to not finding or discovering, but cultivating room for the unanticipated to emerge. We are given the honor of awaiting those holographic and hieroglyphic mobilities that might come. We cannot anticipate subjectivities to come, or even rightly call them "bodies," because it accosts our agreed-upon requirements for sufficient identification. Indeed, the subject as it might come, as it might emerge, cannot be known beforehand and thus might always—out of definitional necessity—be castigated for its inadequacy, its wrongness. But it is this gesture of subjective wrongness that we must embrace if we are to engender the onset of radically reorienting what might be.

WYNTER IS COMING

What might trans/figuration be, especially one that indexes blackness, other than a black metamorphosis? If trans/figurative blackness bears an affiliative kinship with black metamorphosis, the inimitable Sylvia Wynter will prove deeply instructive. "Black Metamorphosis: New Natives in a New World," Wynter's massive unpublished manuscript, was initially meant to be an essay to be published by the Institute of the Black World, in which she would attempt to conceptualize black cultural life in the West in relation to colonialism. She meant "only" to "explore the Minstrel show as the first Native North American theater—and why Amerika distorted it . . . and the way in which the blacks created a matrix to fuse disparate and yet archetypically related patterns."[17] This preliminary sketch, though, exploded the written and verbalized intentions and became a manuscript of over nine hundred pages. It is an unruly text. With ever-expanding length expectations, missing pages, unpaginated sections, and a proverbial open-endedness in its unpublication, "Black Metamorphosis" might be impossible to summarize, to close. "Metamorphosis" bears a deep etymological relationship to transfiguration, the Greek μεταμορφοῦν—literally, to transform—having a wider application, and appearing in the Biblical gospels with the sense of transfiguring. Wynter's text is, in other words, "Black Trans[/]figuration." Her project is an overthrow of the "world system" of "blanchitude," a system that produces analytic boxes that confine us to the singular genre of humanity structuring the world. This genre and the categories that comprise it need to be undermined, as "each and every such category, 'race' included, belongs to an Occidentalist register."[18] There is no place for this register.

"Black Metamorphosis" is a "*macrological* maroonage, ultimately—unbound, unlimited, unreserved."[19] As a text, it is quite literally unbounded by the paratextual filigree of publication and marketing and was unlimited to its original essayistic length.[20] The text itself, as well as the contents therein, exhibits and contains "a multiplex of marooning actions, practices, or activity," where "maroon" "has now become synonymous with cultural resistance" (70, 71); "[the Maroons] were 'wild' in that they negated the plantation system" (72, 73); and what was emphasized was "escape from . . . intolerable conditions of existence. As with the maroons who fled into the interior fastnesses" (182). In marronage's insurgent heft, blackness is trans/figured in the sense that it becomes away from sedimentation and marks a capacious subjectivity that denotes a relation. As Wynter writes, "The situation of resistance" dictated a maneuver away from homogenized ethnic or racial affinity and toward a robust collective, since "both the Maroons, and the plantation slaves, consciously reconstituted a group identity." Indeed, to occupy the political identity of mobilizing one's situation of resistance means that one becomes a "'wild animal' [and] thus negate[s] Christianity, civilization, and the concept of property" (71, 72). Maroons and marronage in "Black Metamorphosis" cite slaves and blackness, but exceed the ways in which these categories have been established by hegemonic "colon-settlers" (62), making it synonymous instead with a "feral" disposition antagonistic to the "humanism" Wynter so painstakingly examines in her larger intellectual corpus.

To understand blackness through the ambit of maroons, marronage, or marooning is to bear in mind a critical interrogation of gender as well. Though Wynter's work has often been maligned for eliding the specificities of gender, there is a marked "gendered" critique in her larger concern with genre. As her primary analytic for critiquing Man, genre and Wynter's critique of humanism always "occur[s] in and through gender and sexuality."[21] "Black Metamorphosis" and Wynter's critical corpus sets sights on undoing the "axiomatic normative man as bourgeois," as "white, male and pure intellect" by way of a kind of transed blackness, or by way of blackness's transness, its trans/figuration. The overrepresented way of being human occurs through and is achieved by "processes of gendering and racialization (among others)"; indeed, to the extent that overrepresented Man—that "primary subjectivity [that] serves as the basis," James Martel might assert, "the bedrock of all subjects"—is a particular hegemonic genre, meaning "gender is a key constitutive part of genre."[22]

Blackness *transes*—goes beyond, moves across and outside of, breaches the confines of—and the fugitive slave "disrupts the code which separates him [*sic*] from the master" (606), a master that is self-driving, normative, and bourgeois. The fugitive slave "move[s] outside the permitted activities of the system" (606) and proceeds to hold, but not possessively have, the very denigrative qualities normative order has ascribed to it. Using Mr. Covey of Frederick Douglass's 1845 *Narrative* as a paradigmatic example, Wynter writes of his self-driving, which constitutes Covey "as belonging to the Single Normative Class—the bourgeoisie—and constitutes those he drives as, to borrow a term from Deleuze and Guattari—the les hors-classe—the lumpen, the outlyers, the maroons—marron, w ld [spacing in original], undomesticated—the hors-caste—outcaste, the hors-la-lol—outlaws" (598). To render the destruction of the normative, one must not refuse that one is this maroon, or the black, or the Negro, or the nigger, but to refuse its immobility, its ontological capture. One can and must. Move toward being other than this; one must transfigure this quintessential blackness, as it were, without conceding to what da Silva calls a categorical blackness. One must be "w ld," omitting the culminatory "i" that foundations subjectivity and rejecting individuation. One must be an outlaw, an outlier, unhomed, cast out and must choose to stay out because then one can engage in activities that are not permitted, those activities that have been banned because they threaten the integrity of the "Single Normative Class"—activities characterized by something like an "ontological sovereignty" without, if I may push on Wynter's phrasing, the dominative ethos connoted in the notion of the sovereign.[23]

To this end of "w ld" marronage, Wynter's sprawling unpublished manuscript provides keen insights into how to understand blackness in a way that ushers in a trans underpinning to black studies' critique of the Human, Wynter's overrepresented Man. Indeed, blackness trans/figures the Human by way, in part, of its necessary counterrepresentation (917), which is not merely, on my reading, an alternative imagistic proliferation of black bodies but a more fundamental and disintegrative counter to or subversion of representation as a genre of subjectivity. Blackness exceeds representation—its trans/figuration is the spillage outside of and in troublesome outskirted relationship to representation; it is presentative, as Hedva says. This representation that refuses to represent emplots a new kind of reality from the purview of the unrepresentable—what does reality look like from the vantage of those who reject reality as such? I cannot presume to have uncompromised access to such a reality, but I might wager that it is one that continues and perhaps achieves "the task of the post–Middle passage voyager," or engages in a "revolutionary praxis" of transforming the hostile landscape encountered (917).

Such a revolutionary praxis takes place in what Wynter calls the "underlife." Where blackness undergoes a "chain of innovations" in service of "reconstitut[ing] new social identities, new social bodies," the underlife is a space of radical trans/figuration where otherwise modes of, not merely being, but *living* transpire (849). Things look different under here, unlike what we might expect them to. And this demands an openness, a commitment to seeing the undone and undoing oneself even if—especially if—it feels wrong. It likely won't feel right because ain't nothing right about being down here. In the underlife is where the Spillersian "retooling" happens, where we Ellisonian "thinker-tinkers" create anew and make heretical assemblages that elude the expectant grasp of capitalism while forming askew affiliations, relations and rhizomes, affinity groups and conspiratorial connects. Forming these new social identities and social bodies is indeed unsettling, as we lose ourselves—or who we thought we were—in the process and can no longer recognize ourselves and others, throwing us into a disoriented smog of unrecognition. The task, then, in this proverbial insanity is to maintain it without delirium: to make a life in the unsettling of the underlife without being unsettled by it—to, in the parlance of La Marr Jurelle Bruce, go mad without losing our minds.

The madness engendered in the underlife, where we can trans/figure and be trans/figured by blackness's constitutive transness, is Wynter's "revindication" of the sociality of blackness through the transformative properties of "black cultural underlife." What results from this revindication is a "contingency," Wynter writes, a "non-official heresy. The heresy of the non-norm" (934). That the resultant underlife is contingent—because failure always occurs when we grope for coherence, to paraphrase Wynter—is significant insofar as it unfixes blackness from sedimentation and demands its perennial openness.[24] Unfixed, revindicated black sociality takes on a differentiation as itself, becoming a force for differentiation *as* its sociality. This sociality is heresy, and a non-official one. It is important that we see Wynter's lexical precision here: she writes "*non*-official" rather than "unofficial," the latter connoting an invalid modality that has failed to be authorized and thus is ersatz. "Non-official," in turn, undermines officiality and renders the lawfulness of the official negated. Sufficient heresy is one that is unconcerned with the reign of the official. Underlife dwellers become heretics, those who refuse to abide sovereign or divine law, and fugitively create otherwise ontological schemas when the omnipotent, the dogmatic, the scriptural—all of which have commanded the limits of the ontological terrain—purported to have a monopoly on what constitutes life and livability. That is the life of the norm, normative life. Heretics, dwellers of underlife, make life nonnormed, nonnormative life: black life, trans/figured.

Heretical nonnormativity captures precisely what trans/figurative blackness strives for: a life other than this, a life in and through the trans *that*, exceeding racialized and gendered requisites for valid subjectivity. Chaos becomes the weather, and in the chaos-that-is-not-chaotic we become away from fixity. Indeed, we are in a period of chaos:

> In this period of chaos, as we move into the twenty-first century, undergoing another great transformation of human existence, the nomadic traveling gods of black underlife, have seated themselves in the technology that diffuses the music which celebrates the act of exchange between themselves and men [*sic*] into every area of the globe. There they will meet with other submerged gods discardable and replaceable by the new Gods, new cults when and where. Like jazz musicians, like hunters, they are accustomed to find their footing in an un-sign-posted world. And they specialize in nativizing exile. (560)

Those of the underlife are nomadic, wandering, diffuse. They live submergence, an agential subjectivity from beneath without being submerged. They emerge via submergence because the deprivation of the validating tenets of existence is the condition, the first step, of what we might become after the abolition of this. Their "footing" becomes no footing at all: footing on no ground, trekking along, still nomadic, in an "un-sign-posted world" because signposts are too predictive, too overdetermined, too closed. The black underlife must have openness. And they make a home in exile, become through being exiled. Banished from the realm of the Gods, they claim exile and live when and where life is supposed to be impossible. Exilic life. And this is maroon life, insurgent life, because "maroonage" is the "veritable epitome of unbroken or unbreakable life."[25]

It cannot be overstated that "Black Metamorphosis," as a text and as a way of saying trans/figurative blackness, "is sutured to black life as the rebellious impulse to indict and overturn the dominant values that engender and profit from black nonbeing and nonpersonhood."[26] Thus blackness, on Katherine McKittrick's account, is always about life. Moreover, that life manifests in struggle and away from the known noun-place.

> The affirmation of black humanness is both relational to and in contradistinction to the dominant order of consciousness because rebellions— *which are activities! not identities! not places!*—honor black life as an ongoing struggle against what is truthfully represented as and believed to be preordained dysselected objecthood and placelessness. It is the process of

creating blackness anew within the context of antiblackness that shifts our focus away from perceiving a range of New World inhabitants as differently occupying resolved knowable and distinct noun-places (settler/property holder/autochthonous/labor unit) and toward the politics of being human as praxis.[27]

Importantly, McKittrick is here expanding blackness to the realm of praxis (we *do* blackness) and insisting on our subjectivity—the possibility of our "being human"—arising in our quotidian praxis. Rather than having only distinct and known "noun-places" to subjectivate ourselves, a praxis subjectivity enables the possibility of finding ourselves outside of these distinct templates and perhaps in the political valence of our subjective praxis. At the fundament of this praxis, this new human subjectivity, is a constant struggle that we might call, with staccato hesitancy, freedom.

This perpetual struggle that engenders life latches to a sociopoetic force that Nijah Cunningham deems a "daemonic" departure from normativity because it "destabilizes the racial logics that undergird the modern idea of the human." The daemonic foregrounds potentialities, unanticipated potentialities that invite the consideration of "how black sociality is operative of life's flight from embrace."[28] Fugitive flight constitutes black sociality, sociality in blackness, which trans/figures blackness as tied to the epidermal, breaches the logics of racialization, and demands a more capacious blackness in which those who flee can thrive in underlife living. The "we" of those who corral around and in blackness becomes unified to the extent that they are moving and dancing. "Unity is not if it merely is. Unity is because it is danced," Wynter writes (548). Blackness is a praxis, a "performative expression [that] generate[s] alternative forms of social life."[29] Man's shadows are unseen and unnormed and this is where normative embrace is eluded, where "Black Metamorphosis" tries to situate black life.

The ultimate goal, then, is to expand "the 'outlyer' consciousness of Blacks" (896), a consciousness that claims the "outlyer" as a mode of encountering differently. To advance the outlyer modality demands a destabilization, as the outside to which outlyers belong is volatile and unhinged by the stabilizing forces of the inside. It is active rather than possessive, agential and performative rather than identitarian and exclusionary. This outlyer consciousness is steeped in blackness insofar as it not only stems from an identifiable physiognomic demographic but from a fugitive, capacious underlife as well, where inhabitants generate themselves inasmuch as they take up the call "to maroon. To become Maroon. To go Maroon on . . . To marronize. To make Maroons of ourselves," all with the aim of "expanding or extending beyond temporal as well as spatial limits, boundaries, 'reservations.'"[30]

ETCETERA

> of the etc of negroes
>
> **M. NOURBESE PHILIP,** "Dicta" in *Zong!*

What would it mean and what would it look like to be, as Susan Stryker says of her transness, "groundless and boundless movement," "furious flow," "one with the *darkness* and the wet"?[31] Another way of thinking about Stryker's movement and flow and darkness might reside in the etcetera of trans/figuration, to make a slight change to M. NourbeSe Philip's words above. There is wisdom in etymology here. According to the authoritative tome that is the OED, "etcetera" stems from the Latin *et cētera*, meaning "the rest" or "the other," and used "as substitute for a suppressed substantive, generally a coarse or indelicate one." To be "the rest" is to always be becoming, to always be extending beyond oneself into an open to-be(come), while to be "the other" is to always be unbecoming, to constantly be dismantling the consolidation of self, again opening oneself, which is necessarily an undoing of oneself. The etcetera is that simultaneity. Different from what Butler calls "the embarrassed 'etc.,'" where there is a kind of shamefaced acknowledgment of the inability to note and account for all of the proliferative identities that one might, and at times is demanded to, reference, Philip's "etc of negroes" works subjectivity in the space of the failure of completion. Subjectivity in incompletion, necessary incompletion, is where blackness hangs its snapback because in its crisis point, of an escaping and doing that exceeds hegemony, is where trans/figurative blackness becomes itself as "suppressed substantive," which I understand as the latent, simmering robustness underlying categorization that necessarily, if/ when released, saturates the limits of the categorizations. It is hostile to, but constitutive of, categorization, and thus is indeed "coarse or indelicate." Living the etcetera is to reside in the transitional site of trans/figuration, becoming and unbecoming, being otherwise and the rest. Or, put poetically differently:

> but it's the other way   a negro.[32]

Note the space between "other way" and "a negro," a space of transition and trans/figuration immediately followed by the saturating blackness of "negroes." The space *is* the other way at the same time it is "a negro," or, the etc. It is an/other way to be, an otherwise that exceeds normative frameworks for ontology. The etc of negroes marks the potentiality that exceeds actuality, exceeds perhaps even our epistemological limits for thinking the potential. And it is troublesome; it troubles our sensibilities.

If "negroes" can serve, at least in tentative capacity, as a synecdoche for the disruptiveness of blackness (or, following Wynter, a "function as the Chaos to the new Norm of the human," as a "mode of Nigger Chaos"), the "etc of negroes" is meant to allude to the radically disorienting and volatile multiplicity of blackness.[33] All throughout *Zong!* the (black) dead appear beyond legalistic, ledgered logics; they dis/appear as overflow. In short, they are excessive, exceeding through the interstitial. The sea on which the historical *Zong* sailed—though it is imperative to note that blackness is not fixed only in what Michelle Wright calls "Middle Passage Epistemology"—is nowhere and in "constant autodislocation," perennial elsewhereness. It is the space of the between, the transitional, that concerns me. Negroes'-cum-blackness's "etc" is a transfigurative space, "a space of transition . . . that allows us to understand the queer relationship" between blackness as paraontological and bodies deemed black that takes seriously the perpetual instability of blackness and further destabilizes it.[34]

If we wish to make the world anew, to dislodge all the normative, and hence violent, frameworks from their hold over us, then we must commit to the terrifying work of radical thinking. Such a radically undone world would necessarily look very different than it does now. Refusing to open ourselves to the openness of gender and racial self-determination—both of which refuse the normativity of pragmatism and live freedom in a radical trans politics—can only be a troubling attempt to hold on to normativity when it seems convenient or less scary. Only in the unrecognizable and unintelligible do we have chances to escape the grasp of captivity. It is captivity and the subjugation to legible logics from which we are running, after all. Living in the space of becoming other than what we were is where living unbounded happens.

I want to make a claim here that may strike many as provocative or dangerously wrongheaded: trans/figurative blackness might be a modality of subjectivity that refuses the limits of history's claim to subjectivating us in culturally legible ways, in ways that render flesh as artifacts of intelligible consumption to be fitted into patriarchal, cisnormative, racially readable schema. Because, as our Lorde and savior wrote in an unpublished poem, "we seek beyond history for a new and more possible meeting."[35] Where might the unpassable, undigestible parts of history be found, the occurrences that vomit up the tyrannical making-legible history and start again? What does starting again look like? What I intend to proffer is the claim that history is tyrannical inasmuch as it exercises an unwavering power over subjects. It is a cultural-metaphysical claim on one's ontology, a narrative that disallows life outside its logics by seeking to capture and make legible all within a kind of narrative totality. Blackness's trans/figuration refuses this tyranny, always and perpetually, and decorates the space of transition with interregnous life—it is a life in the interregnum, literally between (sovereign) reigns. History has as its aim a dominative making-legible with respect to the legible past. But what of the illegible past, the past that escaped the brush of history? Because trans/figuration is concerned with fashioning new and hitherto unknown ways of becoming, and because history often promotes sedimentation (or is invoked in service of sedimentation and teleology), there exists between the two a bit of an antagonism. My proposition operates more closely to what Lisa Lowe calls the "past conditional temporality," a temporal schema that enables a conception of the (legible) past not as fixed or inaugurative of the present moment "but as a configuration of multiple contingent possibilities, all present, yet none inevitable." Resulting from this, as Lowe continues, are "alternatives that may have been unthought in those times," which permits us to "imagine different futures for what lies ahead."[36] Though it purports to be, history is not a totality and thus is subject to fissures. It is those otherwises of history that I want trans/figurative blackness to cite, because those otherwises—to "plunge outside history," à la Treva Ellison—are definitionally transformative. They think underneath the legibility of history, providing new, maybe even unknown, conditions of queer emergence.

UNANTICIPATION

"How do we think about the conditions of possibility for queer emergence?" C. Riley Snorton asked in the fall 2016 semester of his Black Queer Studies course. The question could not be answered, at least not in any sufficient way, and perhaps did not demand a definitive answer as it served primarily as a call *without* response. It elicited participation in its rhetorical character yet refused to accept participation, obviated participation because it gained life through the absence of participation (and it is not lost here that participation bears a sonic similarity with anticipation). The question floated, unable to be grasped or captured, its asking an unanticipated occurrence.

Emergence is fundamentally a state of emergency, which is to say that there is a necessary rupture of normative order, as normative order cannot hold what will become, only what is permitted to *be*. The unanticipatory nature of trans/figuration's condition of possibility for emergence is always an emergency, its etymological "arising, sudden or unexpected occurrence," which is to say its unanticipated breach onto the scene.

Heeding Snorton's intellectual excitation is to insist on queer unanticipation. If to anticipate is to attempt to corral under the grammars of normative legibility, to "seize or take possession of beforehand," then a queer unanticipation is a modality of inhabiting the world that refuses knowability "beforehand" and negates the (non)possibility of Other(ed) ness existing ahead of itself. It is marked by the un- of "pure negation," but a negation I want to contend is fueled by the critique underpinning the black radical feminist tradition articulated by Erica Edwards, a "kind of negation and other world-building that is necessary for the survival of Black thought and Black being."[37] Unanticipation, then, is to flit on the edges of legibility while being radically and hesitantly ambulatory in open fields of play that lead us, always, to different and differing terrains of otherwise-being.

There is a strain of thought, particularly that of Foucault, that favors conditions of emergence over conditions of possibility, as the latter too closely resembles transcendentalist originary thematics. Foucault remarks that "for statements it is not a condition of possibility but a law of coexistence," a materialist and genealogical insistence on how we might come to emerge within the world differently. Foucault's genealogical posture sits in opposition to searches for conditions of possibility and characterizes itself through emergence's conditions as the "very irruption at the place and at the moment at which it occurred," but there might be a way to think Foucault in excess of himself and his own intellectual proclivities.[38] There may be a way—or, better, an insistent hope—to think Snorton's inquiry as valid in its uptake as conditions of possibility alongside conditions of emergence. The black queer and trans rhizomatic lineage from which Snorton, indeed, *emerges* emplots such subjectivities and their persistent shade-throwing existence as precisely a kind of impossible emergence that entails thinking about possibility.[39] If trans subjectivity is indeed the subjectivity of an impossible people, then to insist on the possibility of this impossibility, to *emerge impossibly*, is necessarily to think about possibility—the very possibility of emerging alive.

Yearning for the conditions of possibility for queer emergence is a rhizomatic antigenealogy that, troublesomely and contentiously, refuses the purported clutch of origins. If we are to strive toward the trans axiom of self-determination systematically articulated in the introduction, it is imperative to contend for the increasingly difficult task of encountering others—indeed, encountering our very world—without the given ontologies of legibilizing frameworks. One cannot presume that another exists ahead of themselves in any capacity and thus must approach others with an incessant openness to being opened. The extent to which such a notion disturbs those who commit to thinking that radical openness and self-determination is an impossible task due to our always-already subjection to power and logics of recognition for our very viability is the extent to which I will continue to stubbornly insist. Power may indeed form the subject and provide the subject's condition for existence; indeed, "power is not simply what we oppose but also, in a strong sense, what we depend on for our existence and what we harbor and preserve in the beings that we are."[40] But I genuinely, tremulously think that I *want* to want something in excess of this. *If* power, purportedly axiomatically, produces the very possibility of legible subjectivity, then I want to gesture toward a very difficult notion: subjectivity on the outskirts of power. In other words, I want to gesture toward subjectivity that cannot be anticipated, that cannot be known in advance of itself, subjectivity that exists radically futuristically. *If* we are, as Butler goes on to say in *The Psychic Life of Power*, "stubbornly attached" to power's subjectivating qualities, the only "outside" being a constitutive one dependent upon the hegemony of the "inside," and if we might understand power in a Foucauldian sense as being the instantiation, implementation, and utilization of a relationship of force (and force, it follows in a Derridean lineage, is necessarily an *en*forcement, an iteration of violence), then I want to insist on the outside for itself, on life and livability that skirts the structuring frameworks of a relational embeddedness in power. Perhaps all I can do is insist on my wanting as a naïve whine for something more, but, nevertheless, I want the outside, life in the outside, on its own terms.

This outside on its own terms is where I'd like to think the queerly unanticipated resides. It is a place that refuses that which is deemed, and maybe even simply *is*, a requisite for subjectivity as such. This is an unanticipation that comes from a radical black and trans abolitionist tradition but bears on the ontological fundamentality of how to live in the world. In other words, unanticipation as a modality of world-living, world-subverting, and world-building is necessarily a black and trans modality since, as Che Gossett writes, they "are the refusal of power's grasp."[41] So it is through the blackness and transness, the blackness and queerness, the transness and queerness of Snorton's intellectual provocation that unanticipation must be thought. So: "Imagine what it would be like," Ashlee Marie Preston begins,

> to not spend every waking moment guarding your life. Picture a world in which you weren't always pressured to explain or defend your identity, your humanity or your right to hold space. What would it feel like to experience deep intimacy without fear of your lover spilling your blood because they're incapable of spilling their truth about their attraction to trans women? Consider what it would be like to navigate a world in which you weren't criminalized for merely surviving the best way you knew how.[42]

What Preston might be urging us to imagine is the unimaginable. Insofar as trans women of color are circumscribed overwhelmingly by narratives of violence—insofar as "trans woman of color" *means* to be imminently met with violence—it seems impossible to extricate violence from trans subjectivity. To envision such a world free of the variegated forms of violence Preston enumerates, to the extent that such violence foundations the world and serves as its condition of possibility, is to not imagine the world at all. It is to imagine an unimaginable world. Preston demands that we imagine, impossibly yet insistently, another world; Preston demands that we unanticipate the world.

Trans life has so frequently been forced to consist and, indeed, subsist in avoiding groups of those who might clock them, expecting the ontological disorientation their corporeal transgression portends while they themselves brace for the hit; carrying out extravagant parties, balls, dances, cultures in the undercommon underground; growing adept at what looks and gestures, imperceptible to most, might portend. There is violence pervading the landscape, around every corner and even in one's postcoital bedroom, and that violence impacts some more than others. But life still happens even in those interpellative moments that subject nonnormativity to the violent, reality-crafting limbs of the hegemon. The vitriolic shouts from across the street; the queer-antagonistic institutional barriers; the material, social, discursive, historical, and ideological erasure of the life of queer life presume that they can anticipate, and thus interpellatively subject, any instantiation of queerness to its deadly and immobilizing will. But they cannot. In the moments that exceed such attempts, queerness exceeds itself as externally defined, as the abject, and festers joyously in those places where it cannot be anticipated.

There is a way to read incorporation into the present world as a way of being ontologically anticipated and thus domesticated in the racial and gender Order, a violent primitive accumulation. It is then a violent tearing away of one from oneself, so one *is* only insofar as they give themselves away from themselves and allow themselves to be captured, rendered intelligible. The conditions of possibility for queer emergence would be a stealing of oneself back. Of concern is the creation of space for life, which is to say space to be unhinged, which is, furthermore, to say space to be unanticipated. One necessary practice that will need to be put forth is a radical detachment or unattachment, since unanticipation demands that we peel ourselves off of the stickiness of already given forms and templates. Rather than a Thoreau-esque escape from the woes of civilization—which is not to castigate Thoreau but only to highlight the sickening privileged nostalgia his retreat to the rustic invokes—here the unattachment is a life-in-unattachment breathed into by the very indexical lives of those deemed deviantly unlivable. Put another way, being ontologically uprooted, with all the painful extirpative history the word has specifically for black and trans flesh in the Western world, sets in motion devilish flights of fancy as to how to live as uprooted, or how to existentially thrive through the habitus of doing uprootedness.

The desire at the base of trans/figurative blackness, this other world, is the terrain following abolition. Trans/figurative blackness, in other words, might be the name for this world, it might be what Nat Raha calls the "*expression after the shatter of these* [racial and gendered division of labor under capitalism] *hierarchies*," a reparative future here and now, in the epiphenomenal present, begotten by "the legacy of our being as trans women, trans femmes, of colour, migrant, white, queer, dis/abled; where, against the cells and borders of capital's dailiness, our actions and labour, our minor insurrections and collectivisms, are legible."[43] I'm not sure we know this world, or can know it now, anytime before it comes. But it is imperative that we hope for this world and, even if it comes to pass that such a world is not possible, love it and live it *regardless*.

Allow, please, a series of passages:

> An ethico-political program that does not reproduce the violence of modern thought requires re-thinking sociality from without the modern text. Because only the end of the world as we know it, I am convinced, can dissolve cultural differences' production of human collectives as "strangers" with fixed and irreconcilable moral attributes. This requires that we release thinking from the grip of certainty and embrace the imagination's power to create with unclear and confused, or uncertain impressions. . . . A figuring of The World nourished by the imagination would inspire us to rethink sociality without the abstract fixities produced by the Understanding and the partial and total violence they authorize. . . .

> . . . After breaking through the glassy, formal fixed walls of the Understanding, released from the grip of certainty, the imagination may wonder about reassembling the fundamental components of everything to refigure the World as a complex whole without order. Let me consider a possibility: What if, instead of The Ordered World, we could image The World as a Plenum, an infinite composition. . . .

> . . . For decades now, the counter-intuitive results of experiments in particle physics have been yielding descriptions of the World with features—*uncertainty** and *non-locality+*—that violate the parameters of certainty. Experiments that, I propose, invite us to image the social without the Understanding's deadly distinctions and lethal (re)ordering devices. . . .

> What will have to be relinquished for us to unleash the imagination's radical creative capacity and draw from it what is needed for the task of thinking The World otherwise? Nothing short of a radical shift in how we approach matter and form. . . .

> . . . What if, instead of the Ordered World, we imaged each existant (human and more-than-human) not as separate forms relating through the mediation of forces, but rather as singular expressions of each and every other existant as well as of the entangled whole in/as which they exist? What if, instead of looking to particle physics for models of devising more scientific or critical analysis of the social we turned to its most disturbing findings—such as nonlocality (as an epistemological principle)

and virtuality (as an ontological descriptor)—as poetical descriptors, that is, as indicators of the impossibility of comprehending existence with the thinking tools that cannot but reproduce separability and its aids, namely determinacy and sequentiality?

DENISE FERREIRA DA SILVA, "On Difference Without Separability"

The above guide quotes come from Denise Ferreira da Silva's text about the possibility of imagining ourselves and our world not beneath the weight of "Understanding" and its determinacy and separability, underlain by an "ethico-political program" of trans/figuration. What she argues for (and I argue by extension) is a radically ethical gesture, one that attends to the sociohistorically marginalized but, perhaps more urgently, impossibly attends to the nonexistent. It is an ethics radically reoriented toward those who might emerge in a terrain whose constitutive ligaments refuse hegemony—indeed, are hegemony's refuse.

The modern text is what we've been reading this whole time, and all the things we know to be true about our relations to one another, to history, to structure, requires rethinking. Or unthinking. Or something else. The modern text has cordoned off relations that might have been but for purportedly irreducible and given ontological essences that, again purportedly, presume not only that cross-fertilization cannot occur, but that the fertilization that would occur might not even be "cross" since such a cross-ness is predicated on the instantiation of identifiable and exclusionary boundaries. Strangers are not strangers in this livable rubble we have shorthanded the end of the world as we know it; strangers comprise the village. Villages, social milieus, of uncertainty. Indeterminacy is the constant possibility of the stranger being the subject for whom we knew not that we were waiting. It is something we cannot understand, something about which we are uncertain, and that uncertainty is an imaginative refusal of doing violence.

Unfix the walls. Make walls made of water, pores, perforated fabric. Unfix Understanding, the Reasoning that clutches our sensibilities. Our imaginative otherwise, the trans/figuration of our onto-epistemological subjectivity. Can it be unordered? That is what we hope might be possible. We hope it is impractical; practicality is too fettered to being doable on this unchanged terrain. Our Understanding is too ordered and does not want to change the order. We do; we must; we have, in big and small ways. We frolic in the plenum: the assemblic totality, a saturated and burstingly full nothingness. Composed infinitely, unanticipatedly. Bodies to come, nonbodies and nobodies, weird subjectivities, strange kin. We want all of that.

In praise of counterintuitiveness. The intuitive has always been suspect to me, primarily, though, because I distrusted my mother's use of hers as a trump card for decision-making. But the intuitive rests on a subjective archive of what has been in order to discern, and to demand, what ought. I want something other than what has been and don't want to draw on it for much insight. Or, while the what has been is great for continuing the things that have been, it lacks the radical potentiality I want, the radically trans/figured otherwise that houses what might emerge. Particle physics, oddly enough, has shown us the wondrous acumen of the uncertain and nonlocal/nonlocated. Those particles violate certainty and its parameters, peering out into the vast unbounded unknown. These uncertainties are an invitation. And it is terrifyingly difficult to accept it. We are indeed still holding on because we need to be held. But there are other ways to be held.

There is so much that will have to be relinquished, so much we will have to give up, so much we will have to let go of. So much. So much violence will be done to ourselves, and we are tired of being violated. But, too, so much to gain, so much life to live, so much love. We would only be doing violence to the violated stitches of our subjectivity. This is all to live in a different world, *right here*, other than it has been said to be. For abolition does not launch us into outer space where we terraform another place; abolition stays here while simultaneously disallowing here to be *here*. We will be not what they said we are. What might arise is da Silva's "radical shift in . . . matter and form," a trans/figuration in other words, where we look and act differently. Like, we literally change our matter and the form that matter takes; we'd be doing some sci-fi–type stuff in this world. Imagine ourselves as we cannot be, until we imagine ourselves precisely as that—what we cannot be, as what we have not been permitted to be, as what has been said to be impossible. Imagine ourselves, just that, not *as* anything. Maybe we cannot be whatever we want, but we can certainly not be what we are.

I can only insist on such an Other world, an insistence that stands in tense contrast to existence—the latter a definitive claim, tangible and knowable; the former, by contrast, something that makes itself felt, something that beckons us from elsewhere, solicits us, lures us. Insisting on this world we cannot, and indeed must not, anticipate marks an embrace of something odd. We are beckoned to be on the run toward something terrifying, runnin' toward a queer and hella strange nonplace, a nonplace with a "completely other history of paradoxical laws and non-dialectical continuities, absolutely heterogeneous pockets, irreducible particularities, of unheard of and incalculable sexual differences."[44] That's where we wanna be at—or, rather, where we wanna become at. Irreducible particularities and unheard-of sexual differences populate a trans and trans/figured world unanticipated by logics of legibility. Transness comes to signify not merely, or *even*, changing from one option to another but something not even heard of yet; something different and emergent when the abolitionist dust still swirls is what transness comes to reference here, not even subject to the purported laws of sexual immutability. And unhierarchized, the slashed trans/figurative. All of which is to say, it is not this. And that's all I want. I want another here.

Trans/figurative blackness keeps black trans feminism radical, as it must always be, by refusing relations of exclusion and segregation. The radical force, indeed all radical forces, come from multiplying in unanticipated ways, ways that subvert and traffic outside the expected, ways that courageously welcome different socialities and configurations.

In this chapter I have attempted to tease out the mutability endemic to blackness, drawing a more explicit link between blackness and the capacious alteration hailed by transness. As the concluding chapter of part 1, it has capped the theoretical articulation of black trans feminism as a project toward unfixation, paraontology, abolition, and radicality. The project of black trans feminism, part 1 has shown, is poised toward other ways to be held that are vehemently not predicated on any of the ontological violences that predicate the current world in which we live, which requires a profound letting go and leap into other ways to become a subject and live, unfettered and unbounded. Part 2 will turn to literature—specifically essays, poetry, and interviews—of variously gendered black women in order to demonstrate how the abolitionism and gender radicality of black trans feminism get expressed through the discursive production of those who are hailed by and write within the forces of the black and trans and feminist.

PART **2**

Feminist, Fugitivity 4

Because black feminism has never only been about black women, it's never been this. It's been about a more just world.
FARAH JASMINE GRIFFIN, "On the Legacy of Black Feminism"

But just cuz they name a thing, a thing,
Don't mean it ain't still named God
in some other language.
EBONI HOGAN, "Cardi B Tells Me about Myself"

What has been given to us as the totality of the world is not, in fact, the totality of the world. Indeed, black trans feminism does not claim a legitimacy in "totalities," as all systems, all modes of structuring subjectivity and life, are perpetually open to invention, revision, and reimagination. The open-endedness is a marker of a refusal to foreclose the radical possibility of things being not this, of the onto-epistemic insurrection. The assertions are tentative, never final as if the last word can be said on ourselves; we struggle in bliss acknowledging the perennial incompletion, which serves as a blessed invitation to continue to be vigilant of the violences of certainty and the terrors of congealed axioms that manifest as normativities.

Alexis Pauline Gumbs establishes in her three texts—*Spill: Scenes of Black Feminist Fugitivity*, *M Archive: After the End of the World*, and *Dub: Finding Ceremony*—a discursive ensemble of symphonic racialized gender cacophony.[1] Each of her texts strike one as poetic inscriptions of ancestral wisdom or nonbinaristic radical musings (or, better yet, listenings) on who we are and who we might become as manifested in writing-with black feminist thinkers (i.e., Hortense Spillers, M. Jacqui Alexander, and Sylvia Wynter). Her poems in all of the texts do not read as poems as such; the poems do not read as adhering to identifiable metrics, rhythmic schemes, forms, lineages, or traditions per se. At times one forgets one is even reading a book of poetry, as to approach the genre is to presuppose a certain expectation as to what one should encounter. But Gumbs pens something else on the pages. They are poems, surely, though poems not as objects but as *events*: irruptions of language that throw shade on language's attending requisite forms, unable to be categorized in given ontological schemas of recognition. The poetry of Gumbs's trilogy, or what she refers to as a "triptych," ushers in "a field force which reinterprets and reinvents anew the meaning of the sign"; Gumbs's poetry, in the language of her interlocutor for the final installment of the triptych, "depends on the 'openness' of the sign to be able to reinvent it."[2]

In an interview, Gumbs reveals that *Spill* in particular, though such sentiment can apply to each book she has written, each word she has breathed, is "a celebration of the fact that Black women have not been contained."[3] *Spill* is a celebration of the black and woman/femme, emphasis on both, not a mourning of racialized sexism doled out by the disseminators of white and cis male supremacy. This celebration combats perspectives that emphasize the violences that occur to black women and femmes, a celebration possible by way of Gumbs's commitment to the "anti- and ante-categorical predication of blackness" and gender, which "subordinate[s], by a measure so small that it constitutes measure's eclipse, the critical analysis of anti-blackness to the celebratory analysis of blackness." And all of this "is done not to avoid or ameliorate the hard truths of anti-blackness but in the service of its violent eradication," in the words of her mentor and advisor Fred Moten.[4] This celebration pervades her triptych. M *Archive*, she writes, "is about long visioning about what the material evidence will be of this apocalypse we are going through," and *Dub* "is another way of saying yes, this is an oracle."[5] These books, these oracular gifts, are for us all, and specifically for black women, which might be to say for us all—or, rather, for all of our freedom. *Spill*, M *Archive*, and *Dub* are "for Black women," Gumbs says, "all of us by the way, cis and trans, to recognize ourselves, each other, our ancestors and what we've been through. And to recognize the love and life-making that has also been there the whole time and is still there. And the secondary ceremony is for everyone who doesn't identify as a black woman to also understand that their healing is bound up with ours too." This ceremonial capaciousness inflects black feminism through a massive project of re- and desubjectivation for everyone, a project of abolition and gender radicality under the heading of, for Gumbs and the meditative Spillers, black feminism, and, for me, black trans feminism.[6] The variegated ceremonies are anti- and antecategories *by way of* black women—Spillers's going through gender to get to something wider, as discussed in chapter 2—that fracturative nexus that possesses particularity and, if I dare say, universality, possesses opacity and an open abolition.

Gumbs's triptych (an artistic term that typically references a visual image divided onto three panels hinged together side by side and often used as an altarpiece) is an experimental poetic trilogy. Experimental here means a kind of writing that violates grammar and disallows "normality" in terms of reading and encountering. It is more than the avant-garde or innovative; experimental forms, to take apt language from Shelly Eversley, are black feminist praxis, which fundamentally "transform[s] our understandings of race" and, necessarily, gender.[7] To say, then, that Gumbs's triptych is experimental is to assert that it inaugurates a different imaginative terrain in which another kind of lifeworld is imagined as inhabitable precisely by way of the destruction of the world in which many of us live—the world that is imposed upon many of us as the only world in which to live. Gumbs presents what other worlds in the world, after the world, under the world, might be, and who we might be in those worlds. As an experimental poetic writer, Gumbs offers in *Spill*, м *Archive*, and *Dub* a disruption of the grammatical and discursive economy orchestrating what we can imagine ourselves as. In this sense, this black feminist sense, she alters the stabilized tenets upon which valid life rests and provides different ways to be-with that open up gendered, racialized, and species taxonomies, giving those of us who commit to her thinking some imaginary forms of life that do not look like Forms of Life.

SPILLAGE

Spill, written in a poetic open form or free verse, spills all over itself. Purposely metrically inconsistent, rhyming occasionally, and lacking in regular structure, *Spill* is written with the making and breaking of narrative in mind. In this sense, we can say that it is not simply written by a black woman but, more substantively, written through black feminist fugitivity; *Spill* makes and breaks narrative in its fundamental poetic subjectivity as an instantiation of radical black feminism.

A self-described black queer troublemaker and black feminist love evangelist, Gumbs sets as her task in *Spill* to depict "what every moment of my life is": it is "Freedom wanting to be free. Life wanting to be life. Love wanting to be love," as she describes it in our interview.[8] Black feminist fugitivity, unapologetically gendered-in-excess-of-Gender, is the spillage of historicity and sociality, an incendiary surface, which the various definitions of the title allude to and Gumbs enumerates: to kill or destroy; to flow over the edge; to empty, in a kind of fugitive kenosis that renounces the strictures of the omnisovereign; to move out or escape quickly; to reveal; to drop; to fall. These various definitions demand more room to explode that which curtails black women's subjectivity, room to imagine. Gumbs's "scenes" demonstrate a specifically *black feminist* fugitivity by way of both an urge to expand racialized and gendered lexicons of possibility, and an urge to abolish their categorization while simultaneously excavating these categories for their untrackable generativity. The former I want to theorize, via Gumbs, as an unfixation from tenets of race and gender as they confine one to replaying scripts imposed by normative forces. Urging for an expanded lexicon requires opening up, say, blackness to those who may not even be understood as adhering to its historical requisites; it requires opening up gender to be vitiated by those who refuse its normative hold and seriously considering organizing our worlds around that expansion. If fugitivity marks an escape from and subversion of normative modes of seeing and knowing, Gumbs's black feminist fugitivity takes the position of black women at a nonexclusionary angle that denotes the illegible edge poised to find how we stretch meaning and open things up so vastly that they explode the sky. In brief, her black feminist fugitivity hitches to Kara Keeling's understanding of the black femme, as the figure describes not an identifiable subject but a subjective posture, an illegible "figure that exists on the edge line, that is, the shoreline between the visible and the invisible, the thought and the unthought."[9]

Readers of *Spill* are first greeted, as with most books, by its cover, which features Kenyatta A. C. Hinkle's 2014 drawing *Now There Are Three Ways to Get This Done: Your Way, Their Way or My Way*. Originally made for the Tituba Black Witch of Salem Drawing Series, the image shows a figure spewing a map from one of its mouths. It is uncertain how many faces the figure has (two, perhaps three?); it is uncertain how many breasts the figure has (three, maybe four; or more, as it is uncertain whether the things atop the figure's heads are breasts); it is uncertain what gender the figure is;

it is uncertain what this figure looks like below its breasts, as the rest of the figure is obscured by blackened scribble. The figure, quite simply, spills all over the place in gendered unmappability. The map spewing from the figure's mouth is distorted and gestures toward mappability writ large. It becomes incumbent upon us to note our inability to "map" the figure as "woman" or even human, and, too, our inability to track where the figure begins and ends, or where the map leads and what it depicts. We have no metric, no ground by which to anchor our encounter with the image. So if Sylvia Wynter warned us against mistaking the map for the territory, the cover of *Spill* alerts us to how the scripts we receive for interpreting something are always spilled over by the territory those scripts, as maps, attempt to bind. *Spill* is thus a refusal of racialized and gendered normativities, which incites the possibility of other worlds and epistemologies. It is fueled by a fugitive impetus: "Love, it is freedom, it is older than me, it has not stopped, despite all of the physical and ideological structures we could mention."[10] The escape is constitutive of love, and love is constitutive of escape, as it is precisely because of the impetus of love—love for self, love for others, love for life, love *regardless*—that can and must escape.

In a poem from the first third of the book, Gumbs highlights Harriet Tubman, she who, like Phillis Wheatley (who also has a scene in the book dedicated to her), "spilled out of and upset the container of gendered and racialized slavery."[11] Gumbs opens the poem, introduced by the words "for Harriet Tubman," with a radical singularity ("this can never be equal to this" [39]) and tallies monotonous practices given to the enslaved. But it ends in a flourish. She writes, "So she renamed herself after her mother, left her dirtbag husband, looked up at her north star god and said 'let's go'" (39). Tubman's flight is tied to the claiming of her mother and the rebuking of that masculine instantiation of the patriarchal ceremony: the husband. Flight in this way has a distinctly gendered texture; indeed, her fugitive flight is enabled by the gendered decisions to rename herself by way of the mother and refuse patriarchal masculinity. The "let's go" is particularly of note, as it, on my reading, is polysemous. It marks a demand to move. "Let's go" beckons one's subjectivity to become full of motion, to engender subjectivity through a go-ness that in a sense interpellates, or inaugurates, that subjectivity. Too, though, "let's go" can alleviate the contraction and expand the phrase without redaction as "let *us* go." Expansion of the contraction reveals another intention: it is a demand to free "us," an undetermined demographic inclusive of which is, perhaps, all those who wish to engender their subjectivity through go-ness. It is a liberatory call for the cessation of captivity from external chains—a demand, as it were, for a validation of fugitive subjectivity, via Tubman.

The book's dedication is "TO BLACK WOMEN who make and break narrative." At the outset, not only do black women cast a presence over the text but a disruptive and wayward black woman presence. Black women fracture the linearity of normative narratives. They sabotage, in that black feminist practice of life and living, of "disruption, rupture, and imagined futures."[12] Such a claim necessitates, at least in part, the troubling of all kinds of narrative. So, certainly, the narrative form of *Spill* in many ways defies typical linear storylines, but what the poetic "scenes" of *Spill* also produce is a troubling of racial and gendered narratives, particularly for black women. Black women (re)make and break these racial and gender narratives and produce other ways of coming into subjectivity that are not predicated on such frameworks. Immersion in the black feminist subjectivity of black women is to inhabit another racialized and gendered world in the world, a black feminist *trans*versal world begotten through the possibility black women engender. This engendered world, a certain kind of becoming, is articulated through never-described figures, or figures that are never given intentional physiognomic form. Gumbs's figures emerge instead as wayward movements across and beyond imposed boundaries of racialized gender, marking how Gumbs is inscribing the iterations of "she" throughout the text. This "she," then, coupled with a black feminist transversality, makes one's assumptions of these figures as black women grow into an understanding of "she" as what I've termed a becoming-black-woman. "She" is not the spitting image of "the" black woman; "she" is a modality of life and living, and a beckoning to how one might live differently. Her scenes are glimpses of what life might become if we listen to the fugitive whispers begotten by black (trans) feminism. If we, that is, listen to how their waywardness teaches us another mode of living life, a waywardness that Saidiya Hartman beautifully articulates: "To inhabit the world in ways inimical to those deemed proper and respectable, to be deeply aware of the gulf between where you stayed and how you might live. Waywardness: the avid longing for a world not ruled by master, man or the police."[13] That this is given to us in *Spill* by black women who are becoming—becoming-black-women—black feminism's fugitive scenes are angles of vision into *that*.

It is also the very pages that follow the dedication to the narrative-making and -breaking black women that speak to a kind of waywardness as well. Gumbs writes:

the wide-eyed women the walking women the worst
the water washes the war wrung women
the wailers the whistle the first
the water waists of the undrowned women
the hope floats women the strong
. . . .

the fast-ass women the fall-in-love women the freaks
the fire is full of the all-out women
the walk-out women the sweet
the fire is finding the love-lost women
the worth-it women the ones
fire is blazing the brash blues women
the black-eyed women . . .

our work here is not done. (n.p.)

These women, undoubtedly, these black women who are becoming-black-women insofar as they are moving toward a veritable subjective freedom, inflect the multiplicity of blackness, inflect a multiplicitous gender-radical blackness. The alliterative /w/ sound brushes through one's lips, puffs of air escaping, whooshing on as miniature instances of that escaped air from the vestibule of one's mouth. These brief, aestheticized puffs of air used to adorn the polyvocality of black women escape the body but engender the flesh, might leave the body but articulate through their ethereality a way to live outside the body. All of these women—fast-ass, wailing, undrowned, wide-eyed, walk-out—are nodal points of how multivalent the very category is and thus offer a profound critique of its meaning. It is a meaning that, by virtue of their movement otherwise, becomes undone. Which is to say, *they* become.

A return, then, to chapter 2's articulation of becoming-black-woman. Black women have historically set as their protoblack feminist task to interrogate the capacity of the category "woman," and that this task has continued into 2016 with *Spill* (and no doubt long after its publication) shows that, indeed, our work here is not done. As Spillers is the primary interlocutor of *Spill*, what she calls, at the outset of her germinal essay, a "marked woman" is deeply instructive here as it relates to Gumbs's black women and their becoming, their becoming-black-womanness. The marked woman: a figure who perhaps needs no introduction, or a figure who, perhaps, cannot be introduced, as the marked woman is a pervasive, haunting presence of modernity, conditioning modernity's possibility. Spillers is referencing herself and, more broadly, the nexus of black and woman. I want to maintain the troublesomeness of the "marked woman," the words serving as indices for the disruption and interstitiality of un/gendered subjects proximal to blackness. A problem for thought, the marked woman is not merely, or even at all, a figure that exists as such and unmediated in sociality, but a figure that is figured, which is to say an assemblage fashioned to affix to and as subjectivity. To say that the marked woman is a problem for thought is to understand them not solely, or even primarily, as an actually occurring subject.[14] The marked woman describes not a subject in the world but a disruption that is corporealized, discursive, and created—a set of disruptions rather than a bodily occurrence or Ellisonian "matter of a bio-chemical accident to [the] epidermis." Insofar as the marked woman can be linked to un/gendered blackness, they name a deployable disruption of normativity that, at least in this context, is irrespective of physiognomy. If the figure of the marked woman is mired in a veritable un/gendered blackness, and if it is a problem, where are we to locate it in the world? Black women's bodies serve here less as exemplary representations of racialized cis womanhood's discontents—which itself is a troubled and fractured terminological rendering on the grounds that black women have long been withheld from "womanhood" and its constitutive cisness—and instead as an excessive figuration that retains the possibility of an otherwise ontology, an ontology that refuses the logistical machineries of racial capitalism, gender normativity, settler colonialism, and other hegemonic regimes. An ontology that turns out is not an ontology.

Gumbs's descriptions of these women, too, are descriptions that all attest to a kind of fugitive posture: women who walk, and walk *out*, perhaps in protest of domestic confinement or, more generally, of gendered carceral logics; women who wail and whistle, making noise and vocally flouting decorum; women who hope, despite historical conscriptions of their livability; women who go undrowned, refusing to go gentle into that oceanic abyss of death; women who are fast, who demonstrate, in other words, sexual autonomy *and* the abolition of sex—the act and the perinatal assignation—as compulsorily hemming how one relates to others; women who are brash, caustic, fire-tongued. The polyvalent, repeated (black) women of this opening cascade of what might be a black-girl-magic augur of the feminist fugitivity to come indexes a reiterative, incantatory chant that calls into being an abolition and radicality. All of this operates, textually, in a nonspace, an unlocatable and unfixing fugitive space, because it is *unpaginated.* There is no page number for this section, no numerical way to cite it, maybe because it plunges outside the historical ledgers of legibility, maybe because pagination cannot hold these women, maybe because these fugitive enactments cannot be located. The refusal of pagination implies a wayward, nonlinear lineage, an unlocatable and dislocated anteorigin that is an anarchic dispersal rather than a singular origin from which each page progressively reveals more through a teleologic. These fugitive black women were never meant to survive, so they escape being fixed by numerics.

This is a bold display of waywardness. Gumbs illustrates waywardness as a life practice. It is a practice that black feminists inherit. To imagine that *"i be that walk a piece of the way home wayward woman"* (116; emphasis in original) is to inhabit a wayward lineage. Not a lineage fixed to straightforward causation or a linear historical trajectory with identifiable foremothers, but an inherited lineage from the disparate tremors of the underside of history. The "i" of the declaration refuses the comfort and stasis of home, as she only walks *a piece* of the way home, resting in the between, on the unstable and ebbing and flowing shorelines, in the unplaceable interstitial. This wayward woman partway home will inevitably meet other wayward women, and they will commune together in their waywardness. Coming together is conditioned by waywardness, by "refusing the straightness of railings or streets," and it is this refusal that makes them "the asphalt community of black enough to dance stretch flex" (147). Their black enough-ness contingent upon how they refuse straightness, how they dance and stretch; their black enough-ness always enough when they get outside of things and subvert normative gestures. When they, in other words, spill, where such a spillage is characteristic of the blackness and feminism of fugitivity. They are "sidebody," ecstatic reconfigurations of corporeality around a corporeal waywardness, their "wings" poised for flight (147). So, yes, "we perceive no one to be where they belong" (138), but that's right where "i," where "she," is going to stay.

One also notices that *Spill* is slathered with descriptions of women walking out of doors. The outdoors and out-of-doors look off into the wilderness as an unsettleable settlement. The women about whom Gumbs writes refuse to be contained and confined to the sphere of domesticity, indeed to the sphere of property. Their very bones say "this house would not win she was free she was getting out" (35). As one of the most potent manifestations of propertied ownership, given to allusions of mortgages, wealth, and territory, houses and housedness in the text are gotten out of. Her freeness is contingent upon getting out of the house. She is taking up Nael Bhanji's critique of "homing desires," preferring the transgressive interstitial. Out of the house is where she achieves her freedom, the house's exit the threshold of such freedom. To get out of this house she must, naturally, walk out of its door. Ultimately, then, "she decided to walk out the door barefoot, hands empty unburdened by everything" (36), the emptiness indicative of an openness rather than a barrenness, a sloughing off of all the Morrisonian "shit that weighs you down." She carries nothing, so she is refusing to possess anything. Too, digging into this reading seems to yield the conclusion that she refuses possession itself, both possessing things contained in the house as well as the ways in which she was possessed in and by the domestic sphere of propertied confinement. She will neither be the subject she was said to be nor carry the things that are said to be meaningful for recognition outside of the house. The door is indeed one of no return, but going through it outside into the wilderness is where one can finally subjectivate oneself as unfettered by the normative baggage of legibility tellingly "housed" indoors. Inside those houses might be undesirable specters, spooky astral projections we don't have time for. They get in the way sometimes, those boogeymen. Getting out of the house, then, is less a running away due to fear and more an "inherited swiftness" trained in the wilderness. Those "boogeym[e]n didn't," and couldn't, "quite catch her. so thanks" (47), because they brought online the penchant to leave, to get out there with the others who are getting out there by getting out of here.

The walking-out extends even to her social network. Or, rather, if *Spill* as a text contains the boisterous sociality of all the various instantiations of "she" and "her," the walking-out extends to all those doing black feminist fugitive work—that work *is* walking out of doors. When "she" "decided to call up everyone," they were not home. And I imagine she smiled, too, knowing that missed calls meant breached doors, the outdoors where she'll see them all again. So once she hung up the phone, smiling about the missed connection that was in fact a made connection, she, too, "walked out the door to see where they were and that's how she started to roam" (36). Roaming, or waywardness, is the condition for "see[ing] where they were"; it is integral to sociality. Sociality happens when you walk out the door and roam, amble about in the wild and begin to understand what me-ness is like when you're free. What do you look and feel like without being reflected back to yourself by gazes that can't caress you and that result in your deformation? What do you look like to optics and haptics that don't break on you? We know that walking outdoors and out of doors meant that "she walked out the door over mirrors she broke" (33), so the question becomes, What do wilderness mirrors look like? Is it the reflection of a river, the pupil of another wilderness woman, the glimmer of raindrops, the shine of a star? She won't recognize this person staring back at her, and that is good, because her unrecognition is perhaps the first time she'll be recognized.

To be recognized in one's unrecognizability is a profound escape. But, as Gumbs said in our interview, "the escaping isn't easy." And damn is she right. In the pursuit of the joy that will lead to the black feminist fugitive life one seeks, they will come for you, as they have been doing this whole time. It is true that "when she escaped she was fully free" (43), but that freeness amounts to an illegibility that, while the aim of the one in fugitive flight, invites various means of capture. We, and Gumbs, too, already know from Spillers that not everyone knows our name. So they create them as a way to make legible the illegible, as a way to capture the runaway: "her nickname changed to nutcase. no-name. that crazy bitch." (43). The nutcase, the crazy bitch, the no-named are all demonstrations of the ways that black women break narratives. Black women's subjectivity poses an imminent threat to the order of hegemony, so the aforementioned names are attempts to nonconsensually interpellate their unruliness into negative foils for hegemonic order. Language is broken when trying to ensnare black women, and the nutcase, for example, names not the illegible being onto which it tries to attach itself—indeed, the being it tries to inaugurate into a knowable (pathologized) subjectivity—but the event of language disintegrating. These names are evidence of the nontotality of hegemonic language, its constant rehashing of not a changing-same but a desperate attempt to hold on to what it purported to have already wrapped up. It loses its grip, its muscles weaken, the buildup of lactic acid burning it out. This is the black and trans, the radically black feminist, effect of black women's anagrammaticalizing (per Christina Sharpe) of language that tries to make sense of volatility. That language is the manifestation of untrackability—like, yo, the names they're coming up with are showing us, clear as day, that they can't keep up, that they can't track that which runs so fast it doesn't leave tracks. What they're serving is nutritionally evacuated. Don't consume it. So "drop the spoon, girl. run" (40).

In this space Gumbs is thinking deeply about a different way to do and be gender. She is breaking that narrative to open it up and dig around inside it, discard things, add some seasoning and sauces, or scrap it entirely. But it starts with a mirror, or at least "she thought it was a mirror" (11). Women's literary history, and trans literary and cultural discourses, too, have lengthy lineages of looking into mirrors. Mirrors are often understood as objective reflective surfaces that occasion one's assessment of one's selves, whether that self is erased or obscured or in flux or a combination of the three. The mirror, in a world that throws your image around and makes it difficult to see it for what it is, has long been believed to be the unmediated mediator of one's "I," the symbolic object that Lacanians would deem as formative of the I function or, as such, an identification. But even when we look at, or think we are looking at, a mirror, there is still the omnipresent possibility of seeing something else, or of misreading the mirror itself even when "it had always been a mirror" (11). We might look and something will be off, something might be in the mirror "that wasn't back here"—like "that woman" (11). That woman in the mirror may be no woman at all; that woman may not be the being that is back here looking, because, Gumbs inscribes, this is another woman. No, really, another kind of woman. This is a woman whose "eyes [are] on fire, smile almost inviting." And then it is asked: "what *is* she doing with my only face?" (11; emphasis in original). How can another woman, who is you looking into a mirror, be not-you but have the only face you've got? Well, when that other woman is the woman that might be said to emerge when one's gendered subjectivity is altered, opened, while not changing a thing—what Gumbs calls in M *Archive* the "you beyond you." What this early section of *Spill* is offering readers is the possibility—and it is a radically open one, so nonpresumptuous it cannot even know when it arrives—of a kind of feminist fugitive flight without moving, Morrison's flight without leaving the ground. It is offering, perhaps, what gender *but for* the regime of Gender might be, a way to do and be gender after, and during, abolition. A subjective gender radicality in abolition.

It might be that Gumbs's experimentalizing of gender here by way of blackness's and womanness's nexus is the beautiful mess that "spills" out when breaking and bending gender, when making gender do what it thought it couldn't or wasn't supposed to do. This other woman, then, is "split open like achilles," and her (their? its?) "body" cannot be said to properly be a body. This body that this other woman has is "only pores, only wet spaces, vessel, opening" (15). What is an opened, porous body when body-ness, properly speaking, is a closed entity? This uncertainty is reflected in the text, Gumbs writing "was she possible? . . . was she real?" (15), leaving the questions open. We are left with something strange; we are left with Gumbs's articulation of what gender *might* be: "the new female being, first of her kind, couldn't believe herself" (95). She is unbelievable. And that's the kind of gender that might be our salvation. When all the baggage, all the symbolics predicated on cisness and whiteness and maleness, are breached, we emerge into something else. Spillers might say we emerge into flesh, others might say we emerge into a queer utopia. But, for Gumbs, this new female being that indexes the category-critical analysis that is blackness, the gender vitiating penchant that is transness, is perhaps a term for a subjectivity that arises from engaging black feminist fugitivity.

Such a subjectivity is a conceptual one that hinges on "the disruption of [gender- and] race-biopolitics," as one scholar put it in thinking about Gumbs alongside others like Fred Moten and Stefano Harney, James Bliss, Katherine McKittrick, and José Esteban Muñoz, and "requires a seizure of the biopolitical arsenal, and a queering of the future through decolonial, abolitionist, and fugitive practices . . . to undo the grammar that binds us to a narrowly defined human future."[15] Fugitive black feminism becomes less an epidermal or gender descriptor located in measurements of sufficient melanin or codified sex characteristics and becomes more of a critical, subversive, fugitive praxis. Black feminism is what holds us together in coalitional solidarity, in conspiratorial anticapitalist, antiracist, feminist, anti-imperialist communion, not particular ontologized identities. This hold is how we remain held even when we are on the way to holding without having or possessing. It is an intention, a willful act that rhizomatically affiliates itself with others on political grounds in excess of normative subjectivities. Exceeding these normative subjectivities is fundamentally a pursuit of livable life otherwise.

And who is seeking this life? What kind of subject pursues this other kind of life, making it another kind of subject? Gumbs theorizes, succinctly, a specific black feminist fugitive gesture of subjectivity. Hers is an alternative interpellative call—the, as she writes, "you had me at hell no" (105). If Louis Althusser offers interpellation as the manner through which subjects come into existence as subjects, Gumbs fashions a critique by way of a refusal. Such is her fugitivity, and notably the feminist fugitivity at the fundament of another kind of subject formation. Interpellation in the traditional sense can be thought of as the romantic cliché upon which Gumbs is Signifyin(g): you had me at hello. The traditional call to subjectivity—interpellation—is the being "had" at the "hey you," the "hello." It only takes a space and an additional letter for Gumbs to shift this. "You had me at hell no" reconfigures how one inaugurates oneself by way of and intimately through a quotidian refusal. The inaugural call here is refused and traded in, as it were, for an inauguration through refusal.

The "me" that is "had" is constituted through a "hell no," which begs the question of what a hell-no-subjectivity might mean. At the very least, it is the "her" and the "she" throughout the text that is metonymically indexical of Gumbs's black feminist fugitivity. One continues to ask while reading *Spill*, Who *is* "she"? It is my contention that "she" is the name Gumbs uses as proxy for, or volatile nominative nexus of, the one that "know[s] not what you are" (71) and the one who "was inventing a language. herself" (20). The former is in fact what LaMonda Horton-Stallings calls the "trickster trope" black women use to exceed regulative norms, as claiming the "I'm not what you say I am," Stallings says, is a way that black women "unname" themselves in order "to deny oppressive regimes."[16] In other words, knowing not what one is, here the existential habitus of black women, is the condition for being and becoming something else. It is a kind of trans encounter with the imposition of racialized gendered ontology: rather than being given an ontology and simply wanting the "other" one and buttressing a binary, this more fundamentally refuses to concede to the "gendered" terms, opting out and suspending oneself, holding ontological description in abeyance *as* one's subjectivity—a suspended, always incomplete subjectivity, radically open to the otherwise, the "not what you" (or anyone) "are." The latter quote from Gumbs on inventing a language of/as "herself" advances Spillers's claim that black women, historically, serve as the invented necessity for the West as the negative foil for the nation's superiority. "Herself" becomes the new, unknown thing that black women might invent themselves out toward.

Black feminism is a task: to love, to do and undo, to cause discomfort, to live-despite, to dwell with the breakers and saboteurs. A black feminist fugitive subjectivity is open and opening, inhabitable by all who commit to the radical task of doing and thinking its inhabitability; open is black feminism to radical women of color who are not epidermally black, to antiracist epidermally white feminists, to cis and trans men committed to rendering the destruction of patriarchy's tentacles—because it inherits the Combahee River Collective's refusal of all "biological determinism" that says one's identification begins and ends at any asocial, biological characteristic. Black feminism holds as "sacred" a "trans-inclusive non-exclusive understanding and practice of womanhood" (to be a woman is indeed a practice), "challeng[es] woman as a category, [and] chang[es] the meaning of woman as a category," as well as questions blackness as an epidermal measurement, recognizing that these categories as endowments of a physical body are insufficient, exclusionary, and will, in a liberatory world, ultimately be discarded.[17] When we conspire together and insistently disrupt the consolidating powers of normativity (gender and racial especially) with black feminist force, we inhabit a milieu with one another, and it is in this black feminist milieu that we become-together: become queer, become trans, become black, become fugitive. And that's who we be when we do that work.

METAPHYSICAL ARCHIVES

What might occur if we imagine, and indeed enact, ourselves and sociality through an insistent beyond? That is, so often moves that valorize the beyond are cast as ahistorical or refusing to grapple with the present conditions. This is sensible, perhaps, because the beyond is often brandished by those on the political right who wish to move "beyond race" and "beyond identity politics," rubbing leftists wrongly, justifiably so. The intent here, however, is to dwell in the beyond: truly, to *dwell* in the multiplicitous beyond, to inhabit the beyond as a place where one can move and stretch, a place where one stays and creates a livelihood.[18] The beyond that abolitionists seek to bring about, in echoing reverberation with the "after" that generates radical sentiments seeking to abolish the terrors of this world, is fundamentally a black feminist metaphysics, in Gumbs's terms. Black feminist metaphysicians examine and assess the beyond; indeed, find in it a place where we might wish to live.

As *Spill* thought racialized gendered subjectivity outside of given ontologies and as "fugitive from patriarchy," so, too, does M *Archive* assert a different analytic evaluative frame for what happens when the current regime is abolished. To the extent that it is thought to be easier to imagine the abolitionist end of the world and capitalism than gender's structuring binary, Gumbs takes this to task and has her black feminist metaphysician at the end of the world assess the (racialized) gender rubble. A writing with and after M. Jacqui Alexander, M *Archive* takes breathing as a project—an absurd project, to be sure, because "shouldn't it be a given?" Gumbs asks, knowing that it is certainly not a given (and often something that is taken). The book, or prayer, or oracle, or meditation, is one of possibility: as the note opening the text declares of itself, "This book offers a possibility of being beyond the human and an invitation into the blackness of what we cannot know from here" (xi). Ontology itself has inscribed into it the expurgation of blackness, which is to say ontology qua Ontology is the expurgation of blackness's paraontological fugitivity. Thus, a black feminist metaphysics is not concerned so much with ontology itself or trying to access ontology; rather, the metaphysics Gumbs writes into M *Archive* is an invitation to inhabit precisely blackness's para- and perhaps nega-ontology. Such a space is unknowable, refusing to capture blackness epistemically prior to its being inhabited and hence refusing to circumscribe it. What this black feminist metaphysics implies, then, is a way of coming into being outside of Being, a shadow Heideggerian abandonment of subjectivity that manifests in Gumbs's text as the search for what she calls a "you beyond you" (xi).

The you beyond you is not "you." We can read this "you" through an early passage in *Dub*, where the "you" might come to signify an anoriginary subjectivity, "the you that was us. before" (23), a you not subjectivated by rules of recognition and legibility but one that emerges into itself by refusing and exceeding those rules—ontological rules that structure Being, the excess and refusal of which Judith Butler calls an "insurrection at the level of ontology."[19] The you beyond you and the you that was us before do not wish to hold the you that you were because that you is insufficient and would sully the you that is beyond you. The you beyond you is another way of living. It is a living that has departed from what was permitted to be you, a permission that excluded so much. The you beyond you is what you become after abolition, a you with a radically (un)gendered subjectivity. It is a you that is not contained in a singular, individuated body, because "this thing about one body, it was the black feminist metaphysicians who first said it wouldn't be enough, never had been enough" (6). It was the you before the beyond you that had only one (or was believed to have only one) body, but now, after the metaphysical assessment using un- and anagrammars of black feminism, is more than one body. This "core construct" of one body was a problematic one, a requisite for purported sanity. At base, as Gumbs notes, the myth of the individuated body is a denial of black femininity since it is black femininity that stitches together the universe. The universe—that is, everything—is a simultaneity of blackness and black femininity, and thus the presumption of discreteness is to reject that axiom. And that axiom is what is deemed a black feminist pragmatism of an intergenerational scope (7). Key here is the intergenerational. The you beyond you has inherited a vast archive that makes up and constitutes the you beyond you, such that the you beyond you is many yous, a testament to our living and becoming together through others; the inherited archive, which is to say the ancestors, are "th[e] work [that] began before I was born and it will continue" (6; emphasis in original), work that forms us and, through our being, manifests. We are the work.

As work, our identities are no longer fixed. We are neither static nor settled. Our identities get retooled as flowlike and mutable substances given to alteration, indeterminacy, breach, excessive departure from origins—the abolition and gender radicality at the heart of the black and trans and feminist. What identity comes to be rethought as is a constant practice indexical of the convergence gotten to by Fred Moten and Wu Tsang, that identity is "the act of putting yourself together each day."[20] As Gumbs describes this from the perspective of black feminist metaphysicians, the challenge for those who live after the end of the world is "to create oneself anew on a regular basis" (151). She is setting forth an argument that it may be a misnomer to say what or who we are, as that will undergo alteration, as it should, the next day. Gumbs's quotidian putting-together is an allowance to become with and through others without having to be beholden to previous scripts, and it is the veneration of the possibility—and subsequent, if worked at, actualization—of fashioning and refashioning and reinventing aspiring toward "re-creating a self unrecognizable (to both your former self and the expectations of others)" (151). Offered here is a method of subjectivation that is self-determinative, yet devoted to the collective ("they said it was towards the evolution of the community" [151]); it is a method devoted to coming together, deeply, by way of becoming unrecognizable, because this would be the most open, nonviolent ground on which to encounter others. To refuse any presumptions of who one is before they arrive on the scene and to practice, in the encounter, a perpetual openness to failing to recognize another is how we honor another's creation of themselves. Because they, like us all, are re-creating themselves constantly, putting themselves together all the time, "every three years, every year, every season, every month, every day" (151).

In the constant re-creation it is impossible not to re-create, dramatically, gender. Explored in the text is something that exceeds so many feminist imaginings of the world in which the world after the world is simply the inverse of the old world, its logics held intact. But the black feminist metaphysical world after the world is one where the radical imagination is indeed radical, accounting for gender radicality. This is a world in which "human was human beyond gender" (12) because, as this black feminist metaphysician assessing the detritus of the fallen world notes the dust, what is found are many loved ones, of course, but they lie amid a "rubble that didn't segregate or care" (12). The rubble that is now our loved ones' resting place shows that in the after/world the artificial segregations that before presided over our lives were just that, artifice. Amid even what can be thought to have been the crescendo of a more just gendered world just before the end of the world, one wherein pronouns proliferated and institutions were built to protect rights—rights that were, still, bestowed by the state—and people declared themselves intersex and representatives from marginalized demographics achieved prominence, there is still a critique being made. Even after all that, the (neo)liberal's orgasmic utopia, an after/world black feminist metaphysics requires that "we let that go and t[ake] a different approach" (12). The aforementioned rights- and recognition-based justice is still insufficient, necessitating something more. Required is a gender radicality stemming from a desire to "emulate the amphibians," as Gumbs writes. Needed now is a multiplicitous combination of "slick skin and webbing and genital adaptability" (12). Slickness, which might be to say slipperiness or even evasiveness, is a necessary quality of the skin; webbing to facilitate movement in or on different terrains; genital adaptability—yes, you see what we're getting at. The trans.

Even the "small brown women" who are not simply identifiable people who are brown and woman, not even close to being just that, show the ways that identificatory terms are not mere physical descriptors. They are, in some way, names for "ha[ving] been trained underground" (38). The underground training is a profoundly political training, a way of coming into "small brown womanness" through the underground political training. These women, who are not what you think "women" are, are not only a site where it is difficult to discern gendered categorizations; these women themselves are the reason why "it was very hard to make generalizations about their skin, their hair, their piercings and markings" (38). They catalyze a blurring of race as embedded in the skin and gender as mapped onto locations on the body. It is because of them that "no one ever mentioned a gender or size" (38); they damage the optics and haptics used to determine gendered physiognomy, forcing a disturbance of both gender and individuation. That "people never reported an encounter with 'one of them' they only spoke of 'they' and of 'them'" (38) becomes an implicit assertion of the ontological disruption caused by gender nonnormativity and nonbinariness. And, too, "small brown women," or those women to whom "coloredness" or a conceptual blackness is attached, come to offer themselves as gender nonnormative subjects without reference to anatomical arrangement. These women, who again are not women as we may think of them—but also may not *not* be women in the way we think of them—are nonbinary and nonnormative, *trans*, irrespective of a certain legible arrangement of anatomy or so-called sex characteristics. They bring forth the traniflesh, the un/gendered, and the becoming-black-woman.

The transness of the metaphysical matter in Gumbs's meditation is to be found in its black feminism, and on those grounds I am asserting *M Archive* as well as the other two books in the triptych as expressive of black *trans* feminism. In an interview for *BOMB* magazine, Gumbs says:

> The fact that we are always crossing, even though so much of the structure of our lives is designed to convince us that we are in a stable situation and to sacrifice everything and everyone for that fictional stability. But we are in the borderlands, in the sense that Gloria Anzaldua—a major influence on Jacqui Alexander, by the way, and on me too—talks about it. We are crucially crossing between the many different oceans between us. And not necessarily by choice. Even once we reach each other, the crossing isn't over.
>
> All of the different markers allow us the opportunity to see that there is distance between what we recognize and what we are becoming, which is unrecognizable. I feel like in this book I wrote a lot of strangeness, a lot of queer Black possibility, a lot of out-of-this-worldness, but I think that everyone who reads it will find it all familiar at the same time.[21]

Crossing is endemic to transness, it taking its definitional characteristics from crossing, as its etymology attests: to cross over, to move beyond—acrossedness. It must be noted, however, that the crossing need not be between distinct platforms or terrains; crossing need not be from one place to another, separate place, a logic that maintains the integrity of the places themselves. The crossing, and thus the transing, referred to here and in black trans feminism can reside in the intramural and in fact acknowledges the multiplicity within a single terrain, worlds within a world that can be traversed without leaving. Intramural crossing rejects the cohesion and discreteness of singularized bodies and terrains, the structures of our lives designed to convince us of their stability. The trans is an aspiration toward the unrecognizable rather than from already-disclosed, recognizable places. The trans *is* the crossing, and it is not always an identifiable mobility across established geographies that require economic and sociocultural dexterity and privilege. The crossing can and must happen even when we go nowhere, even when we get to others ("the crossing isn't over"), because there are many, many oceans between us *and* within us.

The trans written into *M Archive* reveals the convergences of blackness and transness in Gumbs's amplifying of "queer Black possibilities" and "out-of-this-worldness," ways of designating that which breaches normativity (abolition) and departs from settlement ([gender] radicality). And its expression is achieved through black women. So often cast as a parochial demographic, black women are reimagined in the text as what Evelyn

Hammonds terms a "metalanguage," a universal sign that bespeaks the nuanced texture of the world *through* the rich particularity of black women. The fundamentality of the world and of coming into a more substantive subjectivity (the "you beyond you") is that density at the meeting point of black and woman. Evidentiary of this, Gumbs notes, "they were all, in their origin, maintenance, and measure of survival more parts black woman than anything else" (7), a placing of black women at the spawning of life. Further in support of this is how the very universe is thought as a black woman, indeed a *fat* black woman. "And no part of you could ever live without them"—that is, fat black women—and "if you think you would have survived without the love of fat black women you are wrong" (146). Fat black women and all such a signifier entails are the reason you are here, we are here, and thus fat black women are not aberrational but universally constitutive. They are the universe, and because of the decimation of the earth, the cursing of the gods, the ravaging of resources, and of course the violences of white cis male heteropatriarchal supremacy, fat black women are pissed and demand the end of this. Indeed, "this is why the universe (huge, black, unfolding, expansive) shakes and shakes her head. you fools. you wasteful fools" (146). It might be that the head-shaking of a fat black woman, a head-shaking that casts judgment and interrogates and demands transformative justice and side-eyes the ways we have ravaged the earth and each other, is what is meant, in large part, by black trans feminism.

That fat black women can stand, in their opacity, as universal signifiers shows *M Archive*'s larger argument of paraontology: the escape of blackness and womanness, or black womanness, even gendered subjectivity, from the "given ontologies" of racial and gendered categorization. Those occupying the space of the pages in the text are not properly the kinds of people we may think they are. Ongoing throughout is a disheveling of the buildup that masquerades as the only kind of people we can be, a buildup cast onto us by regimes of discursive, sociohistorical, and institutional power. We have been forced to be ontological gunk, our identities clogged with what we have been told we can be. What we may have been calling "race" before— or, in Gumbs's words, "all that we had been calling skin before," were simply "layers of accumulated scars" (83). She echoes here Spillers's desire to strip away all those "layers of attenuated meanings, made an excess in time, over time, assigned by a particular historical order, and there await whatever marvels of my own inventiveness," meanings that were imposed and must be discarded in order for an invention to take place.[22] To strip those meanings away *is* the end of the world, this world, and the invention is the "after."

And to get to the after, "they stole themselves, which was a break with everything, which was the most illegal act since the law that made them property"—the law of *partus sequitur ventrem*, the law of de jure and de facto enslavement, the law of chattel as equal to dark skin—"and they had to re-rhythm everything, re-tune bass in their chest, and immediately and perpetually they gave themselves away, the selves they had to give, the re-claimed flesh and bones and skin" (100). Breaking from everything is the only way we might steal ourselves and come to be something different, something "beyond you." Stealing life and becoming something different comes in the deviation from the very things thought to bestow life; it has long been believed that life and existence come from being recognized, and to be recognized one must be interpellated, adhere to the legible scripts that precede one, but it may in fact be not nonlife but life lived otherwise and life stolen that happens when one is not recognized. To have to rerhythm and retune everything away from the previous rhythm and tune does not look or sound or feel like life, but it is too hasty to say that, because of this, the rerhythm and retune are not life, are not music. If the name we have been given for life is "life," the black feminist metaphysician says "*i come to break names apart*" (88; emphasis in original). Rerhythming and retuning are indeed modalities of life. They are life outside of life.

м *Archive* is a deeply paraontological text because it emphasizes the things we are not but might be, the things that we almost were but for "the seemingly white seemingly male ostensibly straight founding fuckers" (155) who stifled our breadth (and breath), the things that we don't know we can be yet but yearn for anyway. The things we hold onto dearly, even those of us who are marginalized and see our statuses as our right to claim differently and to Signify on, must be let go. The tethers to this world do not serve our interests; they impede them. We believe they are immutable, but they are deeply mutable; they may feel like birthmarks unable to be expunged from our bodies, bodies that seem so real and material and never able to be forsaken. But there is, or can be, such a thing as "rebirthmarks" (101), the ability to change the unchangeable; there is the imperative to "*release the heaviness in your body and get gentle with darkness on the move*" (95; emphasis in original) because what we've been given, what has been imposed—even something as seemingly solid as our bodies—is to be refused for something else we cannot know but need to strive toward anyway. Moving with the darkness, which Gumbs writes, it seems, in a harmonious chant with Toni Morrison's "five or six different kinds of" dark which "don't stay still, it moves and changes from one kind of black to another," means that you do not find comfort in the heaviness of what's been imposed.[23] You find a discomfiting comfort, if you will, in the "getting" of getting outside. This is all in service of reworking what kind of world is created after the end of the world. The reworking is a testament to the mutability of things presumed immutable, it is a shapeshifting, a shifting of shapes and shapedness, which is ultimately "towards less collective dependence on a former world" and an independence from that world, toward a mutual creation and living-with the after/world (151).

BETRAYING MYTHOLOGIES

This section, on the third installment of Gumbs's triptych, *Dub*, takes its title from what Gumbs says in the opening note: that "freedom requires a species-scale betrayal of our founding mythologies" (x). *Dub* is an interspecies communion that attempts to go beyond taxonomic structures, beyond taxonomizing gestures, and find the kinship between those entities said in no way to be kin. What this attempt makes plain, then, is its combating of anthropocentric relations to justice, valorizing "modes of life beyond or in excess of the temporality of Man" and further rethinking the expansiveness of the "we." *Dub*'s interspecies, nontaxonomic betrayal of the regime of Man, with Man's constitutive whiteness and cisness, advances a "'we' that is before, after, and beyond every state-sanctioned or exclusionary 'We the People . . .'" If indeed we "need a language for this different, non-statist we-ness," *Dub* is it.[24]

Again, I begin with the note Gumbs pens preceding the text proper. Her commitment is one of thinking and living differently. A constant refrain throughout the triptych is the mutability of ourselves, of our world. Rejecting discourses that posit the steadfastness of the current situation, unable to be altered, she writes that if the ways of thinking that engendered slavery and colonialism were historical creations, and if those creations were "heretical" to ways of thinking that preceded them, "it must be possible to understand life, being, and place differently by now" (ix). We must do things differently, think differently, "tell a different story" (x) that permits us to finally live. Our hope rests in the different story we tell, and it is thus ethically imperative not to rehash the same story, because to rehash the same story is the foreclosure of a story that is not this same one. The stories we have been told of ourselves, and the stories we've told to ourselves, deserve no uncritical glorification. Those stories, too, must go. *Dub* inscribes the "eviscerat[ion]" of "origin stories" also (xi). The stories that have kept us from being in coalition with those who supposedly are not our kin demand evisceration, so we must ask, as Gumbs does, "What if who we think we are, what we believe at a gut level about our kinship loyalty and our perceived survival needs are responses to a story we made up and told ourselves was written by our genes?" (xi). Even though we believe in our bones that the story we tell of ourselves now is the true, unadulterated story, a story that has formed us in such a fundamental way, it is nevertheless a reaction to a story that has been made up and in fact does not rest in our genes. Required is a radical delinking of who we think we are from who we believe we can be, and that snowballs into an effective opening and breach of even the minimal taxonomizing gestures we use to find a place in the world. The ultimate aim of such narrative rebuking—because, as Sylvia Wynter, Gumbs's primary interlocutor in *Dub*, says, we are not *Homo sapiens* but *Homo narrans*—is to extricate ourselves from our humanity, in a way. To unbecome humans is to be in kinship with beings across taxonomy, to find and be "kindred beyond taxonomy" (xii), in search of interspecies coalition in order to save the earth and ourselves as, not inhabitants of, but kin with it.

To do this, we must let go. We must let go of the stories we have told ourselves, the stories that fit us into the world; we must let go of the very notion of ownership, of holding on, of clutching as a form of love; we must let go, yes, of the things that we hold so dearly—of our "race," of our "gender," of our "humanity"—because those things were imposed, violently, nonconsensually, and in fact impede our ability to come together. *It is not problematic to say this*, like, seriously, it's really, really not.[25] "When you think you gotta hold onto something (like who you think you are)," Gumbs says, lovingly, "let go" (xiii). We must, and there is only, practice, she says, so "practice letting go" (249). Our practice must be one of letting go, for the problem is in the holding on. So practice. And the practice, that fugitive "quotidian practice of refusal," is to say letting go, abolishing.[26] The letting go can save us, even though and precisely because it scares us, for the fear we may feel is simply the threat of eradicating the very violence that formed us. We owe nothing to that violence, for letting it go does not leave us formless and void of security in the world; letting go leaves us unviolated, and it is only because we have been, from our inception, formed via violence that we believe unviolation is akin to death. Letting go allows us to attempt to find unviolated existence.

Gatherings. I would contend along with Sarah Jane Cervenak that "gathering itself subverts the grid," and a grid is something that tames unruliness and imposes order, and, too, gatherings "create a sense of wholeness that threatens 'an impulse to name and represent.'"[27] To gather things brings them together into a collective, which does not necessitate the sameness of the things gathered. But in the gathering, a gathering that manifests a collective if and only if the things choose to stay, the gathered things—which also, to be sure, participate in their gathering and staying gathered—bring about a refusal of sanctioned taxonomies. *Dub* seeks to gather as many entities as possible, irrespective of their purported fit with one another. The "them" to be gathered, if gathered, "would be everyone." And we are to gather them still; we are to "recognize in them your jawline, your wet eyes, your long-fingered hands, seeking what but this multitude, if you gathered them they would not fit on this island, they would spill back into the ocean whence they came, when you gather them they will have fins and claws and names you do not know. / gather them anyway" (8). From a poem entitled "opening," this passage cracks open taxonomies that seek to separate and, thus, isolate. Coalition is antithetical to exclusion and isolation premised on arbitrary grounds, grounds that include the taxonomic classification to which you have been told you belong. Across taxonomies, a proxy for identities nonconsensually given or presented in limited options, we must acknowledge that others have not just a similar but *our* jawline and eyes. Even those said to not be of our group possess features that are ours. This performs a dissolution of the borders of the categories; Gumbs, through interspecies gathering, what Cervenak might deem a "black gathering," is engaging trans mechanisms by way of interrogating the texture of the boundaries that define supposedly mutually exclusive categorizations. Gumbs is performing transness inasmuch as "trans" denotes the vitiation of the disposition toward categorization, especially binaristic categories. Finding solace in the molten movement of the multitude, Gumbs venerates the spillage, the overflow of the island that was made for a certain population, arguing poetically that the island cannot contain everyone who might have affinities for the characteristics the island is meant to house. But the sea, with its massive space and its untold depths, is where the spillage goes, and it is because that is where the spillage is from.

This isn't even the positing of origins, which would deserve critique, because the sea does not possess the dictates said of origins: static, immutable, locatable. The sea is constantly in motion. The sea is enigmatic, unknown in its deepest depths. The sea is not in a particular place. To return to the sea, where the spillage—a demographic that is not a demographic but the excess of demography—was forged, is to return to a dispersal. In other words, returning to the sea in whose image the spillage was made shrouds that spillage, an unruly mass of promiscuous gatherers, in a fluid, mobile subjectivity subject to mutation and flow. Gathered at this nonsite, what one presumed were "people" or "animals" will trouble those delineations, having fins and claws, maybe even feet and tails and opposable thumbs all at the same time. What is important is that you, and I, will not know their names. Their names are unnameable, defiant of legibility and referents for hailing. But even though we do not know their names, we are to gather them anyway, because our gathering does not need to know names, does not need to know. The work happens in the gathering, and we find out all we need to when we are gathered together.

Another prevalent thematic topic throughout the text is, of course, color. Permit me, please, reader, to understand her various iterations of color to inflect processes of racialization. And, further, I ask to be permitted to think of this process of racialization as, in the orbit of Lewis Gordon, a blackening.[28] With this, then, the moments in which Gumbs references color are instructive. First, color (specifically "brown") initiates the possibility of interspecies commingling. Brown is the color used to facilitate an interspecies gathering: "there was a thick brown we used, to remember all of it. muck and how we got here, mud and how they stole it. land and what it didn't mean, trees and what they remembered and how they cracked and what they were used for" (31). Brown is what permits remembering one's relation to the muck. It is, in fact, the muck's color too, as well as mud's color, and thus the hue of the skin of people called black is a nodal point for initializing community with other nonhuman entities. The color and the things it is said to describe are in some sense sacred things on the grounds of its color. But, I would assert, not only its color, which assumes that it is *merely* the color that allows for a community, the color itself, as descriptive of the amount of light refracted or absorbed, the thing that gathers. Instead, what the color signifies or what it serves to highlight does the gathering. Brown gathers here because it is the color of mud that was stolen (like "us"), or muck, because it facilitated our getting here.

There is a theorizing here being done about color. It is being expanded to connote something more than itself. Surely it is not a parochial designation meant to delimit and exclude; color and the attending connotations of it are trying to be more than mere description, in a literarily rigorous way. The most potent of those attending connotations is no doubt *skin* color. Even cursory readers of *Black Trans Feminism* will know that it holds, in these pages at least, a suspicious view of the weight of skin as a politically efficacious analytic around which to rally. Nevertheless, the meditation on it here is seen as a different conversation, one Gumbs intervenes in to illuminative effect. If I have demonstrated a suspicion, it is the suspicion Gumbs describes as the "thought [that] our village was the whole world," a village viz. skin color that is presumed to be the totality of the world and its import. But, she remarks, thankfully, "it wasn't that we were provincial about skin, it was what they wanted, what they did and what they tolerated, that let us know they could not be of the worlds (terrestial or celestial) that we knew" (54). Those worlds that we knew are prefigured and prefiguratively apprehended "world[s] anew," worlds that do not provincialize skin or categorical delimitation—a world, that is, after abolition—wherein we are, as Denise Ferreira da Silva intones perceptively, "without separability, determinacy, and sequentiality presumed in the very categories and concepts—that is, the forms of the subject."[29] We become new and different subjects, subjects we could not have been if we had not abolished subjectivity. We become subjectless. For now at least. We see here in Gumbs a rejection of an exclusionary disposition regarding race. It wasn't, she says, a provinciality concerning the skin, a nod to the capaciousness of racial blackness that links in the lineage of Alice Walker, and also Du Bois when he notes in *Dusk of Dawn* that "within the Negro group especially there were people of all colors"; it was instead a critical and strategic engagement with the very given ontology placed upon them. This engagement, though grappling with the modes of subjectivity nonconsensually mandated, was poised toward other worlds. It is perhaps now that the skin, though it cannot be the end of our strivings, cannot be the sole focus, cannot be the thing that even when we get outside of this maelstrom we devotedly covet as indispensable, was one opaque purview to the expansive coalition beyond taxonomy.

Dovetailing with her discussion of skin is, relatedly, color, in a way extracted from the skin and thought about, theorized, on its own to open up another avenue of thought. If I am to read Gumbs's meditation on color as one, indeed, about how *skin* color operates on the assumption of a notion of purity, Gumbs takes on the task of desedimenting the project of racial purity on which racial distinction rests. White supremacy cannot persist without the generalized notion of racial purity, a purity that hierarchizes some "pure" "races" over others, and pure races over impure races. (We must also acknowledge that the gender binary and cis male supremacy are, too, predicated on notions of purity that preclude the possibility of genders of the binary from intermingling as well as preclude nonbinaristic genders and nongenders from muddying—miscegenating, we might say—the purported purity of male-man-masculine or female-woman-feminine.) At some length, within a poem entitled "unlearning herself," Gumbs intervenes in dialogues on color and race, on my reading: "she would go home and try to draw dark rainbows using every crayon color until the paper became wax thick breakthrough dark and layered like the universe and none of her crayons could ever call themselves clean. . . . all the colors, all the colors pushing hard against white paper with the core creative craving for it. Black"(168). Vitiating racial purity and thus racial distinction or hierarchized races (i.e., racism) requires the unlearning not only of various epistemic trends but, in a visceral sense, oneself, as one's very identity is permissible, at least in modernity, only through adherence to legible races. This is fundamentally about unlearning the mechanisms that allow for one to exist in the world, while recognizing that one, if one is to seek an unviolated life, must demand not to exist in this world and to perhaps exist, possibly, in another world in the world. This demand is where Gumbs writes toward. It is a place that cannot abide purity and its presumptions. Every crayon is used to make rainbows, not just those approved by the spectrum of ROYGBIV. In the darkness, a metonymic blackness, is not where there is void but where the very notion and possibility of color converges. That waxy-thick dark rainbow, the site of blackness, is akin to the universe, our universe, and is expansive and, well, universal. Contributory to that expansive fabric is everyone, not a privileged few with distinct identities. Here is a meditation on what happens when one commits to the worldmaking project of blackness: it becomes impossible to parcel out, in neoliberal and capitalist fashion, who deserves what credit and compensation for what they, purportedly individualistically, did. Here, under the helm of the dark rainbow, it is not that we are all the same and homogenous; it is that we cannot ever call ourselves clean, purely the color that has been tagged onto us. When *Black Trans Feminism* makes the claim that blackness can be entered into by anyone willing to do its work, it is recognizing that all who take on such a task—even those said to "be" black—do not become phenotypically black and subject to the same history and contemporary as the people who are called black (people who, even intramurally, nevertheless have different histories and relationships to history, and are subject to it in different, substantial ways). It is to say that entering into blackness, as we all can and must, sullies us, makes us unclean, unable to say that we are pure, that we are the given colored ontologies bestowed upon us. It is to say that when we all put in abolitionist work, pressing hard on the "*white* paper," we engage the creative force of blackness and become, proximally, anoriginally, in communion with blackness.

Much of the normative gesture to taxonomize comes from a sense of identities and knowledges being ownable only by those who occupy certain classifications. Too, it often goes unnoticed that classifications are not self-evident; classifications are in fact constructions. This mode of thinking pervades many realms of life, from the presumption that there are only certain classes of people who can speak on a subject, that there are only certain classes of things worthy of respect and intrigue, that there are only certain classes noteworthy enough to be of scientific or social interest, that there are only certain classes that count as classes as such. All of this presupposes an ownership and that one, or a group, can own a certain kind of relation to others and to knowledge. Gumbs critiques this presupposition. It is easy to critique notions of ownership resulting in the claiming of lands, people as property, or knowledges codified in the Academy. Such ownership is the product of white and cis male supremacist beliefs in superiority and exclusionary practices that marginalize and expunge those who do not approximate the genre of Man. But it is the fundamental notion of ownership itself, irrespective of the body that deploys it, that Gumbs critiques, which extends to those, say, Black Nationalists who covet and proclaim ownership of all things shrouded in a (racial) blackness—cultures, languages, knowledges, and so on. Ownership as such is problematic, and, as Gumbs writes, "this is the problem with owning": "it gets into your blood, it replaces your blood with something like a self-justifying story" (197). To presume ownership is to obscure the processes that precede the moment—instantiated as always already—when ownership appears self-evident and originary, in your blood, always having been there, the ownership becoming simply the revelation of something one had no role in instilling in themselves. The stories we tell ourselves about ourselves, which masquerade as axioms, are in fact "thinner than blood if only slightly younger, it can belong to you and distract from other longings, unlike blood it only binds you to one life, the life you think they gave you. the life you made yourself" (197). Coveting anything as belonging to you and justifying it by saying it has always resided inside you, is natural and endemic to you, only proves to distract you from other, more just, more expansive and capacious longings. The longings for other ways to be or alternative modes of desiring are impermissible when you (can) only double down on a thing you think you own. You do not, nor can you, nor should you. Because these owned things are the paltry scraps given by a hegemon that limits the full flourishing of life. Making something out of what they gave you—rewrapping a gift given by the drunk, abusive uncle—is still to have what they gave you. So, let it go. Gumbs implies the salvific effects of insurgent life instead, life outside the taxonomies and the givens. The getting outside of what has been given is the *"anagential movement of the thing* [that] disowns or unowns knowledge (of slavery, of desire) in the name of another, inappropriate knowledge, a knowledge of the inappropriable."[30] It is in the name of another and an other, where this references those beings (be they human or otherwise) who engage in the preservation and proliferation of life, that we conduct a movement in unownership of what they have given us. Because those things, those desires, those knowledges and ways of being, they cannot be appropriated, and if they cannot be appropriated, which is to say owned and claimed, then they are, in no uncertain terms, radically free. As we shall be.

Dub is a book about how different things can be for us. To imagine something radically different is necessarily a grappling with the meaning of the future. *Dub* is thus about, in so many ways—in the vein of м *Archive*—what happens after. Such being the case, Gumbs posits unequivocally that "the future is black" (191). What is meant here, possibly, is referential of the unanticipation mentioned in chapter 3. The unknownness of the future is "black" by way of a generative density. To be unable to peer into the future, knowing its outcome, marks a way of encountering the future in a way that occludes knowability, which in turn disallows its captivity. In some regard, knowledge works to limn the boundaries of what counts epistemically. The veritable blackness of the future, its unknowability, is a signifier of something in excess of void—it signifies the density required for the unimaginable. We do not know the future's depths, nor should we; all we might know is "the staying power of the dark," knowing that it will be there, and the task is to find a discomfiting comfort in its staying, a staying that can persist precisely because we cannot know it. In the future that is black, "whatever you do there," whatever you might insufficiently imagine yourself being able to do and become, cannot be enough, cannot be accurate, because "there is still more you cannot, do not know" (191). And the not knowing might very well save our lives. Which is to say, blackness might save our lives. Because of the not knowing: "how can you know that you are unknowable? how can you know that you cannot know that which knows you best, how can you best note the knowing that won't happen here. nope, how can you know the unknowing that is ultimately the test. see. you don't see. that's what's black about it" (244).

Blackness can save us if we "let go" in Nash's sense, or if we commit to unknowing and unowning. Blackness sustains, if we let it, our lives. Because "black is air," "black is water," "black is land," "black is the storm that comes from West Africa every year at carnival time" (243). Indexical of the fat black woman of *M Archive*, who has mothered us and nurtured us, blackness in *Dub* characterizes "the hands that clear the brush and rebuild the broken buildings again" (243). And in an interrogative statement reminiscent of the black women who grace the earth, a question posed as a statement, Gumbs writes, "how black are the ways you wind up here, how black the staying sound" (243), ended with a courageous, unbending period. Blackness is that which, for Gumbs, promotes life. It characterizes necessary life-sustaining resources like the land, like water and air, like hands that till the soil and build shelter. To the extent that the world is habitable (for now), blackness made it that way.

Some might wrongly, though it is only a slight wrong, think of Gumbs's triptych as concerning race and gender. But the books are in fact, to my lights, about *blackness* and *gender transgression*, about *abolition* and *gender radicality*. They fracture the ontological in myriad ways, these texts, forsaking even cherished identities, reconfiguring and interrogating and dissolving those identities because they are fundamentally given ontologies. The texts, as the late Cheryl Clarke, a mentor and interlocutor for Gumbs's work, has written, "accept or reject allies on the basis of politics not on the specious basis of skin color"; the texts operate under varying "modes of wayward gendering" we might call trans.[31] In imagining the unimaginability of interspecies coalition and different worlds, worlds in which those who rest at the nexus of black and woman and black and femme might live, might, as Gumbs writes in *Dub*, "bec[o]me muscled approximations of freedom" (58), what is glimpsed is simply another possibility for doing life. The glimpse is gotten to by reconfigurings and reimaginings of race and gender through the abolitionist and radically (un/)gendered effects of blackness and transness, through black trans feminism, which is articulated succinctly in an interview with Gumbs in which she speaks of *Spill*: "The masculinity and the femininity of the people in the book," she says, "are fugitive from patriarchy. It's also fugitive from binary. It really is trying to escape that."[32] There is no normative way to be here, only salvation in being on the run from *a* way to be. The triptych showcases just how expansive and liberating our world could be if we only destroyed the world, ran from it, and found peace with kin across all taxonomic boundaries. With each other, outside of a desire for a certain form of life as ideal, we find freedom.

Questioned, Gendered

No one ever offered a name for what was wrong with me. That's
what made me afraid it was really bad. I only came to recognize its
melody through this constant refrain: "Is that a boy or a girl?"
LESLIE FEINBERG, *Stone Butch Blues*

In the previous chapter I sought to demonstrate how Alexis Pauline
Gumbs poetically depicts what subjectivity might look like if such subjectivity were predicated on a broad-based abolition. I sought to show how
Gumbs could be read as articulating black trans feminism through an inscription of figures who are moving toward an escape from patriarchy and
white supremacist taxonomizing and the attending modes of supposed life
that these regimes entail. Here, I argue for the efficacy of gendered suspension and interrogation—or, rather, for the intriguing space of holding
subjectivity in the *query* of gender, and how such is integral to an understanding of blackness.

It is a peculiar thing to have one's gendered ontology questioned, considering how gender is purportedly transparent and immediately knowable.
It has been made clear that one's gender cannot be discerned simply by
making recourse to the corporeal surface; outside this discourse, though,
normative optics and logics presume that one can *only* adjudicate one's gender, just like that, from a glance. Yet time and again gender nonconforming
folks are met with the question and its many subtle iterations: "Are you a
man or a woman?" "*What* are you?" The question is, at base, an attempt to
capture one's gendered ontology, indeed to subjectivate one intelligibly by

making recourse to gendered ontology, itself a chief form by which one becomes a subject. It is a means by which normative tentacles try to corral gendered unruliness back into the violence of the binary. Those who are nonbinary and those who are gender nonconforming deploy a subjectivity that is not properly a subjectivity: one is not a valid subject if one commits to nonbinariness since subjectivity under the logic of gender normativity disallows breach of the binary—to be a subject *is* to be within the binary.

The work being done by refusing the binary's containment invites the law of the binary; there is an antagonistic relationship inherent to nonbinary subjectivity. This antagonism, by which is meant the mutual exclusivity of gender nonbinary subjective validity and the integrity of hegemonic gender binaristic laws, generates the demand to conceptualize what might, or might not, or cannot, arise after the refusal of the gender binary—that is, how we can possibly, finally, hopefully live in the "?" To be asked the question "Are you a man or a woman?" reveals the seams of the gendered order, which presumes of itself to never have to ask the question in the first place; that it asks and often is not given a sufficient answer—which is to say, is met with the subversive antagonism doing the work of undermining it as an impenetrable system—signifies the order's dissolution. Precisely in these moments of refusing to *be* a sufficient answer to "Are you a man or a woman?" is where the interrogative spirit of transness converges with a history of blackness provoking various interrogations. Trans subjectivity incites a question by way of posing the question of the (in)adequacy of the gender binary. This dovetails with that oft-quoted scene in Du Bois's *The Souls of Black Folk* in which blackness marks a being who is asked the question "How does it feel to be a problem?" Blackness is queried because it itself queries, the posing of a problem a kind of questioning of the adequacy of the given order. If transness and blackness converge in this way, it is my aim in this chapter to excavate the texture of a transness that carries with it the spirit of interrogation with the goal of opening up, destabilizing. In other words, this chapter is a romp through the intriguing confluences of "How does it feel to be a problem?" and "Are you a man or a woman?"

Jess Goldberg, the protagonist of Leslie Feinberg's *Stone Butch Blues* (who carried around, interestingly enough, a copy of *The Souls of Black Folk*, gifted to Jess by a butch lesbian), faced similar inquiries. Jess was "the child who couldn't be catalogued," a testament to Jess's indeterminacy, Jess's escape from frameworks that attempt to situate certain bodies into castes from which they can never deviate. This peculiar predicament is ripe for excavation: the predicament of residing in the interstitial vortex of not-boy and not-girl. In this, it is argued, is not merely despair, violence, and a kind of homelessness—all of which Jess certainly experienced, having been rejected by lovers and intimate kin for Jess's unplaceability, losing jobs immediately after being misgendered by someone in Jess's past, being met with violence on the subway resulting in a broken jaw, being subjected to rape by police officers—there is also the chance for the emergence of a radical alternative in subversion of the stultifying and constricting binary. Jess's experience with the question "Is that a boy or a girl?" and indeed Jess's ultimate refusal of the question's assumptions (e.g. that one *must be* and can *only be* a boy or a girl), while certainly an onerous livelihood to bear, provides an avenue for the realization that, as Edna told Jess, her face close to Jess's, "There's other ways to be than either-or."[1]

TO BE A QUESTION

One of these other ways not confined to the either-or is perhaps the question itself. The very question—"Are you a boy or a girl?" or "Are you a man or a woman?"—is a place to be. Enter jayy dodd. dodd writes: "This dude at a party asked, 'Are you a man or woman?' I'm like, 'I'm your question.' That's as whole as I can be right now. . . . So whenever someone asks, my response is, 'I am your question.' It is yours. I don't have a question. You do. And your question, that is who I am."[2]

I am your question. dodd generatively collapses Du Bois and Feinberg, becoming a question via being a problem—or, put differently, becoming a problem via being a question. Here is a moment, a pervasive and ongoing one, in which gender anomie is displayed, where one undergoes an assault on the normativity of their assessments by others, an uncertainty that causes a pause ("Are you . . . ?") by way of this intensifying "state of uncertainty and behavioral inhibition."[3] The question "Are you a man or a woman?" is reconfigured in and by and as dodd, the question serving, now, as an/other gender. dodd's gender is the nonanswer to the question, which becomes a problem since it is, indeed, not an answer to the question that demands an answer. Crafting a gender in the space of the unanswered question, we now have a problem: the gender that has been crafted. What arises, then, is an/other kind of gender that is fundamentally problematic, that *is* a problematic. That is the gender attempting to emerge and in its inchoate emergence is the problematizing of the general order of things, expressing disdain for closure. In the dissolution that occurs in the problematizing is where this gender peers through. The question becomes a habitable geography, a "very different geography," foundationed by "demonic" ground that brings "alternative geographic perspectives and spatial matters that may not necessarily replicate what we think we know, or have been taught."[4] In the question resides a different way of occupying space, so to mobilize a subjectivity through "Are you a man or a woman?" means that one becomes a different kind of subject, a nonsubject that does not bear the necessary frameworks to be grasped by current grammars. And it is an other-than subjectivity given rise to by the specificity of (gender) nonconformity, which is to say simultaneously, as dodd does, a peak blackness. In other words, the specificity and particularity of the nexus of black and trans (and femme) is an opacity that exceeds itself as particular and engenders a kind of politics or sociality that urges us all—if we wish to live life in the otherworld that arises after the abolition of this one—to get in on it.

Indeed, black trans feminism is the analytic that encapsulates this recurrent encounter between dodd and "this dude at a party," which can be any dude, any party, as she is not describing an isolated moment in her life but the texture of the social world predicated on gender binaries and transparent gender ontologies.[5] The question is the space that refuses to adhere to the logics embedded in syntactical possibility. If the only legitimate question to ask of dodd is locked in the binarisic logic of "Are you a man or a woman?" then she becomes a mobile precipitation of the question's unresolvability. The question is threatened by the imminent erasure she engenders.

jayy dodd. A "blxk question mark," a "volunteer gender terrorist," a manner of living forged as abolition and gender radicality.[6] She is the constant interrogation of the very grammatical dictates that ground subjective semiotics. That is why she is a question mark, a "blxck" one at that, as I'll discuss below, because such ontological desedimentation can only be black and gender transgressive. She is a *volunteer* gender terrorist because there is no place for coercion or nonconsensuality in abolition; she volunteers, anarchically directly participates in the destruction of this world that is the creation of another (kind of/way to live in the) world. dodd as volunteer blxck question mark gender terrorist exceeds a simple respite from violence; she configures "the unreasonable, irreverent wilderness that exceeds and undermines any infrastructural attempt to 'develop' its lands, even in the service of revolution"—dodd as such becomes through abolition and gender radicality.[7]

Fear. "Recently, I was afraid of leaving my house," dodd says, echoing a sentiment so many trans and nonbinary and "post-gender" folks (to use her preferential term) feel when occupying public space. Transantagonistic violence pervades her inhabitation of the world, invoking fear—a fear, I want to highlight, that is as much about the transantagonism as it is about the antiblackness saturating the world; indeed, the transantagonism and those given ontologies of gender *are* an antiblackness, considering the transversal referentiality of blackness and transness. dodd's fear was one "of being caught." This catching is one of optics, "under a gaze," dodd says, that makes her "feel like a wild thing in eyes-locked cage."[8] dodd is not a wild person, nor a wild one, nor simply wild; dodd is a wild thing, a non-one that troubles oneness and Man. Wild because of her radicality, her gender trouble, dodd's troubling of gender trouble insofar as blackness and transness exponentiate one another in their relation to troubling what gender is and what gender does. We have already been told, in fact: this might be what dodd means by "blxk question mark."[9]

A face. What mitigates the fear is a face. dodd searches for faces that look like hers. The face here is more than a Levinasian affective relational interruption; the face, dodd seems to be arguing, stands in for more than itself and the being on which it appears. To search for a face that looks like hers signifies something other than her attempt to find other black or transgender people with whom she could be in solidarity, if only fleetingly. No, this facial recognition is in search of another "face that looks over its-own-back, too." It is a face that does something, that signals something in excess of what it "is"; it is a face that is on the lookout and, because it is looking out, poised to escape. Yes, this is the kind of facial kin dodd seeks, a face "smiling-watchful-escaping capture."[10] This is what molds a face into its faceness for her: how is it looking out, when and at what does it smile, to whom does it look, how does it keep an eye out for the ways it is forcibly positioned in order to flout that positioning? Smiling at the face that comes into its own face via its watchful fugitivity is how dodd might be offering an embrace of those ready to flee that won't slow them down.

The fear that pervades dodd's life on the grounds of her blackness and transness, and her feminist unsuturing of regulative gender regimes, is not to be understood as abject. To the extent that her body—unruly as all hell—is subjected a priori to render dodd a "he," and the extent to which this subjection is the predicate for dodd being encountered in the world violently, the fear stemming from this subjection is being weaponized. She

writes, "Been weaponizing the fear that makes my body subject," an asubjective bellicosity embedded in the constant, gritty struggle of escape that
characterizes her living-in-the-world. A perpetual striving—*hear the Du
Boisian echo*—that is the asubjective subject of/that is dodd's existential
and paraontological torsion. It is an unruly striving, a *"trying to,"* she says,
that works toward the aim of "not get[ting] caught"—an ongoing project
of anticaptivity. Engendering this unruliness is that dodd has "been
feeling antagonistically Black as of late."[11] Importantly, the omission of
"I have" from both dodd's weaponization of fear and her antagonistically
black feeling syntactically instantiates an otherwise mode of thinking when
it comes to ontology. The syntactic omission is a paraontological syntax
of sorts, a way to think through agency without subjectivity, or an agency
that has as its subject a radically different, a radically elsewhere locus. The
subject might be in the realm of the impossible outside, a subjectless subjectivity made possible in the radical impossibility engendered by the convergence of black trans feminism.

TO BE BLXCK

The way that dodd writes the word "black" raises insightful questions that
can cultivate grounds for generative inquiry. She writes the word in a number of places as "blxck," supplanting the "a" with an "x." A peculiar practice,
but what does it mean? We might read "blxck" as a significatory marker
of blackness's interruption. That is, "blxck" could function as a discursive
denotation of the *work* dodd intends for blackness as commingling with
her trans femmeness. "Blxck" becomes an invitation to think blackness differently insofar as it subsequently contains no vowels, as is regulated for
every word in English, making the term a breach of vocabularic constraints,
which is further to say semiotic and normative constraints; and, furthermore, insofar as it suggests an interruption of typical ways of coming to
an understanding of what the very word means. The *x* leads readers to an
exorbitance—or, in Gumbs's language, a spillage, forcing a fundamental
interrogative posture within the term. To read "blxck" and its solicitation
of exorbitance, its abolitionist spirit, is to solicit readers into blackness's effects. The *x*'s placement, insofar as there is a misguided understanding of
blackness as a categorical containment that serves to allow the figure of the
black to "exist," marks here Nahum Chandler's configuration of the *x* as
"an irruption within the fabric of existence," expressing the being of the

black and trans as itself that (non)being that is an ontological issue from which an alternative subjective, paraontological conception of existence might stem. The convergent relationship that dodd advances between blackness and transness in particular manage to bring forth the traniflesh of a becoming-black-woman which harbors them "(within the problem of the Negro which poses a question beyond historicity or sociality as given)," making dodd's blackness, transness, and radical feminism expressive of that "which is other than a relation of knowledge, other than concept or category," Chandler would conclude.[12] Blxckness ushers in the antecategoricality of how one moves through blackness as a deployable and fugitive antiepidermalization toward the radical alternative.

It is a blackness that cannot be contained by or abide its description. To pen blackness on the page, as dodd does, necessarily, in her essayistic and poetic writing, is to commit it to fixity. But "blxck" gestures toward a blackness that exceeds itself as written; "blxck" posits right within its center the inability of the word to express itself fully when written, or, more specifically, inscribed with the intent of exuding transparent meaning. Indeed, how does one pronounce "blxck"? It cannot be folded into legible speech, as it questions its own legibility, enfolds its own blackness onto itself insofar as blackness engenders a certain kind of obfuscation of transparency and semiotic legibility. What's more, the letter is a signifier of gender nonnormativity and nonbinariness, perhaps a linguistic transness—"blxck" is a *transed* blackness, a blackness graphemically inscribed with a trans and gender nonnormative signifier, indexical of dodd's claim that gender nonnormativity and nonconformity is peak blackness. Thus, "blxck" lays bare the intimacy of blackness and transness. And this fuzzies meaning. A kind of refutation of a Derridean axiom: if, supposedly, meaning must await the verbal or written word in order to inhabit itself as meaning, dodd offers here a paraontological semiotics begotten by a(n un)fixation on a conditioning blackness. Meaning, for dodd, is sedimented and cannot mean *in excess of meaning* when said or written. Thus, placing the *x* there alludes to a different semiotic terrain in which one is alerted to the inscription's inadequacy in capturing the word's meaning—indeed, alludes to a terrain in which the inscription's meaning is one that is located in an otherwise realm, a realm that refuses the meaning-making pillars of a binary opposition, a realm that might accurately be understood as trans.

And why wouldn't it be such, as dodd's blackness—or "blxckness"—is inextricable from her trans femmeness. Her "blxck" is, I would assert, a mode of inscribing, or making graphemically apparent, blackness's gender trouble, its indexation of the departure from normative gender symbolics. I will speak more at length about the specificity of dodd's transness later in this chapter, but here I simply want to note that dodd's *blxck* makes plain the manner in which blackness operates as a disruption, too, of gender. dodd's blackness is one that, following (without direct but certainly subjective and lived citation) Denise Ferreira da Silva, possesses the profound "ability to disrupt the subject and the racial and gender-sexual forms that sustain it."[13] The gender trouble embedded within her blackness disrupts the fundaments of valid subjectivity (alluded to in others' question "Are you a man or a woman?" whereby the need to ask the question is an attempt to give legible subjectivity to dodd's nonsubjectivity). Since the subject is sustained and constituted by a "racial and gender-sexual form," by which da Silva means that one cannot *be* a subject without being a raced and gendered subject, dodd's disruption of subjectivity—her questionness— via "blxckness" is a way to attest to this, the word never fully being the "subject" of a sentence or utterance.

What dodd's understanding of blackness culminates into is her perpetual curiosity with the "black condition." Constantly, she inquires into the texture, the gizzards and guts, of the black condition. It preoccupies her, but only because she is preoccupied by it—in fact, all those mobilizing its anoriginal force are preoccupied by a perturbation that initiates them in and through blackness. Consider dodd's poem "Ask Two Different Niggas 'What Is the Black Condition?'" She writes:

> Black control,
> govern Black,
> meaning the Black
> be uncontrollable
> or Black be
> ungovernable
> condition the
> governed Black
> controllable.[14]

This passage is more than a simple meditation on governability, that black people are subject to unjust forms of governance. While the aforementioned is true, dodd interrogates the very fundamentality of governance to blackness's conditioning and subsequently subverts such a definitive characteristic of blackness. She, in other words, seeks to rework the understanding of blackness as that which is given to us by way of the thing subject to oppressive control ("Black control," the opening stanza). While we often understand blackness as the "govern[ed] Black," the corralled image of how blackness has been made legible, what we quickly come to instead is the "meaning [of] the Black": it "be uncontrollable / or Black be ungovernable." This is dodd's blackness. Or, I would submit, this is the blackness she wishes to proliferate. If dodd's interest in the "blxck condition" is one that seeks to examine the current state of things, such is an examination of the governed black, the controlled black. It is this preoccupation with the black-as-abject that in fact leads her outside of this toward the ungovernable and uncontrollable black. Fixation on the condition of blackness in the white gaze, as it were, conceding to how Claudia Rankine has elsewhere described the condition of blackness as one of mourning, for dodd precipitates a more profound (un)fixation on the various subterranean ways that blackness reveals itself as ungoverned or uncontrolled. It is not conceded, by dodd or by this book, that pervasive antiblackness should lead one to frameworks of cynicism, pessimism, or nihilism. A depth in the study of the "blxck condition"—a condition that indexes the uncapturability and elusiveness of that signifier that serves, in the first instance, as a problematizing fugitivity—reveals not merely *anti*blackness but the inextinguishable insistence of its breach onto the scene of sociality *regardless* (that black feminist Walker-esque signifier) of the purported pervasiveness of antiblack oppression. Examination of this condition is aimed not at a simple examination of this condition, skewed in scope to highlight its negated aspects, but at the eradication of this condition that we must examine *in order to*, firstly, eradicate its violent aspects.

There remains the question of dodd's own blackness, how her blackness commingles with her trans femmeness. What is the qualitative shift that occurs when blackness's always already queerness is transed? Where Andrea Long Chu in "After Trans Studies" castigates transgender studies' deployment of transness as insufficiently different from queerness—trans and transing as "queering's unasked-for sequel"—a discussion provided by LaMonda Horton-Stallings brings blackness to the conversation, as it must always be, and asserts that "I transblack literary studies and sexuality studies to demonstrate how black communities . . . provid[e] alternative knowledge about imagination and sexuality."[15] Perhaps this is to say that inasmuch as queer theory had, as it were, a "white problem," trans studies more readily infuses sociality and theory with blackness—or, another possibility, that Stallings's use of "transblack," suturing the words together, implies, as I have implied throughout this book, that blackness and transness operate alongside parallel tracks and are in a similar abolitionist and gender radical struggle. Stallings writes of "transblacking" precisely because the exploration of alternative knowledges and modes of being cannot merely be a "trans" practice but must always be a practice that entails transness's blackness, its politicized deregulation of gender achieved by way of (black) feminism.

I want also to take seriously the *my* in dodd's "My Black Condition" as intimate with her femmeness. The femme of dodd's gender must be read as "not an identity, not a history, not a location on the map of desire. The fem(me) body is an anti(identity) body, a queer body in fem(me)inine drag. . . . Fem(me) is the *je ne sais quoi* of desiring difference prior to any determination of sexual preference or gender identity," write Lisa Duggan and Kathleen McHugh.[16] Femme becomes a modality of longing or desire for something that dissolves sexual and gender determination from without. The femme is desire for movement outside of being ontologized—femme is trans insurgency and desire for the mutinous lawlessness that blackness anoriginally names. This kind of body or identity, it is said, is an impossible one. But it is precisely the impossible that brings together blackness and, for dodd, its abiding transness, as impossibility is the precise thing that these two analytic terms signify: that which, in the current state of sedimented and congealed hegemony, is disallowed. To identify the impossible as that which characterizes the black condition, and, more specifically, dodd's black condition, which is always already a gender-troubling trans femmeness that refuses the gender binary, excavates more of the heft present in dodd's poetic and essayistic theorizations. If dodd's black condition, she writes in the subsequent stanza, "is being caught up, in being. / Conditioning yourself for capture," then the conditioning of the condition of blackness is antithetical to that capture. To the extent that dodd is "caught up," her blackness is not only conditioned by capture but does the work of conditioning that blackness for capture—that is, putting in work to get outside of capture.

Blackness for dodd is inextricable from trans and transed genders in a way that exceeds trite intersectionalist axioms. Blackness foundations the mutability endemic to transness, dodd noting that "the Black body is, in many ways, always capable of being non-conforming." Blackness, then, becomes a conditioning analytic for *all* of those "who find themselves presently & actively on the outside of the restrictive gender binary."[17] If blackness is always already gender nonconforming, which is to say that blackness always already excites a mode of transness (not, it must distinguished, the *being* of transgender necessarily), it requires a more sophisticated understanding of precisely what is meant when the word "black" is uttered. It has been noted in various scholarly and para-scholarly discourses that blackness troubles the symbolic whiteness upon which gender is predicated.[18] My aim is not at all to diminish these claims, as they are, to my mind, thoroughly apt. I want instead to radicalize the claim. When noting that blackness troubles gender, I wonder if we stop short of exceeding the intact gender that is subsequently troubled, presuming that "troubling" is the end. I'm simply curious about what comes after the trouble: What happens when troubling shakes just hard enough that that which was troubled is, effectively, no more? In short, what happens when we finally, if we ever, get to those other genders?

Perhaps what happens is that we are called to do some radical rethinking of things. The rethinking and a reworking of our relationship to our subjectivity and to one another is captured in dodd's notion of being "presently & actively on the outside of the restrictive gender binary." Presently in that we situate ourselves on the outskirts of a general order that gains its existence on the outside's repudiation, and presently, too, in that in our situatedness on the outside we are effectively not situated at all. The outside is not a place where one resides but a dispersal from placedness. We are actively present on this outside when we move toward such a milieu as an ethical and subjective gesture of communing, where communing is a striving for the commune inasmuch as the commune inscribes not a being-together but a coming-together, a coming-together that engenders our *be*coming-together in differentiation.[19] The coming together is facilitated by an agential willingness to engage and be engaged by the ethereal spirit, if you will, of blackness's vitality. dodd's articulation of this relationship— this theorizing of, as her essay title describes, gender-nonconformity as peak blackness—is expressed in C. Riley Snorton's description of blackness's and transness's relationship as a Fanonian "real leap" in which they describe the convergence of radical analytics that "constitut[e] being to the degree that it exceeds it."[20] I might finally read "blxckness" in line with my previous meditation on opacity and its weavability, its exceeding of itself as confined in the opaque subject. dodd has remarked in another poem, "Presently, I Only Want to Understand Being Full & Feeding," that she—or, at least, the speaker of the poem—undergoes a "chronic oscillation of Light & opacity."[21] Her "blxckness" is one that is not only fixed to its epidermalized opacity, unenterable by those not of its same hue. The "x" of "blxckness" implies, on my reading, the oscillatory nature of a different understanding of blackness, a blackness that *moves* and is not only dark but light. "Blxck-ness" indexes an ongoing, perennial movement between being hidden or specific to a certain demographic while also, always, being characterized by a lightedness allowing all to see. Permit me a riff, will you: How do you see the work of someone who, and that, is totally black? By, simply, seeing and seeing again, differently. We are left with the excess, and in the excess is where we might rummage around treasure troves of what we didn't even know existed. Because they don't.

TO BE TRANS

Let us dwell at some length on dodd's poetic conveyance of her gender:

> My gender is going to the corner store in [an] oversized black thermal with jean booty shorts revealing a landscape of thick black thighs, my long slender hands punctuated with royal purple polish, & my lips a severe black matte & being called baby. Or sweetie. The next day, my gender is grungy sweatpants & tall white t-shirt with backward fitted cap, nails still royal, lips now bare & being called bro. Or buddy. My gender is delicate as the season & unforgiving as the weather. My gender is cackled at by beautiful Black girls getting off [a] crowded bus at the end of the school day. My gender is cornered in the club's bathroom by gay men hoping my big polished hands hold other secrets as beautifully. My gender is being followed home at night by a manic holler of a man & wielding the bass in my voice as fully loaded weapon ready to strike. My gender is a tank made of sugarcane & saltwater. My gender is boyish wonder & womanly strength. My gender is more than my body will ever tell itself.[22]

The first day: a gender that travels to corner stores but is never cornered, cannot abide corners for their hedging. She adorns herself with a black thermal that is (too) big for her while simultaneously sporting booty shorts. dodd fits into something oversized—and, very important, *black*—because her gendered girth, or her un/gendered shifting capacity, fills the empty spaces. Indeed, the spaces thought to be empty and unoccupied because one was too small are in fact filled to the brim with modes of embodiment that cannot be perceived. This is what another kind of gender might have the capacity to do: fill in and exist within spaces via its unspaced capacious-ness. And what other color could hold such capacity but that color that cannot be peered, cannot be discerned in its entirety? Black.

What is the climatic occasion for such an outfit, a thermal and booty shorts? Could it be warm out, necessitating short shorts to combat the heat; could it be brisk and cool, requiring that one warm one's torso? Neither? Both? A confusion of the atmospheric texture is only the result of a gender that is not measurable in terms of current metrics. Her gender is one that perplexes us because we understand the natural world on the grounds of a mistaken universality and criteria for legibility. That is, we assume that our metrics for determining the temperature outside are not crafted metrics at all but sound, obvious observation. When met with an illegible gender we are confused. In this confusion is an alternative avenue of doing gender—a gender encased in, or given away by, blackness; a gender that is indiscernible; a politics that decidedly walks about, confusing our metrics, being mobile and going to gain sustenance. And all of this occurs outdoors, in the open. What to make of our uncertainty as to the *weather* outside? If Christina Sharpe describes antiblackness as the weather, simply there, all the time, so mundane and always everywhere that it is simply what we live with, dodd demonstrates, in her opening sentence here, that the weather is not simply to be passively received. The weather and its accompanying antiblackness—which is to say, too, its accompanying hegemony that oppresses all breaches of normativity—does not have a monopoly on meaning-making. The weather might be antiblack, might be 96 degrees and humid, but we can enact our subjectivities in ways that refuse such weather; we can adorn thermals and booty shorts, making others question, indeed, *is it* 96 degrees and humid? Even if for a second they do not believe the normativity of the weather, we, in our otherwise genders, make them question.

And what is one who engages gender like this called? How are they interpellated, *mis*interpellated, neither, both? The melding of masculine readings and feminine readings orchestrate various kinds of commingling subjectivities. Colors potent with significatory allusions clash with sartorial reads, which clash with corporeal understandings. Or dovetail seamlessly. Nothing is certain, nothing determined. And this is where dodd's gender perhaps rests restlessly. Baby, sweetie. Man? Woman?

The second day: baggy, grungy sweats that cannot give straight answers. Long white T-shirt, a signifier of a certain geographical and racialized demographic, backward fitted cap, all of which muddy gender's buttressing luminosity and symbolic integrity. Anything to make it cave in on itself or work to its own detriment. What yesterday expressed oral femmeness is now left bare, yet still clashing—or dovetailing—with nails that do different work. Today, no baby or sweetie but "bro." A question arises: Is today's "bro" a shift or a continuity from yesterday's "baby," "sweetie"? Are these interpellative calls right one day and wrong the next, right both days, wrong both days? What we are left with is a surfeit of questions rather than further archival evidence as to dodd's "true" gender. Or perhaps we are left with, precisely, her "true" gender: the questions. She is here calling attention to the ambiguity of gender's location(s). Where do we extract and extrapolate assumed ontological gender? In the femininity of the nails, making one "woman"; in the bareness of lips, making one "man"; in the donning of too-big shirts; in the wearing of too-short shorts?

dodd's litany of experiences saturated with gendered significance evoke the turmoil in which her gender resides: the confused, uncomfortable, ridiculing laughter of schoolchildren who have recently sedimented gender, but who, in their black girlness, are still beautiful; the lustful arousal of gay men in nightclubs who seek strong hands to caress them; the spectral violence portended by men catcalling one at night but being met with another, (unexpected) bass-filled voice in response from a body not supposed to have such a timbre; the commingling of "sugar in the tank" and bitter saltwater; the convergence of youthful boyish wonder and mature womanly vigor. It is delicate and unforgiving, and in short it refuses the binaristic connotations embedded in the gender binary's appropriate roles. This is a gender—among many others for which we may not have names and that also get questioned incessantly—that pokes holes in the haughty hubris of a normative gendered regime that touts itself as impenetrable. dodd is making another kind of gender out of the fallen rot of given gendered ontologies. And that gender, whatever it can or cannot be called, or is refused to be called, is what dodd, and this iteration of black trans feminism, is after.

And this gender, as she concludes, "is more than my body will ever tell itself." dodd's traniflesh is showing. This kind of gender cannot be reduced to what is (thought to be) present on the body, perhaps cannot be understood, properly, as a body. The body, whatever we take that to mean, cannot tell the entirety of this kind of gender because the body is limited in its predication on the gender binary. That is to say, to be understood as a body it must adhere in some way to binaristic gendered logics. To yearn for and engage the substantiveness of the questioned genders is to, definitionally, subvert bodiness and reach for traniflesh—subjectivity that is uncapturable, liberated, disruptive of the body's systematicity, legible only in its departure from normative constraints that limn the body. The body cannot tell itself these otherwise genders because the body does not know what it cannot be: other than body. A radically trans and transed gender discards the body in a multitude of ways because in order to do transness one must refuse binaristic gender's reign, and to refuse binaristic gender's reign is to undermine one of the central tenets of how bodies emerge into recognition. In short, we cannot trust the body, cannot live in it because it is the thing impeding, at crucial times, the emergence of the trans.

On this score dodd asks a question: "What happens to the body when every truth it tells is denied by someone with the power to kill it?" This is the plight of, as she goes on to say, "living Trans as unapologetically as possible."[23] To live trans unapologetically is to risk one's subjectivity in a way that one is both at risk of being killed by hegemonic forces and at risk of, in a poetic and literal sense, killing oneself. Deployment of a trans and, importantly, *transed* subjectivity is an ontological breach that renders one illegible to the very frameworks that permit one to exist as a subject. Transness vitiates subjectivity insofar as subjectivity's recognizability is dependent upon logics of legibility and recognition. Living through this in a way that is unapologetic means that the answer to dodd's question might be: the body becomes no more. The body dissolves and what emerges is what was discussed in chapter 2: traniflesh. Traniflesh is the gender-that-is-not-Gender that dodd's unapologetic transness reaches for; it is expressive of what she notates as "the antagonism of subjectivity," or a subjectivity that is definitionally antagonistic to normative frameworks. This is a flesh one will "be a passenger to," because in its guidance it will lead to a mobility characterized by the "travers[al of] / broken ground and swallowed foundations."[24] On no ground will it walk and on no foundations will it stand. The things presumed to enable existence—grounds, foundations— are unnecessary when living in this kind of subjectivity. It is subjectivity that subtends and subverts the foundationalizing principles of the body if we come to an understanding of the body as the ultimate foundation for grounding one's inhabitation of the world. dodd transes this. The body cannot hold the girth of unapologetic transness. It is, indeed, unholdable by bodiness, as bodiness relies on the regime of the normative for its existence. The truths told by this body are trans truths, which do not and will not abide bodiness.

Whence, then, does the urge to truth-tell stem? So long has the worn conversation surrounding agency been restricted to one's ability to command one's body in ways that one wishes. Is there agency without the body? If the body is ultimately inadequate and is discarded by unapologetic transness, how does one engage in the thing formerly called agency? dodd would posit that what enters is elasticity. "To be Trans, here in Amerikkka, means to be elastic," she writes, "to traverse the pulling apart and remaking of your identity each day and nearly with every interaction."[25] This is what I mean by subjectivity: pulling apart and remaking one's identity, so much so that what culminates is not properly an "identity" if such a term is meant to denote an adherence to (limited) options given to us to choose from. dodd's subjectivity, the only "identity" that she can have while expressing her unapologetic transness, is fundamentally a pulling apart and remaking, a retooling and rewinding and undoing, where the very process of re-, re-, un- *is* the subjectivity being fashioned. An elasticity the very meaning of which is elastic, flexing and stretching and breaching form; an elasticity the meaning of which is to undo form by way of refusing "a" form. dodd is yearning for something else, and that is, I think, all she yearns for—something else, the not what we've been given. She is fashioning on the fly via improvisational subjective alchemy. She, as she put it herself, "know[s] I been changed":

> My new language is flight
> At my shoulder blades an expanding
> Without ache—wide as freedom
> This body prophesied transfiguration[26]

An epistemological claim, dodd *knows* she's been changed, a change precipitated by an illegible truth unforetold by her illegible traniflesh that we only have recourse to call, loosely and misguidedly, a body. The language—that articulation of that which might exist, the pneumatic ether that gives over what is permitted to exist—that dodd discovers for herself is one of flight, which is to say fugitivity, which is, finally, to say, differently inflected, black and trans and feminist concatenated into an abolitionist gender radicality. She speaks herself into another kind of existence via fugitive flight, and if that Heideggerian assertion holds true, the "man [*sic*]" that this language speaks is one that seeks to vitiate that upon which man [*sic*] and man [*sic?*] and Man [*sic!*] rest. Even dodd's physical "body," here metonymized in the shoulder blades (which, barring anthropological limitations, might sprout wings that could engender liftoff) signify breach. Expansion is what dodd's new subjectivity will pray to, refusing containment and limitation, always seeking more capacity to get outside of it all, "without ache," so the pain that the body's systematicity might expect is jettisoned because this new thing is not a body. It is "as wide as freedom." It is an unbounded capacity that will not buckle under the weight of sedimentation. What many understood dodd's body as (all that dodd was, purportedly) was only an imprecise glimmer into something else, as it foreshadowed, as we've seen before, "transfiguration" and trans/figuration.

There is an immense refutation of the order of things present. All up in some serious feelz, dodd begins "hoping my gender is future or whatever."[27] *Or whatever*. This is precisely what is meant. The "or whatever" is not flippant; it is the closest approximation to the future gender that dodd envisions for herself. The space of the whatever is a miasmic, nebulous, *trans* kind of ethereal otherwise enfolded in on by blackness's and transness's fugitive inflections. Conversant with Rinaldo Walcott's whatever as an uncertain and radically open blackness and Stallings's whatever as a funky "imperiocorporeal" modality of perception and living, and also Omise'eke Natasha Tinsley's Kreyòl and queer and *mati* meanings, dodd's futuristic gendered whatever marks that (non)thing to which she wants her gender to aspire, an uncapturable otherwise elusive of the current regime in which gender is ensnared.[28] Too, the overt futurity of another kind of gender as a "non-binary blxk homie (*remember homie is gender neutral*)" folds into a spectrality, connoted by its characteristic historicity insofar as specters, ghosts, are presumed to have lived and then died only to come back to haunt. dodd has been calling her body a ghost, "an astral projection," because of its ecstatic outsideness from its given ontology of masculinity. "i have always felt my body as outside of itself," she writes, "masculinity under the guise of a Man(hood) honestly terrifies me. being a man has no urgency to me. while i never want to be absolved of blind spots, i don't think identifying exclusively as male is safest for me to understand this / my body."[29] Despite what some might call the facticity of dodd's masculine body (dodd is 6 feet 5 inches tall, has a markedly deep voice, and is very often read by strangers as a black man), she refuses masculinity's hold and yearns for something outside or in excess of the binary—outside and in excess of being itself. Astral spectrality is the start of another kind of being, a being outside of being that dodd seeks to subjectivate for herself. It is an otherwise being that is fueled by the black and trans unsuturing of gender. dodd's gender-as-future-or-whatever dovetails with the kind of future Jordy Rosenberg yearns for: one of radical anonymity, an opacity that engenders a radically open-to-claim insurrection.[30] A future that is illegible and perhaps unanticipated is a future that does not bear the grammar of our current moment, which is all we might wish for because it is not this, though we do not know what else it might be. That future we do not know precisely because it is not this is what we desire, and to fashion a gender through this not-known future, this radical anonymity of the future is to forge an identity not through constitutive bodily markings (that is, markings that constitute and engender our bodies) but through how we engage the sociopolitics, how we do politics.

TO BE FEMINIST

"Now, for the record: I'm not a feminist. Never been. Never wanted to be," dodd writes in her essay "Stop Dude Feminists."[31] The essay is an admirable one, detailing how the United Nations' #HeforShe campaign centers men as the gatekeepers of feminism and reduces gender social justice to a violent biological dichotomy. dodd insists that feminism is much more nuanced than simply "gender equality." But the claim that dodd is not, and never wanted to be, a feminist is a peculiar one. It does not seem like the typical gesture often made, where black people distance themselves from feminism because of its association with whiteness (as if whiteness has sole claim to feminism, which it demonstrably does not). Rather, dodd's never being and never having wanted to be a feminist is a temporal claim. This essay was originally published in November 2015. In a December 2013 essay, however, dodd, in writing about the simultaneous blackness *and* feminism of Beyoncé, says "Beyoncé is the reason I can call myself a feminist now."[32] This is not to mention the above-quoted passages from essays that span 2017–2019, all of which, in their radical gender politics and insistence on centering race viz. blackness, engage feminism. What is to be made of this?

Though dodd does not unequivocally and consistently claim the title of feminist, that is of little matter to me, quite frankly. The kind of feminism advocated in this book is one that emphasizes dispersal and engagement, praxis and deployment, rather than declaration and position. Conversant with Imani Perry's feminism as a verb and focused on the dismantling of patriarchy as a force of sovereignty, property, and personhood, I am reading dodd as fundamentally a feminist, even if she has a temporally vexed relationship with the term. In other words, I care very little about dodd's declaration of herself as a feminist or not, but rather am interested in how she enacts tenets of feminism, does, as it were, feminist work.

Coming to feminism as a critical praxis alleviates the requirement to consider as feminist only those who declare themselves feminists. It becomes in fact a modality of inhabiting the world, deploying one's subjectivity in nonnormative ways, and interrogating hegemonic patriarchal edifices. I refuse stilted definitions of feminism as the slogan-attractive

"The future is female" or "Feminism is the radical notion that women are people," not for their inaccuracy—though there is a substantive critique to be made of asserting the superiority or inherent goodness of a (binaristic understanding of one's) biologized accident—but for their woeful insufficiency. Doing the feminist work entailed in black trans feminism invites a radicality hardly contained in the aforementioned catchphrases. Following Perry here, dodd is ripe for gleaning what Perry calls "the vicar of liberation," which expresses feminism as "a call to pursue becoming different kinds of subjects from that demanded by the political economy."[33] Given an ontology of gendered embodiment from the hegemon, it is imperative that, if we are to dismantle the violences of the hegemon, we discard those ontologies in favor of something different. When given "Are you a man or a woman?" as dodd is constantly given, giving the question back, indeed becoming something else through the illegibility of the question unanswered, is the start of perhaps a different form of radical feminist engagement.

Such is the texture of dodd's feminism, her black and trans feminism. This is a feminism that does not need to proclaim that it is feminist because its feminism exceeds proclamation; its feminism resides in the radical praxis of illegibly inscribing otherwise modalities of subjectivity. It is a question that goes unanswered, given back, and refused for its externalized origins and inherent violences. This is a feminism that is interested in dissolving gender's normative hold and creating something else that might be a more just and ethical way to form subjectivity. It attends to violent histories that have traveled along lines of what have been consolidated into race and gender by seeking a way to live in excess of these still-normative identities, these given ontological skins we have come to love so dearly. Because of their normative and at base hegemonic bestowal, they cannot be the home in which we dwell for the duration of our lives; we demand something more capacious and of our own coalitional choosing. Here is a specifically *black trans* feminism. It is a commitment to alleviate violences in all of their forms, chief among which are the violences done by whiteness's racial taxonomy and gender's unbreachable binary. The feminist work dodd is doing rests on a foundation of refusing to "reproduc[e] a biologically violent dichotomy of HE and SHE," as she says later in "Stop Dude Feminists." Inherent to trans feminism is both a radical skepticism of the efficacy and validity of the gender binary as well as an ethical commitment to refusing to reproduce violence, which the binary serves to proliferate. Her trans feminism does not adhere to the reproduction of biologized genders forced into a he or she, nor does it even concede that such a biologized understanding of gender is anything but a fundamental violence. Posited here, then, is a way of linking the trans and the feminist through a self-expropriative interest in service of becoming, in service of a challenge to given gendered ontologies, and in service of being and becoming something in excess of ourselves.

The above *trans* feminist argument dodd makes is also a *black* feminist argument. As has already been shown in the preceding pages, dodd's trans femmeness, the ways she unsettles gender's constitutive stability, is endemic to her blackness. To operate at "peak Blackness" is to inhabit gender nonconformity (or to *ex*habit gender). The peakness of blackness cannot not be excessive of the gender binary. It is because blackness, especially when peaked, operates under a (gender) nonconformance, yes; even more, though, it is because the mechanisms that respond to the fugitive paralaw of blackness must also maintain a strict hold over the gendered law that maintains the integrity of (identificatory) law qua Law—thus to *do* blackness is to fracture the law's various load-bearing vectors, gender chief among them.

All of this black trans feminism is a textured attempt to do something quite intriguing and a bit close to blasphemous in the context of black liberation: to kill black boys and men. Be clear that this is surely not the murdering of black boys and men so pervasive in the United States and elsewhere, the images of which populate social media. This is assuredly something very different. This is a different kind of death that engenders a different kind of life. In discussing her gender transitionings, dodd writes, "i consider my own body, how i have seen it has changed since the beginning of this process. i've begun transitioning from male-identified to non-binary, & i'm working on physical & professional shifts with that transition. so one of the bodies that is most present in the text is a Black *boy* body i have begun to kill quietly."[34] Transitioning is characterized as a shift. This shift encompasses the body as well as one's profession; the shift is pervasive enough to extend beyond the subject that is transitioning. For one to transition, say, from male-identified—from AMAB, cis, masculine—to nonbinary or trans femme is a process of quietly killing the black boy. This killing is a quiet one, not the loud variety of white cops or vigilantes exterminating black boys and men. This killing that dodd embarks on is sonically muted, a slow murder that eradicates the tenets upon which male-identification rests: toxicity, violence, rigidity. dodd is understanding male-identified as a signifier of a particular modality of being interpellated into enacting masculinity, and that is what is being killed quietly. Black boys and men are not to be conflated with masculinity, though the dissolving of such a conflation renders the terms "boys" and "men" troubled and subject to reconsideration. The signifier of being male-identified is the culprit responsible for the violent adherence to masculinity's cult, as it were; thus to kill it is perhaps the apogee of a trans feminism from dodd's subjectivity as black, trans, and femme.

This amounts to something quite profound: "i'm like both the lady & man but i'm killing him & showing up to his funeral. i expect i'll leave me everything in the will," dodd goes on to say. First, dodd is here making a subjective claim, a fractal-subjectivity claim, by which is meant a dispersive and fluid mode of enacting oneself. This is not an ontological claim that presumes one is some*thing* in one's entirety. dodd is *like* the lady and the man; dodd is not *the* lady and the man. This opens up being "identified" to something more mobile: a subjective plenum where one moves through always shifting iterations of who they continue to become. This is an insistence on transed gendered ways of living, never settling on a gender that is fixed. A refutation, of sorts, of ontological gender. dodd then goes on to kill the man—or, rather, kill "him" and subsequently show up to "his" funeral. "He" is dead, killed, because "he" is a materialized signifier that points toward a performative gendered violence. To actualize her trans femme subjectivity, dodd must kill "him." It is the killing of "him" that allows trans femmeness to emerge, as it is, in a sense, the analgesic mitigation of the ontological violence that is "he" and "M/man." The funereal scene that comes after becomes a recalibrated funeral unlike those historically occurring in the long tradition of black death. We do not mourn at this funeral; we celebrate the death for which this new funeral commences. We kill the violence imposed upon us, a killing that is nonviolent since it eradicates (gendered) violence. The last thing that readers must wonder is who is this "me" that shows up to the funeral and is left—curiously, left by themselves—everything in the will? I am interested in "me": who they are, where they get their understanding of their gender, what they might call that gender, and to what end they enact their gender. I'm interested in the possibility of "me" being a ghostly figure, a tranifleshy figure who lives gender other-than Gender; I'm interested in the possibility of "me" bearing a subjectivity that seems paradoxical and impossible to us only because "me" has in fact abolished Gender and lives through and as something else, a trans/figured subjectivity. It must feel lovely, "me," to have gotten outside, basking in the sun, having been given nothing that you did not give yourself. Go 'head with your bad self.

(And a bonus final question: What is written in the will?)

The goal is ultimately "to rupture gender," which does not, importantly, serve as the end for dodd. In rupturing gender, one is then tasked with the "need to imagine ourselves more free."[35] That is "all that is wanted," freedom—or, more precisely, freeness, the condition of freeness as that which enables what one will become. The blackness of the trans feminism dodd deploys and makes possible is one that fashions different kinds of subjectivity, subjectivities that shroud, or unshroud, "bodies" in trani- flesh; subjectivities that can only, as dodd writes, "[be] called elusive" as they swing from "ungovernable vines" between unfixed poles we forgot the locations of.[36]

TO BE SOMEPLACE NOT HERE

dodd's 2019 poetry collection, *The Black Condition ft. Narcissus*, offers further insight into her conceptualization of blackness and gender, as well as how life might be lived. It is a collection that spans many subjects, from the body to visibility to music to religiosity and spirituality. To be dwelled on here are only two of its entries, "We Cannot Grieve What Doesn't Leave Us or I'll Be at Every Function" and "Babylon *After Ajanae Dawkins*," as they round out a meditation on dodd's gendered and racialized subjectivity and her theorization of what the future holds for such subjec- tive insurgency.

But, as a kind of preface, the title page of the collection, which is usually reserved solely for the title of the book, is accompanied by something else: an addendum by dodd. She writes, just below her name,

> Live! From Wilderness Records
> (Some Place Not Here, USA, 20i7)

The collection is thus opened by not only the author's name and publisher's information; it is opened, and thus initiated, by an immediacy—live! The content of the collection is happening now, as we speak; we are unable to relegate its occurrences to the past as it is all happening as we read. The "studio," as it were, that is providing a forum for these live events hails from the wilderness. The context and its black trans femme aura come from the outside, the wilderness, the wild. As coming from the wilderness where beasts and the unknown romp around lawlessly, as coming from the wild, from wildness, the black and trans and fem(me)inism in *The Black Condi- tion ft. Narcissus* likewise "nam[e], while rendering partially opaque, what hegemonic systems would interdict or push to the margins."[37] They are opaque, operating under a specificity and an opacity available only to those within it; they also, though, in Glissant's weavable opacity, are names for the onto-epistemic space of the margins. This is to characterize the black and trans and femme flashing from the poems.

Interestingly, too, is what follows the liveness from the wilderness. Situated parenthetically, we have the location, presumably, in and from which dodd writes. That place is someplace that is not here, and it has the geographic name of "the USA," in the year "2Oi7." The United States is the place dodd occupies, but it is a place that is not here. dodd does not occupy the United States in the same way as others do, nor does she perhaps occupy the United States as such. In other words, dodd lives on a certain ground and in a certain atmosphere and at a certain latitude and longitude that has been given the name "United States of America," but she does not live the life of the United States, does not live life by virtue of the United States. She is some place not here, the United States, because her subjectivity is one that cannot live here. So, while she occupies this place corporeally perhaps, who she is (becoming) is a subjectivity disallowed in the United States and thus she—dodd and the black, trans, femme identities she holds and that subjectivate her—are someplace else. And since to be located requires both space ("USA") *and* time, the date she lives in is, interestingly, 2Oi7. It is so subtle one might miss it, presuming, of course, that it reads 2017, all numerics that make sense. But 2Oi7 jumps out first because it is not the ostensible year in which the collection is published, causing astute readers to double-check; 2Oi7, supplanting the "o" (zero) with an "O" (capital O) and the "1" (one) for an "i" (lowercase I), first signals a break from normative temporality. If dodd has said her gender is the future (or whatever), perhaps the future could be, not 2017, but 2Oi7, as it is a date that appears not entirely legible—or, further still, perhaps 2Oi7 is a *whatever time*, a time that is not a time. Dates in this future get composed of alphanumerics instead of just numbers, literally altering the grammar, amending the American, indeed Western, and further worldly, grammar book.

"We Cannot Grieve What Doesn't Leave Us or I'll Be at Every Function" titularly announces black trans life and livability. It announces an argument that though there are numerous headlines about slain black trans people and dried tears on mourning faces that testify to kin taken away too soon, we needn't grieve because they have not entirely left us (and if they did, because of dodd's commitment to black trans people, she'd be at every function). It is a poem that does not mourn even though someone, a man that used to live in dodd's body, is now dead. The death is a time for celebration, for laughter. It is a poem that dances. In essence, the poem is in two parts, though not signaled as such. The first, a solid chunk of text partitioned by slashes, attends the funeral and observes. The first half of it reads:

> The only man I have ever killed lived in my body / / At his funeral / I'm in the back of the mezzanine wearing black-jean booty-shorts / oversized white t-shirt / with my own face air-brushed / metallic lavender / / I am his widow / & his only son / / Below / people are laughing / not weeping / because they are in on the joke / / This cathedral / tailored / & fitted for a casket / is a new unspeakable familiar / / Safer than mother's heels / was double knot tie / & monogrammed cufflinks / / The gag is: even in rigor the corpse smiles / / The coffin is rented / / The suit mine / / All of this is to be burned[38]

Forget sartorial propriety implicitly expected for funeral attendance—a propriety that I personally know all too well, frustratingly castigated for not dressing "properly" for a funeral (as if [or, *because*] respect[ability] sticks to adorned fabrics)—dodd shows up in booty shorts, no gown or decorative hat, and certainly no suit, which I've come to learn is a sartorial instantiation of coerced masculinity and cisnormative ideality. When attending the funeral of the man who used to live in dodd's body, a man she killed, you wear what you wish. You wear a white t-shirt and shorts that show off thighs because you are able to show up precisely because that man lies in the casket. You show up as simultaneously the man's widow (you are the person he was wedded to, told by others that you would spend the rest of your lives together) as well as the person who was birthed by the man. If permitted to understand the speaker as dodd herself, or at least someone with whom dodd shares an experiential affinity, then the gendered personhood spoken of is one in which her pronouns are pluralistic: dodd's "she" can hold both a widow and a son, signaling the abandonment of an immutable gender binary as well as, in a literal sense, multiple gendered subjects having lived as oneself. dodd is dead (the man in the casket), alive (the widow), and recently born (the only son). And knowledge of this arises precisely where the speaker stands: in the back of the mezzanine. The mezzanine, the liminal space, the interstitial where indeterminacy reigns. The speaker's gender is an interstitial indeterminacy.

The others who have gathered at the funeral do not weep but laugh. They laugh because, as dodd writes, "they are in on the joke." What joke? The joke is, or might be, that the man in the casket for whom they have gathered is not dead, really. Others not in on the joke might assume that simply because someone no longer lives that they are dead and gone. But the joke is that the man, while no longer living, is not dead. That man has changed form, has trans/figured—has mutated into another subjectivity, was not to be held to this world but transformed, de-personed, engendering something and someone unanticipated. To kill the man *is* the gender of the speaker, and perhaps the gender of dodd. dodd's understanding of herself as a "blxk trxns womxn" who at the time of this writing uses she pronouns is the result of killing the man who used to live in her. She has devoured that man, killed him, and he is not dead, because, in devouring him and killing him, it remains that "nothing is ever / gone if / devoured / completely."[39] The corpse smiles even in rigor mortis. And that is the joke, the "gag": "Oh, but wouldn't they gag," we hear from Treva Ellison (and interestingly, in Signifyin(g) referentiality to Ralph Ellison's *Invisible Man*, the joke of the funeral and dodd's sitting in the back of the mezzanine resonates with Ellison's protagonist noting that "the *joke*, of course, is that I don't live in Harlem but in *a border area*"). The joke here is that all of this is not what it seems. The coffin is rented, meaning that the man inside won't be using it for long (again, he is not dead); the suit is the speaker's, who let the man borrow it. The joke is that perhaps it is not actually safer to don cufflinks and suits and ties than to wear mother's heels; that, after all, led to this funeral, to someone being killed. Adhering to normativity is not always the safest option because, in the end, "all of this is to be burned." It will be burned, this whole shindig, because the genders implicit in the coercion to wear cufflinks and ties and suits, to not wear mother's heels, is an utter joke. So burn it all. There's the gender we want. "Gender is . . . a field of signifying roses you can walk through . . . / Eventually the flower wilts & you can pick another, *or burn the field.*"[40]

The second part of the poem is almost entirely right-justified, a structural allusion to a feeling of being pushed against a surface, cornered. To quote this half in its entirety:

> At the repast, I dance.
> I pink my hands in lipstick.
> I shift weight in sea-foam skirts.
> There are never enough eyes to question,
> if I had always been here.
> So when someone calls for me
> To reveal
> —my trained smile-mouth
> lifts the veil—

I perform my favorite tricks again.
Called an apparition so often,
I longed for the familiar ghost.
My mother will tell someone
how I am, now, divine;
That she always discerned
I am a conjurer.
Every prayer required a sacrifice.
I call this look everything I got away with.
In the wake,
I am a different kind of breeze,
in heaven, holding whatever
binds me to this earth.[41]

At the repast, a feast to satiate hunger, the speaker dances. Sustenance makes one want to move joyously. Femme accoutrements reserved for lips are used for hands. The body is undergoing reconfiguration, trans/figura-tion. Eyes wander across this trans/figured body that may not be quite a body and wonder. Those eyes question if the speaker has always been here. The answer is no; the answer is yes. What the speaker is, a gender trans-muted with "sea-foam skirts" covering (or uncovering) who-knows-what (or who-cares-what), has been here all along, though may have fallen in the cracks, indeed may have characterized the cracks. But the speaker's gender didn't show up—didn't, properly and etymologically, exist—so few others saw it. Called on to reveal themselves, the speaker lifts the veil. But what the veil reveals may not be legible. So perhaps the questions continue, unsatis-fied with the answer. Unable to see what has and has not always been here, a here that is someplace else.

Unable to see because the speaker's gender is a ghost. As noted previ-ously, ghosts, those astral projections, elude the grammar of the mate-rial. The speaker's gender is ungrammatical, anagrammatical, unable to be caught by the legibilizing sinews of others. That gives them over to con-juring, to creating things out of thin air or concocting unreal things. The spiritual machinations and wizardry, witchcraft even, requires sacrifices. The man in the casket is the sacrifice. The genders imposed and coerced are the sacrifices necessary to allow for conjured spectral ethereal genders to manifest. What manifests is "a different kind of breeze," one that blows unlike no other breezes before. Neither gust nor zephyr, neither gentle nor harsh, this different breeze is a defiant atmospheric (mis)calculation. What culminates as the subjectivity and gender of the speaker: *everything I got away with*. Their new look, the one that gets questioned incessantly, is the consolidation of all the things gotten away with. One of them is the murder of a man. Another is the burning of a funeral scene in which coerced ties and suits and the prohibition of mother's heels were the cause of its occurrence. This part of the poem—notably, the only part that has broken free of the confinement of the right side of the page—is the breach of the gender nonconforming (the gender radicality and its peak blackness). It is the consolidation of all the tiny insurrections, the little ways that one holds on to their refusals. Trans femmeness woven into and from blackness is an accumulation of criminal acts, getting away with things not permitted.

dodd meditates further, now on the status of the body, in "Babylon *After Ajanae Dawkins*," this time from a theological perspective. Here she wonders about those who might be taken up in the rapture, a rapture that has been assumed to be akin to freedom. But only "to those who believe." But dodd notes that this rapturous freedom is only "probably" linked. There is doubt as to whether being taken up in the rapture is actually a freedom, a doubt cast over a heavier shadow when we "reimagine / the fear of being left behind" after the rapture. Long has it been told to us that we should desire to be one of the 144,000 "who had been redeemed from earth" (Revelations 14:3), but what of those who did not ascend? What is life on earth like for those left behind? We are urged to reimagine the purported fear we've been told to have of being left behind. It may not be as trepidatious as we once thought. We must ask:

> what is power
> if the entire land is damned?
> could we even know liberation here?
> *if we bodied the revolution over land or*
> *landed the body in revolution or*
> *revolted the land we call our bodies*—[42]

Let us say that those left behind in the rapture are the damned, the wretched. If all who inhabit the land, postrapture, are the damned, meaning that they are all in the space of the unchosen-by-the-divine, in (sinful) opposition to sovereign power, then what, pray, *is* power now? Might there be no more power, all of us damned people in the same nonnormative position? We wonder if liberation can be known here, if liberation is affixed to a prepositional mandate; that is, need liberation be liberation *from* something? A something that is hegemony, power? No power, no need to be liberated—life, now, is the after of "after the end of the world," since indeed the world has ended, the messiah has come.

The italicized lines muse over bodies and revolt. They serve as responses to the preceding question about knowing liberation. They are onto-epistemic responses, bringing the ontic (*"bodied"*) to bear on the epistemic ("could we even know . . . ?") through revolution. Introduced by an "if," the italicized lies are conditionals that, if met, would precipitate, indeed, a liberated life. The damned will be living a life of liberation if the revolution over land was bodied. And "bodied" can be read here in the vernacular as "catching a body" or "bodying," meaning to kill or eliminate. Land cannot be territorialized, thus to eliminate such a pursuit might be one node of liberation—a liberation for nonsentient life. The second conditional for liberation is if the body lands inside, or comes into existence as, a revolution. What is a body-as-revolution? What is a body given form through revolution, a revolutionary body? Our bodies are themselves normative sites of cohesion the limits of which have been dictated by a power that is no longer present postrapture. The aim is to situate the body within revolution such that the body lives in and as revolutionary. Lastly, the third conditional seems to follow directly from the first and second: if we are no longer to presume that we can own and territorialize the land, and if our bodies are a kind of land that has been territorialized (by the divine) that are now urged to live within revolution, to "revolt the land" we call our bodies is the actualization of bodies living in revolution—our bodies revolt. We discard our bodies, revolt from them, and live in and as something else. We live now that we have officially been damned in a subjectivity that is not body but something fashioned by revolution and revolt.

Part 1 of "Babylon" concludes with asking whatever divinity scattered us—referential of the Tower of Babel, but also to the forces that may have created diasporic identities—"what will we make of our new cradles of tomorrow?" It is a question, an open one, that yearns for an answer that may never be given. But, in being an open question, it is also an invitation to await tomorrow without divine decree, creating that tomorrow, that future, for ourselves. It is a tomorrow that part 1 of "Babylon" picks up, as tomorrow's "issue" is one of "decolonizing the body." This phrase serves as an introductory clause to a list, or an expansion on the issue of the potential of a decolonized body, as the colon that affixes to its end signifies the onset of an explanation or enumeration. Perhaps it is both. It reads thusly:

the limited imagination we are offered
past the ships leaving the shore.
what happens to our mouths,
when the last shards of ivory finally flow out,
spitting all back into the ocean.
will our bones begin washing up out of the sea—
a railroad mob of salt marrow? we have never
completely known the expanse of the deep.[43]

Those "ships" are referential of Middle Passage ships, and it is necessary, then, to breach the imaginaries those ships inaugurated. Those imaginaries are limiting; that "Middle Passage epistemology," to draw on Michelle Wright's language, is the given ontology inaugurating us into racialized (non)personhood, circumscribing our expansive becoming in excess of such scripts. Having left the shore, the ships initiated an entire worldview that was then used as the subjectivating force for the ships' inhabitants' racialized descendants. That worldview is inhospitable to alternative worldviews, worldviews that are not only views but ways of inhabiting different kinds of worlds. The kind of being said to be in the pathologized lineage of those ships' inhabitants is a kind of being disallowed other ways of being the beings they've been told to be. The ivory (coast) has embedded itself into our mouths, corporeal apparatuses for speech acts that performatively promulgate desires and wills attempting to manifest. Spit it out. Spit out the fetters, the chains with the sweat of the dewy air on mornings in the coffle at Elmina. Spitting into the ocean might show all those who have been thrown, or threw themselves, overboard that what sent them over the nautical edge is being discarded, thus it is, perhaps, not safe but inviting to come back to the surface. It shows that world of bodies down there that we survived, as they did, on different terrain.

I meditate on dodd because she seems to capture the gender radicality of black trans feminism. Her disinterest in boundaries ("*uninterested in boundaries,*" she claims) presents a radically open opening of subjectivity, where the incessant critique of boundedness calls into question a variety of things; the "mad black, mad queer" maternal inculcation she had from her mother, a mother who both mothered and other-mothered dodd into the madness—which is to say, the deep commitment to radicalization—of blackness and queerness; the insistence on possibility and life in excess of death ("Even in their [two black queer friends of dodd's who completed suicide] deaths, they showed me a possibility. I want to honor that by becoming one for somebody else."), retooling her subjectivity as possibility, not a known or fixed subjective referent to which she aspires; the refusal of the purported facticity of the body ("Even when I'm in my highest femme, I know I'm a black man to somebody on the street. So I think that our bodies fail us." Yet dodd is unwavering in asserting that "I'm not a black man"), understanding that the body can be and is, and might become, something other than body, something fleshier; and the "gender work," as dodd calls it, that "is alive. Is black. Is here. Is now."[44] They will question us, as they have been doing all along, but we are their question, in need of no resolving answer. The questions hold an infinite possibility of what might be, and they are out there in the wild, dodd writing for us "more wilderness revival than congregation"—writing for us, indeed, the curvature of "The Somebody Else."[45]

Questioned. Gendered.

Black. Trans. Feminist.

Her [sic] *name is Selenite.*
Learn the way
it slides
through your mouth
like a song
you just can't
catch I've been
practicing my dance.
Spins, dips
floor work
anything to
dodge the
teeth of men.
GODDESS X, "Biting Your Tongue"

Yall gone be mad as hell when you transport to a world beyond worlds & get greeted by a bunch of Black Trans women . . .
NEREYDA @TwittaHoney

"Trigger." A catch or lever that, when pulled or pressed, releases a spring and mobilizes some force to action. That which releases the hammer of a gunlock. Quick to act, momentously and instantaneously. To cause something else to occur; to stimulate, activate, "set off," or to spark. To initiate a change or shift in a cycle; to reroute a state of affairs. "Trigger," in a word, is incendiary movement, the fomentation of something that's about to pop off.

Triggers, though, are also warnings. As a term mobilized in feminist circles to alert others to potentially (gender-based, typically) violences (e.g., provocative language or sexual assault), triggers also portend a kind of break. I am certainly in no position, nor do I have the desire, to critique the efficacy of trigger warnings at the present time. What I seek to do is excavate the polysemous work that triggers and triggering do with respect to aspects of black trans feminism. To the extent that I would argue that blackness and radical deployments and undoings of gender act as profound onto-epistemic triggers, this chapter is decidedly about how it may be necessary to, put crassly, trigger the shit out of those who stand in positions that are rarely, if ever, the audience warned in trigger warnings. If the social world rests on hegemonic, normative foundations that themselves engender the conditions that enable the violences about which people need to be trigger-warned—these foundations themselves in fact trigger-*happy*—it becomes necessary to trigger those very foundations. Like the 2017 exhibit on gender by the same name, the import of "trigger" as a way of challenging us "to experience the mess itself as a productive model for both the conception and display of gender"—Maggie Nelson's inhabitable and useful analytic of "messy shit"—asks for a different understanding of "trigger," one that demands of us something quite intense.[1]

It is through the poetic works of two black trans women that I explore this: Venus Di'Khadija Selenite, about whom Goddess X, in the opening epigraph, is speaking, and Dane Figueroa Edidi. To my knowledge, neither of these women have received the sustained meditation and analysis their work deserves. Their writing has been given no scholarly treatment, so I am beginning that work here. Selenite's essay collection *The Fire Been Here* and xyr collection of poems, *trigger*, will serve as my primary objects of analysis, in addition to Edidi's poetry collection, in all its titular realness, *For Black Trans Girls Who Gotta Cuss a Mother Fucker Out When Snatching an Edge Ain't Enough: A Choreo Poem*.[2] Both of their works put into bold relief how black trans womanness articulates itself as a song that, indeed, "you just can't catch." Goddess X elucidates just what it means to read the work of Selenite, and Edidi as well, I would argue: to witness the ongoing practice of dance, spinning and dipping, uncaught. Their lifeworlds written into prose and poetry is the floor work that is constantly dodging teeth.

Venus Di'Khadija Selenite has chosen to forgo working a traditional nine-to-five job. Such a decision, of course, can be read as a refusal of capitalist demands of productivity, labor exploitation, alienation, and the Marxian like. But, more fundamentally, this decision is one that has been informed by the persistent specter of violence. Xyr career as a poet, writer, interdisciplinary artist, and sex worker is a self-employment decision informed by the increased likelihood of the traditional career path forcing xym to "navigate misgendering, trauma, anxiety, and depression," jobs in customer service, for example, inevitably "leading [xym] to misery."[3] Life as a black queer gender-fluid trans woman subjects xym, almost inevitably, to various violences that dictate xyr very livelihood. And we (should) know this all too well, the constant influx of reports detailing the murders of black trans women—including black trans suicides, which Selenite maintains are murders once removed—the prevalence of misgendering, of being maligned in media and policy, the list goes on. These violences that seem inextricable from black trans life are not to be overlooked and are certainly not overlooked in Selenite's or Edidi's work. The task, then, is to heed the mechanisms that structure the conditions that give rise to those violences while also engaging the fissures that generate room to move that enlivens, that *lifes*, black transness. No doubt Selenite is met daily with forces undesirable, specters of violence portending xyr murder; no doubt, as xe says, it is unknown "if strangers will openly object or if this is my last day on Earth." That threat is all too real. It's no surprise to xym that, as the eponymous words of xyr essay collection state, *the fire been here*. Nevertheless, "I survive every time" ("Trans Women of Color").[4] Death is always here, but our persistent survival is testament to the fact that life wins each day we survive.

For Selenite, what sutures the violence to the liveliness of black trans life and saturates it all is disruption, which doubles as a kind of queerness, which xe understands through the nonnormative, the "justified disruption," exceeding the strictly sexual or gendered.[5] The place from which it seems Selenite's work arises is what I would call xyr black trans axiom: "To be a Black trans person in America means to exist as a disruption, to fight every day." Working one's subjectivity in and as the nexus of black and trans and woman is more than a purported ontological fact. This is to say that xe both identifies and is identified as a black trans woman, but it is because, I would argue, xe puts xyrself to work in a certain way as to draw sustenance, retribution, joy, and liveliness from the paraontological fissure that blackness, transness, and womanness index. Black and trans are textured echoes of the fugitive, they give weight to what it "means to run for your life from powers designed to hurt, or kill, you," by which we might read xym as arguing for a way of living that is itself a running from power. "Run[ning] for your life" is, to be sure, a visceral escape from those attempting to harm one on the grounds of antiblackness and transantagonism; too, however, Selenite is setting up life *as* running—a constant escape as freedom—or, playing with syntactic inflection, running *for* your life ("Letter on Mother's Day").

Selenite operates from the understanding of a blackness that is entangled with queerness, transness, even disability, and thus in excess of its consolidation and sedimentation onto the corporeal surface. In a Twitter post of February 11, 2017, xe writes, "You can't be pro-Black if you're anti-queer, anti-trans, anti-woman, anti-disabled, etc. because all those kinds of Black people EXIST." If I may read this a bit askew, or exert more analytic pressure on an expected reading, this sentiment seems to be more than an articulation of the fact of black queer folks, black trans folks, black women, and so on. Xe is of course echoing Audre Lorde's argument that there is no hierarchy of oppression, in which Lorde refuses what has come to be called "oppression Olympics" by asserting the entanglement of various marginalized identities and movements. But, in addition to all of this, Selenite might also be asserting, if only implicitly, that to say "black" *is to say* "queer," "trans," and the like. Pro-blackness necessitates that one also be pro-queer, -trans, -woman, -disabled, not only because there are black people who intersect with these other identities, but also, and more substantively, because these marginalized identities all inflect what Selenite calls the "work that came before me."[6] Queerness, transness, and so on, in referentiality with blackness, index the *work* that antecedes them as historical phenomena; they all, in different but paraontologically related ways, are kinds of work stemming from a force of refusal. Pro-blackness, then, denotes a pro-ness for not simply or solely what has come to be consolidated as people deemed sufficiently black, but for that movement otherwise than normative sex/gender/ability/et cetera. So indeed, one cannot be pro-black and not be pro-queer, pro-trans, because they each reference low-key anoriginal mutiny.

There is an intimate togetherness between blackness and transness—a sociality endemic to the two, or the multiplicitous One, this radically dispersive singularity that, in gender nonbinaristic glory, is in fact a they—that manifests in excess of violence. As Selenite grieves over the death of

Tamara Dominguez, xe is told, "You're not alone," by a fellow trans woman whom Selenite watched battle emotional violence from a middle-aged cis man. Those words, for Selenite, "came as reassurance that we were going to be alright" ("Trans Women of Color"). The transness of blackness and the blackness of transness, as it were, demand a more-than-oneness; black and trans "don't go it alone" because, with them, "it's a social dance, unruliness counterpoised between riot and choir," Moten writes in *Black and Blur*, the first installment of his trilogy *consent not to be a single being*. "Our numbers are queer, they won't come out right, 'cause we keep moving like simple giving in the remainder."[7] In these queer numbers that are more than one yet singularly together in their more-than-oneness, the black and trans of the (ante)matter indexes a constant sociality, a haptic "You're not alone," that finds in its veritable queerness an unruliness that does the work of reassuring that we gon' be a'ight. Together we come out wrong, which is more important than coming out right or just or correctly revolutionary. As long as we are together in doing it wrong, where "it" is the ways of the world in which we know we are made to live, we keep it moving in the remainder.

Selenite operates under the understanding of blackness and transness as political postures, as alignments and affinities that do not adhere, first, to a presumed ontological state; instead, xe affixes it to a kind of fighting, an active, intentional irruption at the scene of one's subjectivity in the midst of sociality. When Selenite was offered a "Black Trans Lives Matter" button, xyr reluctance to wear it stemmed not at all from xyr disbelief of the importance of black trans lives but from the fact that "the person who gave me the button later announced his support for Hillary Clinton, and that's what made me reluctant to wear it" ("The Problem"). With Clinton's alleged violent imperialism and neoliberal politicality (her, in a word, whiteness and uptaking of masculinist nation-state practices), "Black Trans Lives Matter" was only a titular announcement on the button.[8] Ironically, it held little blackness or transness. Selenite demands that black and trans do subversive work, that they unrelate to power. Implicit in this is that, first, Selenite reworks black and trans as agential postures that must have a political rather than identificatory alignment, and, second, that the black and trans of "Black Trans Lives Matter" titularly designated on the button is in fact a manifestation of Clinton's brand of political and politicized whiteness. It is because whiteness as the nonrelation to power, the sine qua non of power, is a rather indiscriminate beast, and it finds whomever will concede to its validity and instrumentalizes them. Whiteness will claim whomever it wants, and whomever will listen. Even black cis men who murder trans women, Selenite says, are "pawn[s] for white supremacy" because, by contrast, to enact blackness is to already operate via trans subversion, thus the attempted extermination of transness (and, indeed, it is always attempted and never entirely succeeded in) is a rejection, a textured exiting, of blackness. Blackness, in Selenite's formulation, is to "dismantle . . . violent shackles," the work of which characterizes the work of blackness, gender radicality. Blackness and transness cannot be extricated; "our chains"— which is to say the fixities that curtail us, whether we wear these chains ourselves or not—"are all interconnected." Black trans women demanding freedom and abolition "isn't just for them," because to make such demands in the name of blackness, transness, and refusal of the gender binary is a wide-reaching demand. In this is a marked black feminism the likes of that of the Combahee River Collective, for the demand to free and abolish in the name of blackness and transness is a demand to free everyone, to abolish all oppressive systems ("When Our Sister"). The concern, thus, is radical change for Selenite. And radical change, the only change in which I and Selenite and black trans feminism are interested, "consist[s] in the time of 'blackness,'" to quote Hortense Spillers following Ellison, and blackness is that configuration harboring radical change because it is a critical postulate "of *transformational* possibilities."[9] Blackness must be thought in and through its insurgent openness, its unfixing, and thus be able to be mapped and unmapped on and off of a vast range of subjectivities, or its ability to change form, to transfigure. Misreadings of epidermal sufficiency are inadequate for a theorization of blackness, which is to say that blackness is deployable, that it is volatility, that it is trans—that it is, as theorized in chapter 3, to think trans/figuratively.

Ultimately, Selenite articulates a blackness and radical transness that is ecstatic, volatile. Xyr conveyance of black trans feminism is always molten, as it must be, shifting and transmogrifying. Xyr conveyance of black trans feminism, to use xyr language, is a daily occurrence of failure:

> It is one of my most often thoughts, one that doesn't stem from a traumatic past, one that questions on repeat. I'm constantly searching for the answers until the answers arrive on my plate. And when they do, I have entered an atmosphere of biting and stinging. These occurrences are supposed to happen. This atmosphere I speak of is failure. I have recently realized I have failed more times than I think. Of course, I am not exempt from accountability and atonement. In addition to

spending hours on thinking of what my tomorrow brings, what I will have for breakfast in the morning, and what is still to create, I spend much time wondering how I have failed and where that failure lies. I have failed many times—and through failure is where much work begins. ("Failure")

Black trans feminism cannot be circumscribed simply by trauma; it "doesn't stem from a traumatic past," but from a multifaceted relation to life and living, in the quiet moments. It happens in the moments when one is thinking about breakfast, planning for the day, brushing one's hair. These moments are meaningful and in fact the moments that comprise life. And these moments, because of their bite and their sting, are, too, constituted by failure. This failure, though, is necessary because of its destruction of sedimentation. I want to understand this as a kind of autoimmunity, as a necessary, welcomed self-interrogation, ("questions on repeat," as Selenite writes) that refuses to let its conceptual host become a structured hegemony. As intent on what might be possible *after* the self-destruction, autoimmunity yearns for the not-quite insofar as what it seeks is the refusal of present conditions without the presumption of knowing what can or ought to emerge from the rubble of present conditions. Blackness and transness as sites of black trans feminism cannot become sedimented or normative and thus must, a bit paradoxically, bring about their own self-destruction precisely because they name not themselves but an otherwise mode of life that cannot be contained in the nominative I have given it. Black trans feminism tries to name that which exceeds black trans feminism as a mode of theorizing and living—indeed tries to name *that excess* and therefore never in fact names that which it means to name. In this sense, as Selenite says, it is always a failure, but a failure from which work begins because the work is the unnamable excess.

Selenite's brand of black trans feminism is one that places a profound demand: "We demand that you move for our liberation to happen," xe says for the Rally for Trans Women of Color on March 5, 2017. Black trans feminism happens, liberation as such happens, when we, all of us, move to liberate trans women of color. "Your shackles cannot fall off," xe goes on, "unless you exhaust yourselves for the removal of ours" ("Message"). An ongoing state of perpetual exhaustion in the name of black trans feminism, a potent synecdoche of which might be black trans women, is what we mean by black trans feminism. This is work we all must do. In the work is where liberation happens, and in the work is where we become. To slightly repurpose Selenite's words, if you think *being* is enough, "you are not motherfucking ready to be our accomplices." To be ready to do black and trans work "you must be prepared to be down in the fucking dirt and grime for our liberation" ("Message"). That is the work that engenders who we are together: the getting down in the dirt, the driving of the getaway car, the Lorde-esque living and loving in the trenches. In being accomplices in black trans feminist struggle—that is, in as certain terms as can be mustered, to *work toward the eradication of (one's own) whiteness, cisness, and masculinity*, one engenders black trans feminism. I am finding support here in the paraontological as the necessary mode of relation; I am finding, in short, a way for anyone to become—indeed, the necessity of becoming—through black trans feminism, one's identity and subjectivity emerging *as such* through the engendering of black trans feminist politicality. This politicality and subsequent subjectivity is to soil oneself in grime. In the grime is where we become identified together, a grimy people.

Might we then consider Selenite's theorizations, essayistic or poetic or vernacular, as a way to understand the queer kinship of a black trans feminist "family," as it were? If Selenite has "long believed that blood is thicker than water," a common tropological thread for tracing familial lineage, "but sometimes blood is contaminated and you must create your own gel in the world," is it possible to think of affiliates and accomplices of black trans feminism as belonging to this "gel"? Though it is often believed that "blood" is immutable and rather sectarian when it comes to family, the creation of this new gel provides a different kinship analytic that is not bound by such worn metaphors of given, biologized families. You are with us, fam, as black trans feminist kin, without qualification, if you are down with being in this new gel. This gel is fluid, it feels atypical, and it works differently, but its bond is a kinship nonetheless. This kinship does not end or begin with birth; it is forged, demanding ongoing and active support. Only when you put in the work of black trans feminism, repping your fam, puttin' 'em on, do we have an affinity for them. We become family, are not simply born into it, so if they do not do the work of love—that name for an "indefinite openness," a black/trans being-in-the-world—then you "do not have an allegiance or responsibility to them" ("Diary").[10]

I want to turn now to select poems from Selenite's collection *trigger*.[11] *trigger* "is a gigantic 'f*** you' to those [systemic] powers," powers that curtail black and trans flourishing: white and cis male supremacy.[12] It is an ode to triggering, to being a trans/feminist killjoy, to "reclaim[ing] triggering" and cultivating room to "empathize and hold necessary space for marginalized people, especially black queer and trans people, collectively." The poems are "intend[ed] to disturb and call out individuals who hold power, prejudice, and/or privilege," as xe says in the introduction and, also, the Content Warning. Selenite is triggered every day, and it has mobilized xym to do the work xe does. The collection, then, seeks to trigger others to mobilize around a certain kind of liberatory work. This chapter will focus on, not to the exclusion of a number of xyr other poems, "cosmetics," "black lives matter, d.c. 2015," and "trigger," as they provide a representative cross-section of the collection and Selenite's poetic theorizations as a whole with respect to blackness, transness, and black feminism.

Few black feminist texts would be complete, or even possible, without reference to one's mother(s). "cosmetics" is an ode, of sorts, to xyr mother, a mother who was "pressed away into respective caskets to remember what made her / beyond disability / beyond single motherhood / beyond making a living." Xyr mother would not be lodged into death-bound boxes awaiting the state-sanctioned vulnerability to premature death, as Ruth Wilson Gilmore might suggest. The repetition of "beyond," strategically placed to initiate each hardship, prioritizes an excess of these hardships of disability, single motherhood, and scraping to make a living. These are instantiations of Jared Sexton's "social life of social death," of which I will offer an implicit critique, but which is useful here nonetheless to denote how black life lives amid—indeed, *beyond*—imposed and unaccommodated hardships. Life and love persist in the space of pervasive "disdain," even from xyr mother's mother, Selenite's mother always loving, as she couldn't not do, as she "cradled and sustained us."

Selenite's mother is deaf, a detail that brings attention to the prevalence of black people in deaf communities and with disabilities in general. This disability is woven into the specificity of xyr mother's black womanness, which is then used to index a kind of black feminism.

> despite her mother's disdain.
> my mother cradled and sustained us
> through welfare checks
> readied us from a feminism we couldn't learn from college.
> her deafness allows her to coordinate life
> on her own terms.
> we have never used sign language.
> we have learned feelings and sentiments
> from reading mouths and signaling hands.

Xyr mother's life is life done in ways other than normative; she navigates sociality differently, which, as Selenite implies, gives her over to a nonacademic feminism. Feminism is here a way to "coordinate life," a modality of living that is radically self-determinative—"on her own terms." A feminism that is self-determinative and further outside the bounds of normative discourse since this different kind of sociality happens in gestures, signed words, haptic affects, and ethereal moods, synesthetically. All of this is the grounding, or the un/grounding, for black feminism: there is a different mode of intellectualizing here, a hieroglyphic theorizing (per Barbara Christian) that retools intellectualism not as "a function of getting a degree" but as "the outcome of black feminism and black feminist practice in general."[13] Colleges and universities are institutional sites that do not seem to be able to hold this kind of feminism, which makes this feminism, definitionally, a black feminism. Writes James Bliss, "Black feminist theorizing names the critical practice that operates, that invents, at the impossible limits of institutionality," making black feminism—like the women of color feminism of Grace Hong, unapprehended by normative ideality and suggestive, definitionally, of an unimaginable subjectivity and coalition against nationalist frameworks—a relational method.[14] What Selenite's mother taught xym with her cradling and welfare (queen) checks, alluding to Cathy Cohen's critical queerness, was a feminism that was always and necessarily "out of place," as Bliss terms it, unable to be placed and fixed. Elsewhere, Selenite's black feminism is unapologetically trans and paraontological. Xe writes in "on intersectionality," "i'm teaching this kid / a zora lesson; / how skin ain't always kin." If, as one Twitter user, @PettyPendergrass (or Ashon Crawley), remarks, the "paraontological distinction is just fancy talk for 'all your skinfolk ain't your kinfolk,'" then Selenite, as I will show momentarily in xyr poem "black lives matter, d.c. 2015," is making a black/feminist intervention into how we understand blackness. Through Zora Neale Hurston, Selenite's brief haiku makes a profound claim as to the capaciousness and elsewhereness of blackness, its Cohen-esque queerness. The transness that is always present in xyr work and that must always be read in its spectral present when encountering xyr poetry is given haiku form in "rebellion haiku," in which Selenite writes,

> we are the girls
> defying false tongues from your
> parents on gender.

By titling the haiku "rebellion" Selenite affixes transed genders and gender nonnormativity to a spirit of rebellion. Much like what *Black Trans Feminism* has attempted to tease out thus far, Selenite argues for transness as a force of gender "def[iance]," self-determinative and abolitionist toward inherited legacies of gender normativity. Xyr transness is a fracture of given genealogies. Xyr transness is xyr black feminism.

This out-of-place, unincorporable black feminism—black feminism as such—is carried in xyr mother's language. Xyr mother spoke "in what the average american would deem gibberish," a vernacular that escapes discursive confines. This language is loved for its nonconformity, Selenite revealing that "when i love her vernacular / i am loving her." I want to refrain from a shallow reading that would simply render that which has been disparaged (purported "gibberish") into something to be venerated. Such a move maintains operative, hierarchical, valuative logics, fails to interrogate the integrity of such logics. But when Selenite loves this language of xyr mother, it is "to honor her," and, most tellingly, "to fellowship with our rebellious hymns." Loving, not merely accepting or tolerating, the language of xyr deaf mother marks the means by which Selenite engages a black feminist praxis of fellowshipping with rebellious hymns, communing with rebelliousness. The different texture of speaking, molded into a kind of song whose lilting tenor *is a fundamental escape from captivity* (to offer a critique of James Baldwin's words), is the formless form that a black feminism begotten by xyr mother takes.[15]

The next poem on which I want to meditate briefly, "black lives matter, d.c. 2015," provides a critique of BLM and the Movement for Black Lives (M4BL) in service of black trans women. Selenite poetically inscribes a common critique, that "the movement doesn't come across our intersections," meaning, of course, the intersections of black/trans/woman. While certainly not a new critique, frustration with some of the movement's iterations' erasure of trans and gender nonconforming folks *in practice* (since, at the level of documented herstory and commitment by its founders, it is clearly inclusive of such people) manifests here as a demand to make the movement more capacious. It is a demand, in other words, to be more radically open, and, more specifically, a demand for the radical openness of blackness. Selenite writes:

> [BLM doesn't] uplift the names we chose for ourselves
> or retweet the hashtags we become every morning
> when we are always in mourning.
>
> i've walked out of the rectangles

Implicit in the first line of the above excerpt is a reference to the #SayHer-Name campaign, created by Kimberlé Crenshaw to address the dearth of notoriety given to black women and girls who are slain by state, law, and vigilante forces. In this campaign, however, there might be read an uncritical lack of interrogation for how those names come to be attached to the very women they are relied upon to summon in the national memory. When black trans women are killed, which names are being said: the deadnamed and misgendered nominatives proliferated throughout the media, or the names these women "chose for [them]selves"? What Selenite is putting forth is a critique of a critique, one that is certainly not malicious, that excavates the ontological base of how we remember our dead. It is xyr commitment to the (un)gendered imbrication of blackness at work, what I would argue is a node of xyr black trans feminism.

Demanding retweets and hashtags for the black and trans women who are murdered—Papi Edwards, Lamia Beard, Ty Underwood, Yazmin Vash Payne, Taja Gabrielle DeJesus, Penny Proud, Kristina Gomez Reinwald, Keyshia Blige, London Kiki Chanel, Mercedes Williamson, Jasmine Collins, Ashton O'Hara, India Clarke, K. C. Haggard, Shade Schuler, Amber Monroe, Kandis Capri, Elisha Walker, Tamara Dominguez, Keisha Jenkins, Zella Ziona, Monika Diamond, Johanna Metzger, and all those who have gone unnamed and unnoticed in media spotlight—is a way to summon the specters of these women's lives, to present the nominative space for mourning, which publicly testifies to the death of people who indeed lived. It was, at least in part, the rigid categorizations these women breached that then demanded their deaths, categorization touting itself as the arbiter of life. Categorization demands closedness. Selenite, then, notes that xe has "walked out of the rectangles," which presents xyr inhabitation of another way to live; life outside of those deathly gender categorizations become, in this moment, inextricable from the necessity to open up categories. Rectangles stand in as rigidity and boundedness, so to walk out of them (note the plural, implying that it is not only gendered rectangles) is to breach categorizations of all kinds, making space for living. Since it has been argued throughout this book that gender cannot be thought, or unthought, outside of blackness, it stands that the more obvious reading of the rectangles as gender binaristic boxes cannot, consequently, be thought outside boxes (or, the box) of blackness, da Silva's categorical blackness. This is a demand to open, radically, blackness, to figure blackness as radically opened, and as a space for life. It is life as possibility through thinking gender differently elsewhere, because "painting gender / in unconventional ways was sanctioned elsewhere" ("rites of passage").

The nexus of black and trans and woman make a protest out of Selenite's body. Xe is "a protest" precisely because of how xe agentially engages the world, how xe politicizes xyr subjectivity and how xyr subjectivity is politicized.

> where i live
> i don't go to any more protests
> because I'm a protest repeating the cycle
> of living
> surviving
> being threatened
> escaping
> and glorifying
> because I'm not dead.

Selenite, sure, might argue that *being* a black trans woman makes xym, by definition, protestatory. It seems also that xe is describing something more here, a recurring mode of inhabiting worldliness and doing a certain kind of politics. Xe is a "repeating . . . cycle," a reiterative crisis ("protest") that irrupts at the scene of one's embodied subjectivity; xe is agentially living, surviving, being threatened, *escaping*. Xe does not rest or sit still in xyr purported being but moves, does, makes a practice out of this protest. That is what we mean by radicality. At the most basic, intimate level, radicality is a theorization about living a kind of life we have not been permitted to live yet, a liberatory kind of thing that we might call freedom—and that won't occur until a futuristic "once upon a time" in which "no trans women were murdered / and we all got free" ("deliverance haiku"). It is living in the world, as xe writes in "a night spiritual (for jes grobman)," "demanding abolition." Black trans feminism is abolitionist, it is in the tradition of black feminism, it is escaping "being threatened," it is rejecting those normative drinks they keep trying to serve us.[16]

The title poem of the collection, "trigger," asks at the outset, "why we cry?" With a notable syntactical elision—a testament, perhaps, to a necessary black/trans breaking of the fetters of language—Selenite does not ask why *do* we cry, which might place the act inside a formation of causality. The causal "do" would imply a specific cause, an agential external imposition that engenders one's crying. But self-determination advances, paradoxically, without a cause, and thus the formulation of the question here is a self-determinative crying that is not fixed definitionally to an external agent. While the crying of presumably black and/or trans and/or women has an external locus that may have set in motion one's current lachrymosity, it is a crying that is not only a question expecting an answer (e.g., What is making us cry?), nor simply a vernacular elision of the verb, but in supplementation of both of these also the question that inaugurates, or is inaugurated by, their radical subjectivity. Quite different than an ontology reduced to a state of tearful grief, "why we cry?" is a question the answer to which lacks a sustained and locatable locus, but is nonetheless a constant interrogation of that locus, a refusal to allow it to appear natural. To ask the question and thus engender a subjectivity from the *asking* of that question is a perennially interrogative and destabilizing posture of paraontological refusal of that which is making "we" cry.

The subsequent lines index an anoriginal refusal given over by a lineage of the consolidated and corporealized forces that act in subversion of the subsequent things to be triggered, about which I will say more in a moment. "We," Selenite writes, "are already prepared. / we inherited roles as fighters." The preparedness is an a priori inauguration of a subjectivity inherited by fighting predecessors. Selenite is making a nuanced move here. Instead of asserting that we have a genealogy of fighters backing us, what xe draws out is the inheritance of our "roles as fighters," an urge to fight, distinct from the act of fighting. Splitting proverbial hairs aside, this delineation between fighting and the roles of fighting marks the former as an act or acts of resistance commonly known and referenced in histories of the marginalized; the latter, however, asserts something more: the spirit, as it were, of those who are given to fighting. This is a distinction that highlights the preferential dismissal bequeathed by one's forebears, a disposition toward rebellion and maroon philosophy, rather than an overt display of resistance. Important, then, is how this can be read as an ante-anti, an insistently previous rebellious lawlessness endemic to precisely what has been theorized up to this point—abolition and gender radicality.

Selenite continues in the vein of this force, which is accurately given expression in the title: trigger. Triggering serves to function as the radicality to which a black trans feminism refers.

> they have prepared us
> to trigger.

trigger the white people.
trigger the hoteps.
trigger the binarists.
trigger the woman haters.
trigger the respectable.
trigger the jesus freaks.
trigger the crucifiers.
trigger the silenced.
trigger the slut shamers.
trigger the transmisogynists.
trigger the straight people.
trigger the presidents.
trigger the faux prophets.
trigger the capitalists.
trigger the laws.
trigger the uniformed.
trigger the complacent.
trigger the powers.

and you will join us
the sea of disruptions roaring
calling forth the sun after the storm.

Naming the various ways in which one might be violently captured via whiteness, hoteps, binaries, haters, transmisogyny, Selenite urges us to trigger all of them. Triggering here acts in tangential and skirted differentiation from dismantling or fighting against or even destroying. We are to trigger, to unsettle, rattle to the core, quake, provoke discomfort. There is no "warning" attached to this triggering, which usually allows those it accosts the ability to opt out. The triggering here is only that, a triggering, with no regard for assuaging the provoked discomfort. What is peculiar in the list of things to be triggered is that all of them strike readers (at least those liberals/leftists inclined to read Selenite's work) as negative or oppressive things to combat—except one. We are also told to trigger "the silenced," the only marginalized demographic in the serial poetic list, a curious inclusion indeed. Considering this, and according Selenite's poetry the nuance, craft, and precision at the level of language that would be given to any other more visible poet, I can only take this deeply seriously. What are we to make of triggering, then, if it is not reserved only for the bad stuff?

I would conclude, tentatively, that triggering serves as Selenite's enactment of provocation and fire-stoking. That is, even those who are marginalized are required to do work, a reading of which might lead to the conclusion that it is not about one's given ontological status but the way one mobilizes themselves in excess of the impositional ontology that has given them to silence. Another of Selenite's poems, "loud haiku," gives support for this:

holding your peace is
a lie told for your silence.
be interruptions.

Holding one's "peace," it is implied here, is a misnomer, as it is never peaceful to be silent, echoing Audre Lorde's famous axiom that one's silence will not protect them. Such peace is a lie told only to make silence more appealing. What we must be, Selenite urges, are interruptions. We must trigger. While capitalism and whiteness and transmisogyny and all the rest are to be interrupted, too, silence is to be interrupted, whether that silence is imposed internally or externally. Triggering is Selenite's means of interruption, xyr means of deploying the fissuring tremors of xyr black trans feminism.

Triggering interrupts the stasis, a stasis that is itself a death. We never die, though you might think we do all the time. We do not, though we are viciously, terrifyingly close all the time. But we stave it off because we sing our "survival haiku":

we are routinely
four five seconds from dying
then rising at dawn.

GODDESS

When we rise, the pinnacle of our ascent that never rests might aptly be called "the goddess." Dane Figueroa Edidi, whom Selenite refers to as a "phenomenal multifaceted goddess," precedes and exceeds herself. She is not only deemed a goddess for her spiritual connectedness, her anointing as priestess ambassador of Mother Africa, but also because of her transtemporality. "Goddess" functions doubly: in the typical fashion of a feminine-gendered—or, more specifically, a femme—deity, but also, in trans women of color communities, as a crown for those who have transitioned by murder, had only their given names, or unknown chosen names. "Goddess" names both immortalized divinity and visceral mortality. "Goddess" is an impossible inhabitation of the interstitial space between life and death, which presents the opportunity to begin thinking deviantly insofar as goddesses don't follow rules of existence. Goddesses live somewhere else (here), knowing death intimately and living anyway, living any and all and other ways.

Edidi was given over, in part, into a familial black transness, her uncle having been a trans woman (who Edidi honors in pronoun usage by using her uncle's preferred "he/him/his" pronouns). She is clear and intentional about herself, claiming unequivocally that "I'm a woman. I am trans. I am black. I am the daughter of an immigrant. I'm Nigerian. I'm Cuban. I'm Native-American."[17] All of these identities coexist within her as more than things that she is; they are things that compel her to do a certain kind of work. Her blackness, transness, womanness are "gifts" and "skills," describing, then, a subjective deployment and agency that asks of its bearers more than it proclaims given ontologies. They call for the utilization of, the doing and working of, the gifts and skills of blackness, transness, womanness. They present a different mode of encountering the world, allowing one "to see the world in a way that is deep."[18] Blackness, transness, womanness, indigeneity, and the like become the textured names for deep world-seeing.

Edidi also makes a paraontological distinction between "trans" and "transgender," reserving the latter for that "very westernized American concept" fixated on "proper" transgender subjectivity, while the former is something that existed before its name (anoriginal), something that speaks to a nonnormative cultural gendering. "Trans" is a politicized statement for Edidi, a way to allow those of trans experience to evade dismay and trauma, which is why she never writes about trans people who are in dismay. This conception of trans identity is sutured to white supremacy insofar as white supremacy dictates that, as trans, "you must be traumatized in order for me to care about you." Transness cannot be tied to trauma for Edidi, because it comes before and exceeds the frames of trauma.[19] Transness lives and incites life, refusing to be hemmed in by cis white supremacist logics of deathliness. In this regard, transness takes on an inherent agency and, in that agency, a movement that mushrooms over the ways that transgender has been circumscribed by hegemonic logics to be situated in near-death and existential impossibility.

When she is asked about the concerns in need of the most attention in the world, Edidi responds:

Honoring blackness is something that needs to be poured into. Honoring trans and gender non-conforming folk, especially TGNC people of color, for continuing to be awesome in this society that tells us that we are nothing. . . .

We need to remember that we are stronger than those who want to enslave us. We must make sure the most oppressed is ok because when we do it's like a geyser: it breaks through the ground and sprays up, but it starts at the bottom. As it goes into the air it becomes a waterfall and sprays the whole area. When we are honoring the most oppressed it shifts everything.[20]

What would it mean to pour into, not blackness, but the *honoring* of blackness? The honoring of transness and gender nonconformity? The honoring of blackness and transness concedes that we cannot "be" in our ontological totality black and/or trans but, rather, as with all types of identities, do them, rummage around in them, deploy them, dig into them. In other words, honoring them is what we can and must do, venerating and amplifying them through us so they can turn the world inside out. Our attention should be paid to these modes of living and to those who are continually forced into, given into, these modes of living. Those folks who are told they are nothing. But in the face of being accosted with one's nothingness, which should not entail a rejection of the status of nothingness but a stringent excavation of it, one can be awesome *as* nothingness, which is then a generative onslaught of sociality. The awesome entails a break, a surreal suspension of the predominating logics under which one has heretofore operated, so to be awesome as nothingness might be what defines the conditional force of blackness and transness.

Blackness and transness are not defined or confined by their subjection to violence. To be stronger than forces of capture is characteristic of, indeed endemic to, blackness and transness as names for that which spills over those forces. Herein lies Edidi's black feminism, again, like Selenite, citing without citation the Combahee River Collective: when the most oppressed are "ok," that would necessitate the dismantling of all regimes of hegemony. It is notable that she writes simply the "most oppressed" rather than providing a noun to "complete" the phrase, indicating, on my reading, that it is the state of oppression, the entering into and inhabitation of a certain power relation—an "(under)privileged" relation to power, one given to a nondeterminative understanding of the subversion of power even though it subjects one to oppressive scrutiny—that needs to be "ok."[21] This relation, which is implied as the names of blackness and transness, is that which is the aim. It is a bottomness, a dwelling in deviancy, a lowdown lowness in the dirt and trenches that breaks the ground: a narrative making and breaking that pervades sociality to engender a new mode of living. Etymologically abiding by the terms of blackness and transness, and their inflective and indexical fugitivity, is to understand them as modalities that demand something of us in order to allow the radical world transformation we seek to ensue. What this fugitivity, this radicality, will bring is the shift in everything. And Edidi means this; she means that *everything*, all that we know, will shift, either massively or ever so slightly, but shift nonetheless because thingness is predicated on a normative logic that renders things "things" inasmuch as they adhere to normative constraints of legibility. Hence why it is imperative for black trans feminism to demand abolition, as abolition names the radical shift noted here. To honor blackness and transness (or gender nonconformity) is to shift everything. To abolish.

Turning now to her poems, I highlight specifically two of her suites, "The Other Four Women" and "For Black Trans Girls Who Love Black Trans People," in addition to more briefly drawing from her title poem, and from "Mythos." As the first suite of poems in "Libations: Of Gods and Goody Bags," "The Other Four Women: A Suite" queries how Edidi might be named. Whether "unknown woman," "redbone woman," "Didi (sister)," or "Peaches," all of these various interpellative nominatives bear a tense relationship to Edidi's subjectivity. The first suite opens:

> My skin
> Is the universality of Black
> I have been born on many continents
> Across many lifetimes
> Born again
> And again (27)

Blackness has a universality that is consolidated into her dark skin. This universal blackness is not a characteristic of her epidermal corporeality; rather, her skin is a manifestation of that universal blackness. That she is indexical of this blackness, constitutive of which is her black trans womanness, means that this blackness—a fundamental "unknown woman[ness]," as the section's title attests—is promiscuously multivalent in its universality. We might all, if we put in the work, align ourselves in and near this blackness, which has been born on every continent, beholden to no geographical specificity. (It is also important to make clear that this is not a mere testament to diasporic blackness, that black people can be found everywhere on the globe by way of diasporic dispersal. Edidi writes that she, a proxy for this universal blackness, is *born* on many continents, not that she traveled there or found herself there. Blackness begins in geographic multilocatedness; it does not get there post hoc.) Blackness's being born, too, occurs repeatedly, undoing and redoing itself, never settling or congealing.

What is more, the "universality of Black" is stitched to a rebellious spirit to dismantle racialized and gendered structures. Institutional and structural hegemonies are not obviated in this recalibrated sense of blackness. Systemic patriarchy, Edidi writes, "tried to end me / But my divine fire he could not tame"; and, indeed, again, "destruction of misogyny in the music of my stride / The death of White supremacy finds its place here" (27). Structural critiques are in fact enabled by this recalibrative sense of blackness, a blackness constituted by a critique of patriarchy and transmisogyny. In Edidi's black trans woman movement, white and cis male supremacy find their demise, since they disintegrate in the melodious music of her "stride." "Mere" being is not the demise of these systems, but movement, motion, agential enactment is. "Stride" becomes the poetic analytic for politicized embodiment through flesh. Striding in and through her black trans womanness is the political identity Edidi takes as an "unknown woman."

The concluding part of the suite, "Peaches," alludes to Spillers's opening line of "Mama's Baby, Papa's Maybe," Spillers's enumeration of those markings that attach to black women whose names we do not know, among them "Peaches," the first in that litany of "overdetermined nominative properties." As a term used to hail black feminine sex workers, "Peaches" lashes a critique of this negatively connoted naming practice and claims that "monstrosity" right at the outset: "My skin is / Whatever the fuck I please" (31). She claims autonomy over the iconographic reflexes attributed to her skin, which, reading in a bit, might be to say that she claims the radically autonomous terrain of flesh. That is the name that cannot be known or tracked, so Edidi inaugurates herself through that untrackability, calling it simply "the One," a name that "was lost to history" (27).

Part 1 of "For Black Trans Girls Who Love Black Trans People," titled "Life Turns," is what I would call a meditation on the genre of flesh. Neither about black trans*gender* or trans*sexuality*, the "transness" of these black people is what Sandy Stone has called "transsubjectivity," as distinguished from transsexuality. Transsubjectivity "better helps us see that the body is an instrument for involvement with others." It is, importantly, "a genre rather than a gender."[22] Transness marks a particular subjectivity of disordering and deforming Order and Form, a modality of worldly inhabitation rather than an innate and biologized/sexualized characteristic of an already known and formed being. Less a specific gender, it is the disruption of gender; it is, conversant with Sylvia Wynter, a genre that highlights the proliferative possibility of other genres. Transsubjectivity, as a genre, a disordering and deforming genre—or, more precisely, the genre that attests to the disordering and deforming heft of noting generic specificities—weakens the strong metaphysical truth claim of the gender binary, "healing" us from the violence of the metaphysics of the imposed ontology of dimorphic, binaristic gender and sex. This healing genre of transsubjectivity comes in that which was "back when bodies were an after thought" (64). Bodies, captive vessels initiating us into legible recognition, used to be an afterthought. Something precedes and exists in excess of the body, something that Edidi calls "a different whisper." This different whisper, breaking free of the hold of the optic and breaching the realm of the sonic's muted decibels of the lowdown frequencies, offers another kind of subjectivity, another genre of being that becomes, echolalically and ethereally, in resonances so quiet they may not even register in aural ledgers of comprehension. When we go there, we enter into new life where "life turns [and] / we gain new flesh" (64). Edidi goes, as perhaps was the inevitable destination that is not a destination, to flesh—a new flesh that might be best conceived of as traniflesh, flesh that doesn't sit still but "turns / And . . . turns / And . . . turns" (67). In this turning flesh, mobile flesh that whispers differently, there is another kind of coalitional subjectivity we inhabit, or can possibly inhabit. While turning, Edidi says that "we still we" (67). But the very phrasing of the claim raises questions as to the initial "we" that is, supposedly, still "we." In other words, does we$_1$ equal we$_2$, or is it that we$_1$ is—still—we$_2$? What unexplored caverns are present in "we" that hold a capaciousness capable of being simultaneously itself yet still something different? Might this be reminiscent of Gumbs's "you beyond you" or other woman with one's only face? The provocation of these questions in three brief poetic words alludes to the very questioning of collective subjectivity. We are forced to ask, "Who? We? Who is this we? Who volunteers for this already given imposition? Who elects this imposed affinity?"[23] If "we still we," then it is necessary to interrogate deeply who this, these, we's are to the point where we-ness itself is questioned, shuttling into the mix the possibility of the imposed we-ness (the "given imposition") being agentially supplanted for another we-ness, a recalibrated we-ness arising out of a transsubjective place that is claimed in the interrogation of how we become we.

Parts 2 and 3, "Passions/New Love" and "Nature," further meditate on flesh and movement. In "the rivers of my flesh" (68), a flowing flesh that does not stop to conform to corporeality but, rather, makes subjectivity in flow, Edidi writes of an "emotion that creeps into my flesh and rewires / my past" (67). This emotion, unnamed and perhaps unnamable, reworks and refashions the past. Fleshy emotion is what this is: its function is to rewire pasts that have long been said to be "written in stone." This fleshy emotion and its constitutive black and trans un/gendering necessitate a recalibrative relation to the past, because, as suggested by Snorton, the transitive relation between blackness and transness "entails a confrontation and rethinking of the past as it has been rendered into History."[24] The past cannot remain what it has been said to be, and it is the transitivity of blackness and transness that confronts this claim, rendering History as something different—a "new love," perhaps. Rewired now, the past is unable to hold such claims as fact and fiction or true and false. It is now "beyond binary benediction" (68). The divine blessing long bestowed onto (gender) binaries can no longer hold, if it ever could. The fleshy emotionality Edidi advances is a vitiation of binaries, divine or not. This is traniflesh, a recalibrative, ethereal subjectivity. Edidi actualizes this in part 3, giving readers a glimpse of how such a fleshiness might manifest. For her, it manifests in love—the poem being largely about her romance, really, with coming to love—and in the movement of her body.

> Wild is wind
> This dance of body
> . . . .
> This waltz of hips
> . . . .
> Trust this embrace
> Baptize you in it's [sic] whirlpool (70)

Always dancing, hips moving in a waltz. This is how love in the flesh and love of flesh happens. Edidi shows an impossible embrace without being bound. We are urged to trust this embrace that may seem unlike an embrace; we must be willing to be baptized—a spiritual, retooled divinity in the image of Africanic religious spiritualities—in a whirlpool. There is no stillness in this embrace, only a fast-moving rush of water (*rivers of my flesh*) that holds us without letting us stop. We are held in a way that facilitates our radical escape, which is to say we are loved. It is a new kind of love. Fleshy emotion creeps into us, as Edidi writes in "Interlude IV," in "new / ancient / and / radical ways" (131).

Cast over the entire collection is a transitivity, an anoriginal force of density. The subtitle of the prologue is "All Beginnings Have a Before," and already we inflect the before of before, an elusive uncategorizable anoriginality. The claim of origins falls short, always, because there is something that precedes it. Natal originality and all that it is used to support—gender assignments at birth, Africanic origins of authentic blackness—undergoes a critique here. Edidi ushers in a Selenite-esque "defying" of natality. This critique is fueled both by Edidi's spirituality and her transness. In an interview, she remarks that when she operates in "Goddess space," a term she uses to describe the full functioning of her spiritual apex, she understands fully that "my being is older than time."[25] She precedes herself. Who she has become is a becoming that was a long time coming, a coming with no locatable starting point. What she has become, then, a black trans Goddess woman, is the result of a trans beginning. I want to make the claim that Edidi's older-than-time-ness, her before-beginning, is a veritable, and fundamental, blackness and transness. If we understand transitivity as a "not-yet differentiated singularity from which distinct genders, race, species, sexes, and sexualities are generated in a form of relative stability" and furthermore understand blackness as an "(open and anoriginally proper) field" of "the flaw that attends essential, anoriginal impurity—the flaw that accompanies impossible origins and deviant translations," then my claim, albeit oblique, is illuminated.[26] If the "beginning" is always, as Spillers writes, "really a rupture and a radically different kind of cultural continuation," there must always be a before that beginning.[27] However, this before, if laid a finger on, also constitutes another beginning, which, by extension of Spillers, is preceded by something before it as well. I want to posit, then, that the "before" is no point in time but an index of a transitivity, a dense singularity that is itself, blackened and transed, a rupturative force. It is this that Edidi references, and, further, it is this that she understands as birthing (her) fugitive subjectivities of black and trans woman. The nothingness from which distinctions consolidated into race, gender, and the like stem is a generative, before-before force unable to be contained or limned. And it is that force that might be called black and trans, both of which are irreducible in their names for this force and nonsubstitutable. "There was no gender" in this before-beginning, and "there were no pronouns" (33), Edidi says in the prologue of "Mythos: A Play in One Act," because those are categories that come a posteriori. This before-beginning, this blackness and transitivity, is not and cannot abide categorization; it is itself that which precedes categorization. A singularity that harbors all the denseness the word connotes, this before-beginning that Edidi taps into in her Goddess space grounds her black trans womanness. Say it for us, Omise'eke: "She—a black woman—dances the beginning of humanity and the genesis of creativity itself."[28] It is, maybe, this Goddess space, blackness's trans feminism, black feminism's transness, trans feminism's blackness, embodied.

REBEL

More etymology. The infinitive verb "to rebel" comes from the Anglo-Norman and Middle French *rebeller*, meaning to rise up, to revolt. In its current use, it means to resist, oppose, or be disobedient to, a higher authority; to rise in opposition against an established ruler or government. Those who do this work—because, indeed, it is work—are naturally called, in the noun form of the word, "rebels." There is a beauty in the homonymic "rebel," readers not knowing to which it refers, the verb or noun. Its multivalency is indicative of the black trans feminism to which it is, here, attached, it connoting both doing and being, a being-as-doing: a becoming, which is perhaps the word for the simultaneity of verb and noun. Selenite and Edidi are rebellious rebels, manifesting this in their own ways, via triggering or cussing motherfuckers out and snatching edges. That is what black trans feminist rebels do. It is a rebellion that disobeys, undermines, and refuses authoritative calls, opposes forces of governance. It can't help but do this, as its very existence as black trans feminist abolition and radicality demand that governance cannot hold, power cannot be obeyed, order cannot be established. We don't want any of that. We've had enough. So, we yearn for something else—indeed, we hope for it, fugitively.

Hope, Fugitive

They will not claim me
Today
. . . . . .
Will not
Mark the way I move
For death
I
Mean to survive
Live
Love
Thrive

MORGAN ROBYN COLLADO, "I"

To engage in critical analyses . . . to refuse [the] biopolitical and necropolitical machinations; to refuse the representational structures that present some deaths as the requirement for the optimization of life itself; and to insist on different vocabularies for living, which involves asking more and better questions as well as laying claim to the survival of the damned.

C. RILEY SNORTON, "On Crisis and Abolition"

Make no mistake: the stakes are high. We live amid so many different kinds of violence, find ourselves in such a fatal and oppressive mire, feel the weight of an impending (and extant) doom. We want out, but it has grown exponentially more difficult to believe that "out" even exists. Why hope for something that has been shown continually to fail us? The world is burning, many of us are being violated on massive scales. What is this life, if it can even be called such?

Not only are we met with external forces curtailing and extinguishing us and our kin—which is all of us; we must see all of us as kin to one another—but we are also met with modes of thinking that increasingly attempt to deem black trans feminism unthinkable, and indeed to deem (black) trans people as a demographic impossibility. We got feminist theorists talking about "one comes from a man and a woman, and one remains a man and a woman, even in the case of gender-reassignment or the chemical and surgical transformation of one sex into the appearance of another," reinvesting in some second-wave, transantagonistic white feminist nonsense for the sake of a return to the "real Real."[1] We got TERFs out here with their "adult human female" t-shirts and pink pussy hats and supersuspect political commitments. We got Hoteps on some "My African Queen" and "We were Kings and Queens back on the Continent" shit. And then we got literal pandemics and widespread fatalities precipitated in no small part—which is to say, a very, very large part—by that bell hooksian white supremacist heteropatriarchal imperialist capitalism, affixed to that a transantagonist ableist militaristic Judeo-Christian Western modernity project. We are dying out here, in droves.

But it is so very easy—and maybe even, on some accounts, sensible—to heed Inferno's threshold dictum to abandon all hope. There are some in a similar struggle as black trans feminist projects who ascribe a dutiful virtuousness to relinquishing hope and proclaiming nihilism.[2] How, and why, should we be hopeful in such excruciating times, times that have, seemingly, been *all of time*? The questions resound with a fury and an unwavering demand to be answered in the face of their pervasiveness. How does one insist on black life mattering when contemporary and historical evidence points decisively to the fatal, fatal contrary? I am not here to quibble over the last word on the current and historical state of affairs. I do, however, want to skirt such questions in a way that does not dismiss or avoid them. My aim is to alter, slightly, the terrain upon which we come to ask questions, to alter how and when, and for what purpose, we ask particular questions. So I want to begin with my own litany of queries that I hope will serve to supplement, complement, and, most important, interrogate claims for hopelessness; I want to focus on how claiming that, say, Black Lives Matter is important not simply because that demonstrates that they should but because *we can still make the claim in the face of black (and trans and feminist) lives not mattering.* Let us say that my responsibility is not nihilism or its obverse, optimistic zeal, but, rather, simply, *life.* That is the aim of black trans feminism. If black trans feminism can be called, rightly, rigorously critical thought qua thought—where thought is a hieroglyphic and radical commitment to concerning oneself with the livability of life lived otherwise—it is in the first and last instance a fundamental critical analysis. And as critical analysis, we learn from Snorton's epigraph above repurposed slightly away from its original, but still related, context of HIV/AIDS that such a critical analytic modality involves at base how we can sustain the life and survivability of the damned, the most marginalized, the nonlife and the unthought, the black and trans and feminist and black trans feminist.

How, then, might those who take up the call to deliver the hard truths that antiblackness (not to mention transantagonism and sexism) disallows any hope for black *life* respond to me and my articulation of black trans feminism? "How dare *you!*" they might shout. "Who are you to say, in the face of black 'bodies' being gunned down day after day, their murderers acquitted time and again, the afterlife of slavery clear as a sunshiny day, that you are responsible to life? Where, we ask, do you see this life, when all we can see are the bodies piling up around us?" I like to think I would kindly wait for them to finish. And then: "Is that the only life you see blackness living? Are there not modes of being black and, more pointedly, doing blackness that are about liberation? What of the underground ball scene and clandestine gatherings where life is stolen? Why does it seem that the modes of living that move beneath the radar of social and literal death, which is an understanding scarily aligned with (white cis) hegemonic representational gazes, do not register, are not deemed valid as representative of blackness, too? Does not this very *insistence* of mattering, of wanting something other than this, make a difference, however illegible it seems to the powers that be (which are not the only powers that matter, nor is 'power' itself all that must be appealed to)? Is not the obliteration and ending of the world, the burning shit down, as it were—which, it seems, is one of nihilism's demands—a decidedly masculinist endeavor that forgoes black feminist movements of living in the turmoil (living here precisely because here is where we deserve to be) while refusing to concede that here must remain how it is, while bringing the kids, the laundry, the bills, and the Nina Simone records with us; that foregoes black queer untying of tongues, veneration of the non-normative, and refusal to let death sentences end one's joyous, exuberant livelihood on the dance floor and in the bedroom even when AIDS wracks your communities; that foregoes a black trans 'even-so and as-yet of living'?[3] That is, 'the world' is not to be equated with the idea of Europe or the conception given to it by whiteness; there are, indeed, black and trans and feminist worlds that have as their central aim our life and livelihood. Is not our aim instead to 'Imagine otherwise' and '*Remake* the world,' as Christina Sharpe notes?[4] And, finally, have we not already come to the understanding that how we are treated and what betides us is not the totality of our subjectivities, that there is a way we inhabit ourselves not beholden to colonialism, white supremacy, heteronormativity, and cisnormative modes of sense-making, that there is a subjective sensibility to which we have access that exists in excess of the violated body?"

So we've come to this: How do we *live* black trans feminism, what does its uptake and practice look and feel like in what Bertolt Brecht has termed *finsteren Zeiten*, or "dark times"? How are we to do our black trans feminism in the world we can't not live in? One avenue for living—among others, I'm sure—is a living and livability that begins from fugitive hope.

Hope has been construed in the popular imaginary as a virtue, a defense against nihilistic despair. At first, it was widely understood that hope or hopefulness was a perceptual positivity concerning the likelihood of goal attainment. This definition, however, was refined to describe hopefulness more acutely as operating along two axes: pathways and agency. Hope and hopefulness thus became definitional of a belief that those pathways were findable, that at the end of those pathways were desirable goals, and that one had the capacity to be motivated to traverse those pathways to their end. The driving force behind all of this, hence, was deemed hope.[5] Put simply, hope as a general concept acts in conflictual, perhaps even antagonistic, relation to nihilism, pessimism, and cynicism. These things arise in the context of a largely sober, astute recognition of the political and social, as well as historical, climate being one that has time and again dashed the likelihood of real progress and liberation. What has been given to us has proved, in short, rotten, despite promises for freshness, for reparation, for actual change. More of the same in different garb is all we have been given, many remark. And the shrug-worthy feelings persist precisely because of a measured assessment of the terrain in which we live. But it is held here in these pages that a certain mania could serve us well, a mania coughed up when we are constantly choking, relieving us of our tracheal constriction. Instead of formulating or recalibrating or reconfiguring—trans/figuring— the world in which all other worlds are possible (and this, I submit, is what is not taken seriously enough, the worlds that may be possible in the world) to concede to the fundamental antiblackness, say, of the world requires nothing to be done, for nothing can be done. There must be a preconditioning force for engaging in struggle to refuse to let the world remain as such despite its longevity. Different futures are possible; radically altered presents are possible; and, further still, the historical record is mutable, for even when we ponder, "What language in the archive is only used for the purpose of capture?," we can respond, as Cameron Awkward-Rich does, with another question: "Can you make even that language do something else?"[6] And we can answer, "Yes." And it is because the world and its constituents are never, and have never been, finalized.[7] As well, and in a different disciplinary light, rather than shallow, platitudinal notions of hope as an unwavering and uncritical happiness or blind faith, more robust and nuanced accounts of hope articulate it as not denying dismal realities but "facing them and addressing them by remembering what else the twenty-first century has brought, including the movements, heroes, and shifts in consciousness that address these things now."[8] Hope is not the belief that all will be fine, nor is it a "sunny everything-is-getting-better narrative, though it may be a counter to the everything-is-getting-worse narrative"; hope, as Patrisse Khan-Cullors writes, is the grounds for "inspiration for collective action to build collective power to achieve collective transformation, rooted in grief and rage but pointed towards vision and dreams."[9]

More pointedly, it is a fugitive hope that concerns this chapter, a "radical hope" that Junot Diaz writes "is our best weapon against despair" because it "demands flexibility, openness."[10] It is my contention that fugitive hope rests not in a belief of the essential goodness of the political sphere, but in the "possibilities with which 'all reality is fraught,'" and its fomentation of "room for imagining the world differently and in doing so, for transforming the scripts of gendered [and racial] embodiment."[11] Fugitive hope asserts itself as the necessary condition under which possible futures might have the chance to emerge. Fugitive hope aspires for life in and through blackness; fugitive hope is an escape from fixed rootedness, which is thus a radical opening of possible futurity. Grounded in black feminist grammars, it concerns the tense of futurity colored by deviancy, one that *does* a future that has not happened and perhaps is thought not to be able to happen, but insists on it happening nonetheless. It is to perform a future that must happen, *regardless*. It is the power to imagine beyond current fact, a prefiguration of living the future now as imperative rather than subjunctive. Because we "have more than the bodies of the slain around which to organize, even within a strictly necropolitical sense," there is always a lively elsewhere in which to place our hope. So, far from conceding blackness and its affiliates solely to an ontology of fungibility and social death, imbuing a constitutive fugitive hope into blackness—or merely revealing its presence therein—enables the "possib[ility to] understand *how* [the enslaved] created families, communities, sociality; how they fled and loved and worshiped and defended themselves; how they created the world's first social democracy."[12]

Necessary is a "noticing," as Katherine McKittrick would say, an insistence that characterizes the shifting of the analytic frame "away from the lone site of the suffering [black] body" and "toward co-relational texts, practices, and narratives that emphasize black life."[13] This is inflective of my iteration of fugitive hope, which references in a paradefinitional sense the ways we persist in a world that despises us by way of living in another world in the world. The antiblack, transantagonistic, cis male supremacist world that structures dominant history is not the only world we have; there are, most definitely, other worlds within and beside, beneath and above that world— the undercommon covert gatherings in the library and grad students' apartments, the roguish underground drag coalitions, the underfunded organizations putting in work for the proliferation of black queer and trans life—and these worlds, too, are worlds worth understanding as valid in the world. It is because these other worlds exist, irrespective of their mass and ontological gravity in the grand scheme of things (a grand scheme that is nevertheless exclusionary and should not be the only scheme we think of as grand), that one persists. Such marks a kind of hope, a hope designated as fugitive because of the way this persistence allows one to get outside of, and escape the treacheries of, the violence of the world that looks on in amused, Du Boisian contempt.

What animates my claims is this: I refuse to concede that the world, irrevocably and fundamentally, is "antiblack," as is so often the go-to terminology (whereby this is to say nothing of the elision of antitransness, antiqueerness, antifemmeness), which is not to say that there is not a saturative antiblackness to the world. There no doubt is. My refusal, and thus my fugitive hope, operates under the assumption that the world is in fact the "total context of meaningful connections in which we exist with others" rather than an immutable, hegemonically imposed template for existence.[14] The subterranean and submerged queer kinships, the clandestine circles in which things are quiet as it's kept, the other-mothered and mother-*out*-law nurturance we receive are all ways in which we do and can connect meaningfully with one another. And those connections matter a great deal; those connections are the world in which we (can) live.

(Before continuing, I want to alert readers—warn them, even—of the heavy citational texture this chapter will have. I will, in other words, call upon a range of thinkers to say things precisely because I want to illuminate an *archive* of black trans feminist life. The citational practice herein is an attempt to inundate readers with how, over and over, blackness, transness, and feminism assert life and livability despite, over and against, in excess of, or irrespective of discourses and materialities of death and deathliness. It's come to my attention that many of those who ascribe to discourses of nihilism or pessimism in black studies, when sometimes rightly and sometimes wrongly accused of obscuring gender, rejoin with their position's entrenchment in black feminism, then name-drop one of the, like, four black women who seem most closely amenable to their position [though it must be noted that *none* of these go-tos would understand themselves as within the intellectual framework their work is often used to support]. What I seek to do is show that in fact the archive and *dozens* of black feminists and black trans thinkers, and indeed the black radical tradition, theorize life and livability and hope. And I am naming them, quoting them, fleshing them out, pointing to the texts-less-cited. In short, I am showing my work, teacher.)

JOY

> So how do we transmute our grief? Never let it exist without also bringing joy. That we are able to mourn, still means that we are here.
> JAYY DODD, "A Poetic beyond Resilience"

The question of ethics has been present throughout this book. Of utmost concern is how we might come to live together differently, wherein all of us can indeed finally *live* together, can do life on nonviolent (under)grounds and permit a way to exist that is not tied to death or violence or normative constraints. This is the commitment of black trans feminism, its abolitionist and radical desires, necessitating a steadfast emphasis on forging new modes of life and living. It is for these reasons that I express here a celebratory life in excess of a deathly sociality. That celebratory life is the enlivening injection of fugitive hope.

Forgive me, then, for yet another Hortense Spillers quote. Spillers homes in on a crucial ethical relation between agential life and blackness. At length, she writes,

Whatever conclusions we draw about a particular Black person should be complicated in relation to who that person *is*, but if you have decided that all of Black life fits a template then you can call on the Black rage argument every time and that means that you can anticipate, empirically, millions of people every time on the basis of some kind of configuration that you just apply wholesale to those persons. It's also a way of breaking into that cozy, comfortable sense that we have already been able to predict and determine who you are on the basis of something called "Black Experience" or whatever you want to term it. I want to break into that presumption, open up that closure to see instead a question mark, or an interrogation; who is Colin Ferguson, or Dolly Jones? I want to see an *attending*, a *waiting* for the subject to reveal what *it* is. That hasn't happened enough in the culture, in two loci primarily. It hasn't happened in the community enough and it hasn't happened in the larger world. Everybody wants to determine where, who, what the Black person is before you get to the ballpark to find out who they in fact are. If you can look from the outside at the person, then the person can also look out from that perspective, can then begin to think himself/herself [*sic*] as a possibility that can in part define its own possibilities, its own self-possibilities. One is not simply put here by forces of oppression or police brutality or the shape of the economy. All of those are very powerful forces that are moving and operative in the world and there's no reason that I would want to try to deny them. But I would also want to place more emphasis on agency and agentification—I think that the latter may be a Kenneth Burke word. In the quote that I pulled from Habermas in *Knowledge and Human Interests*, self-consciousness does not necessarily revise laws or change them, but it can make them inoperative or ineffective *if* we can begin to talk about *agency*. That's missing in the discussion, it's there sporadically, but I would like to see it there systematically; it seems to me that the ethical is a way of putting that on the table in a systematic way.[15]

What Spillers asks for is the dismantling of the black experiential monolith. The way that blackness has been conscripted into an impenetrable milieu of death is a template that allows one to presume that they know what blackness is prior to its appearance. The force of open interrogation indexes the

waiting and attending of the subject's revelation of itself. Its openness disallows its totalizing knowability, which carves out an always and already
hopeful possibility of it being other than what it is or has been forced to
be. Blackness is not only seen and acted upon, it sees and acts, it thinks
itself "as a possibility that can in part define its own possibilities." Beginning from agency, or Burke's agentification, a subjectification that arises to
the extent that it is agential, is the beginning of dealing with various subjectivities ethically because it makes laws from without inoperative. A self-
determinative demand, the ethical gesture alluded to is opening what might
become in the interstitial caverns between who and what we are permitted
to be and who and what we have not yet become. Refusing to succumb to
circumscripts—circumscribing scripts tethered to positional identities—is
a "fugitive move that generatively builds a new, alternative future within
the land," refusing to leave while refusing to let here, this place, remain as it
is.[16] This refusal is animated, literally and etymologically, via what Rebekah
Edwards calls a "trans-poetics," or here a kind of fugitive trans-poetics that
makes generatively discordant music on the incommunicability of trans,
"writing the 'resistance of the inarticulate'" for illegible bodies, bodies that
mobilize the trans feminist possibility in performative error.[17]

It is a different enactment of oneself that fugitive hope calls for, an agential otherwise enactment that is in fact engendered by blackness's creative,
generative capacities. Living otherwise—or, rather, the otherwise than
being that abolition and gender radicality engender, and the penchant for
blackness to live in excess of, as Sarah Jane Cervenak says, "its history of
promiscuous uses and abuses." What she calls a "deregulated togetherness" indicates a lively sociality valid on its own terms, refusing to concede
to hegemony's hold. This world has only begun to see its breadth; in this
world, "something else is never not going on."[18] This something else is the
coalition, one adamant about its coalitionality, by which is meant not a solidarity but, really and truly, a *coalition*. Black trans feminism, I posit here, is
moved toward fugitively hopefully, and that movement takes the shadowy
texture of a coalition understood as "requir[ing] a rethinking of the subject
as a dynamic set of social relations. Mobilizing alliances do not necessarily
form between established and recognizable subjects, and neither do they
depend on the brokering of identitarian claims"; this kind of coming together means that

> when such networks form the basis of political coalitions, they are bound
> together less by matters of "identity" or commonly accepted terms of

recognition than by forms of political opposition to certain state and other regulatory policies that effect exclusions, abjections, partially or fully suspended citizenship, subordination, debasement, and the like. In this sense, "coalitions" are not necessarily based on subject positions or on reconciling differences among subject positions; indeed, they can be based on provisionally overlapping aims and there can be—perhaps must be—active antagonisms over what these aims should be and how best to reach them.[19]

This is to say that coalitions are irreverent toward established identifiable vectors that might be called identities, parties, groups, organizations, and the like. It is a promiscuous, polyamorous love affair with a kind of relation that ever-shifts and must remain open to undoing itself, desedimenting itself, rolling with punches that capitalism and white supremacy and transantagonism have gotten so good at throwing in order to protect itself. Coalitions are black trans feminism's praxis in one sense, and this means *a radical togetherness on grounds that do not abide the categorical or taxonomic* because that is where black feminism must go (curious minds, again, will want to read this note);[20] and, in another sense, coalitions are the doing of fugitive hope. In other words, it is urged that we, as CeCe McDonald writes from prison (which is to say from institutional incarceration and violence and captivity), "go beyond their natural selves and do things that were unimaginable to their own mind. . . . My message to everyone is to go beyond your natural self, live and love free!"[21] Coalitions recognize and make clear that, sure, perhaps there have been no identifiable moments in which black or trans or femme or black and trans and femme people have been unwaveringly free, but the coalition persists, black trans feminism persists and insists, that, yes, "We have never been free, *but we have been being free.*"[22]

That kind of freeness is striven toward in myriad ways, one of which is a self-defense that is also "a radically transformative self-endangering, self-ungendering, degeneration of self in regenerative selflessness."[23] Such wordiness, but beautifully so: the movement toward getting free, radically free, is to endanger oneself inasmuch as the notion of one's very self is predicated on captivity. This freedom is an abolition because it ungenders the self, unhinges the self from the very things that constitute selfhood, degenerating that self toward something regenerative—selflessness, which is not merely a kindness in giving of one's time but quite literally a state of being (-ness) wherein the self is negated (-less): the state of being less a self. If the self, in the modern world, *must be* a raced and gendered self, and if these constitutive characteristics are nonconsensual, coercive bestowals, then abolition and gender radicality necessitate a selflessness. And in this selflessness is a regeneration, one we are hopeful about because of its being unable to be anticipated. The imagining entailed in a tough, almost painful, spiteful hope is linked to a black feminist lineage that puts its faith in flight, but a flight that escapes without leaving, a flight the likes of Pilate Dead, who flew without leaving the ground, a flight—a fugitivity—"whose radicalness can be understood in concert with what Grace Hong has conceptualized as the 'leap' in her discussions about Black feminism. . . . [which] implies a work of imagination, the ability to believe that a different future might be possible, despite the seeming inevitability of a crushing present." The right-here is amid struggle, not already cashed in as solidified in its terrors. The right-here, as Michelle D. Commander concludes through her discussion of Hong and black feminism, is "something that can be fought over."[24] And we must be, and are, and have been, fighting for it. Imagining ourselves, our black and trans and feminist selves, in mobile excess of our circumscripted "role of pain porn, totems and inspirational mammies" is what will "reveal whether we are feminists in name only, or truly committed to the liberation of all" people.[25] Our feminism is inextricable from being able to live otherwise, hope, and move escapefully, so black trans feminism becomes our ability to handle the excess of trans women's role as pain porn and totems and mammies, to handle alleviation of violence against women, as Shaadi Devereaux argues. When joyful living operates in excess of mournful death, which is not to the exclusion of mourning and grief but is grief's fracturous breakage, living in and through abolition and gender radicality becomes a celebratory matter. Lucille Clifton's black feminist imperative to "come celebrate / with me that everyday / something has tried to kill me / and has failed" is given in an ante- and anticategorical blackness that by just the tiniest hair of a fraction subordinates the fixation on oppressive antiblackness to ebulliently celebrating blackness. And this is done, we are reminded, "not to avoid or ameliorate the hard truths of anti-blackness but in the service of its violent eradication."[26]

It is wrongly assumed, to whatever extent it *is* assumed, that fleeting moments of escape from subjective theft add up to little more than individualistic or negligible instances of subverting hegemony and enslavement. Each of those captured blackened subjects who attempted, in whatever small way, to abscond to the hush harbor, the North, the sea, maroon communities, Africa, or elsewhere was not merely a singular reaction to plantation servitude; they must be understood as refusals of an entire ontology and worldly habitus. That is, the literal and proverbial slave, in every instance of escape and self-determination, refused slaveness, unbecame a slave irrespective of the structure that is indifferent to such unbecoming. This posture of being and becoming *back*, not only having being imposed from without but doing oneself as altered subjectivity in response, in excess, from within, in subversion—back. Fugitive hope, from this genealogy, asserts that we can be back and in this being back negotiate a space for *living*.

Truthful is it that "black social life has been the constant emergence of abolition as the grounding of its existence, the refusal of violence and violation as a way of life, as quotidian," as Ashon Crawley asserts; black life "is the ongoing 'no,' a black disbelief in the conditions under which we are told we must endure."[27] Truthful is it that, black feministically, we must "refus[e] to disappear and . . . refus[e] to comply."[28] Truthful is it that, even when utterly fracturing gender binaristic logics, "we also reckon with the fact that we exceed every possible legible node."[29] As the (necessarily trans and feminist) politic of blackness, fugitive hope strives toward "life beyond present life," a Derridean empirical and ontological actuality predicated on perpetual, unregulated movement "not toward death but toward a *living-on*."[30] In the stretch toward living-on is the never-ending end of Crawley's ongoing "no" that is engendered by disbelief in the unacceptable conditions of the present moment. Commitment to the abolitionist dreams invoked here demand that we know there is life in self-determined, unbounded, inveterate socialities that refuse external circumscription that different life does not and cannot live here.

More generally across the mode of thinking blackness as antithetical to the sociopolitical world, there exists a disdain for revolutionary abolitionist acts that don't in their singularity topple the acropolis of slavery's many afterlives. Such smaller acts are dismissed as either capitulations or ineffective, faux acts of abolition. These "forces of mitigation that would transform the world through a coalition of a thousand tiny causes," seen disparagingly by some notable game-changers in the field, are subordinated to more macropolitical conflagrations that will spectacularly incinerate contemporary slavery in a fiery blaze.[31] Until this happens it appears that nothing will qualify as real subversive abolitionist politics. An oversight is present here, though—namely, David L. Kline's critical query of "what the proper level of abolition could possibly mean *other than* a pragmatic coalition—or a micropolitics—of a thousand tiny causes," a simple yet trenchant acknowledgement of how abolition can only occur: in the processual making and tinkering, in experimental lab work, that takes time to produce the unanticipated "absolute turning of this motherfucker out."[32] And, further, radical abolition, in these micropolitical moments, might look unlike revolutionary radicality. Thinking with the black feminist fugitivity articulated by Alexis Pauline Gumbs necessitates recalibrating the look and feel, the optic and haptic, of abolition. Gumbs's black feminism believes in life and in that visceral "network of microscopic balloon cells in her chest [that] had a say and could collaborate with oxygen to make some small decision called live."[33] The small decision, the minutiae that is feminist fodder, insists on all those miraculous tiny breaths we were not meant to breathe, insists on living—insists, always, on life. This is to say that overt, explosive abolition so couched in masculinist terms is a tired and ineffective way of understanding what abolition can be. Revolution must follow the unanticipatory transness that Jack Halberstam imagines "not as a masculinist surge or an armed confrontation" but as and in "a form we cannot yet imagine"—a black and trans form that refuses capturability by fleeing to, as Halberstam concludes, the "wild beyond."[34] That wild beyond is abolition and gender radicality, straight up. If Gumbs asks, "What if abolition isn't a shattering thing, not a crashing thing, not a wrecking ball event?," then perhaps inhabiting the fugitive space of black feminism means that abolition might be "something that sprouts out of the wet places in our eyes, the broken places in our skin, the waiting places in our palms, the tremble holding in my mouth when I turn to you."[35] Abolition, the world-making of fugitive hope, occurs in the mundane places of our subjectivity, or the minutiae of our living.

Abolition happens in the lachrymose moments of pain and joy, in the rekindling moments of brokenness, in the openness of awaiting palms, in the infinite lacuna between thought and speech. In these little moments of the crumbs of our living is where abolition explodes in stentorian silence, radiating as unintelligible registers that escape the grasp of hegemonic legibility. The minutiae of life are the structures by which we engage in the world, indeed make and remake the world, which is the only way we can do ourselves in the world liberationally. Living in the flesh must always insist "on the importance of miniscule movements, glimmers of hope, scraps of food, the interrupted dreams of freedom found in those spaces deemed devoid of full human life"—there is no other way.[36]

To think black trans feminist social life is to stand unwaveringly in the assertion that it is not reducible, nor understood best primarily through, a history of violence and terror. It is, in fact, "the rich remainder, the multifaceted artifact of black communal resistance and resilience," as Terrion L.

Williamson argues.[37] Black feminist understandings of blackness and its life necessitate a pointed feminist recalibration of how blackness has been fixed in death, even if those claims of blackness's death attempt to account for a kind of life. Fugitive hope, what I am trying to get across as the fueling force that compels black trans feminism to be *lived in the world*, is, as J. Kameron Carter writes, *"far from being trapped in social death*, is 'mystical' and stateless," this latter point echoing Gumbs' black feminist fugitivity.[38] It is life that ain't got time for the purportedly validating gaze of white cisnormative patriarchy, choosing instead to imagine itself through itself, its own (non) rubrics, and creating something else. Black feminist legacies have long been concerned not with whether one is seen as fungible or deemed a "dead relation" by state powers but with interiority. The concern has been on what those living black life, trans feminist life, think about the life they are living. In short, the concern is on living life and living lives rather than living deaths. Ain't that why they try to kill us in the first place, because we live so loudly, so feverishly, all the while loving too? Williamson's specific black feminist critique of the thinking of blackness as proximal to (social) death deems it impossible to align blackness with death. The cogency of her argument comes not merely from a sustained treatment of scholarship but more from the experiential, the unapologetic love for the (black women) folk that have edified her for decades, who live the most potent counterargument to social death theorizing. When she discusses her "Grammy," how she took care of her home as an act of love and a rejection of the idea that her life was "circumscribed by the conditions of its possibility," or when she conveys how her black women friends of various ages would "go *in*" in a "slain-in-the-spirit takeover" kind of way—these women vitiate the very possibility of social death even daring to timidly rap on their doors. These women, disseminators of black feminist theorizing, make a profound argument that "black social life, the *primary* measure of black subjectivity, is . . . fugitive—it coheres, accumulates its sociality, in the wild. Black social life is therefore irreducible to the codes of (white) civil society that it brings into being; the *outside* of value is *its* tabula raza."[39]

To put it simply, by way of Ashlee Marie Preston's experiential black transness, "it's time for trans women of color to consider how we're going to surthrive instead of survive."[40] To do more than simply stay alive but to thrive in life, to "go in" on life even amid pervasive extermination, is to declare profoundly that living is the best counter to forces that have as their aim your demise—indeed, that have as their foundational condition of possibility your contentment with their deathly valuative rubrics. Even in the face of black trans women's average lifespan of only thirty-five years (a statistic that, despite its pervasive citation, is debated), there is, as Preston's quote above speaks to, the demand that they, we, you, not only stave off death but imbue living life with a kind of joy, a kind of pervasive refusitive exuberance, a kind of fugitive hope.[41]

Relegating an implicit whiteness and thus antiblackness to the realm of the social a priori disallows blackness from touching the social realm. Blackness and the life it lives, when it is even said to live life, particularly without affixations to some kind of death, is written off as something that must leave and live out of this world, in outer space. The sentiment compels marginal understanding, as the history of the world is one not too chipper with the presence of blackness. But we have heard this before: the Negroes cannot stay here, it was said, send them elsewhere so they do not seek vengeance upon the whites for crimes past. Send them to Liberia, to Ile a Vache. But whatever you decide, they do not belong, nor do they deserve to stay here. We are indeed living in the afterlife of slavery. And we are living in the afterlife of its parasentiments, the residual debates and discourses running alongside that "Great War." But I must make a plea, that blackness lay claim to this world, that queer and trans life lay claim to this world. I want to believe in the world; I want blackness, transness, feminism to pervade the world of which they, too, take hold. Only when one concedes to the utter ineffectiveness of these to infect sociality, perhaps pathogenically, does one think only in outer space can we thrive. Nah. I do not make that concession, that we cannot do the damn thing right here, where we be at, where we stay at. I do not concede to the luminous, overwhelming whiteness of the world ("I do not weep at the world," Zora Neale Hurston proclaims), of sociality—constitutive of one another, to be sure—because, as Jimmy Baldwin says, "the world is not white. It never was white. It cannot be white."[42] Blackness lives here. Transness ain't goin' nowhere, it has been here from the jump. Black feminism reconfigures sociality, anagrammaticalizes it, annotates it.[43] I possess a persistent looking-forward-to-it-ness because it is the posture of fugitive hope that must refuse the theorization of colonization and emigration efforts, as if we must leave. I want the world, because it is mine, too. I want the world because I cannot not take it; the world has made and unmade me, and I refuse to disown its inhabitation of me. Messy as the world is, I heed Spillers because we are here, right here, "everywhere *in* it and *of* it—the world's mess."[44]

> We have to show the world that we are numerous.
>
> SYLVIA RIVERA, "We Should Not Be Ashamed"

There is, to my mind, a profound hope in thinking multitudinously. To think multitudinously is to think in excess of the singular and the abject because a multitude's many-ness offers possibility. And in possibility is where another kind of life might be found. The multitude does not abide implicit coherences and discrete categorization, nor does it abide binaristic thinking that disallows the in-between or the outside (e.g., the nonbinary). The multitude carries with it a resilience via its plasticity, its ability to be more than and excessive of the unitary. In black trans resilience, an embodied "antagonism of subjectivity," as jayy dodd calls it, there is flexibility. The multitude is a way to think dodd's ability to be both the lady and the man, the dead man in the coffin and the widow, as well as the son. This many-ness is subtended by a blackness and transness, multitudinality integral to blackness and transness. Being and becoming trans "means to be elastic," undoing and redoing one's subjectivity in excess of its circumscription and normative inauguration, "pulling apart and remaking . . . your identity each day and nearly with every interaction." That is, after all, what identity is: "The act of putting yourself together each day."[45] When we put ourselves together in myriad ways, or, more interestingly, take ourselves apart in defiance of legibility, we are proceeding from the protestatory and tiny revolutionariness of transitioning. Even in moments that might be historically circumscribed by pervasive or certain death we must demand that we will survive. Even purportedly certain death must not shake our drive to transition, and transfigure, ourselves and the world in which we find ourselves into something more, to do the gritty minutiae of work required of liberatory and radical change. The multitude, in more ways than one, illustrates the space of the black and trans to believe in survival when we jump.

Using Kai M. Green, CeCe McDonald, and Treva Ellison's forum on "Trans Multitudes" as a theoretical apparatus, and CeCe McDonald's poem "Death Reality" as an object of analysis, here I will dwell on how the nexus of black and trans expresses a fugitive hope.[46] At the outset, I want to quote McDonald's poem:

> I've come to accept that I will die.
> I know this.

And frightening it is
But I refuse to live in
Fear.
You try so hard
To make me deny
Myself
To inherit a lie.

McDonald begins with a fundamental acceptance that she will die. This, however, is far from conceding that her life, as resting at the intersection of black and trans and femme, is deathbound. She will die, yes, but it is not because an external force will deem her dead, socially or literally. She will die but she is not dead. Death is a living in fear, or a life constituted by fear. Even more, she will not deny the life that saturates her. There are various ways that the world attempts to have her inherit a lie—a lie of her "biological maleness," a lie of her nonright to defend herself, which is to say to live boldly. She will commit to living, to hoping that her next day will come even when she is surrounded by white and cis male supremacist vitriol, accosted by it, even. Fugitive hope as constituted by an insistence on black trans life looks like when you are sentenced to forty-one months in prison for second-degree manslaughter after defending yourself from the racist and transphobic vitriol being lashed at you, or, in other words, refusing the given ontology of abject black trans womanness in favor of one that agentially decides that it "won't die," as I speak to later in this chapter; it looks like a self-defense that is radically transformative. That is, CeCe McDonald's self-defense was an instance of a praxis that seeks to regenerate black trans womanness—that self-determinative, ungendering force of disruption—through agency and life rather than imminent death. This self-defense is indexical of one's ability to imagine oneself possible and alive in another way. Since the violence faced is ultimately about controlling unruly movement, by extension the alleviation of violence is precisely the mobilization of that unruly movement. It is her "imaginative abolition," as she calls it, where walls are dissolved, and also where "we will have free cookies for everybody, unicorns, and really cute clothes": a "trans-topia" in which—in truly abolitionist and gender radical fashion (*trans*-topia)—"we do the work, and *we all* in on this."[47]

McDonald thinks "beyond identity" into a space where her subjectivity as black and trans and woman—though so often it is presumed that this nexus is defined hegemonically through abjection and death; the syntactic instantiation of black trans woman as emergent only in their heightened proximity to death and violence—is imagined beyond this legible identity as something that is yet to exist: black trans life, through and through, unfettered by terror. McDonald imagines herself in excess of black trans deathboundedness without jettisoning how violence pervades black trans experience. As Green, McDonald, and Ellison write, "The re-memory work Black trans, gender non-conforming and gender fluid writers, artists, dreamers, thinkers, performers, and activists are doing is multifaceted: we have to remember against modes of remembering that forget how transgender . . . is grounded in the materialities of anti-black racism and Black resistance." There is a shift, however, a shift toward something that I might argue is more foundational: "We *also*," they say, "have to actively forget ways of seeing and remembering ourselves and communities as nothing: we have to practice being as an active attempt to forget what we look like through Western eyes."[48]

> I am alive.
> And I have died
> An infinite death.
> I am here.

McDonald is alive even though she has died an infinite death. She is still here, an echo of Miss Major's oft-quoted assertion that she is "still fucking here." Green, McDonald, and Ellison's commentary on the poem notes that "life and death are written and re-written through struggle and articulated via praxis," making death and life always malleable, always shifting in meaning.[49] Death only wins, so to speak, when the work ceases, when it is deemed impossible that things will change. They continue, "If death is a lurking shadowy presence that attempts to parameterize life through the metric of time, then how are we living outside of time and the quantum logics of civilization?" Fugitive hope is the living outside of time and civilization because it yearns for something not legible in current frameworks. And that happens in what Treva Ellison calls "an anti-social social" created by transgender, gender nonconforming, and gender-fluid people: nonbiological and nonnuclear kinship formations, "crafting ranges of genders and vectors of desire and pleasure that vex binaristic and explanatory logics," imaginative remembrances and critically fabulated memories, and "trying to forget and outlive the strictures of life, death, pain and trauma." This is all, as Ellison concludes, neither living nor dead nor living-dead—it is "deathless."[50] We fugitively hope for a deathless world.

This rejection of the necropolitical frame motivates Erin Durban-Albrecht's trans Haitian narrativity. Durban-Albrecht's intentional movement "alongside and beyond" death-bound narratives of blackness understands blackness and its constitutive transness as excessive of death and violence, constituted by and through life—those "life-building strategies of survival" specifically for trans Haitian lives. Durban-Albrecht indexes a fugitively hopeful outlook by focusing explicitly on "unsettl[ing] the proximity of black and death," the living archive, and thinking black trans subjectivity through this frame.[51] They (Durban-Abrecht) ultimately hunker down in the life of fugitive hope, as it reaches for the vestiges of life that are themselves worlds and reveal that this world must recognize that we are not going to lay down and die.

McDonald again:

> And whether it be.
> By me.
> The world.
> The love of my life.
> I push.
> To live.
> Seen and unseen
> Thriving.
> Striving.

No matter where the specter of death comes from, because it can come from anywhere, she still pushes to live. It does not have to be seen, or unseen, because its efficacy is not predicated on optics that we know. It is a living that thrives and strives, a living that comes about in escaping the very logics of life and death defined by normative rubrics; it is a living that comes from multitudinous rupture. Multitudinous black and trans life "script[s] that alternative/surprise ending," an ending that must be capped with a question mark because we cannot know what it has in store for us. Black and trans convergence is somethin' else, you know, because "it is a simultaneous living in spite of and in intimate partnership with death, premature and otherwise, that we Black Trans, gender non-conforming, and non-binary writers, artists, thinkers, makers, and doers, be. We be making ways out of no way, rising as the phoenix do and bowing knees prayin' like granny too. We believe that we can do all things, *all the things*, through our Black radical feminist fierceness."[52]

Angela Davis says:

> But as I always like to say, we have to act as if it is possible to build a revolution and to radically transform the world.[53]

James Baldwin says:

> One is responsible to life.[54]

Assata Shakur says:

> I believe in living.
> . . . .
> I believe in life.[55]

Nahum Dimitri Chandler says:

> For, we must prepare ourselves to practice a commitment to that which is otherwise than what has for too long been understood under the heading of death; instead, we must practice an inhabitation of that non-place beyond the thought of death as a form otherwise than being.[56]

Imani Perry says:

> I have never believed in theories of social death.[57]

Greg Burris says:

> No system of thought—no social science, no economic model, no governing ideology—is ever as hegemonic or dominant as we pretend it is, and there are always cracks in the ruling regime, holes and gaps from which other forms of thinking, being, and imagining can emerge. [The] project is thus a radically open-ended one, and [it] refuses to give existing structures and institutions the final say.[58]

Keguro Macharia says:

> . . . the noose the bullet the lynching the poisoning
> the bombing the camps the mass graves the
> killing that makes futures difficult

but not impossible

never impossible.[59]

Kokumo says:

> and what is death, to a muthafuckin' Phoenix
> when resurrection, is your morning yawn
> you arise each day after they kill your spirit, hopes, and sanity
> and still manage to find enough of it to keep moving on
> you have survived trips across the ocean in ships
>   that you should never have known
> whips dancing on your back fasta' than
>   Step N' Fetchet combined
> and dodged bullets like the rain
> and now
> here you are
> standing in front of the world
> daring it to bring on the next apocalypse
> because when the bombs make impact and the smoke clears
> there you will be
> Black, trans, and still breathing[60]

Julia R. Wallace and Kai M. Green say:

> There are indeed other ways of being and knowing that challenge the notions of a pathological native.[61]

Roderick Ferguson says:

> [Vincent] Harding was standing before a class at Spelman, doing what he usually did, talking about how "slavery had dehumanized our people." And then he said, "That day something moved me to ask myself: who are these young people before me? These are the great-great grandchildren of those folks I'm saying were dehumanized. If those folks had truly been dehumanized, then these students wouldn't be here. There wouldn't be anybody out there struggling, washing, scrubbing, stealing, hustling to make sure they were here. There would have been no tradition in the family that said, 'You've got to be there.' There would have been no encouragement that said, 'Get out of bed in the morning; you've got to go to school.'" Here Harding rebuts those discourses—seductive as they

are, erudite as they seem—that tried to reduce black life to its social repressions. This determination to meet life with life is a vital ingredient.[62]

Saidiya Hartman says:

The significance of becoming or belonging together in terms other than those defined by one's status as property, will-less object, and the not-quite-human should not be underestimated. This belonging together endeavors to redress and nurture the broken body; it is a becoming together dedicated to establishing other terms of sociality, however transient, that offer a small measure of relief from the debasements constitutive of one's condition.[63]

Shit, it don't even matter if you're black and poor, because you are here and you are alive and all these folks surrounding you encourage you and persuade you to believe that you are beautiful too. This collective endeavor to *live free* unfolds in the confines of the carceral landscape. They can see the wall being erected around the dark ghetto, but they still want to be ready for the good life, still want to get ready for freedom.[64]

Ashlee Marie Preston says:

We were, are, and will always be here, unapologetically holding space. . . . We're now shifting toward an existence that knows no boundaries. We are no longer accepting censorship over our identities. The process of erasure begins in the mind and works its way outward. It guts us of our potential, dreams, and our sense of self. We can combat it by imagining ourselves in places other than an open casket.[65]

Shea Diamond says:

I refused to believe I couldn't be successful because I'm trans. I refused to believe that was the end. There were family members who said I wouldn't make it, friends who said I wouldn't make it because I was trans. They tried to get me to de-transition. I had to prove that I was possible.[66]

Cherise Morris says:

How does it feel to be a **possibility**? they ask me
it's an-always-kind-of-knowing
I'm here.
it's *an-always-sort-of-knowing   we will always be here*
and that there would be no *here* without us.[67]

José Esteban Muñoz says:

> As strongly as I reject reproductive futurity, I nonetheless refuse to give up on concepts such as politics, hope, and a future that is not kid stuff.[68]

Adrienne Kincaid says:

> This is the story of a black transgender lesbian. Before you steel yourself for a long litany of pain, let me not bury the lede; this piece is largely innocent of the long litany of pain. Part of why I wrote this is because I can tell a story about transition and, while being perfectly honest, have not a scene that involves the back of a police car, or being arrested for prostitution, or even engaging in any kind of sex work. There's no period of homelessness and no vignettes where I wake up in a hospital, lucky to be alive. My life is quotidian and it is that very character that makes my story worth telling. . . .
>
> To hear the Internet tell it, black transgender women only have one of two fates—celebrity or a desperate, marginal existence ending lonely, too young, and possibly violently. Laverne Cox, Janet Mock, or one of the many black transgender women who were murdered in 2015. There is another possible future.[69]

Dixa Ramírez D'Oleo says:

> What are the usual responses to foreign Afro-descended subjects, or mixed-raced subjects born in the United States, when these subjects insist on self-descriptors [or a paraontological understanding of blackness] . . . ? The retort is, "Would a cop hesitate to shoot you just because your mother is Thai?," as people joked about Tiger Woods, or "Would a cop hesitate to shoot you just because you grew up in Martinique and insist on saying you're Martinican instead of African American?" If this is the case, then blackness seems to be defined by the authority figure, especially at a moment of potential violence.
>
> The cop would not hesitate.
>
> But having the military power to end our lives is not the same as having the power of being the word of "God." When did those of us interested in defying white supremacy collectively decide that the white supremacist hail—from the cop, the nurse, the teacher, the president—had the ontological power to define us?[70]

Aaryn Lang says:

> When we remember trans people, we must understand that we've lived
> first. That we have loved and been loved in return. That we made art,
> raised families, made our mamas proud, and fought for our people.
> Every day a trans person gets to wake up and pursue their dreams,
> that legacy breathes on. Expanding what we believe love, justice, and
> affirmation for trans life looks like is not just convicting murderers,
> or being featured on magazine covers. It's also, as Miss Major Griffin
> Gracy says, "the personal things"—the things that we all live for, to be
> able to experience our lives to the fullest. Trans people need to know
> we're being murdered, yet we've also been thriving throughout. We are
> our ancestors' wildest dreams coming true, and this is what I allow to
> lead the way.[71]

Nat Raha says:

> A politics of intersectional feminism, anti-colonialism, anti-capitalism
> and prison abolition exist in opposition to the establishment and lib-
> eral status quo. Radical transfeminism has been claimed as the banner
> for this, with the understanding that another world is necessary and
> is already being created in which trans lives may flourish. This is a life
> praxis that understands the everyday of trans lives as struggles against
> transmisogyny and sexism, white supremacy and precarious work; that
> understands the herstory of trans and queer struggles as rooted in this.
> This is a politics that must understand the centrality of anti-colonial
> and migrant struggles and black liberation to the transformation of the
> world; that trans women of colour—and our experiences—are funda-
> mental. This is an activism that understands solidarity with disabled
> people and sex workers must be part of its constitution; that supports
> and builds alliances with people fighting for safer and self-determined
> working conditions for sex workers free from police harassment, many
> of who[m] are trans people—and that creates space for the articulation
> of knowledge, experiences and creativity from those most marginalised
> in an ableist world. This is a world-making practice articulating a fresh,
> politicised culture as we develop a consciousness of diverse trans expe-
> riences, expressed through art, poetry, film and performance. This is a
> trans politics and praxis that answers to the challenges of our time, to
> challenge the fundamental, structural inequalities of the "wrong soci-
> ety" [Juliet] Jacques astutely highlights we are trapped within.[72]

Cameron Awkward-Rich says:

> Sometimes you don't die
> when you're supposed to[73]

Fred Moten says:

> But, somehow, we have lived, and continue to live, in a climate that
> doesn't support life. It is as if black social life breathes out the air it needs
> to live in the pockets and folds and spaces it makes, despite seemingly
> irresistible external pressure and internal strife.[74]

Hortense Spillers says:

> I am really not a pessimist, of the Afro or any other sort, and continue to
> believe that as long as we are conscious of what is happening to us, we
> have a chance. There are no excuses now. We do not know everything,
> but we know enough, from the dangerously shifting biomass and the
> massive damage we do to our planet and its ecological systems daily,
> down to diet and health. But where's the determination to handle what
> we do know? . . . Here we are once more. At a beginning, and perhaps we
> will find the wherewithal to rise in joy to meet it, despite our knees! As
> feminists, our work is, as usual, cut out for us.[75]

WON'T DIE THINGS

Zora Howard's poem "Won't Die Things," a veritable praise song for black
excessive life, discursively manifests an abjected subjectivity as in possession of "rebellious lungs" and "riotous blood." We live through the demands
of black trans feminism by "beef[ing] with death" because it is death that
seeks to lay claim to and subjectivate us, but will not and cannot.[76] In excess of "the expropriative violences of the post-Enlightenment" because
its characteristic ether—its won't die-ness, as it were—"countermythically
moves alongside wounded black flesh as the safe house and harbor at
world's end."[77] Insofar as corporeal extermination via legal and extralegal
means is a profound regulation of blackness, the fugitive hope I affix to
blackness indexes "blackness's very deregulatedness," a life in/on the run J.
Kameron Carter and Sarah Jane Cervenak designate as a "queer generativity" that arises with a being accosted by the inadequacy of regulative forces.

Won't die things are enabled by their subjectivation through what Carter and Cervenak call "parahuman life": "Life not caught in the stultifying state framework of a life/death binary."[78] Death and the state's regulated iterations of "life" are inadequate to these things that are things that won't die. In refusing death, these won't die things implicitly assert that they, too, can claim life in this world.

This is not to slander the axiom of pervasive black and trans death or the legitimacy of mourning, but rather to assert *that we live*. I want to insert fugitive hope as designation of a black and trans and feminist *won't* die-ness—an agential, volatile refusal of death, combating of death, belief in itself as that which will not submit to or be acknowledged by the logics of death. We are won't die things.

Howard's poem is an elegy, but it is one dedicated precisely to those who will not die, those who "defy the grave." She distills what the black elegy does and dramatizes black life even in black death, nullifying the very possibility of black death—blackness is that which will not die, so to elegize blackness is to always speak of life. Here is an impossible hope, a fugitive hope: even in the face of "objective," demonstrable death, still, blackness refuses death; blackness "won't stay dead somehow," which is to say will continue to live.[79] Because, indeed, "we know the fall, but we know better the flight." Fundamental to the black radical tradition is inexhaustibility, that "irrepressible response to social injustice" Cedric Robinson finds in the undercurrent of black radicality—a kind of unceasing, in spite of everything, hope that does not and cannot die. It is hope in the persistence, in "black life politics [that] persists, unapologetically," in the performative "repetition" of "the N****r they couldn't kill."[80] This black elegy as a poetic analytic for fugitive hope will always survive and thrive, as the colloquial saying goes, and makes clear that instead of concerning the "death-bound subject" it concerns the almost impossible liveliness of black subjectivity, of black *life*.

At the level of aspiration, how we breathe and how our heart beats, we must maintain a "stubborn heart and indignant breath," a heart that beats even after it's been pierced by smoldering lead, a breath that sucks in air as we are choked. I am speaking of the impossible, yes, I know. I am speaking of a dream, a fallacy, that has been shown yet again—and again, and again—to be untrue, our hearts stopping when we plummet to the earth after our john or our intimate partner "discovers" our transness, our breath ceasing when the state is fed up with the loosies we sold. I am speaking, though, supplementarily, of the only possibility we have. I am speaking, of course, of the possibility of us living. And I will not stop speaking of it. We, as Howard says, "don't stay dead somehow." I am speaking of that, of how we won't stay dead and exceed in and as life. I hope, against hope, fugitively, I suppose, that we won't stay dead even when they kill us. Black trans feminism's fugitive hope demands this, at least of me; it demands that we live here, otherwise, refusing to remain dead because we have to live. We have to live right here because, as Howard concludes, "We ain't goin' nowhere."

Howard: "We here, still. You hear me—we here, still!"

If I repeat myself, so be it. Black trans feminist life bears repeating. Is it (im)possible to unwaveringly maintain that the blackness of transness, the blackness of feminism, the transness of feminism, and their inverses and proliferations can mean that, as won't die things, we become "endless"? Without end, we live and live, we "is endless," Howard says. Our is-ness is constituted through endlessness, which is to say a refusal of closure; our is-ness is "boundless bow." How illuminating. The bow, or, synonymously, the hold, of the ship—the ship's underbelly—is an endlessness. It is not confinement, nor is it capture. The bow is endless, and parts of us got made there. How can one not hope, grittily so, when we've become through endlessness?

Howard: "We won't go, and sure won't go quiet. We won't go, and sure won't go quiet."

My concern is oriented not through a social life of social death, a syntactical formation that subordinates the life to a death implied to be more fundamental, but to the fundament of social life. And the social life as intensified and reworked by the force of un/gendering, by the texture of what it might mean to throttle through a becoming-black-woman, by how bodily "misalignment" and the journey of one's transition might impact how we see the fullness, nonexclusionarily, of sociality and, most important, what sociality can be. And this necessitates that we continue to live, and live differently, and gain insight into how others live differently. My concern is oxymoronic: "I'm a surviving, walking oxymoron / Obviously I can say that I am alive and I'm tryna die this way," raps hip-hop artist Royce Da 5'9".[81] Life remains even in dying; black life persists even in death.

The ways that Black femmes, in particular, and Black people, in general, create and exercise power through the production of social life and social underworlds that are always already denaturing and deforming the "world as we know it." The over-representation of social death as an axiom of Blackness also relies on a dismissal of gender and sexuality as one of the staging grounds of Black fungibility. The idea that Blackness is related to death relies on the reality of natal alienation for enslaved Black women as a defining characteristic of "Blackness as social death," but then twists that fact to render anti-Blackness as the primary structuring mode of the human project, relative to gender and sexuality, which, under this framework, become strategic modes of oppression. This logic de-particularizes and abstracts gendered anti-Black violence to do the work of rendering anti-Blackness as a universal or axiomatic theory of Blackness.[82]

Fugitive hope makes its living in the volatile den of underworlds booming with life. In these underworlds of exuberant sociality, these queer and trans "anti-social networks," "transgender, gender non-conforming, and gender-fluid people are . . . innovating kinship structures outside of nuclear family and blood frameworks, crafting ranges of genders and vectors of desire and pleasure that vex binaristic and explanatory logics, inventing memories where there are none, and trying to forget and outlive the strictures of life, death, pain and trauma."[83] These things that won't die are "wild and profusive" because "things exceed the imperative of this. Specificity, *this* event, *this* thing, *this* one inaugurates the order of things."[84] Things are *that*, Eva Hayward and Che Gossett argue, drawing on Foucault. *That*, a kind of (black) trans (feminist) (im)possibility, "is demonstrated as the exotic charm of another system of thought, is the limitation of our own, the stark impossibility of thinking that," which primes trans—"(which is always, here, about the conditions of trans life)"—as that which "works in relation/resistance/reification to colonial and racial violence."[85] Further saturating fugitive hope with the legacies and theorizations of black feminism is Denise Ferreira da Silva. In a talk titled "Hacking the Subject: Black Feminism, Refusal, and the Limits of Critique," the precursor to her article with the same title and slightly altered subtitle ("Black Feminism and Refusal beyond the Limits of Critique"), da Silva implicitly shows the black womanness elided by theorizations of blackness as equivalent to nonbeing and (social) death and adds a useful feminist intervention in the notion of refusal. She says, as if to make explicit the gendered elision of Frank B. Wilderson's "I am nothing," that "the 'no' and the 'nothing' that the *black female body* has consistently been punished for signifying" is where one should look for the nothingness of blackness. It is the black femme body, for da Silva, that is properly historicized as "nothingness."[86] Additionally, da Silva adds supplemental integrity to fugitive hope's claim to the world when she says, "Black feminism is a double refusal: the refusal to disappear and the refusal to comply," marking black feminism as a refusal to leave while simultaneously refusing to play by the rules required to stay.[87] This double refusal is a profound statement of love for and in blackness. The black feminist double refusal refuses to disappear because feminist blackness is loved enough to be seen as validly existing here, as it always has been; it refuses to comply because compliance would be to submit to antiblackness, and it loves blackness too much for that.

....

I end with a call for effusive openness and vulnerability to what comes after: a black trans feminist call for abolition and gender radicality. For, as Jennifer Nash has written, "black feminist theory"—which is, we know, another way of saying or another angle into black trans feminism—"has long been an anticaptivity project, one fundamentally invested in radical conceptions of freedom. Thus, underpinning my investment in letting go is reanimating black feminism's radical imagination, its capacity to continue to ask: What if we imagined relationships with what we cherish beyond the racially saturated conceptions of property and ownership? Can we untether care and love from ownership? Can we express our deepest and most cherished investments otherwise?"[88] There is so much we have not yet become. Black trans feminism is an opening up into those other things. We have been curtailed and ontologically hemmed, and sometimes we venerate our hemming because it is the only way we knew how to persist: to claim what has been pathologized in us. But I wish for us to imagine ourselves as more than only what has been given us; I wish for us to imagine even more than what has been taken from us—what are the things we have neither been given nor have had taken, but haven't even fathomed yet because the parameters of fathoming have been clipped? How radical do we wish our conception of freedom to be, which is to say, How radically free do we wish to be? I know we want it, but what will it mean to actually be that free, a freedom that is less concerned with unfettered access to things once forbidden and way more interested in what has never even been an option? Black trans feminism's abolitionist disposition will indeed, to bring Hartman back, make us freer than we want to be; gender radicality will make us freer than we may want to be, and it is because all of this cannot commit to partial liberation. We are all in, ripping that Band-Aid off and biting that bullet because this shit is going to hurt. I mean, why wouldn't it? We will be, in anticapturing ourselves, tearing away some fundamental parts of ourselves and leaving the only homes we've known. We have invested so much in the things we have been given, in part because capitalist logics have said that caring about something equates to an investment in it with the expectation of a return on that investment. Nash's expression of these investments otherwise is a subversion of the commitment–investment conflation, the identity–property conflation, the assumption that all we have is all we see before us. Come, radically imagine with us, with black trans feminism. Radically imagine what a world and our relation to others could be if we did not predicate sociality on transactional exchanges or violent presuppositions or ontological foreclosures or skewed life chances (indeed, *life* chances, chances for ways of being a life). Imagine what abolition will feel like, that world in which prisons and logics of captivity—all forms of captivity—are, by definition of the existence of such a world, impossible. Imagine the kinds of beings we might dream ourselves into becoming when we do not have to adhere to such narrow templates to even be given acknowledgment. Imagine that.

Hmm, imagine that. My, my, my . . .

Notes

INTRODUCTION: ABOLITION, GENDER RADICALITY

1. Readers may take note of my separation of "trans" and "feminism," uncommon among most usages of the term, which is often combined as "transfeminism." My hope is that this does not strike readers as uninformed or unethical, as, I assure you, it is not my intention to imply either of these about its usage here. I am following Julia Serano's insistence on their separation, Serano writing: *"Many trans feminists prefer spelling 'trans feminism' as two separate words, where trans is an adjective that modifies feminism. The single-word version—'transfeminism'—looks somewhat alien, and seems to suggest that this is not actually a strand of feminism but something else entirely (just as the single word 'transwomen' suggests that trans women are something other than women). Along similar lines, we do not describe people as Catholicwomen or lesbianwomen"* (emphasis in original). It is because I concur with Serano's rationale that I replicate the practice in these pages. Additionally, of note is my pervasive use of "trans" instead of "transgender." The prefixal use of "trans" rather than a more specific "transgender" or "transsexual" is intentional, since it allows for the open-endedness I seek. Following Bobby Noble and Sarah Lamble—and this thinking can be extended to blackness and black feminism—rather than as a mere "umbrella" term I am deploying "transness" as "a political approach that questions, disrupts, and transforms dominant ideas about what is normal." Because the more explicit "identity" that "transgender" signifies, and the "pedantic" distinctions between "transgender"/"transsexual"/etc. "cannot hold," as Noble says, "trans" is my preferred term because it "signif[ies] subjectivities where bodies are at odds with gender presentation, regardless of whether that mis-alignment is self-evident in conventional ways or not." See Serano, "Trans Feminism." See also Johnson, ed., *No Tea, No Shade*, 237; and Scott-Dixon, ed., *Trans/Forming Feminisms*, 102.

2. Hartman, quoted in Wilderson and Soong, "Blacks and the Master/Slave Relation," 30.

3. Villarejo, "Tarrying with the Normative," 69–70; see also Brown, "World on Fire," 581–82. Villarejo clarifies further: "In its most benign form [normativity] appears as a bullying insistence toward obedience to social law and hierarchy, and in its most lethal form it carries the punishment of death for resistance to them. In my view, queer theory brings immense resources to the analysis of, engagement with, and critique of normativity, resources precisely calibrated to the degree to which 'queer' is deployed as a catachresis, as a metaphor without an adequate referent." Brown also brings in black feminism as integral to queerness, writing, "Radical black feminisms, my subject in this essay, are already queer, as they critique normativity and normativizing processes."

4. Tate, *Psychoanalysis and Black Novels*, 10.

5. Preciado, *Testo Junkie*, 107; see also Lauretis, "Eccentric Subjects"; Chandler, *X*; and Bey, *Problem of the Negro*.

6. Puar, *Terrorist Assemblages*, 213. There is also a way that intersectionality might, as Mark Rifkin explains in his meditation on black and indigenous "irreducible differences," advance as if, say, one's race and gender "have determinate boundaries . . . [which] can end up reifying those boundaries in ways that not only rigidify" them but also naturalize them. As Anna Carastathis has noted, some models of intersectionality "also naturalize politicized identities, constructing the boundaries between groups as pre-given and obscuring their genealogies," such as the shifting and nebulous ways the very meaning of "black" and "woman" have come to emerge. See Rifkin, *Fictions of Land and Flesh*, 33.

7. See, for example, T. Ellison, "Flex, Conjure, Crack."

8. This is a bit of a vexed subject, one I have long avoided. It used to be (and somewhat still is) a common practice, especially back in the 1990s and early 2000s, for those in critical race theory or feminist/gender studies, if they were not of color and/or women, to make clear that they were *not* of color and/or women and could never know those realities. That is, white people studying "race" and cis men studying "gender" or "feminism" would often make clear, to sometimes spectacular and yawn-worthy effect, the limits of their epistemological reach due to their identity. There is a monstrously large archive of text after text noting how one's whiteness disallows them from *really* knowing what the life of blackness is like or how one's (biological? assigned?) maleness disallows them from knowing the depths of women's lives. All of this is fine, I suppose. It is, however, something I have not really done.

And why is this? On one hand, the aforementioned rhetorical moves often struck me as disingenuous at worst and nowhere-going at best. The same song and dance—I'm white so I can't know black stuff, or I'm a dude so I can't know woman stuff, and, later in the game, I'm cis so I can't know trans stuff—got old very quickly, seeming perfunctory and cordoned off from the theorizing or intellectual work that followed (which I must admit was much more interesting to me). And now I'm putting my own song and dance, as non–sing-songy and non-dancey as I might think it is, into my own text, albeit in an endnote, which I hope you know, reader, is intentional; let me not make another spectacle likes the ones I feel so iffy about. On the other hand, I am still unsure as to where my "identity" lies, and to what I may lay "claim." For instance, I am black. That has never been questioned, as I identify as and am identified as black all the time. After this, things get tricky (or maybe *because* of this they do). I would not be as unwavering in saying that I am "straight," though "gay" does not accurately capture me in any substantive way, nor does "bisexual" or "pansexual." I have come to find a comfortable kind of home in "queer," though many would say that my sexual history (which is not to say, at least for me, that queerness is only concerned with sexuality) does not qualify me for queerness. My queerness comes from a commitment to gender self-determination and the axiom that gender cannot be determined simply by looking at the body. To say that I understand myself through queerness is to say that I may be (and have been) attracted to a non-op trans man or trans woman, or a trans woman who passes as cis but is adamant about holding onto the transness of her womanness, or a nonbinary person, all of which do not map onto straightness. It would be at the very least simply *off* to say that I am straight when, say, expressing attraction for a trans woman, as it would possibly, in a sense, disqualify her transness from being *constitutive* of the body and identity to which I am attracted.

I do not intend to do that thing, you know, where ostensibly "straight" people perform their lament of their straightness—*Oh, god! Straight people are so problematic, so basic, and I hate that I'm one of them. I wish I could just, you know, not be.* I kind of get it, I do: it seems at times *politically* necessary to distance oneself from heterosexuality, and its accompanying cisnormativity, in order to be sufficiently radical and given to liberatory politics. I don't want to knock y'all for that desire. But this skews too close, for me, to a biological determinism and the retroactive naturalization and purported inherency of a sexuality that is in fact a historicized construction. Sexuality is not some innate thing, with its parameters all in place beforehand. That is not to say one can choose to be gay or straight or bi or pan; rather, it is to say that straightness and gayness and bi-ness are predicated on historically and culturally delimited understandings and requisites for where one locates both one's sexuality as well as where one locates the operative erogenous hotspots on one's desired object. To the first part, I wish to quote Eve Sedgwick: "It is a rather amazing fact that, of the very many dimensions along which the genital activity of one person can be differentiated from that of another (dimensions that include preference for certain acts, certain zones or sensations, certain physical types, a certain frequency, certain symbolic investments, certain relations of age or power, a certain species, a certain number of participants, and so on) precisely one, the gender of the object choice, emerged from the turn of the century, and has remained, as *the* dimension denoted by the now ubiquitous category of 'sexual orientation.'" "Sexual orientation" or "sexuality" is the product of an a priori delimitation and foreclosure of other weighted criteria that might have come to take the lead in determining it. See Sedgwick, *Epistemology of the Closet*, 8. Emphasis in original.

(Not to mention, too, that my sexual desire, and the desire of those given to sexual and gender radicality, is one very much unconcerned with reiterating the script of one's ostensible sexual identity according to a given definition of proper usage of sex organs, proper identification of sex organs, proper alignment of sex organs between partners, and proper connotations and implications resultant of proper usage, identification, and alignment. This would be what Paul Preciado calls "realists," "genitalists," or "straight/homosexual 'naturalists.'" By contrast, I and the sexual and gender radicalist approach sexuality (if it can be called such) on untethered and unfixed grounds, being and becoming "those for whom the organ (biological or synthetic, alive or technosemiotically incorporated) is merely the interface by which they access certain forms of pleasure or affects that can't be represented by sexual difference, gender, or sexual identity." These are called, in Preciado's lexicon, countersexualists. Abolition and gender radicality asserts a countersexual relation to imposed ontological sexual identities. See Preciado, *Countersexual Manifesto*, 9–10.

To the second point—that of where one locates erogenous hotspots on desired objects—that we can say one's gender does not reside in perinatal gender assignation (not least of which is to say that genitals, themselves not readily given to transparent meanings as "penises" or "vaginas" [perhaps the "or" should also be in scare quotes], are largely hidden from view when one even determines their sexual attraction to another person or thing) means that how we *know* the gender of our desired object is mired in something(s) that have, as it were, been prechewed. In short, to "be" a "man" attracted to other "men" bypasses that where one locates, reads, sees, *knows* another's "manness" is tainted from the start, which is to say our sexualities, though feeling so deeply rooted, are damn dirty liars. Take Judith Butler on this front: "Anatomy is a *condition* of sexual fantasy, but it also gets radically transfigured"—an apt phrase, considering chapter 3 of this book—"by sexual fantasy, so I think we would be making a big mistake if we thought that the sex between Barry Winchell [a proclaimed straight man] and his lover [a drag performer] was straight or was gay." Butler continues:

> I'm not sure we can say. I'm not sure we *should* say. It may well be that it is romantically and even sexually very straight for both of them, extremely straight, even though there are two penises in play. That just means that the *meaning* of the penis is going to be transfigured within the sexual scene. Or that penis may well be put out of play; we don't know what kind of play it was in. But if it's put *into* play, the question is, 'In the service of what sexual fantasy is it put into play?' For example, think about *Boys Don't Cry*. Are we going to say that Teena Brandon/Brandon Teena was having straight sex with her girlfriend/his girlfriend? Or is it lesbian sex? My sense is that their sex puts the distinction into crisis and that it is probably all the more interesting and exciting by virtue of the fact that it eludes the categories that are available for it. Where's anatomy in that? (J. Butler, in Olson and Worsham, "Changing the Subject," 756. Emphasis in original.)

In fact, the meaning of genitals is radically displaced when we interrogate their role, the affixed subjects, and their function, which dissolves the question of sexuality, indeed, into a question itself. One cannot maintain the discrete categories of homosexual or heterosexual, for example, unless cisnormativity is maintained, a cisnormativity that necessarily violates aberrant subjectivities and identifications. Thus, with my own nebulous and timid nonbinariness, my they/them pronouns (see below), and with the nebulousness of others' identifications and somatic meanings, sexuality cannot be so vociferously clutched as if innocent. In part what I am arguing is that to presume the innocence of sexuality is to overlook its violation of otherwise identifications that have not been sanctioned by what Butler would term the heterosexual matrix, or, put differently, cisheteronormativity.

Neither am I so sure I would identify as "cisgender" or "cis," though most would say I surely do not qualify for transgender or transness. Sure, there have been a decent number of occasions when someone assumed that I was transgender because of the work that I do (fourteen times [that I know of], and counting), and sure I use and am hailed sometimes by they/them pronouns and think my subjectivity through nonbinariness, but does that mean I have "access" to saying that I "am" trans? But before answering so quickly, two things must be noted: first, that it is well known, at least in trans studies, that transness is not simply, or even primarily, about *being* a certain kind of (gendered) body. Transness lies elsewhere, in short. Can one "access" transness and be validly woven through the subjectivity of transness via other realms that both lie outside the body and that *assert the meaning of the body in a radically different way*? Can bodiness itself be transed by the engendering of sociality and interpersonal semiotic meaning-making in ways not beholden to the normativities of this world? Second, because of my blackness and the fact that blackness makes for gender trouble—that blackness's somatic endowment and its anoriginal desedimentary problematizing of ontological mandates are not given over readily, or perhaps at all, in the gender binary, in cisness, per Hortense Spillers and Che Gossett and Kai M. Green and C. Riley Snorton and Diane Detournay and Hari Ziyad and, and, and . . . —am I automatically unable to claim cisgender status even if I wanted (which, to be sure, I so vehemently do not)? (Though someone like Savannah Shange would say that it is not a matter of jamming black people into the category of cisgender, which black people and blackness do not fit within, but rather one of recognizing that we are *nontrans*, which acknowledges the cisness disallowed black people and blackness but does not relegate those who might otherwise be called cis to the status of trans, relinquishing them, unjustifiably, from what could be called "cisgender privilege.") I, though, am not simply talking about privileges and double standards; it is, and must be, about different and differing modes of subjectivity.

So, where I'm at right now is understanding myself in the following way: I am black, or more accurately, I do blackness, a kind of categorical irreverence unwilling to abide normative impositions; I am not straight, though neither am I gay or bi or pan, but perhaps I do queerness, which is to say, *I have a queer relationship to sexuality*; and I am not trans per se but enact subjectivity in ways that seek a trans and transed engendering of sociality, or inter- and intrapersonality, which is to say *I have a trans relationship to gender.*

9. Glissant, *Poetics of Relation*, 190.

10. I take this phrase from Fred Moten's "Case of Blackness." Moten writes, somewhat famously, "What is inadequate to blackness is already given ontologies. The lived experience of blackness is, among other things, a constant demand for an ontology of disorder, an ontology of dehiscence, a para-ontology whose comportment will have been (toward) the ontic or existential field of things and events" (187).

11. I draw here from Hurston's *Mules and Men*, in which she writes, "The Negro offers a feather-bed resistance. That is, we let the probe enter but it never comes out. It gets smothered under a lot of laughter and pleasantries" (2–3).

12. Raha, "Radical Transfeminism."

13. Raha, "Radical Transfeminism."

14. "Interview: Kai M. Green."

15. Anderson, *Beyond Ontological Blackness*, 11; see also J. K. Carter, *Race*, 159.

16. Halberstam, *Trans**, 8.

17. *Radcliffe College Monographs*, 31.

18. "Fugitive Slave Act" (U.S. Constitution, 1793); "Fugitive Slave Act" (U.S. Constitution, 1850).

19. See Bey, *Problem of the Negro*, specifically the chapters "Paraontology" and "Uninscriptions."

20. Harney and Moten, *Undercommons*, 47.

21. J. K. Carter, "Black Malpractice," 86, 69.

22. N. Butler, *Under False Colors*.

23. See N. Butler, *Under False Colors*.

24. Collins, *Black Feminist Thought*, 15. Emphasis in original.

25. See Gill-Peterson's *Histories of the Transgender Child*, 122. She writes: "It makes sense to say that in its invention gender *was* a form of race. The morphology of the sexed and gendered body was a racial formation in [John] Money's schema of development. Put more simply, gender was a phenotype, much as sex had been during the preceding fifty years" (emphasis in original).

26. See N. Butler, *Under False Colors*. This information is found in the *Charleston Courier*, November 18, 1859, page 4, first column. Interestingly, too, Wilson was identified as "the same gay lothario who was discovered showing the cloven foot in Charleston very recently." It seems that "gay lothario," whether accurate as to how Wilson would identify or not, is a kind of stand in for gender transgression. That is, the language of transness or transgender was unavailable to them to describe Wilson's gender enactments,

so "gay lothario" might be the closest approximation to this—it was the only available spot in the "grid of intelligibility," in Ann Stoler's nomenclature.

27. Lamble, "Transforming Carceral Logics," 254.

28. Shange, *Progressive Dystopia*, 10.

29. Stanley, Spade, and Queer (In)Justice, "Queering Prison Abolition, Now?," 122. Emphasis added.

30. Gossett, "Abolitionist Imaginings," 330. Emphasis in original.

31. Harney and Moten, *Undercommons*, 7. See also Halberstam, "Wildness, Loss, Death"; and Halberstam and Nyong'o, "Introduction."

32. Adkins, "Black/Feminist Futures," 718.

33. Adkins, "Black/Feminist Futures," 719.

34. See Puar, "I Would Rather Be a Cyborg," 49. Puar writes at the outset of the essay, which I draw on here, "'Grids happen,' writes Brian Massumi, at a moment in *Parables for the Virtual* where one is tempted to be swept away by the endless affirmative becomings of movement, flux, and potential, as opposed to being pinned down by the retroactive positioning of identity (2002, 8). For the most part, Massumi has been less interested in how grids happen than in asking how they can un-happen, or not happen." See also Steinbock, *Shimmering Images*, 12. Steinbock writes: "The greater challenge of transgender studies would be to stay with the indefinite period or moment in suspension from the gridded paradigm, while fully acknowledging a tendency or intensity that suggests direction, location, context. With gender transition comes a potential bodily change through self-multiplication across the shimmering passage of unresolvable disjunction in which we all live and breathe."

35. cárdenas, "Dark Shimmers."

36. Quoted in Antwi, *Words of Power*, 73.

37. Walker, "In Search of Our Mothers' Gardens," 402.

CHAPTER 1. BLACK, TRANS, FEMINISM

1. Davis and Lowe, "Interview," 318.

2. J. Butler, *Gender Trouble*, xx.

3. J. Butler, *Gender Trouble*, xxi.

4. Yes, *they.* Think about it: Butler has written, with notable and, I would argue, intentional first-person point of view, "If *I* do not recognize myself as 'she,' does that mean that I fail to recognize that someone seeks to interpellate me within that pronoun?" While the conditional "If" opening the sentence shuttles the question into the proximity of a discursive gesture to illustrate a point, it remains that Butler is un-

derstanding this to apply personally, that this is a moment that *Butler* is expressing via Butler's own experience. See J. Butler, *Senses of the Subject*, 12. Emphasis added.

But in further support of my choice of pronoun here is a talk Butler gave at a workshop hosted by the School of Philosophy at University College Dublin, in conjunction with the Society for Women in Philosophy, on February 6, 2015. During this talk Butler read excerpts from the then-forthcoming *Senses of the Subject*. After reading the above passage, in an aside Butler noted that "maybe people do 'prefer' pronouns now and they state them—I ask sometimes, actually, at the beginning of classes, 'How do you want to be referred to?' and people let me know and I follow that respectfully. *I, myself, don't actually have a preference*, which, I think, makes me a little bit out of sync with the times." Butler, in other words, is pronoun indifferent.

But, lastly, in a final evidentiary flourish, I think here of Jack Halberstam's remarks in "Nice Trannies" in which he writes of Butler: "By any number of metrics, Butler is trans, is a gender-non-conforming subject." Because of all this, it seems to me that a "they" pronoun is quite appropriate to use in reference to Butler.

5. J. Butler, *Gender Trouble*, xxi.

6. See Samatar, "Against the Normative World"; Crawley, "Otherwise Movements"; see also Crawley, *Lonely Letters*, specifically 79 and 197; and da Silva, *Toward a Global Idea*. More specifically, in "Otherwise Movements," which was published just a few months before his interview "Against the Normative World," Crawley writes, "black performance produces an ethical demand for critical commentary, critical change that is radical, change that is grounded and founded in the capacity for any song, any dance, any word to be otherwise than it is. This demand for change, change that is founded in movement, in vibration, produces a critique of the normative world."

I might also make a quick reference to King, Navarro, and Smith's introduction to *Otherwise Worlds*, in which they define "otherwise" as "*in all ways except the one mentioned.*" See King, Navarro, and Smith, *Otherwise Worlds*, 10.

7. I want to make clear, too, that I want to distance myself (though readers may find this to be an inadequate move) from those on the political Right who castigate identity politics as an unthinking mob mentality, and who refuse identity politics for an extreme individualism. Such a logic, to me, seems deeply apolitical and is not at all how I wish to think here, which will hopefully be made abundantly clear. See Taylor, *How We Get Free*, 8–11.

8. Carter and Cervenak, "Black Ether," 221n17.

9. Moten and Harney, "Indent (To Serve the Debt)," 199.

10. Aizura, "Introduction," 609.

11. J. K. Carter, *Race*, 192. Carter is speaking specifically in a theological context with respect to black liberation theology, whiteness, and the Jewish, nonracial flesh of Jesus.

12. See Nash, *Black Feminism Reimagined*, 26. "I want to think about Black feminist defensiveness—which I see as a kind of ethical response to feminism's peculiar

relationship with intersectionality—as actually leaving Black feminists stalled," Nash says further, in an interview on her book. "We expend a lot of energy protecting our turf, policing its boundaries. It is this ongoing effort that I describe as 'holding on' to intersectionality. I use 'letting go,' on the other hand, to describe the risky endeavor of embracing the call to really be a non-captivity political project, to surrender the alluring project of protecting intersectionality. When I say non-captivity project, I mean that Black feminism has had a fundamental commitment to freedom—to thinking about what freedom looks and feels like, to thinking about who we are and how we relate to each other in a world where we are free." See Garcia-Rojas, "Intersectionality Is a Hot Topic."

13. Crawley, "That There Might Be Black," 124.

14. Pierce, "Feeling, Disrupting," 436; see also Ridley, "Imagining Otherly," 482.

15. Górska, *Breathing Matters*, 21.

16. Moten, *Stolen Life*, 159.

17. Green, "The Essential I/Eye in We," 191.

18. Green, "The Essential I/Eye in We," 191.

19. Thomas, "Proud Flesh Inter/Views," 18. I find support for this even in narratives about antebellum U.S. enslavement, which many often understand as possessing a dormant, simmeringly monolithic, homogenous slave rebellious spirit. That is, there is the assumption in many instances that *all* slaves despised slavery, had "freedom dreams," found inherent solidarity with every other enslaved black person if not every other black person, and wanted to either run away or kill all white people (I am admittedly being a bit hyperbolic). But consider Frederick Douglass, who writes in the third chapter of his 1845 *Narrative*, "Moreover, slaves are like other people, and imbibe prejudices quite common to others. They think their own better than that of others. Many, under the influence of this prejudice, think their own masters are better than the masters of other slaves; and this, too, in some cases, when the very reverse is true. Indeed, it is not uncommon for slaves even to fall out and quarrel among themselves about the relative goodness of their masters, each contending for the superior goodness of his own over that of the others" (12).

20. See T. Ellison, "Labor of Werqing It," 1.

21. Rickards, "Watch." Further support for this point, and Walker's, is recognition that "there were black people with rounded features and thick hair, and other blacks with angular features, high cheekbones, golden skin, and hair that they could sit on, as the folks would say." See Ferguson, "To Catch a Light-Filled Vision," 321. Nyong'o's quote comes from Nyong'o, *Afro-Fabulations*, 125.

And further still, in Du Bois's *Dusk of Dawn*, he writes, "Within the Negro group especially there were people of all colors." Epidermal color, in short, is not a sufficient or reliable anchor for locating one's blackness.

22. Da Silva, "Toward a Black Feminist Poethics," 86; see also McDonald and Tinsley, "Go beyond Our Natural Selves." Da Silva in particular, I would argue, also echoes Barbara Ransby's black feminism, which is less about the politics arising from one's identity, "not a kind of essentialism notion that your body determines your politics," which she remarks in the context of a panel discussion of the Comba- hee River Collective's foundational Black Feminist Statement. Gosztola, "Authors of Combahee River Statement," n.p.

Also, McDonald, in context, writes: "I ask that you all will not leave your can- vases undone. Use every color imaginable to show who you are inside and out, for every tint and every hue counts. And as you create your picture remember you are the illustrator, so no one can create your picture but you. So make it the most precious and most beautiful picture that you can, with love, truth, and joy in every color" (251).

23. Moten, "Blackness and Nothingness," 774. Emphasis added.

24. Walker, "In the Closet of the Soul," 545, 540; see also Corsani, "Beyond the Myth of Woman," 113.

25. Garza, "Herstory of the #BlackLivesMatter Movement." I must note, before I get called out for that move of saying "So much has been said about *x* topic" and then leaving it at that, some of the people I have in mind: Ntozake Shange, Michele Wallace, Toni Morrison, the Combahee River Collective, Angela Davis, Audre Lorde, Mary Helen Washington, Keeanga-Yamahtta Taylor, and the list could go on.

26. See Combahee River Collective, "Black Feminist Statement"; Segal, "Genera- tions of Feminism," 6.

27. Segal, "Generations of Feminism," 6. Specifically, Segal is speaking of the fifty or so women of color based in New York and Oakland, as well as other black activists of the mid-twentieth-century, who got left out of the narrative but were not *not* in the historical labor of feminist worldmaking; for black feminism's radical inclusivity, see Stallings, "Black Feminism."

28. Ellison et al., "We Got Issues," 166.

29. First, see Nash, *Black Feminism Reimagined*, 5. She writes, "I advance a concep- tion of black feminism that is expansive, welcoming anyone with an investment in black women's humanity, intellectual labor, and political visionary work, anyone with an investment in theorizing black genders and sexualities in complex and nu- anced ways. My archive of black feminist theorists includes black, white, and nonblack scholars of color who labor in and adjacent to black feminist theory. My contention is that these varied black feminist scholars can all speak on and for black feminist theory, and as black feminist theorists, even as they make their claims from different identity locations."

Additionally, see Gill-Peterson's discussion in *Histories of the Transgender Child* in which she touches on, drawing from the work of Chela Sandoval, how we ought to constantly caution "against this persistent problem, where minority forms of knowledge such as black feminist theory, queer of color critique, or indigenous epistemologies are misrecognized as correlate to a particular identitarian scope that reduces their sphere of applicability, rather than constituting 'a theoretical and methodological approach in [their] own right.'" See Gill-Peterson, *Histories*, 29.

30. Spillers, "Scholarly Journey." Emphasis added.

31. See Zeisler, *We Were Feminists Once*, specifically chapter 1.

32. Snorton, "Transfiguring Masculinities."

33. Boellstorff et al., "Decolonizing Transgender."

34. Snorton, *Black on Both Sides*, 184.

35. Raha, "Transfeminine Brokenness."

36. Garriga-López, "Transfeminism."

37. Espineira, "Q Comme Questions," 114.

38. Awkward-Rich, "Trans, Feminism," 833; see also J. Butler, "Against Proper Objects," 8. Specifically, Butler writes, "what is incisive and valuable in feminist work is precisely the kind of thinking that calls into question the settled grounds of analysis. And even the recourse to sexual difference within feminist theory is at its most productive when it is taken not as a ground, foundation, or methodology, but as a *question* posed but not resolved."

39. Hill-Collins, "Black Feminist Thought," 141–42. Collins writes, "I take issue with Bey's suggestion that blacktransfeminist thought is so distinctive from Black feminist thought that a new name is needed."

40. Koyama writes on her FAQs page, "Emi does not identify with any particular gender, but she does not so strongly identify with the state of having no gender to claim that as an identity either. Honestly, she thinks that having an identity— especially gender identity—is kind of weird." See "Frequently Asked Questions," Eminism.org, accessed March 11, 2021, https://eminism.org/faq/basic.html.

41. All references in this paragraph are from Koyama, "Transfeminist Manifesto."

42. Corsani, "Beyond the Myth of Woman," 109. Emphasis added.

43. Barrow et al., "Models of Futurity," 323.

44. Outrans, "Transféminismes."

45. Kaas, "Birth of Transfeminism," 148–49. Emphasis in original.

46. Stryker and Bettcher, "Introduction," 8; see also Halberstam, *Trans**. Finally, see Combahee River Collective, "Black Feminist Statement."

47. See Nash, "Re-Thinking Intersectionality"; and Nash, *Black Feminism Reimagined*. Encapsulatingly, Nash writes in "Re-Thinking Intersectionality,"

> One "so what" question that remains unexplored by intersectional theorists is the way in which privilege and oppression can be co-constituted on the subjective level. That is, while intersectionality purports to describe multiple margin-

alizations (i.e. the spectre of the multiply-marginalized black woman that haunts intersectionality) and multiple privileges (i.e. the spectre of the [heterosexual] white man that haunts intersectionality), it neglects to describe the ways in which privilege and oppression intersect, informing each subject's experiences.

In painting black women, for example, as wholly oppressed and marginalized, intersectional theory can not attend to variations within black women's experiences that afford some black women greater privilege, autonomy, and freedom. In troubling the monolithism of "black womanhood," intersectionality could be strategically disloyal to dominant conceptions of black women as "the mules of the world," exploding the tendency of radical projects to elide critical differences *within* ostensibly marginalized subject positions. (11–12)

In *Black Feminism Reimagined*, Nash brings intersectionality specifically to bear on its relationship to black feminism, noting how black feminism has become hemmed in by defining itself through the policing of intersectionality's uses (and, I would add, policing overwhelmingly its uses by white women). After articulating the "single affect" governing black feminist politics as defensiveness—which, I will admit, we must critique, as if that is the only black feminist affect out there; a falsity, to my mind—she writes, "I treat black feminist defensiveness as manifested most explicitly through black feminism's proprietary attachments to intersectionality. These attachments conscript black feminism into a largely protective posture, leaving black feminists mired in policing intersectionality's usages, demanding that intersectionality remain located within black feminism, and reasserting intersectionality's 'true' origins in black feminist texts. This book traces how defensiveness is largely articulated by rendering intersectionality black feminist property, as terrain that has been gentrified, colonized, and appropriated" (3).

48. Espineira and Bourcier, "Transfeminism," 90.

49. Santana, "Mais Viva!," 211.

50. Santana, "Mais Viva!," 217.

51. Santana, "Mais Viva!," 217–19.

52. Bey, "Trans*-Ness of Blackness," 278.

53. da Silva, *Toward a Global Idea*, 60–61. Emphasis added.

CHAPTER 2. FUGITIVITY, UN/GENDERED

A shorter version of chapter 2 appears in the *Black Scholar* 49, no. 1 (2019), under the title "Black Fugitivity Un/Gendered."

1. Fournier, "Lines of Flight," 121. Emphasis added.

2. In "Peter's Pans: Eating in the Diaspora," the introductory chapter of Hortense Spillers's *Black, White, and In Color*, Spillers, in doing a reading of Ralph Ellison,

writes, "By revising and correcting 'blackness' into a *critical* posture, into a pre-eminent site of the 'multicultural,' long before the latter defined a new politics and polemic, and by distinguishing it from a sign called the 'American Negro' (and we can make any substitution here that might be appropriate, i.e., 'black,' 'Afro-American,' 'African-American,' as more or less the same lady and gentleman), [Ralph] Ellison harnessed 'blackness' to a symbolic program of philosophical 'disobedience' (a systematic skepticism and refusal) that would make the former available to *anyone*, or more pointedly, *any* posture, that was willing to take on the formidable task of *thinking* as a willful act of imagination and invention" (5; emphasis in original). I might mention, too, that only pages later Spillers writes that "'blackness' [i]s a series of critical postulates and the figure of 'Rineheart,'" from Ellison's *Invisible Man*, "had staged it as a caricature of *transformational* possibilities, [so] radical change would consist in the time of 'blackness' dispersed across predicates" (15; emphasis in original). This also, of course, bears a similarity to Walter Mignolo's epistemic disobedience, defined by Mignolo as a delinking. What is so beautifully pertinent to my overall discussion, too, is how Mignolo writes that those engaging in epistemic disobedience undergo "two *kinds or directions* advanced by the *former anthropos* who are no longer claiming *recognition by* or *inclusion in* the *humanitas*"—and the italics here are in the original, as if he is emphasizing the very things that concern the intellectual life of my project—which is a testament to the requisite for a decided break from the very comfort of our familiarity with our humanity. That is, Mignolo and Spillers are urging for a break, a Mignolo-esque delinking, from the precise category we think is so fundamental for our existence (being human, or Anthropos) and seeking recognition, that which constitutes our existence in the social sphere, elsewhere, by different means. To no longer seek inclusion into the *humanitas* is to find inclusion on other grounds wherein one is not encountered on the viscerally ideological grounds of the human, that of race and gender, among other embarrassingly "etc." things (per Judith Butler). Those other grounds are grounds, or maybe nongrounds, maybe McKittrick-like demonic grounds, of an abolished world, a world after our freedom. See Mignolo, "Epistemic Disobedience," 161. Emphasis in original.

3. Pinto, "Black Feminist Literacies," 27–28.

4. This aligns with Jennifer Nash's interrogation of the ways black feminists have policed the uses of intersectionality, conflating a fidelity to a presumed original intent with care and correctness. If Nash argues that care for a term and its uses means to "exercise a deep fidelity to the analytic's foundational texts," like her I seek to "interrogate *both* the claim that careful reading and textual fidelity are synonymous and the notion that certain kinds of reading practices manifest an affection for"—not only intersectionality, as is her aim, but for these superused Spillersian terms. These terms are tools, used respectfully, of course, but ultimately to engender radical subjectivities and relationalities and the like, not a mere regurgitation of the academic black feminist queen. Her ideas can move in different, unintended ways. See Nash, *Black Feminism Reimagined*, 59. Emphasis in original.

5. Spillers, "Mama's Baby, Papa's Maybe," 222.

6. The phrase "illusive flesh" that Stallings makes use of comes from Hayden's poem "Monet's Water Lillies." Stallings cites this in her discussion: "Here space and time exist in light / the eye like the eye of faith believes. / The seen, the known / dissolve in iridescence, become / illusive flesh of light / that was not, was, forever is" (213).

7. Weheliye, *Habeas Viscus*, 72, 112.

8. Horton-Stallings, *Funk the Erotic*, 206.

9. Horton-Stallings, *Funk the Erotic*, 213.

10. Spillers, "Mama's Baby, Papa's Maybe," 73.

11. Chu, *Females*, 1; see also Gabriel, "Limits of the Bit."

12. Snorton, *Black on Both Sides*, 53.

13. Benston, *Performing Blackness*, 9; Colebrook, "What Is It Like to Be a Human?"; Green, "Race and Gender Are Not the Same!"; Spillers, "Mama's Baby, Papa's Maybe." For Benston, primordial blackness references a kind of denaturalization of history as teleological, and the beginning-as-blackness is a displacement of "white mythology," which can be read in conjunction with a Chandlerian blackness (or African American subject; or Negro) that is a paraontological originary displacement or desedimentation of ontology.

Colebrook's transitivity marks a trans iteration, as it were, of anoriginal lawlessness (indexical, via someone like Moten or Nahum Chandler, of blackness). It is, in effect, a conditioning generativity that has not yet congealed into discrete identities.

Green, in brief, in thinking about the turmoil surrounding Rachel Dolezal, argues that "black has always been a porous entity. . . . Not all black people relate to the category or are marked by the category in the same way. Your blackness might not be legible in certain places perhaps because of your complexion, or language, or accent, or hair texture. . . . Black is a category that we all have the ability to move in and out of to a certain extent" (n.p.).

And, lastly, Spillers notes that black women's claim or relationship to femininity, via captive African American women, is largely "the tale writ between the lines and in the not-quite spaces of an American domesticity" (77).

14. Some readers might also understand this as conversant with Maurice Merleau-Ponty, specifically when he writes, "I become flesh only at the very edge of my perception, and can do so only under the press of the invisible and imperceptible outside that, it would seem, forms the border of that flesh. My body is visible and able to be apprehended like any object, but my flesh is not; it is bounded by my perception and extends proprioceptively into the world." While this proves fruitful and generative in the sense that flesh is distinguished from the body as something much more illegible and unapprehendable to normative rubrics, I part from this inasmuch as this account is fixated on an ocularcentric perception. Too, it seems

to presume that flesh is a matter primarily if not solely of one's own perception, by which it is bounded. This proves somewhat troubling for my account on the grounds that I want to think about a fleshiness that is more coalitional as well as not beholden to one's own perception, delimiting flesh to a knowable boundary within one's own grasp. I want to hold out for something more unknown and unanticipated, more assemblic and coalitional. See Salamon, "Place Where Life Hides Away," 103.

15. Nash, *Black Feminism Reimagined*, 104.

16. "Saidiya Hartman on Fugitive Feminism." Emphasis added.

17. Scott, "Experience," 25. Because of Scott's cogency and unflinching, though measured, critique, I wish to quote her at length:

> When the evidence offered is the evidence of "experience," the claim for referentiality is further buttressed—what could be truer, after all, than a subject's own account of what he or she has lived through? It is precisely this kind of appeal to experience as uncontestable evidence and as an originary point of explanation—as a foundation upon which analysis is based that weakens the critical thrust of histories of difference. By remaining within the epistemological frame of orthodox history, these studies lose the possibility of examining those assumptions and practices that excluded considerations of difference in the first place. They take as self-evident the identities of those whose experience is being documented and thus naturalize their difference. They locate resistance outside its discursive construction, and reify agency as an inherent attribute of individuals, thus decontextualizing it. When experience is taken as the origin of knowledge, the vision of the individual subject (the person who had the experience or the historian who recounts it) becomes the bedrock of evidence upon which explanation is built. Questions about the constructed nature of experience, about how subjects are constituted as different in the first place, about how one's vision is structured—about language (or discourse) and history—are left aside. . . .
>
> To put it another way, the evidence of experience, whether conceived through a metaphor of visibility or in any other way that takes meaning as transparent, reproduces rather than contests given ideological systems—those that assume that the facts of history speak for themselves and, in the case of histories of gender, those that rest on notions of a natural or established opposition between sexual practices and social conventions, and between homosexuality and heterosexuality. (24–25)

18. Spillers et al., "Whatcha Gonna Do?," 304.

19. It is possible and necessary to proceed without the presumption of a coherent subject of representation for our political endeavors. We needn't continually foreground that we know, in "her" totality, the black (cis? trans? non-cis/non-trans? cis *and* trans?) woman and, from this knowledge, proceed with our black trans feminist

politics on "her" behalf. No shade to Toni Cade Bambara, but "the black woman" is ultimately a phantasm that obscures the indeterminacy and complexity that rests at that nominative site, an indeterminacy and a complexity that proves much more utile for abolitionist and radical aims. The black woman "we" is a perpetually unstable category whose named forces cannot in fact be contained by the category, is indeed categorical dissolution. This instability, however, promulgates an opening up of the previous restrictions placed onto the radicalized gendered nexus toward other configurations, toward transfigurations, of not only race, not only gender, but politicized livability.

20. Escalante, "Gynecology and the Ungendering."

21. Colebrook, "Modernism without Women," 434; see also, of course, Stryker, "Transgender Studies."

22. This has been critiqued on multiple occasions by people like Christine Battersby, who has written, "Even the 'becoming-woman' of women is not something that women themselves perform. Instead, the 'becoming-woman' of women results from changes in the organisation of social structures of males, produced by social transitions within capitalism." Alice Jardine, in turn, argues that becoming is pertinent only for those who already sit comfortably within positions of power and wish to simply abdicate that power, those who are, in effect, bored with their power and need a change of pace. As Hannah Stark and Timothy Laurie write in their summative description of the matter, the risk, ultimately, is that "'becoming' contains a trap that attends any philosophical concept imported into a political situation: a desire for romantic abstraction at the expense of engagement with lived realities and the practical demands of living trans lives" or living femme/cis woman lives. See Battersby, *Phenomenal Woman*, 188; Jardine, *Gynesis*; and Stark and Laurie, "Deleuze and Transfeminism," 128.

23. Dolphijn and van der Tuin, "Thousand Tiny Intersections," 132.

24. Deleuze and Guattari, *Thousand Plateaus*, 106.

25. Deleuze and Guattari, *Thousand Plateaus*, 275.

26. See Deleuze and Guattari, *Thousand Plateaus*, 276. They write also that becoming-woman needs to be taken up by men as well. It "should produce a becoming-woman as atoms of womanhood capable of crossing and impregnating an entire social field, and of contaminating men, of sweeping them up in that becoming," which dovetails with my assertion that black trans feminism is to be taken up by anyone, that blackness can and should be taken up by those who are nonblack, that transness can and should be taken up by those who are nontrans, and that feminism can and should be taken up by those who are not its implicit white woman. On the subject of blackness, Jeffrey T. Nealon makes this very claim in "Refraining, Becoming-Black: Repetition and Difference in Amiri Baraka's *Blues People*." Drawing on Nathaniel Mackey, who remarks on the tendency of black people to enact "countering, contes-

tatory tendencies" and engage in the "movement from noun to verb," Nealon writes in a Deleuzian and Guattarian flourish: "So perhaps we could say that if this movement from noun to verb 'is' anything at all, it 'is' what we might call a *becoming*-black (rather than a hypostasized *being*-black). As Baraka writes in 'The Legacy of Malcolm X,' even 'the Black Man must aspire to Blackness'" (86).

27. Nyong'o, *Afro-Fabulations*, 199.

28. Richardson, "Ajita Wilson," 193. Richardson also notes that what constitutes one's girlhood and womanhood, as it were, is variegated and creative, as various as there are people, and that our emphasis must be on how "these are categories of self-definition and creativity and are not fixed in any one kind of body, whether or not socially recognized as 'woman'" (206n1).

29. The Nigerian scholar Oyěwùmí is critiquing the "age-old somatocentricity in Western thought," arguing ultimately that "the cultural logic of Western social categories is based on an ideology of biological determinism: the conception that biology provides the rationale for the organization of the social world. Thus, this cultural logic is actually a 'bio-logic.' Social categories like 'woman' are based on body-type and are elaborated in relation to and in opposition to another category: man; the presence or absence of certain organs determine social position." See Oyěwùmí, *Invention of Women*, x; see also Oyěwùmí, "De-Confounding Gender"; and Riley, *Am I That Name?*

30. Colebrook, "Modernism without Women," 432, 434; da Silva, "Hacking the Subject," 20.

31. Deleuze, "Letter to a Harsh Critic," 11. Emphasis in original. See also Preciado, *Countersexual Manifesto*, 147.

32. Deleuze and Guattari, *Thousand Plateaus*, 279.

33. Wright, *Physics of Blackness*, 109.

34. I have in mind here a Tweet by jade bentil (@divanificent). On March 4, 2020, bentil tweeted for a grand total of over 2800 likes: "'Listen to Black women' is such an empty, essentialist take and seeing it leveraged to legitimise imperialist and fundamentally self-serving political positions is altogether very very underwhelming" (https://twitter.com/divanificent/status/1235315503645839368).

35. Malatino, *Queer Embodiment*, 197. Emphasis in original. See also Deleuze and Guattari, *Thousand Plateaus*, 195. It may be useful to state clearly here, just in case, that becoming-black-woman is quite a "real" and material, or socially substantive, matter, not a philosophical abstraction untethered to "actual" black women. To quote Deleuze and Guattari: "A becoming is not a correspondence between relations. But neither is it a resemblance, an imitation, or, at the limit, an identification. . . . To become is not to progress or regress along a series. Above all, becoming does not occur in the imagination. . . . [It] is perfectly real. But which reality is at issue

here? For if becoming animal [or becoming-(black)-woman] does not consist in playing animal or imitating an animal [or (black) woman], it is clear that the human being does not 'really' become an animal any more than the animal 'really becomes something else.' Becoming produces something other than itself. We fall into a false alternative if we say that you either imitate or you are. What is real is the becoming itself, the block of becoming, not the supposedly fixed terms through which that which becomes passes" (237–38).

I am intrigued by this inasmuch as I am intrigued, and place an emphasis on, what the "something other than itself" is that becoming produces. If becoming-black-woman means neither that you binaristically imitate black women nor simply are a black woman, what is this something else that the becoming produces here? I am interested in that, and I think it might be described in my analytics of abolition and gender radicality.

36. See Quan's chapter "It's Hard to Stop Rebels That Time Travel," 189.

37. Williams, *Transgressive*, 44.

38. Merleau-Ponty, *Visible and the Invisible*, 139–40.

39. Mackey, *Bedouin Hornbook*, 105.

40. Mackey, *Bedouin Hornbook*, 158.

41. J. Carter, "Transition," 235–36; Snorton, *Black on Both Sides*, xiv.

42. Bhanji, "Trans/Scriptions," 515.

43. Bhanji, "Trans/Scriptions," 515. Emphasis in original.

44. Halberstam, *Female Masculinity*, 172.

45. Gessen, "To Be, or Not to Be."

46. Gossett, "Žižek's Trans/Gender Trouble."

47. Morrison, *Bluest Eye*, 138; duCille, "Of Race, Gender, and the Novel."

48. Bowen, "Discovery."

49. Harney and Moten, *Undercommons*, 50.

CHAPTER 3. TRANS/FIGURATIVE, BLACKNESS

1. Crawley, *Lonely Letters*, 234.

2. Spillers, "Idea of Black Culture," 26. Spillers writes, "In a sense, if there is no black culture, or no longer black culture (because it has 'succeeded'), then we need it now; and if that is true, then perhaps black culture—as the reclamation of the critical edge, as one of those vantages from which it might be spied, and no longer predicated on 'race'—has yet to come."

3. Snorton, *Black on Both Sides*, 59.

4. Konitshek, "Calling Forth," 17. Emphasis in original.

5. da Silva, "1 (Life)." Emphasis added. The distinction I am here highlighting is that between da Silva's categorical blackness, which for her is "always already a referent of [a] commodity, an object, and the other, as fact beyond evidence" and "serves the ordered universe of determinacy and the violence and violations it authorizes," and blackness as a formless, vital substance of matter, which, according to the black trans theorizing of Jessica Marion Modi, "nullifies ways of knowing that depend on determinacy (as well as, argues Ferreira da Silva, separability and sequentiality). As matter, it 'invites the possibility of knowing without modern categories' under which difference among humans and matter registers as separability." See Aiken, Modi, and Polk, "Issued," 434–35.

6. Cervenak and Carter, "Untitled and Outdoors," 6; see also Nash, *Black Feminism Reimagined*, 108.

7. McKittrick, "Worn Out," 99.

8. See Snorton, "Transfiguring Masculinities."

9. Howie, "On Transfiguration," 159–60.

10. Howie, "On Transfiguration," 158–59.

11. Moten, *In the Break*, 154.

12. Nyong'o, *Afro-Fabulations*, 206–7.

13. Hedva, "In Defence of De-Persons."

14. Hedva, "In Defence of De-Persons." The comment on privilege as radical incapacity for sociality is Hedva's quotation of an exchange with Fred Moten who makes that keen observation. Additionally, Hedva writes in their "About" section, regarding the body, "There is always the body, but the task is how to eclipse it, how to nebulize it, and how to cope when this inevitably fails. There is no divine purpose other than the purpose of telic nothingness and the warzone of sociality, but both make beautiful garbage, a khoratic plenum" (https://johannahedva.com/about .html, accessed March 23, 2021).

15. Snorton, *Black on Both Sides*, 2.

16. See McKittrick, *Demonic Grounds*. McKittrick, drawing on Sylvia Wynter's work, writes that demonic grounds are the "very different geography" that might be characterized as a "nondeterministic impossibility" (xxv). It's a kind of abolitionist geography about "not . . . only reifying and politicizing marginality in itself (black women's identities = margin/position = difference in/and feminism; or, our present form of life)" (135).

17. Quoted in White, "Black Metamorphosis," 129.

18. Thomas, "Sex/Sexuality," 100. Emphasis in original.

19. Thomas, "Marronnons / Let's Maroon," 65–70.

20. All parenthetical citations in this section reference Wynter's "Black Metamorphosis."

21. Weheliye, *Habeas Viscus*, 42.

22. Haynes, "Sylvia Wynter's Theory," 94; Martel, *Misinterpellated Subject*, 38.

23. Wynter uses "ontological sovereignty" to speak to how black people, and perhaps other people of color, too, including, notably, indigenous people, "move completely outside our present conception of what it is to be human, and therefore outside the ground of the orthodox body of knowledge which institutes and reproduces such a conception." Mark Rifkin understands this as "a new way of understanding potentials for social life." See Wynter and Scott, "Re-Enchantment of Humanism," 22.

24. See Wynter, "Creole Criticism."

25. Thomas, "Marronnons / Let's Maroon," 70.

26. McKittrick, "Rebellion."

27. McKittrick, "Rebellion," 85. Emphasis added.

28. Cunningham, "Resistance of the Lost," 115.

29. Cunningham, "Resistance of the Lost," 117.

30. Thomas, "Marronnons / Let's Maroon," 76.

31. Stryker, "My Words," 247. Emphasis added.

32. See "Block Chapel" in Moten, *Feel Trio*, 30.

33. Wynter, "Ceremony Must Be Found," 36.

34. Snorton, "Transfiguring Masculinities."

35. Lorde, "Age, Race," 123. The poem is titled "Outlines."

36. Lowe, *Intimacies of Four Continents*, 175.

37. E. Edwards, "Cedric People," 252.

38. Foucault, *Archaeology of Knowledge*, 131, 121.

39. I am drawing from black trans woman Juliana Huxtable, who, in response to the question "What's the nastiest shade you've ever thrown?" says, "Existing in the world."

40. J. Butler, *Psychic Life of Power*, 2.

41. Filar and Gossett, "Cruising."

42. Preston, "Guide to Survival."

43. Raha, "Future Justice," 46.

44. Cornell, *Beyond Accommodation*, 83.

1. All quotes from *Spill*, M *Archive*, and *Dub* will be cited parenthetically.

2. Wynter, "Ethno or Socio Poetics," 88.

3. Gumbs, "We Stay in Love."

4. Moten, *Black and Blur*, viii.

5. Gumbs, "We Stay in Love."

6. Gumbs, "We Stay in Love." See also "Whatcha Gonna Do?," in which Spillers remarks, "I have always thought that where the women's movement was moving was towards a society that did justice towards *everyone*. So that for black feminism, radical feminism [which is to say black trans feminism], to morph into a concern with prison reform or health care is appropriate. These and the other big issues of our time seem to me to be an appropriate extension of human rights. . . . So I am thinking that we really make a mistake when we read those movements in their particularity ultimately, because I think that the start is particular, but that their thrust is and must always be outward, broader" (308). Black feminism, and black trans feminism, *is decidedly not a parochial project*. This is what Spillers is suggesting, and what Gumbs poetically inscribes, and what Farah Jasmine Griffin notes in the epigraph. It is a project for all; black feminism operates on a paraontological and radically inclusive modality of thinking and doing.

7. Reed, *Freedom Time*, 9; see also Eversley, "Evidence of Things Unseen."

8. Bey and Gumbs, "Spillage."

9. Keeling, *Witch's Flight*, 2.

10. Bey and Gumbs, "Spillage."

11. Gumbs, "We Stay in Love."

12. Haley, *No Mercy Here*, 200.

13. Hartman, *Wayward Lives, Beautiful Experiments*, 227.

14. Notably, I am using "they/them" instead of a more expected "she" because, if the marked woman references a disruption of gendered categorization, to name the marked woman "she" *might* belie that intent. Thus, usage of the gender neutral— and I would argue, more specifically, gender nonbinary—"they" is both to "ungender" "woman" insofar as it is marked as well as to contend that the un/gendered blackness of the marked woman is not beholden to gender binaristic logics.

15. Smith and Vasudevan, "Race, Biopolitics, and the Future," 216–17; see also Gumbs, "We Can Learn," 61, 1. This can also be linked to her mentors Cheryl Clarke, June Jordan, and Barbara Smith, as Gumbs seems to extend their deployable and capacious understanding of lesbianism, bisexuality, and blackness. In "New Notes on Lesbianism," Clarke writes that "I call myself 'Black,' too, because

Black is my perspective, my aesthetic, my politics, my vision, my sanity." Blackness becomes something that exceeds the epidermis, not to its exclusion but to its radical recalibration and opening. Blackness is dispersed into perspective (a way of seeing and reading) and politics (a way of relating to power). Or June Jordan's use of bi-sexuality as a prefigurative "queerness" meaning not a certain sexuality but "a critical relationship to existing sexual and social norms." (Cathy Cohen's queerness bears strong resonances here, too.) Clarke's lesbianism operates similarly, is imbricated with her understanding of blackness, Clarke thinking with Smith's definition of "lesbian" as an interruptive "negation of identity." In Gumbs's reading of Roderick Ferguson (who is himself reading Smith's reading of Toni Morrison), she writes that "lesbian" is "a way to interrupt the reproduction of identity . . . [that] trouble[s] the process of identification itself," and "a particular critical practice [that] could disrupt the reproductive narrative of patriarchal family providing, in Morrison's words, adopted by Ferguson, 'something else to be.'"

I might note as well, finally, that this kind of understanding of "lesbian" dovetails with Monique Wittig's thought inasmuch as Wittig famously asserts, in radical trans feminist fashion, that "lesbians are not women." Where for Clarke "lesbian" is the negation of an identity—the refusal, paraontologically, of a given ontology—Wittig similarly can be read as arguing for a lesbianism that allows for a trans feminist affirmative assertion of "not wanting to be a woman as a revolutionary process based on a desire for a gender-free utopia"—or gender abolition. This makes "lesbian," and the above-stated convergences of lesbianism with blackness, not about representation or the possession of an identity but "about refusing to do the labour of heteronormativity/sexism/misogyny, remember, not (or not only) about appearance or gender representation!" as Alyosxa Tudor argues. See Tudor, "Im/possibilities of Refusing," 371.

16. Horton-Stallings, *Mutha'*, 37.

17. Check out Gumbs, "We Be"; and Gumbs, "One Thing."

18. I reference here Martin Heidegger's "Building Dwelling Thinking" in Heidegger, *Poetry, Language, Thought*, 141–160.

19. J. Butler, *Precarious Life*, 33.

20. Moten and Tsang, "All Terror, All Beauty," 347.

21. Sycamore, "We Are Always Crossing."

22. Spillers, "Mama's Baby, Papa's Maybe," 65.

23. See Morrison, *Song of Solomon*.

24. J. K. Carter, "Something Else A'Comin' . . ."

25. See McKittrick, *Dear Science*. Katherine McKittrick, in discussing the grimness of the ways discourses of "identity" have reified biologics, writes, "The incorporation of 'identity' into disciplined learning systems—the *institutionalization* of identity within the context of the university—has resulted in a grim reification

of a biocentric order." Let me pause here really quickly just to clarify that McKittrick, on my reading, is saying that the ways we continue to rehash and reassert "identity" as the primary motivator of our disciplinary work—indeed, *as* disciplining—is part and parcel of reinscribing and solidifying biologics and biocentric ordering. She goes on: "Identity is often conflated with flesh. Identity has biologic traces. Identity is corporeal. Studying identity so often involves demonstrating that biology is socially constructed, *not displacing biology* but, rather, empowering biology . . . as the primary way to study identity. Race (including whiteness) galvanizes the biologics of identity" (39; emphasis in original). McKittrick also, in a footnote concluding this passage, writes of Paul Gilroy's *Against Race*, and was, like I was when I read Gilroy's text and the commentary that followed its release, baffled by the resistance to its argument. "The resistance to *Against Race*, particularly (but not only) from black US scholars, has always been curious to me," she writes, "so much so that I thought I was misreading the book, or that my copy was missing a chapter. It is as though the title for the US edition of the book—*Against Race*—is some kind of template implying that Gilroy is, himself, 'against race' and that the text is a refusal of black studies. The discussion of fascism is hard, the journey into black conservatism is hard too, as are the discussions of corporeal authenticities . . . but this book is not a negation of race, blackness, or black studies. It is a monumental critique of race thinking and ultranationalism" (39–40). I don't understand what is so difficult to understand about the violence and colonial imposition *that is race*, and the subsequent need to rid ourselves of this. Why is it that holding onto race as a legitimate mode of analysis is seen as such a virtue? It is a colonial imposition; it is violent; it is not useful to us in the end (though I know y'all will talk about institutions and structures and material effects that are not wished away if we just get rid of race; y'all will say that this is "color-blindness," but y'all will be, I think, willfully misreading the deep argument throughout this book and McKittrick's book, as well as Gilroy's, and if that is the case then I don't know what else to say).

26. Schuster and Campt, "Black Feminist Futures."

27. Cervenak, "Black Gathering," 11; see also Moten, *In the Break*, 139.

28. Referenced here is Gordon's 1997 book *Her Majesty's Other Children: Sketches of Racism from a Neocolonial Age*. In it he writes, "In effect, then, in the antiblack world there is but one race, and that race is black. Thus to be racialized is to be pushed 'down' toward blackness, and to be deracialized is to be pushed 'up' toward whiteness" (76).

29. King, Navarro, and Smith, eds., *Otherwise Worlds*, 43.

30. Moten, "Taste Dissonance Flavor Escape," 218.

31. Clarke, "Lesbianism," 135; Keegan, Horak, and Steinbock, "Cinematic/Trans*/Bodies Now," 2.

32. Gumbs, "We Stay in Love."

1. Feinberg, *Stone Butch Blues*, 236. Previous quotation comes from page 240 of the text.

2. This and all quotes in this paragraph attributed to dodd are from Schwartz and dodd, "Interview."

3. Nordmarken, "Queering Gendering," 38. Importantly, Nordmarken recognizes that gender anomie and those who incite it do not result in a rosy picture. The uncertainty very often leads to violence. Nordmarken goes on to say, "Gender anomie is indeed problematic, as it contributes to the structural inequality gender minorities face, such as physical violence and discrimination in employment, healthcare, housing, education, and interactions with family members and the criminal justice system" (43). The violence and trepidation in these moments are not to be lost, but, concurrently, "there are also positive aspects of gender anomie; it can be understood as a hopeful crack in a seemingly solidified oppressive system, a fissure in which possibilities for a more just society can be imagined and developed" (43).

4. McKittrick, *Demonic Grounds*, xxv–xxvi.

5. Throughout the process of writing and revising this chapter, and indeed across the different sources written by dodd drawn upon for this chapter, dodd changed her gender pronouns three times. Hence, she identified as different iterations of at least syntactic genders, some of her writing reflecting, if only implicitly, how she identified herself in the available language at that time. At the time of this writing she used "she" pronouns exclusively, and I am intentionally using this pronoun for her in all of my references to her, irrespective of the point in time of the relevant source material, because it is not, to my mind—and the mind of other scholars in trans studies—a failing of the implicitly validated linearity of one's gender as the basis for how one should "really" identify but a failing of grammar's ingrained transantagonism. That is, grammar and linguistic dictates disallow certain kinds of gender mutabilities (indeed, virtually all gender mutabilities) that do not house space for different gender pronouns and various inflections of, or altogether different, genders over time for a single subject. Put another way, poetically, the genders one was known by to others after one announces oneself through different pronouns become, because of grammar's inability to hold multiple genders in a single subject over time, "misplaced language," as Cameron Awkward-Rich has written (see "Essay on the Theory of Motion" in *Sympathetic Little Monster*).

In short, there are some who might take dodd's pronouns as a disqualification, of sorts, for certain arguments made in her writing, or in mine—namely, those that pertain to gender nonconformity or nonbinariness. For this writing, her use of "she/her/hers" pronouns does not invalidate arguments pertaining to the impact of nonbinary or gender nonconforming subjectivity and indeed demonstrate the capaciousness of her pronouns, her pronouns' nonexclusivity.

6. "jayy dodd," Nightboat Books. I might also put dodd in conversation with Del LaGrace Volcano, who self-identifies as "a gender variant visual artist who accesses 'technologies of gender in order to amplify rather than erase the hermaphroditic traces of my body'" and as "a gender abolitionist, a part-time gender terrorist, an intentional mutation and intersex-by-design." Where Volcano's gender nonnormativity and intersexuality leads to a gender abolitionism like dodd's, I would assert, the distinction comes in the use of words for terrorizing gender: whereas dodd is a volunteer gender terrorist, Volcano is a "part-time" gender terrorist. If I may read into this, the part-time gender terrorism still has tethers to waged labor, and perhaps a slight tether to the current world as it is, whereas volunteering as a gender terrorist is a complete unseating from waged labor, demanding and taking and desiring no capital. See MoCA Skopje, "Del LaGrace Volcano."

7. Shange, *Progressive Dystopia*, 65.

8. dodd, "Impossible Outside."

9. dodd, "Impossible Outside."

10. dodd, "Impossible Outside."

11. All aforementioned quotes attributed to dodd come from dodd, "Impossible Outside." Emphasis in original.

12. Chandler, *X*, 53–55.

13. da Silva, "Hacking the Subject," 21.

14. Find the poem here: "jayy dodd," Tagvverk, April 18, 2017, https://tagvverk.info /2017/04/18/jayy-dodd/.

15. See Chu and Drager, "After Trans Studies"; and Horton-Stallings, *Funk the Erotic,* 10.

16. Duggan and McHugh, "Fem(Me)Inist Manifesto," 153.

17. dodd, "Gender Non Conformity."

18. See, for example, Spillers, "Mama's Baby, Papa's Maybe"; Gossett, "Žižek's Trans/Gender Trouble"; Ferguson, *Aberrations in Black*; Holland, *Raising the Dead,* 179–80; and Abdur-Rahman, *Against the Closet.*

19. See Stanley, "Affective Commons," 502–3; Marx, *Grundrisse.*

20. Snorton, *Black on Both Sides*, xiv.

21. See "Presently, I Only Want to Understand Being Full & Feeding," 2019, https:// www.baestjournal.com/jayy-dodd (accessed March 25, 2021).

22. dodd, "Gender Non Conformity."

23. dodd, "Poetic Beyond Resilience."

24. dodd, "Horizon."

25. dodd, "Poetic Beyond."

26. dodd, "I Know I Been Changed."

27. dodd, "Homies Don't Come Out."

28. As for Walcott, he writes of the "whatever" of blackness as that where "the uncertainties and commonalities of blacknesses might be formulated in the face of some room for surprise, disappointment, and pleasure without recourse to disciplinary and punishing measures . . . a whatever that can tolerate the whatever of blackness without knowing meaning—black meaning, that is—in advance of its various utterances." Stallings, then, names this "whatever" *funk*, which for her is like the liminal spaces of blackness, the miasmic byzantine web connecting the variegated nodes of blackness, a nonreproductive sex and transaesthetics of cultural art forms. And, lastly, Tinsley links the whatever of blackness to a veritable queerness. See Walcott, "Outside in Black Studies"; Horton-Stallings, *Funk the Erotic*; and Tinsley, *Thiefing Sugar*.

29. dodd, "Homies Don't Come Out." Emphasis in original.

30. Rosenberg, "Trans/War Boy/Gender." Rosenberg writes that he desires "a future that may never know our name or remember us personally. Radical anonymity. I am not talking about anonymity in the present. I am talking about anonymity to the future. I mean politics." And it is this that I am drawing on.

31. dodd, "Stop Dude Feminists."

32. dodd, "To Wake Up Flawless."

33. Perry, *Vexy Thing*, 229.

34. Kelly, "Interview with jayy dodd." Emphasis in original.

35. dodd, "Gender Non Conformity."

36. dodd, "Put Your Hands"; dodd, "Narcissus."

37. Halberstam and Nyong'o, "Introduction," 453.

38. dodd, *Black Condition*, 43.

39. dodd, "I Have a New Obsession."

40. Awkward-Rich, *Sympathetic Little Monster*, 8. Emphasis added.

41. dodd, *Black Condition*, 44.

42. dodd, *Black Condition*, 65. Emphasis in original.

43. dodd, *Black Condition*, 66.

44. Schwartz and dodd, "Interview."

45. Kelly, "Interview with jayy dodd."

CHAPTER 6. TRIGGER, REBEL

1. Roben, "Trigger." Of note: "The artists in 'Trigger' share a desire to contest repressive orders and to speculate on new forms and aesthetics—a desire to picture other futures. For many, developing new vocabularies necessarily entails

a productive reworking of historical configurations." New Exhibitions Museum, https://www.newmuseum.org/exhibitions/view/trigger-gender-as-a-tool-and-as-a -weapon (accessed March 26, 2021).

2. Edidi, *For Black Trans Girls*.

3. Venus Selenite, Patreon, https://www.patreon.com/venus_selenite (accessed August 11,2019).

4. All references to the essays in the collection, since it is unpaginated, will be parenthetically cited with an abbreviated title.

5. Selenite, "*Steven Universe*." I am drawing here from xyr brief commentary on the cartoon *Steven Universe*, in which xe says, "Everything and everyone is queer." In Selenite's summation, the show "centers on Steven, a boy who is half-human and half-gem. Steven's mother was a magical alien combatant that gave up her physical form to give birth to him. She was the leader of the Crystal Gems, who protect the Earth from demolition and wickedness and include gems Garnet, Amethyst, and Pearl, warriors that present a feminine gender expression cast from the magic of their gemstones. They live together and help Steven to navigate and summon his powers with the inheritance of his mother's gem." As a cartoon for children and teens, one would not expect to see much reference to sex and sexuality, which implies that Selenite's understanding of queerness is more than the sexual, or even the strictly gendered (though inclusive of these, to be sure). Queerness is the nonnormativity of the show, the balm for the marginalized, the other-than what typical cartoons provide.

6. Parker, "Passing."

7. Moten, *Black and Blur*, 183.

8. Do not read any particular partisan stance into this. I'm not going there with y'all. Nope.

9. Spillers, *Black, White, and in Color*, 14–15. Emphasis in original.

10. J. Butler, *Senses of the Subject*, 93.

11. Selenite, *trigger,* 2016. Since the collection is unpaginated, I will signal the title of the poem in-text, forgoing the need to give bibliographic citation beyond this citation of the collection as a whole.

12. Chase, "Acts of Intentionality."

13. Williamson and Derickson, "Scandalize My Name."

14. See Bliss, "Black Feminism out of Place," 729; Hong, *Ruptures of American Capital*, xiii–xiv; and Dillon, "Possessed by Death," 115.

15. In *The Price of the Ticket*, Baldwin writes, "I know very well that my ancestors had no desire to come to this place: but neither did the ancestors of the people who became white and who require of my captivity a song. They require of me a song less to celebrate my captivity than to justify their own" (xx). Selenite's poem seems to me to assert that, here, song can be a means to escaping captivity rather than indexical of a contentment with it.

16. This very last clause I draw from Selenite's poem "water as substitution for merlot," in which xe writes, pithily, "we reject the drinks you are serving."

17. Cruz, "Who Does."

18. Stoltenberg, "Magic Time!"

19. Stoltenberg, "Magic Time!"

20. Edidi, "Love and Saying No."

21. See Harney and Moten, *Undercommons*, 47.

22. Quoted in Stryker, *Transgender History*, 159.

23. Moten, "Case of Blackness," 180.

24. Snorton, *Black on Both Sides*, 6.

25. Edidi, "Love and Saying No."

26. Colebrook, "What Is It Like," 228; Moten, "Blackness and Poetry"; Moten, "Case of Blackness," 179.

27. Spillers, "Mama's Baby, Papa's Maybe," 68.

28. Tinsley, *Ezili's Mirrors*, 60.

CONCLUSION: HOPE, FUGITIVE

A shorter version of the conclusion appears in *Callaloo* 41, no. 2 (2018), under the title "Fugitive Hope: The Constitutive Life in Black Elegies."

1. Grosz, *Becoming Undone*, 109–10; see also Hayward, "Don't Exist," 192.

2. In *Ontological Terror*, Calvin Warren is met with vitriol by an audience member. After he presents on the hopelessness of living while black, the nonmattering of blackness, the importance of his "nihilistic responsibility" to convey that there is no hope or meaning for the black, he is castigated for saying that there is no solution to antiblackness. "How dare you tell this to our youth! That is so very negative! Of course we can change things; we have power, and we are free," one audience member tells him, the audience member's intensity rising (though Warren genders the audience member as "she," I refrain from the gendered assumption). After waiting for the person to finish, he retorts with a litany of incisive questions: "'Then tell us how to end police brutality and the slaughter of the youth you want to protect from my nihilism.' 'If these solutions are so credible, why have they consistently failed? Are we awaiting for some novel, extraordinary solution—one no one had ever imagined—to end antiblack violence and misery?' Silence. 'In what manner will this "power" deliver us from antiblackness?' How long must we *insist* on a humanity that is not recognized—an insistence that humiliates in its inefficacy? 'If we are progressing, why are black youth being slaughtered at staggering rates in the twenty-first

century—if we are, indeed, humans just like everyone else?'" See Warren, *Ontological Terror*, 3. Emphasis in original.

3. Snorton, *Black on Both Sides*, 185.

4. Sharpe, "Lose Your Kin."

5. Snyder and Lopez, *Handbook of Positive Psychology*, 257.

6. Awkward-Rich, "Craft Capsule."

7. There is a particular dovetailing and echoing with Henry Giroux I wish to highlight here. He calls his an "educated hope." See Giroux, "When Hope Is Subversive," 38.

8. Solnit, *Hope in the Dark*, xii.

9. Quoted in Solnit, *Hope in the Dark*, xiii–xiv.

10. Diaz, "Under President Trump."

11. Snorton, "New Hope," 89.

12. Kelley, "Black Study, Black Struggle."

13. McKittrick, "Mathematics Black Life"; McKittrick, "Diachronic Loops," 10. Someone like Tiffany Lethabo King, too, drawing on McKittrick, writes that we must be urged "to move beyond simply theorizing or 'analytically reprising' anti-Black violence. For McKittrick, naming violence has never been the only, or the most important task, of Black studies projects." See King, *Black Shoals*, 30.

14. Cheah, *What Is a World?*, 97.

15. Haslett, "Hortense Spillers." Emphasis in original.

16. Ritskes, "Beyond and Against," 81.

17. R. Edwards, "Trans-Poetics," 252. Regarding trans-poetics and its relation to trans studies and feminist studies, I'm noting specifically Edwards's point that

> an example of a trans-poetics relevant to transgender studies is one articulated in feminist translation studies regarding the inevitability and potentiality of error. . . . In the context of gender performativity, error is also conceived as generative, as the imperfect iteration that allows for the possibility of the "improper" (Butler 1993). A trans-poetics making use of both of these understandings of error draws on the discord, contingencies, and multiplicities possible in language in order to narrate and subvert cultural and critical attempts to fix gender and sexual boundaries. (252)

18. Cervenak, "Black Gathering," 2, 7.

19. J. Butler, *Frames of War*, 162, 147.

20. I am in fact quite terrifyingly asserting boldly a claim Hortense Spillers makes in terms of the unpopular fact that we may have to begin making common ground with those that don't look like us, something I gravitate toward eagerly via trans theorizing because transness is, in part, precisely the interrogation of how we come

to understand what it means to properly "look like" something at all, which is often underlain by many normative assumptions that are best served by a forthright critique. Spillers writes on the former,

> There are more black women with whom we have very little in common than we are comfortable thinking about so that a subject of black feminism might at times—and this is rather shocking, I admit!—find greater common cause on some issue with other women than with those women whom she regards as members of her own community. One of the tasks of black feminism in the years to come is to acknowledge these very uncomfortable truths and not anticipated differences and explain how they work. We are also being summoned to look at another truth that stares us in the face every day, and that is the extent to which women in power do not always look and behave very differently from the males who preceded them in power. I am of the opinion that women who reach certain levels of management and privilege often forget something along the way, and that is, the necessity to forge a different image of power; in that regard, male leadership is not exemplary, and I see no need to repeat it or imitate it; in short, we don't need women who really want to be either like men or men themselves, whatever we decide that is, and as hard as it is to say these days, I think we know it when we see it. Spillers, "Scholarly Journey," n.p.

So many times—especially with my students—there is an unceasing assumption that black women are 1) readily identifiable, which is predicated on a host of assumptions that of course do not demand always being spelled out at every utterance (e.g., the demand that one note with brutal clarity how they are defining black women, reminiscent of the annoying sophomore who asks for impossible clarification on a term to make a spectacle out of not having all the answers yet) but that does need to be given more sustained, intentional, explicit thought; and 2) a monolith, even in those moments when one asserts that, surely, not *every* black woman, but the subsequent argument goes on to assume just that. This, then, stands in for black feminism. The tendency, in short, is to make winks and nods toward "knowing better," as it were, but operating on the assumption of the validity of the very thing about which we know better. As I've made clear throughout this book, and as I'll make clear once more here, the assumption that one is on a proverbial team by virtue of ontologized characteristics is, in no uncertain terms, a fantasy. Indeed, "gone was the fantasy that a similar body denotes a similar desire; gone should be the fantasy that a physical body denotes anything about desire or gender at all. So many of the misunderstandings of each other's bodies, desires, or emotional needs that we blame on gender are merely interpersonal failings," as Sophia Giovannitti writes. One's *being* a black woman guarantees nothing of their politics, their concerted relation to power, or even their "common" oppression. Following Giovannitti's argument, which is made in only a slightly different context, I might make the case that the ways that some black women feminists malign white women in particular—again, as my students constantly do, to the spectacular exclusion of white men and those who might be called black (cis) men too—is carried out in order to "reify biologically essentialist notions of our own bodies—as a group—without *really* having to say it." Black women as the embodied site of a definitionally progressive black feminism are secured by way of noting how bad, say, white women are, and thus how inherently good, which is to say sufficiently on the right side of political history, black women *as a whole, a group, and a transparently known demographic* are. If I may repurpose Giovannitti once more, making a parallel not to her specific target of concern with cis men but as a gesture toward similar operations and trends (not in an *analogous* way; let me be clear on this point before y'all come after me for something unintended): the implicit and insufficiently worked-around buttressing of black women as *the* demographic of all things right with the world "is an expression of maintaining our fidelity to the world of distinction, or refusing to break with the conditions of the struggle we observe. In this way, we are simply repeating the belief that a binary gender *can be a stable category*, even as we simultaneously fight against the conditions of the gender binary foisting stable and unwanted categories upon us. We cannot champion a non-biologically essentialist, trans-inclusive feminism *and* champion No Cis Men" (or, alternatively, listen to black women, black women told y'all, black women over and against any other demographic or mode of thinking, and the like); "we cannot have it both ways." See Giovannitti, "In Defense of Men." Emphasis in original.

Put another way, my issue is not with black women being the spokespeople for what is being said but, rather, with the conflation of black feminism with black women and, as a result, the deprivation of *work* and *politics* and *doing* from black feminism. It instantiates black feminism as a being and an identity, negating its reach and efficacy as a way of moving through the world and, more important, changing the world. Because we know that there are myriad problematic black women out there. Spillers is critiquing all of this, beautifully ("a subject of black feminism might at times—and this is rather shocking, I admit!—find greater common cause on some issue with other women than with those women whom she regards as members of her own community.")

Even black women can become enamored of the kind of power already in place, a kind of power that is violent and extractive and expropriative, and those black women do not do black feminism, they do not deserve our veneration. Even black women want to wield what is often deemed toxic masculinity; even black women "want to be either like men or men themselves"—*whatever we decide that is*, Spillers says immediately, delinking "like men"-ness from biological determinism and opening it up to a sociogenic way of inhabiting the world—and this means black feminism neither automatically includes all black women, nor excludes all nonblack women, *nor is about being anything in particular but is about a doing, an engendering.*

So, to put a finer point on this: such a black feminism is about coalition and coming together on ungrounded grounds that index how we seek to change and abolish and radicalize sociality and the world. Coalition does not necessitate a common plight but a common, even if temporarily and intermittently, envisioned future. Put colloquially, it's not necessarily or solely about where you've been but about where you're going.

21. McDonald and Tinsley, "Go Beyond Our Natural Selves," 253–54.

22. Chambers-Letson, *After the Party*, 42. Emphasis added.

23. Moten, *Black and Blur*, 275.

24. Commander, *Afro-Atlantic Flight*, 23.

25. Devereaux, "Trans Women."

26. Clifton, "Won't You Celebrate"; Moten, *Black and Blur*, xiii.

27. Crawley, *Blackpentecostal Breath*.

28. da Silva, "Hacking the Subject," 20.

29. Enke, ed., *Transfeminist Perspectives*, 11.

30. Derrida, *Specters of Marx*, xx. Emphasis in original.

31. Sexton, "Social Life of Social Death."

32. Kline, "Pragmatics of Resistance," 66. Emphasis in original; Moten, "Blackness and Nothingness," 742.

33. Gumbs, *Spill*, 34.

34. Harney and Moten, *Undercommons*, 10–11.

35. Gumbs, "Freedom Seeds," 145.

36. Weheliye, *Habeas Viscus*, 12.

37. Williamson, *Scandalize My Name*, 9.

38. J. K. Carter, "Paratheological Blackness," 595. Emphasis added.

39. Williamson, *Scandalize My Name*, 4–9, 66, 18. Emphasis in original.

40. Preston, "Guide to Survival."

41. See Herzog, "Life Expectancy of Trans Women."

42. See Baldwin, "Black English."

43. See Sharpe, *In the Wake*.

44. Spillers, *Black, White, and in Color*, 40. Emphasis in original.

45. dodd, "Poetic Beyond"; Moten and Tsang, "All Terror, All Beauty," 347.

46. McDonald, Green, and Ellison, "Trans Multitudes and Death Reality."

47. McDonald, "Foreword," 3. Emphasis added.

48. Ellison, Green, and McDonald, "Introduction." Emphasis in original.

49. McDonald, Green, and Ellison, "Trans Multitudes and Death Reality."

50. T. Ellison, "Day 1."

51. Durban-Albrecht, "Postcolonial Disablement," 196.

52. McDonald, Green, and Ellison, "Trans Multitudes and Death Reality."

53. Workneh, "Angela Davis and Gloria Steinem."

54. Baldwin, "My Dungeon Shook," 92.

55. Shakur, *Assata*, 1.

56. Chandler, "Coming of the Second-Time."

57. Perry, *Vexy Thing*, 244.

58. Burris, "Birth of a (Zionist) Nation," 12–28.

59. Macharia, *Frottage*, 166.

60. Kokumo, "Black, Trans and Still Breathing."

61. Wallace and Green, "Tranifest," 569.

62. Ferguson, "Light-Filled Vision," 333–34.

63. Hartman, *Scenes of Subjection*, 61.

64. Hartman, *Wayward Lives, Beautiful Experiments*, 24. Emphasis in original.

65. Preston, "Guide to Survival."

66. Moore, "Shea Diamond."

67. Morris, "Cosmic Matter of Black Lives." Emphasis in original.

68. Muñoz, *Cruising Utopia*, 92.

69. Kincaid, "Why I Had to Come Out."

70. D'Oleo, "Mushrooms and Mischief," 153–54.

71. Lang, "Why I Don't Believe."

72. Raha, "Limits of Trans Liberalism."

73. Awkward-Rich, "Cento."

74. Sirvent, "BAR Book Forum."

75. Spillers and duCille, "Expostulations and Replies," 19.

76. Howard, "Won't Die Things."

77. Carter and Cervenak, "Black Ether," 212.

78. Carter and Cervenak, "Black Ether," 205, 212, 221n11.

79. Howard, "Won't Die Things."

80. Hesse, "White Sovereignty," 601.

81. Slaughterhouse, "Monsters in My Head," 2012.

82. T. Ellison, "Labor of Werqing It," 16.

83. T. Ellison, "Day 1."

84. Hayward and Gossett, "Impossibility of That," 16. Emphasis in original.

85. Hayward and Gossett, "Impossibility of That," 16–17. Emphasis in original.

86. da Silva, "Hacking the Subject."

87. da Silva, "Hacking the Subject."

88. Nash, *Black Feminism Reimagined*, 137.

Bibliography

Abdur-Rahman, Aliyyah I. *Against the Closet: Identity, Political Longing, and Black Figuration*. Durham, NC: Duke University Press, 2012.

"About." A Radical Transfeminist, November 19, 2011. https://radtransfem .wordpress.com/about/.

Adkins, Amey Victoria. "Black/Feminist Futures: Reading Beauvoir in *Black Skin, White Masks*." *South Atlantic Quarterly* 112 (2013): 697–723.

Aiken, Joshua, Jessica Marion Modi, and Olivia K. Polk. "Issued by Way of 'The Issue of Blackness.'" *TSQ: Transgender Studies Quarterly* 7 (2020): 427–44.

Aizura, Aren. "Introduction." *South Atlantic Quarterly* 116 (July 2017): 606–11, https://doi.org/10.1215/00382876-3961721.

Anderson, Victor. *Beyond Ontological Blackness: An Essay on African American Religious and Cultural Criticism*. New York: Bloomsbury, 2016.

Antwi, George. *The Words of Power*. Bangkok: Booksmango, 2012.

Awkward-Rich, Cameron. "Cento between the Ending and the End." Poets.org, 2018. https://poets.org/poem/cento-between-ending-and-end (accessed March 29, 2021).

Awkward-Rich, Cameron. "Craft Capsule: Revising the Archive." *Poets and Writers*, December 9, 2019. https://www.pw.org/content/craft_capsule_revising_the _archive.

Awkward-Rich, Cameron. *Sympathetic Little Monster*. Los Angeles: Ricochet, 2016.

Awkward-Rich, Cameron. "Trans, Feminism: Or, Reading like a Depressed Transsexual." *Signs: Journal of Women in Culture and Society* 42 (May 19, 2017): 819–41, https://doi.org/10.1086/690914.

Baldwin, James. "Black English: A Dishonest Argument." In *The Cross of Redemption: Uncollected Writings*, edited by Randall Kenan, 154–60. New York: Knopf, 2011.

Baldwin, James. "My Dungeon Shook." In *The Fire Next Time*, 1–10. New York: Vintage International, 1993.

Baldwin, James. *The Price of the Ticket: Collected Nonfiction, 1948–1985.* New York: St. Martin's Press, 1985.

Barrow, Kai Lumumba, Yve Laris Cohen, Kalaniopua Young, and Dean Spade. "Models of Futurity." In *Trap Door: Trans Cultural Production and the Politics of Visibility*, edited by Reina Gossett, Eric A. Stanley, and Johanna Burton, 321–38. Cambridge, MA: MIT Press, 2017.

Battersby, Christine. *The Phenomenal Woman: Feminist Metaphysics and the Patterns of Identity.* New York: Routledge, 1998.

Benston, Kimberley W. *Performing Blackness: Enactments of African-American Modernism.* New York: Routledge, 2013.

Berger, Anne-Emmanuelle. "Sexing Differances." *Differences* 16 (2005): 52–67, https://doi.org/10.1215/10407391-16-3-52.

Bey, Marquis. *The Problem of the Negro as a Problem for Gender.* Minneapolis: University of Minnesota Press, 2020.

Bey, Marquis. "The Trans*-Ness of Blackness, the Blackness of Trans*-Ness." *TSQ: Transgender Studies Quarterly* 4 (2017): 275–95, https://doi.org/10.1215/23289252-3815069.

Bey, Marquis, and Alexis Pauline Gumbs. "A Spillage of the Fugitive Variety." *Social Text* Online, March 17, 2017. https://socialtextjournal.org/a-spillage-of-the-fugitive-variety/.

Bhanji, Nael. "Trans/Scriptions: Homing Desires, (Trans)Sexual Citizenship and Racialized Bodies." In *The Transgender Studies Reader 2*, edited by Susan Stryker and Aren Z. Aizura, 512–26. New York: Routledge, 2013.

Bliss, James. "Black Feminism out of Place." *Signs: Journal of Women in Culture and Society* 41 (2016): 727–49.

Boellstorff, Tom, Mauro Cabral, micha cárdenas, Trystan Cotten, Eric A. Stanley, Kalaniopua Young, and Aren Z. Aizura. "Decolonizing Transgender: A Roundtable Discussion." *TSQ: Transgender Studies Quarterly* 1 (2014): 419–39, https://doi.org/10.1215/23289252-2685669.

Bowen, Effie. "Discovery: Geo Wyeth." *Interview Magazine*, July 6, 2012. https://www.interviewmagazine.com/music/discovery-geo-wyeth.

Brown, Jayna. "A World on Fire: Radical Black Feminism in a Dystopian Age." *South Atlantic Quarterly* 117 (2018): 581–97, https://doi.org/10.1215/00382876-6942171.

Burris, Greg. "Birth of a (Zionist) Nation: Black Radicalism and the Future of Palestine." In *Futures of Black Radicalism*, edited by Gaye Theresa Johnson and Alex Lubin, 120–32. New York: Verso, 2017.

Butler, Judith. *Frames of War: When Is Life Grievable?* New York: Verso, 2016.

Butler, Judith. *Gender Trouble: Feminism and the Subversion of Identity.* New York: Routledge, 1999.

Butler, Judith. *Notes toward a Performative Theory of Assembly.* Cambridge, MA: Harvard University Press, 2015.

Butler, Judith. *Precarious Life: The Powers of Mourning and Violence.* New York: Verso, 2006.

Butler, Judith. *The Psychic Life of Power: Theories in Subjection.* Stanford, CA: Stanford University Press, 1997.

Butler, Judith. *Senses of the Subject.* New York: Fordham University Press, 2015.

Butler, Nic. *Under False Colors: The Politics of Gender Expression in Post–Civil War Charleston.* Charleston County Public Library, 2018. https://www.ccpl.org /charleston-time-machine/under-false-colors-politics-gender-expression-post -civil-war-charleston (accessed March 29, 2021).

cárdenas, micha. "Dark Shimmers: The Rhythm of Necropolitical Affect in Digital Media." In *Trap Door: Trans Cultural Production and the Politics of Visibilty,* edited by Reina Gossett, Eric A. Stanley, and Johanna Burton, 161–82. Cambridge, MA: MIT Press, 2017.

Carter, J. Kameron. "Black Malpractice (A Poetics of the Sacred)." *Social Text* 37 (2019): 67–107, https://doi.org/10.1215/01642472-7370991.

Carter, J. Kameron. "Paratheological Blackness." *South Atlantic Quarterly* 112 (2013): 589–611, https://doi.org/10.1215/00382876-2345189.

Carter, J. Kameron. *Race: A Theological Account.* Oxford: Oxford University Press, 2008.

Carter, J. Kameron. "Something Else A'Comin' . . ." Contending Modernities, May 31, 2019. http://contendingmodernities.nd.edu/global-currents /something-else-acomin/.

Carter, J. Kameron, and Sarah Jane Cervenak. "Black Ether." *CR: The New Centennial Review* 16 (2016): 203–24.

Carter, J. Kameron, and Sarah Jane Cervenak. "Untitled and Outdoors: Thinking with Saidiya Hartman." *Women and Performance: A Journal of Feminist Theory* 27 (February 10, 2017): 1–11, https://doi.org/10.1080/0740770X.2017.1282116.

Carter, Julian. "Transition." *TSQ: Transgender Studies Quarterly* 1 (2014): 235–37, https://doi.org/10.1215/23289252-2400145.

Cervenak, Sarah Jane. "Black Gathering: 'The Weight of Being' in Leonardo Drew's Sculpture." *Women and Performance: A Journal of Feminist Theory* 26 (2016): 1–16, https://doi.org/10.1080/0740770X.2016.1185242.

Chambers-Letson, Joshua. *After the Party: A Manifesto for Queer of Color Life.* New York: NYU Press, 2018.

Chandler, Nahum Dimitri. "The Coming of the Second-Time." The A-Line, August 30, 2018. https://alinejournal.com/vol-1-no-3-4/the-coming-of-the -second-time/.

Chandler, Nahum Dimitri. *X: The Problem of the Negro as a Problem for Thought.* New York: Fordham University Press, 2014.

Chase, Sidney. "Acts of Intentionality: A One on One with Venus Selenite." *Huffington Post,* July 7, 2016. https://www.huffingtonpost.com /entry/acts-of-intentionality-a-one-on-one-with-venus-selenite_us _576434e2e4b034ff3eef582b.

Cheah, Pheng. *What Is a World? On Postcolonial Literature as World Literature.* Durham, NC: Duke University Press, 2016.

Chu, Andrea Long. *Females*. New York: Verso, 2019.

Chu, Andrea Long, and Emmett Harsin Drager. "After Trans Studies." TSQ: *Transgender Studies Quarterly* 6 (2019): 103–16, https://doi.org/10.1215/23289252 -7253524.

Clarke, Cheryl. "Lesbianism: An Act of Resistance." In *This Bridge Called My Back: Writings by Radical Women of Color*, edited by Cherríe Moraga and Toni Cade Bambara, 128–37. New York: Kitchen Table, 1983.

Clifton, Lucille. "Won't You Celebrate with Me." Poetry Foundation, 1993. https:// www.poetryfoundation.org/poems/50974/wont-you-celebrate-with-me (accessed March 22, 2019).

Colebrook, Claire. "Modernism without Women: The Refusal of Becoming-Woman (and Post-Feminism)." *Deleuze Studies* 7 (2013): 427–55, https://doi.org/10 .3366/dls.2013.0123.

Colebrook, Claire. "What Is It Like to Be a Human?" TSQ: *Transgender Studies Quarterly* 2 (2015): 227–43, https://doi.org/10.1215/23289252-2867472.

Collins, Patricia Hill. "Black Feminist Thought as Oppositional Knowledge." *Departures in Critical and Qualitative Research* 5 (2016): 133–44, https://doi.org/10 .1525/dcqr.2016.5.3.133.

Collins, Patricia Hill. *Black Feminist Thought: Knowledge, Consciousness, and the Politics of Empowerment*. New York: Routledge, 2000.

Combahee River Collective. "A Black Feminist Statement." *Women's Studies Quarterly* 42 (2014): 271–80.

Commander, Michelle D. *Afro-Atlantic Flight: Speculative Returns and the Black Fantastic*. Durham, NC: Duke University Press, 2017.

Cornell, Drucilla. *Beyond Accommodation: Ethical Feminism, Deconstruction, and the Law*. Lanham, MD: Rowman and Littlefield, 1999.

Corsani, Antonella. "Beyond the Myth of Woman: The Becoming-Transfeminist of (Post-)Marxism." Translated by Timothy S. Murphy. *SubStance* 36 (2007): 106–38.

Crawley, Ashon. *Blackpentecostal Breath: The Aesthetics of Possibility*. New York: Fordham University Press, 2016.

Crawley, Ashon. "Otherwise Movements." *The New Inquiry*, January 19, 2015. https://thenewinquiry.com/otherwise-movements/.

Crawley, Ashon. *The Lonely Letters*. Durham, NC: Duke University Press, 2020.

Crawley, Ashon. "That There Might Be Black: Thought Nothing Music and the Hammond B-3." CR: *The New Centennial Review* 16 (2017): 123–49.

Cruz, Rosana. "Who Does Lady Dane Figueroa Edidi Think She Is?" Colorlines, December 18, 2019. https://www.colorlines.com/articles/who-does-lady-dane -figueroa-edidi-think-she.

Cunningham, Nijah. "The Resistance of the Lost Body." *Small Axe* 20 (2016): 113–28, https://doi.org/10.1215/07990537-3481402.

da Silva, Denise. "Hacking the Subject: Black Feminism and Refusal beyond the Limits of Critique." *PhiloSOPHIA* 8 (2018): 19–41.

da Silva, Denise. "Hacking the Subject: Black Feminism, Refusal, and the Limits of Critique." Barnard College, 2015. https://www.youtube.com/watch?v=T3B5Gh2JSQg (accessed March 29, 2021).

da Silva, Denise. "On Difference without Separability." *32a São Paulo Art Biennial* (2016): 57–65.

da Silva, Denise Ferreira. "1 (Life) ÷ 0 (Blackness) = ∞ − ∞ or ∞ / ∞: On Matter beyond the Equation of Value." *e-flux journal* 79 (2017). https://www.e-flux.com/journal/79/94686/1-life-0-blackness-or-on-matter-beyond-the-equation-of-value/.

da Silva, Denise. "Toward a Black Feminist Poethics." *Black Scholar* 44 (2014): 81–97, https://doi.org/10.1080/00064246.2014.11413690.

da Silva, Denise. *Toward a Global Idea of Race.* Borderlines 27. Minneapolis: University of Minnesota Press, 2007.

Davis, Angela Y., and Lisa Lowe. "Interview with Lisa Lowe and Angela Davis: Reflections on Race, Class, and Gender in the USA." In *The Politics of Culture in the Shadow of Capital*, edited by Lisa Lowe and David Lloyd, 303–23. Durham, NC: Duke University Press, 1997.

"Del LaGrace Volcano: Corpus Queer: Bodies of Resistance 1980–2018." MoCA Skopje, June 7, 2018. https://msu.mk/del-la-grace-volcano-corpus-queer-bodies-of-resistance-1980–2018/.

Deleuze, Gilles. "Letter to a Harsh Critic." In *Negotiations, 1972–1990*, translated by Martin Joughin, 3–12. New York: Columbia University Press, 1995.

Deleuze, Gilles, and Felix Guattari. *A Thousand Plateaus: Capitalism and Schizophrenia.* Translated by Brian Massumi. Minneapolis: University of Minnesota Press, 1987.

Derrida, Jacques. *Specters of Marx: The State of the Debt, the Work of Mourning and the New International.* New York: Routledge, 2006.

Devereaux, Shaadi. "Trans Women: Live and in Color." The Progressive, March 7, 2015. https://progressive.org/magazine/trans-women-live-and-in-color/.

Diaz, Junot. "Under President Trump, Radical Hope Is Our Best Weapon." *New Yorker*, November 21, 2016. http://www.newyorker.com/magazine/2016/11/21/under-president-trump-radical-hope-is-our-best-weapon.

Dillon, Stephen. "Possessed by Death: The Neoliberal-Carceral State, Black Feminism, and the Afterlife of Slavery." *Radical History Review* 12 (2012): 113–25, https://doi.org/10.1215/01636545-1416196.

dodd, jayy. *The Black Condition Ft. Narcissus.* New York: Nightboat, 2019.

dodd, jayy. "Gender Non Conformity as Peak Blackness." Medium, November 28, 2016. https://medium.com/@jayydodd/gender-non-conformity-as-peak-blackness-7834a901dc1d#.tydx3c5qe.

dodd, jayy. "Homies Don't Come Out, They Let You In." Medium, July 12, 2016. https://medium.com/@jayydodd/homies-dont-come-out-they-let-you-in-aaf9ad991d8c.

dodd, jayy. "Horizon." Vagabond City, April 1, 2016. https://vagabondcitylit.com/2016/04/01/horizon-by-jayy-dodd/.

dodd, jayy. "I Know I Been Changed: After Lashun Pace (Rhodes)." Yes Poetry, March 8, 2017. https://www.yespoetry.com/news/jayy-dodd.

dodd, jayy. "The Impossiible Outside (Or, a Zumbi's Autopsy)." Awst Press, August 29, 2016. https://awst-press.com/essay-series/jayy-dodd/zumbi.

dodd, jayy. "Narcissus (Goes to the Market)." Nashville Review, April 5, 2017. https://wp0.vanderbilt.edu/nashvillereview/archives/13619.

dodd, jayy. "A Poetic beyond Resilience." Poetry Foundation, November 20, 2017. https://www.poetryfoundation.org/harriet/2017/11/a-poetic-beyond -resilience.

dodd, jayy. "Put Your Hands Where My Eyes Can See." Big Lucks, October 11, 2017. https://www.biglucks.com/journal/jayy-dodd.

dodd, jayy. "Stop Dude Feminists." Those People, 2015. https://medium.com/thsppl /stop-dude-feminists-1c0693d0126c.

dodd, jayy. "To Wake Up Flawless: Beyoncé as Black and Feminist." Snakes on McCain, December 16, 2013. http://snakesonmccain.blogspot.com/2013/12/to -wake-up-flawless-beyonce-as-black.html.

D'Oleo, Dixa Ramírez. "Mushrooms and Mischief: On Questions of Blackness." Small Axe 23 (2019): 152–63.

Dolphijn, Rick, and Iris van der Tuin. "A Thousand Tiny Intersections: Linguisticism, Feminism, Racism and Deleuzian Becomings." In Deleuze and Race, edited by Arun Saldanha, 129–43. Edinburgh: Edinburgh University Press, 2013.

Donahue, Joseph. "Wind Map VII." Talisman: A Journal of Contemporary Poetry and Poetics, 2011. https://www.talismanmag.net/donahue.html (accessed March 29, 2021).

Douglass, Frederick. Narrative of the Life of Frederick Douglass. New York: Dover Publications, 2016.

duCille, Ann. "Of Race, Gender, and the Novel; or, Where in the World Is Toni Morrison?" Novel 50 (2017): 375–87, https://doi.org/10.1215/00295132-4194984.

Duggan, Lisa, and Kathleen McHugh. "A Fem(Me)Inist Manifesto." Women and Performance: A Journal of Feminist Theory 8 (1996): 153–59, https://doi.org/10 .1080/07407709608571236.

Durban-Albrecht, Erin. "Postcolonial Disablement and/as Transition: Trans* Haitian Narratives of Breaking Open and Stitching Together." TSQ: Transgender Studies Quarterly 4 (2017): 195–207, https://doi.org/10.1215/23289252-3814997.

Edidi, Dane Figueroa. For Black Trans Girls Who Gotta Cuss a Mother Fucker Out When Snatching an Edge Ain't Enough: A Choreo Poem. CreateSpace, 2017.

Edidi, Dane Figueroa. "Love and Saying No: Five Questions with Lady Dane Figueroa Edidi." TransFaith, n.d. http://www.transfaithonline.org/display /article/love-saying-no-five-questions-with-lady-dane-figueroa-edidi/ (accessed March 29, 2021).

Edwards, Erica. "Cedric People." In Futures of Black Radicalism, edited by Gaye Theresa Johnson and Alex Lubin, 251–54. New York: Verso, 2017.

Edwards, Rebekah. "Trans-Poetics." TSQ: Transgender Studies Quarterly 1 (2014): 252–53, https://doi.org/10.1215/23289252-2400109.

Ellison, Ralph. *Invisible Man*. New York: Modern Library, 1994.

Ellison, Treva. "Day 1: When Remembering Forgets, Forgetting Remembers." *The Feminist Wire*, November 20, 2017. http://www.thefeministwire.com/2017/11/introduction-remembering-forgets-forgetting-remembers/.

Ellison, Treva. "Flex, Conjure, Crack: Flexibility and the Uncertainty of Blackness." *C: International Contemporary Art* 132 (2017): 28–33.

Ellison, Treva. "The Labor of Werqing It: The Performance and Protest Strategies of Sir Lady Java." In *Trap Door: Trans Cultural Production and the Politics of Visibility*, edited by Reina Gossett, Eric A. Stanley, and Johanna Burton, 1–22. Cambridge, MA: MIT Press, 2017.

Ellison, Treva, Kai M. Green, and CeCe McDonald. "An Introduction: When Remembering Forgets, What Forgetting Remembers." *The Feminist Wire*, November 20, 2017. http://www.thefeministwire.com/2017/11/introduction-remembering-forgets-forgetting-remembers/.

Ellison, Treva, Kai M. Green, Matt Richardson, and C. Riley Snorton. "We Got Issues: Toward a Black Trans*/Studies." *TSQ: Transgender Studies Quarterly* 4 (2017): 162–69.

Enke, Anne, ed. *Transfeminist Perspectives in and beyond Transgender and Gender Studies*. Philadelphia, PA: Temple University Press, 2012.

Escalante, Alejandro S. "Gynecology and the Ungendering of Black Women." African American Intellectual History Society, December 4, 2018. https://www.aaihs.org/gynecology-and-the-ungendering-of-black-women/.

Espineira, Karine. "Q Comme Questions." In *Q comme queer: Les séminaires Q du zoo (1996–1997)*, by Marie-Hélène/Sam Bourcier, 112–21. Lille, France: Éditions GayKitschCamp.

Espineira, Karine, and Marie-Hélène/Sam Bourcier. "Transfeminism: Something Else, Somewhere Else." *TSQ: Transgender Studies Quarterly* 3 (2016): 84–94, https://doi.org/10.1215/23289252-3334247.

Eversley, Shelly. "The Evidence of Things Unseen: Experimental Form as Black Feminist Praxis." *Journal of Narrative Theory* 48 (2018): 378–98, https://doi.org/10.1353/jnt.2018.0016.

Feinberg, Leslie. *Stone Butch Blues*. New York: Alyson, 2014.

Ferguson, Roderick A. *Aberrations in Black: Toward a Queer of Color Critique*. Minneapolis: University of Minnesota Press, 2004.

Ferguson, Roderick A. "To Catch a Light-Filled Vision: American Studies and the Activation of Radical Traditions." *American Quarterly* 71 (2019): 317–35, https://doi.org/10.1353/aq.2019.0026.

Filar, Ray, and Che Gossett. "Cruising in the End Times: An Interview with Che Gossett." Verso, December 18, 2016. https://www.versobooks.com/blogs/3016-cruising-in-the-end-times-an-interview-with-che-gossett.

Foucault, Michel. *Archaeology of Knowledge*. London: Psychology Press, 2002.

Fournier, M. "Lines of Flight." *TSQ: Transgender Studies Quarterly* 1 (2014): 121–22, https://doi.org/10.1215/23289252-2399785.

Fugitive Slave Act of 1793, U.S.C. ch. 7, 1 Stat. 302 (February 12, 1793).

Fugitive Slave Act of 1850, U.S.C. ch. 60, 9 Stat. 462 (September 18, 1850).

Gabriel, Kay. "The Limits of the Bit." *Los Angeles Review of Books*, November 25, 2019. https://lareviewofbooks.org/article/the-limits-of-the-bit/.

Garcia-Rojas, Claudia. "Intersectionality Is a Hot Topic—and So Is the Term's Misuse." Truthout, October 17, 2019. https://truthout.org/articles/intersectionality-is-a-hot-topic-and-so-is-the-terms-misuse/.

Garriga-López, Claudia Sofía. "Transfeminism." In *Global Encyclopedia of Lesbian, Gay, Bisexual, Transgender, and Queer (LGBTQ) History*, edited by Howard Chiang, 1619–23. Farmington Hills, MI: Charles Scribner's Sons, 2019.

Garza, Alicia. "A Herstory of the #BlackLivesMatter Movement by Alicia Garza." *The Feminist Wire*, October 7, 2014. http://thefeministwire.com/2014/10/blacklivesmatter-2/.

Gessen, Masha. "To Be, or Not to Be." *New York Review of Books*, February 8, 2018. http://www.nybooks.com/articles/2018/02/08/to-be-or-not-to-be/.

Gill-Peterson, Jules. *Histories of the Transgender Child*. Minneapolis: University of Minnesota Press, 2018.

Giovannitti, Sophia. "In Defense of Men." Majuscule, 2020. https://majusculelit.com/in-defense-of-men/ (accessed March 29, 2021).

Giroux, Henry. "When Hope Is Subversive." *Tikkun* 19 (2004): 38–39.

Glissant, Édouard. *Poetics of Relation*. Translated by Betsy Wing. Ann Arbor: University of Michigan Press, 1997.

Gordon, Lewis R. *Her Majesty's Other Children: Sketches of Racism from a Neocolonial Age*. Lanham: Rowman and Littlefield, 1997.

Górska, Magdalena. *Breathing Matters: Feminist Intersectional Politics of Vulnerability*. Linköping: Linköping University Press, 2016.

Gossett, Che. "Abolitionist Imaginings: A Conversation with Bo Brown, Reina Gossett, and Dylan Rodríguez." In *Captive Genders: Trans Embodiment and the Prison Industrial Complex*, edited by Eric A. Stanley and Nat Smith, 323–42. Oakland, CA: AK Press, 2011.

Gossett, Che. "Žižek's Trans/Gender Trouble." *Los Angeles Review of Books*, September 13, 2016. https://lareviewofbooks.org/article/zizeks-transgender-trouble/.

Gosztola, Kevin. "Authors of Combahee River Statement, Which Profoundly Influenced Black Feminism, Mark 40th Anniversary." *ShadowProof*, July 10, 2017. https://shadowproof.com/2017/07/10/authors-combahee-river-statement-profoundly-influenced-black-feminism-mark-40th-anniversary/.

Green, Kai M. "The Essential I/Eye in We: A Black TransFeminist Approach to Ethnographic Film." *Black Camera* 6 (2015): 187–200.

Green, Kai M. "'Race and Gender Are Not the Same!' Is Not a Good Response to the 'Transracial'/Transgender Question OR We Can and Must Do Better." *The Feminist Wire*, June 14, 2015. http://www.thefeministwire.com/2015/06/race-and-gender-are-not-the-same-is-not-a-good-response-to-the-transracial-transgender-question-or-we-can-and-must-do-better/.

Green, Kai M., and Treva Ellison. "Tranifest." TSQ: Transgender Studies Quarterly 1 (2014): 222–25, https://doi.org/10.1215/23289252-2400082.

Grosz, Elizabeth. Becoming Undone: Darwinian Reflections on Life, Politics, and Art. Durham, NC: Duke University Press, 2011.

Gumbs, Alexis Pauline. Dub: Finding Ceremony. Durham, NC: Duke University Press, 2020.

Gumbs, Alexis Pauline. "Freedom Seeds: Growing Abolition in Durham, North Carolina." In Abolition Now!: Ten Years of Strategy and Struggle against the Prison Industrial Complex, edited by CR10 Publications Collective, 145–56. Oakland, CA: AK Press, 2008.

Gumbs, Alexis Pauline. M Archive: After the End of the World. Durham, NC: Duke University Press, 2018.

Gumbs, Alexis Pauline. "One Thing: Toni Cade Bambara in the Speaking Everyday." The Feminist Wire, November 23, 2014. http://www.thefeministwire.com /2014/11/well-being-of-the-community/.

Gumbs, Alexis Pauline. Spill: Scenes of Black Feminist Fugitivity. Durham, NC: Duke University Press, 2016.

Gumbs, Alexis Pauline. "We Be: Black Feminism and Embodiment (Part 3 of Can Black Feminism Be Quantified)." The Feminist Wire, March 22, 2012. http:// www.thefeministwire.com/2012/03/we-be-black-feminism-and-embodiment -part-3-of-can-black-feminism-be-quantified/.

Gumbs, Alexis Pauline. "We Can Learn to Mother Ourselves: The Queer Survival of Black Feminism, 1968–1996." PhD diss., Duke University, 2010.

Gumbs, Alexis Pauline. "We Stay in Love with Our Freedom: A Conversation with Alexis Pauline Gumbs." Interview by Joy KMT, February 4, 2018. https:// lareviewofbooks.org/article/we-stay-in-love-with-our-freedom-a-conversation -with-alexis-pauline-gumbs/.

Halberstam, Jack. Female Masculinity. Durham, NC: Duke University Press, 1998.

Halberstam, Jack. Trans*: A Quick and Quirky Account of Gender Variability. Oakland: University of California Press, 2018.

Halberstam, Jack. "Wildness, Loss, Death." Social Text 32 (2014): 137–48, https:// doi.org/10.1215/01642472-2820520.

Halberstam, Jack, and Tavia Nyong'o. "Introduction: Theory in the Wild." South Atlantic Quarterly 117 (July 2018): 453–64, https://doi.org/10.1215/00382876 -6942081.

Haley, Sarah. No Mercy Here: Gender, Punishment, and the Making of Jim Crow Mo- dernity. Chapel Hill: University of North Carolina Press, 2016.

Harney, Stefano, and Fred Moten. The Undercommons: Fugitive Planning and Black Study. New York: Minor Compositions, 2013.

Hartman, Saidiya V. Scenes of Subjection: Terror, Slavery, and Self-Making in Nineteenth-Century America. New York: Oxford University Press, 1997.

Hartman, Saidiya V. Wayward Lives, Beautiful Experiments: Intimate Histories of Social Upheaval. New York: W. W. Norton, 2019.

Haslett, Tim. "Hortense Spillers Interviewed by Tim Haslett." *Black Cultural Studies*, 1998. https://drive.google.com/file/d/1ktmHlPkd7u6IjT2Qw3oNb-FnI97_FNXR/view?usp=sharing.

Haynes, Tonya. "Sylvia Wynter's Theory of the Human and the Crisis School of Caribbean Heteromasculinity Studies." *Small Axe* 20 (2016): 92–112, https://doi.org/10.1215/07990537-3481570.

Hayward, Eva. "Don't Exist." *TSQ: Transgender Studies Quarterly* 4 (2017): 191–94, https://doi.org/10.1215/23289252-3814985.

Hayward, Eva, and Che Gossett. "Impossibility of That." *Angelaki* 22 (2017): 15–24, https://doi.org/10.1080/0969725X.2017.1322814.

Hedva, Johanna. "In Defence of De-Persons." Guts, May 10, 2016. http://gutsmagazine.ca/in/.

Heidegger, Martin. *Poetry, Language, Thought.* New York: Perennial Classics, 2009.

Herzog, Katie. "Is the Life Expectancy of Trans Women in the U.S. Just 35? No." The Stranger, September 23, 2019. https://www.thestranger.com/slog/2019/09/23/41471629/is-the-life-expectancy-of-trans-women-in-the-us-just-35-no.

Hesse, Barnor. "White Sovereignty (. . .), Black Life Politics: 'The N****r They Couldn't Kill.'" *South Atlantic Quarterly* 116 (2017): 581–604, https://doi.org/10.1215/00382876-3961494.

Holland, Sharon Patricia. *Raising the Dead: Readings of Death and (Black) Subjectivity.* Durham, NC: Duke University Press, 2000.

Hong, Grace Kyungwon. *The Ruptures of American Capital: Women of Color Feminism and the Culture of Immigrant Labor.* Minneapolis: University of Minnesota Press, 2006.

Horton-Stallings, LaMonda. *Funk the Erotic: Transaesthetics and Black Sexual Cultures.* Urbana: University of Illinois Press, 2015.

Horton-Stallings, LaMonda. *Mutha' Is Half a Word: Intersections of Folklore, Vernacular, Myth, and Queerness in Black Female Culture.* Columbus: Ohio State University Press, 2007.

Howard, Zora. "Won't Die Things." 2015. https://www.youtube.com/watch?v=xbtxa1XJ7gA (accessed March 29, 2021).

Howie, Cary. "On Transfiguration." *L'Esprit Créateur* 53 (2013): 158–66, https://doi.org/10.1353/esp.2013.0002.

Hurston, Zora Neale. *Mules and Men.* New York: Harper Perennial, 1990.

"Interview: Kai M. Green on Transracialism—Epistemic Unruliness 21." Always Already Podcast, July 5, 2017. https://alwaysalreadypodcast.wordpress.com/2017/07/05/interview-kai-m-green-on-transracialism-epistemic-unruliness-21/.

Jardine, Alice. *Gynesis: Configurations of Woman and Modernity.* Ithaca, NY: Cornell University Press, 1985.

"jayy dodd." Nightboat Books. https://nightboat.org/bio/jayy-dodd/ (accessed March 29, 2021).

Johnson, E. Patrick, ed. *No Tea, No Shade: New Writings in Black Queer Studies.* Durham, NC: Duke University Press, 2016.

Johnson, Gaye Theresa, and Alex Lubin, eds. *Futures of Black Radicalism*. New York: Verso, 2017.

Kaas, Hailey. "Birth of Transfeminism in Brazil between Alliances and Backlashes." *TSQ: Transgender Studies Quarterly* 3 (2016): 146–49, https://doi.org/10.1215/23289252-3334307.

Keegan, Cáel M., Laura Horak, and Eliza Steinbock. "Cinematic/Trans*/Bodies Now (and Then, and to Come)." *Somatechnics* 8 (2018): 1–13, https://doi.org/10.3366/soma.2018.0233.

Keeling, Kara. *The Witch's Flight: The Cinematic, the Black Femme, and the Image of Common Sense*. Durham, NC: Duke University Press, 2007.

Kelley, Robin D. G. "Black Study, Black Struggle." *Boston Review*, March 7, 2016. http://bostonreview.net/forum/robin-d-g-kelley-black-study-black-struggle.

Kelly, Devin. "Interview with jayy dodd, Author of *Mannish Tongues*." Entropy, January 23, 2017. https://entropymag.org/interview-with-jayy-dodd-author-of-mannish-tongues/.

Kincaid, Adrienne. "Why I Had to Come Out as a Black Trans Woman." *Huffington Post*, August 22, 2016. https://www.huffingtonpost.com/adrienne-kincaid/post_12733_b_11258546.html.

King, Tiffany Lethabo. *The Black Shoals: Offshore Formations of Black and Native Studies*. Durham, NC: Duke University Press, 2019.

King, Tiffany Lethabo, Jenell Navarro, and Andrea Smith, eds. *Otherwise Worlds: Against Settler Colonialism and Anti-Blackness*. Durham, NC: Duke University Press, 2020.

Kline, David. "The Pragmatics of Resistance: Framing Anti-Blackness and the Limits of Political Ontology." *Critical Philosophy of Race* 5 (2017): 51–69.

Kokumo. "Black, Trans, and Still Breathing." The Feminist Wire, November 23, 2017. http://www.thefeministwire.com/2017/11/black-trans-still-breathing/.

Konitshek, Haley. "Calling Forth History's Mocking Doubles." *Hypatia* 32 (2017): 1–19, https://doi.org/10.1111/hypa.12334.

Koyama, Emi. "The Transfeminist Manifesto." In *Catching a Wave: Reclaiming Feminism for the Twenty-First Century*, edited by Rory Dicker and Alison Piepmeier, 244–59. Boston, MA: Northeastern University Press, 2003.

Lamble, S. "Transforming Carceral Logics: 10 Reasons to Dismantle the Prison Industrial Complex Using a Queer/Trans Analysis." In *Captive Genders: Trans Embodiment and the Prison Industrial Complex*, edited by Eric A. Stanley and Nat Smith, 235–66. Oakland, CA: AK Press, 2011.

Lang, Aaryn. "Why I Don't Believe in Transgender Day of Remembrance." Them., November 20, 2017. https://www.them.us/story/why-i-dont-believe-in-trans-day-of-remembrance.

Lauretis, Teresa de. "Eccentric Subjects: Feminist Theory and Historical Consciousness." *Feminist Studies* 16 (1990): 115–50, https://doi.org/10.2307/3177959.

Lorde, Audre. "Age, Race, Class, and Sex: Women Redefining Difference." In *Sister Outsider: Essays and Speeches*, 114–23. Berkeley, CA: Crossing Press, 1984.

Lowe, Lisa. *The Intimacies of Four Continents*. Durham, NC: Duke University Press, 2015.

Macharia, Keguro. *Frottage: Frictions of Intimacy across the Black Diaspora*. New York: NYU Press, 2019.

Mackey, Nathaniel. *Bedouin Hornbook*. Los Angeles: Sun and Moon, 1997.

Malatino, Hil. *Queer Embodiment: Monstrosity, Medical Violence, and Intersex Experience*. Lincoln: University of Nebraska Press, 2019.

Martel, James R. *The Misinterpellated Subject*. Durham, NC: Duke University Press, 2017.

Marx, Karl. *Grundrisse: Foundations of the Critique of Political Economy*. Translated by Martin Nicolaus. New York: Penguin Classics, 1993.

McDonald, CeCe. "Foreword." In *Captive Genders: Trans Embodiment and the Prison Industrial Complex*, edited by Eric A. Stanley and Nat Smith, 1–4. Oakland, CA: AK Press, 2015.

McDonald, CeCe, Kai M. Green, and Treva Ellison. "Trans Multitudes and Death Reality: A Coda." The Feminist Wire, November 27, 2017. https://thefeministwire.com/2017/11/trans-multitudes-death-reality-coda/.

McDonald, CeCe, and Omise'eke Natasha Tinsley. "'Go Beyond Our Natural Selves': The Prison Letters of CeCe McDonald." *TSQ: Transgender Studies Quarterly* 4 (2017): 243–65, https://doi.org/10.1215/23289252-3815045.

McKittrick, Katherine. *Demonic Grounds: Black Women and the Cartographies of Struggle*. Minneapolis: University of Minnesota Press, 2006.

McKittrick, Katherine. "Diachronic Loops/Deadweight Tonnage/Bad Made Measure." *Cultural Geographies* 23 (2016): 3–18, https://doi.org/10.1177/1474474015612716.

McKittrick, Katherine. "Mathematics Black Life." *Black Scholar* 44 (2014): 16–28, https://doi.org/10.1080/00064246.2014.11413684.

McKittrick, Katherine. "Rebellion/Invention/Groove." *Small Axe* 20 (2016): 79–91, https://doi.org/10.1215/07990537-3481558.

McKittrick, Katherine. "Worn Out." *Southeastern Geographer* 57 (2017): 96–100.

Merleau-Ponty, Maurice. *The Visible and the Invisible: Followed by Working Notes*. Edited by Claude Lefort. Translated by Alphonso Lingis. Evanston, IL: Northwestern University Press, 1968.

Mignolo, Walter D. "Epistemic Disobedience, Independent Thought and Decolonial Freedom." *Theory, Culture, and Society* 26 (2009): 159–81, https://doi.org/10.1177/0263276409349275.

Moore, Madison. "Shea Diamond, No Longer In the Rough (Exclusive)." *Out*, November 15, 2016. https://www.out.com/music/2016/11/15/shea-diamond-no-longer-rough-exclusive.

Morris, Cherise. "The Cosmic Matter of Black Lives." August 26, 2017. https://www.cherisemorris.com/blog/2017/8/24/0xw6i92nlpvr4ruz4h3kocs3jrev8a.

Morrison, Toni. *Song of Solomon*. New York: Knopf, 1977.

Morrison, Toni. *The Bluest Eye.* New York: Vintage International, 2007.

Moten, Fred. *Black and Blur.* Durham, NC: Duke University Press Books, 2017.

Moten, Fred. "Blackness and Nothingness (Mysticism in the Flesh)." *South Atlantic Quarterly* 112 (2013): 737–80.

Moten, Fred. "Blackness and Poetry." *Arcade: Literature, the Humanities, and the World* 55 (2015): http://arcade.stanford.edu/content/blackness-and-poetry-0 (accessed March 29, 2021).

Moten, Fred. "The Case of Blackness." *Criticism* 50 (2008): 177–218.

Moten, Fred. *The Feel Trio.* Tucson, AZ: Letter Machine Editions, 2014.

Moten, Fred. *In the Break : The Aesthetics of the Black Radical Tradition.* Minneapolis: University of Minnesota Press, 2003.

Moten, Fred. "Preface for a Solo by Miles Davis." *Women and Performance: A Journal of Feminist Theory* 17 (2007): 217–46, https://doi.org/10.1080/07407700701387317.

Moten, Fred. *Stolen Life.* Durham, NC: Duke University Press, 2018.

Moten, Fred. "Symphony of Combs." The A-Line, February 6, 2018. https://alinejournal.com/vol-1-no-2/symphony-of-combs/.

Moten, Fred, and Stefano Harney. "Indent (To Serve the Debt)." In *Public Servants: Art and the Crisis of the Common Good,* edited by Johanna Burton, Shannon Jackson, and Dominic Willsdon, 197–206. Cambridge, MA: MIT Press, 2016.

Moten, Fred, and Wu Tsang. "All Terror, All Beauty: Wu Tsang and Fred Moten in Conversation." In *Trap Door: Trans Cultural Production and the Politics of Visibilty,* edited by Reina Gossett, Eric A. Stanley, and Johanna Burton, 339–48. Cambridge, MA: MIT Press, 2017.

Muñoz, José Esteban. *Cruising Utopia: The Then and There of Queer Futurity.* New York: NYU Press, 2009.

Nash, Jennifer C. *Black Feminism Reimagined: After Intersectionality.* Durham, NC: Duke University Press, 2019.

Nash, Jennifer C. "Re-Thinking Intersectionality." *Feminist Review* 89 (2008): 1–15, https://doi.org/10.1057/fr.2008.4.

Nealon, Jeffrey T. "Refraining, Becoming-Black: Repetition and Difference in Amiri Baraka's *Blues People.*" *Symplokē* 6 (1998): 83–95.

Nordmarken, Sonny. "Queering Gendering: Trans Epistemologies and the Disruption and Production of Gender Accomplishment Practices." *Feminist Studies* 45 (2019): 36–66, https://doi.org/10.15767/feministstudies.45.1.0036.

Nyong'o, Tavia. *Afro-Fabulations: The Queer Drama of Black Life.* New York: NYU Press, 2019.

Olson, Gary A., and Lynn Worsham. "Changing the Subject: Judith Butler's Politics of Radical Resignification." *JAC* 20 (2000): 727–65.

Oyěwùmí, Oyèrónkẹ́. "De-confounding Gender: Feminist Theorizing and Western Culture, a Comment on Hawkesworth's 'Confounding Gender.'" *Signs* 23 (1998): 1049–62.

Oyěwùmí, Oyèrónkẹ́. *The Invention of Women: Making an African Sense of Western Gender Discourses.* Minneapolis: University of Minnesota Press, 1997.

Parker, L. G. "Passing: Beyond the Body, A Reason to Say Yes—A Conversation with Venus Selenite and Francisco-Luis White." *Winter Tangerine*, n.d. http:// www.wintertangerine.com/conversation-2/ (accessed March 29, 2021).

Perry, Imani. *Vexy Thing: On Gender and Liberation*. Durham, NC: Duke University Press, 2018.

Philip, M. NourbeSe. *Zong!* Middletown, CT: Wesleyan University Press, 2008.

Pierce, Joseph M. "Feeling, Disrupting." *Biography* 39 (2016): 434–37, 508.

Pinto, Samantha. "Black Feminist Literacies: Ungendering, Flesh, and Post-Spillers Epistemologies of Embodied and Emotional Justice." *Journal of Black Sexuality and Relationships* 4 (2017): 25–45, https://doi.org/10.1353/bsr.2017.0019.

Preciado, Paul B. *Testo Junkie: Sex, Drugs, and Biopolitics in the Pharmacopornographic Era*. Translated by Bruce Benderson. New York: Feminist Press, 2013.

Preciado, Paul B. *Countersexual Manifesto*. Translated by Kevin Gerry Dunn. New York: Columbia University Press, 2018.

Preston, Ashlee Marie. "A Transwoman of Color's Guide to Survival." Afropunk, July 7, 2017. http://afropunk.com/2017/07/a-transwoman-of-color-s-guide-to -survival-self-care-is-key/.

Puar, Jasbir K. "'I Would Rather Be a Cyborg Than a Goddess': Becoming-Intersectional in Assemblage Theory." *Philosophia* 2 (2012): 49–66.

Puar, Jasbir K. *Terrorist Assemblages: Homonationalism in Queer Times*. Durham, NC: Duke University Press, 2007.

Radcliffe College Monographs. Cambridge: Ginn, 1888.

Raha, Nat. "Future Justice in the Present." *Radical Transfeminism*, 2017. https://www .academia.edu/34153942/Radical_Transfeminism_Future_Justice_in_the _Present.

Raha, Nat. "The Limits of Trans Liberalism." Verso, September 21, 2015. https:// www.versobooks.com/blogs/2245-the-limits-of-trans-liberalism-by-nat-raha.

Raha, Nat. "Radical Transfeminism." Radical Transfeminism Zine, Autumn 2017. https://radicaltransfeminismzine.tumblr.com/post/165475105432/forthcoming.

Raha, Nat. "Transfeminine Brokenness, Radical Transfeminism." *South Atlantic Quarterly* 116 (2017): 632–46, https://doi.org/10.1215/00382876-3961754.

Reed, Anthony. *Freedom Time: The Poetics and Politics of Black Experimental Writing*. Baltimore, MD: Johns Hopkins University Press, 2014.

Richardson, Matt. "Ajita Wilson: Blaxploitation, Sexploitation, and the Making of Black Womanhood." *TSQ: Transgender Studies Quarterly* 7 (2020): 192–207, https://doi.org/10.1215/23289252-8143350.

Rickards, P. J. "Watch: Artist Lina Iris Viktor on the Misconceptions of Blackness in Art, and Painting with Pure Gold." The Root, March 30, 2017. http://www.theroot .com/watch-artist-lina-iris-viktor-on-the-misconceptions-of-1793694249.

Ridley, LaVelle. "Imagining Otherly: Performing Possible Black Trans Futures in Tangerine." *TSQ: Transgender Studies Quarterly* 6 (2019): 481–90, https://doi .org/10.1215/23289252-7771653.

Rifkin, Mark. *Fictions of Land and Flesh: Blackness, Indigeneity, Speculation*. Durham, NC: Duke University Press, 2019.

Riley, Denise. *Am I That Name? Feminism and the Category of "Women" in History*. Minneapolis: University of Minnesota Press, 1988.

Ritskes, Eric. "Beyond and against White Settler Colonialism in Palestine: Fugitive Futurities in Amir Nizar Zuabi's 'The Underground Ghetto City of Gaza.'" *Cultural Studies ↔ Critical Methodologies* 17 (2017): 78–86, https://doi.org/10.1177/1532708616640561.

Roben, Scott. "Trigger: Gender as a Tool and a Weapon." *Art in America*, December 1, 2017. http://www.artinamericamagazine.com/reviews/trigger-gender-as-a-tool-and-a-weapon/.

Rosenberg, Jordy. "Trans/War Boy/Gender: The Primitive Accumulation of T." *Salvage*, December 21, 2015. http://salvage.zone/in-print/trans-war-boy-gender/.

Royce Da 5'9", and Slaughterhouse. "Monsters in My Head," 2012. https://www.youtube.com/watch?v=rz_wZ39JpmE.

"Saidiya Hartman on Fugitive Feminism." Institute of Contemporary Arts, 2018. https://ica.art/learning/round-table-fugitivity# (accessed September 17, 2019).

Salamon, Gayle. "'The Place Where Life Hides Away': Merleau-Ponty, Fanon, and the Location of Bodily Being." *Differences* 17 (2006): 96–112, https://doi.org/10.1215/10407391-2006-004.

Samatar, Sofia. "Against the Normative World." *The New Inquiry*, April 9, 2015. https://thenewinquiry.com/against-the-normative-world/.

Santana, Dora Silva. "Mais Viva! Reassembling Transness, Blackness, and Feminism." *TSQ: Transgender Studies Quarterly* 6 (2019): 210–22, https://doi.org/10.1215/23289252-7348496.

Schuster, Emma, and Tina Campt. "Black Feminist Futures and the Practice of Fugitivity." *BCRW Blog*, 2014. http://bcrw.barnard.edu/blog/black-feminist-futures-and-the-practice-of-fugitivity/ (accessed March 29, 2021).

Schwartz, Claire, and jayy dodd. "An Interview with jayy dodd." *Los Angeles Review of Books*, July 27, 2017. https://lareviewofbooks.org/article/an-interview-with-jayy-dodd/.

Scott, Joan W. "Experience." In *Feminists Theorize the Political*, edited by Judith Butler and Joan W. Scott, 22–40. New York: Routledge, 1992.

Scott-Dixon, Krista, ed. *Trans/Forming Feminisms: Trans/Feminist Voices Speak Out*. Toronto: Sumach, 2006.

Sedgwick, Eve Kosofsky. *Epistemology of the Closet*. Oakland: University of California Press, 2008.

Segal, Lynne. "Generations of Feminism." *Radical Philosophy* 83 (1997): 6–16.

Selenite, Venus. "*Steven Universe* Is the Queerest Thing on TV, and I'm Obsessed." *The Tempest*, October 15, 2015. https://thetempest.co/2015/10/15/entertainment/steven-universe-is-the-queerest-thing-on-tv-and-im-obsessed/.

Selenite, Venus. *trigger: poems*. CreateSpace, 2016.

Selenite, Venus. *The Fire Been Here*. CreateSpace, 2017.

Serano, Julia. "Trans Feminism: There's No Conundrum about It." *Ms. Magazine*, April 18, 2012. http://msmagazine.com/blog/2012/04/18/trans-feminism -theres-no-conundrum-about-it/.

Sexton, Jared. "The Social Life of Social Death: On Afro-Pessimism and Black Optimism." *InTensions* 5 (2011): http://www.yorku.ca/intent/issue5/articles /jaredsexton.php (accessed March 29, 2021).

Shakur, Assata. *Assata: An Autobiography*. Chicago: Lawrence Hill, 1987.

Shange, Savannah. *Progressive Dystopia: Abolition, Anthropology, and Race in the New San Francisco*. Durham, NC: Duke University Press, 2019.

Sharpe, Christina. *In the Wake: On Blackness and Being*. Durham, NC: Duke University Press, 2016.

Sharpe, Christina. "Lose Your Kin." *The New Inquiry*, November 16, 2016. https:// thenewinquiry.com/lose-your-kin/.

Sirvent, Roberto. "BAR Book Forum: Fred Moten's 'Consent Not to Be a Single Being.'" Black Agenda Report, July 25, 2018. https://www.blackagendareport .com/bar-book-forum-fred-motens-consent-not-be-single-being.

Smith, Sara, and Pavithra Vasudevan. "Race, Biopolitics, and the Future: Introduction to the Special Section." *Environment and Planning D: Society and Space* 35 (2017): 210–21, https://doi.org/10.1177/0263775817699494.

Snorton, C. Riley. *Black on Both Sides: A Racial History of Trans Identity*. Minneapolis: University of Minnesota Press, 2017.

Snorton, C. Riley. "'A New Hope': The Psychic Life of Passing." *Hypatia* 24 (2009): 77–92.

Snorton, C. Riley. "Transfiguring Masculinities in Black Women's Studies." The Feminist Wire, May 18, 2011. http://thefeministwire.com/2011/05 /transfiguring-masculinities-in-black-womens-studies/.

Snyder, C. R., and Shane J. Lopez. *Handbook of Positive Psychology*. Oxford: Oxford University Press, 2001.

Solnit, Rebecca. *Hope in the Dark: Untold Histories, Wild Possibilities*. Chicago: Haymarket, 2016.

Spillers, Hortense. *Black, White, and in Color: Essays on American Literature and Culture*. Chicago: University of Chicago Press, 2003.

Spillers, Hortense. "The Idea of Black Culture." CR: *The New Centennial Review* 6 (2006): 7–28.

Spillers, Hortense. "Mama's Baby, Papa's Maybe: An American Grammar Book." *Diacritics* 17 (1987): 65–81, https://doi.org/10.2307/464747.

Spillers, Hortense. "The Scholarly Journey of Hortense Spillers." Brandeis NOW, February 1, 2019. https://www.brandeis.edu/now/2019/february/hortense -spillers-qa.html.

Spillers, Hortense, and Ann duCille. "Expostulations and Replies." *Differences* 29 (2018): 6–20, https://doi.org/10.1215/10407391-6999746.

Spillers, Hortense, Saidiya Hartman, Farah Jasmine Griffin, Shelly Eversley, and Jennifer L. Morgan. "'Whatcha Gonna Do?': Revisiting 'Mama's Baby, Papa's

Maybe: An American Grammar Book'—A Conversation with Hortense Spillers, Saidiya Hartman, Farah Jasmine Griffin, Shelly Eversley, and Jennifer L. Morgan." *Women's Studies Quarterly* 35, no. 2 (2007): 299–309.

Stallings, L. H. "Black Feminism: The Beginning and End of a World." Black Perspectives, December 3, 2018. https://www.aaihs.org/black-feminism-the -beginning-and-end-of-a-world/.

Stanley, Eric. "The Affective Commons." GLQ: A Journal of Lesbian and Gay Studies 24 (2018): 489–508, https://doi.org/10.1215/10642684-6957800.

Stanley, Eric A., Dean Spade, and Queer (In)Justice. "Queering Prison Abolition, Now?" *American Quarterly* 64 (2012): 115–27.

Stark, Hannah, and Timothy Laurie. "Deleuze and Transfeminism." In *Deleuze and the Schizoanalysis of Feminism: Alliances and Allies*, edited by Janae Sholtz and Cheri Lynne Carr, 127–40. London: Bloomsbury Academic, 2019.

Steinbock, Eliza. *Shimmering Images: Trans Cinema, Embodiment, and the Aesthetics of Change*. Durham, NC: Duke University Press, 2019.

Stoltenberg, John. "Magic Time! 'Trans Lives and Theater as Change Agent: A Q&A with Dane Figueroa Edidi and Natsu Onoda Power.'" *DCMetroTheaterArts*, December 27, 2016. https://dcmetrotheaterarts.com/2016/12/27/magic-time -trans-lives-theater-change-agent-qa-dane-figueroa-edidi-natsu-onoda-power/.

Stryker, Susan. "My Words to Victor Frankenstein above the Village of Chamounix: Performing Transgender Rage." GLQ: A Journal of Lesbian and Gay Studies 1 (1994): 237–54, https://doi.org/10.1215/10642684-1-3-237.

Stryker, Susan. *Transgender History: The Roots of Today's Revolution*. Berkeley, CA: Seal, 2017.

Stryker, Susan. "Transgender Studies: Queer Theory's Evil Twin." GLQ: A Journal of Lesbian and Gay Studies 10 (2004): 212–15.

Stryker, Susan, and Talia M. Bettcher. "Introduction: Trans/Feminisms." TSQ: Transgender Studies Quarterly 3 (2016): 5–14, https://doi.org/10.1215/23289252 -3334127.

Sycamore, Mattilda Bernstein. "We Are Always Crossing: Alexis Pauline Gumbs by Mattilda Bernstein Sycamore." BOMB, March 22, 2018. https://bombmagazine .org/articles/alexis-pauline-gumbs/.

Tate, Claudia. *Psychoanalysis and Black Novels: Desire and the Protocols of Race*. New York: Oxford University Press, 1998.

Taylor, Keeanga-Yamahta. *How We Get Free: Black Feminism and the Combahee River Collective*. Chicago: Haymarket, 2017.

Thomas, Greg. "Marronnons / Let's Maroon: Sylvia Wynter's 'Black Metamorphosis' as a Species of Maroonage." *Small Axe* 20 (2016): 62–78, https://doi.org/10 .1215/07990537-3481546.

Thomas, Greg. "Proud Flesh Inter/Views: Sylvia Wynter." *Proudflesh: A New Afrikan Journal of Culture, Politics and Consciousness* 4 (2006): n.p.

Thomas, Greg. "Sex/Sexuality and Sylvia Wynter's 'Beyond . . .': Anti-colonial Ideas in 'Black Radical Tradition.'" *Journal of West Indian Literature* 10, no. 2 (2001): 92–118.

Tinsley, Omise'eke Natasha. *Ezili's Mirrors: Imagining Black Queer Genders*. Durham, NC: Duke University Press, 2018.

Tinsley, Omise'eke Natasha. *Thiefing Sugar: Eroticism between Women in Caribbean Literature*. Durham, NC: Duke University Press, 2010.

"Transféminismes." Outrans, 2012. http://www.outrans.org/infos/articles /transfeminismes/ (accessed March 29, 2021).

Tudor, Alyosxa. "Im/possibilities of Refusing and Choosing Gender." *Feminist Theory* 20 (2019): 361–80.

Villarejo, Amy. "Tarrying with the Normative: Queer Theory and Black History." *Social Text* 23–24 (2005): 69–84.

Walcott, Rinaldo. "Outside in Black Studies: Reading from a Queer Place in the Diaspora." In *Black Queer Studies*, edited by E. Patrick Johnson and Mae G. Henderson, 90–105. Durham, NC: Duke University Press, 2005.

Walker, Alice. "In Search of Our Mothers' Gardens." In *Within the Circle: An Anthology of African American Literary Criticism from the Harlem Renaissance to the Present*, edited by Angelyn Mitchell, 401–9. Durham, NC: Duke University Press, 1994.

Walker, Alice. "In the Closet of the Soul: A Letter to an African American Friend." In *Words of Fire: An Anthology of African-American Feminist Thought*, edited by Beverly Guy-Sheftall, 538–48. New York: New Press, 1995.

Wallace, Julia R., and Kai M. Green. "Tranifest: Queer Futures." GLQ: *A Journal of Lesbian and Gay Studies* 19 (2013): 568–69.

Warren, Calvin L. *Ontological Terror: Blackness, Nihilism, and Emancipation*. Durham, NC: Duke University Press, 2018.

Weed, Elizabeth, and Naomi Schor, eds. *Feminism Meets Queer Theory*. Bloomington: Indiana University Press, 1997.

Weheliye, Alexander G. *Habeas Viscus: Racializing Assemblages, Biopolitics, and Black Feminist Theories of the Human*. Durham, NC: Duke University Press, 2014.

White, Derrick. "Black Metamorphosis: A Prelude to Sylvia Wynter's Theory of the Human." *C. L. R. James Journal* 16 (2010): 127–48.

Wilderson, Frank B., III, and C. S. Soong. "Blacks and the Master/Slave Relation." In *Afro-Pessimism: An Introduction*, editor unnamed. Minneapolis, MN: racked and dispatched, 2017. https://rackedanddispatched.noblogs.org/files/2017/01 /Afro-Pessimism.pdf (accessed March 29, 2021).

Williams, Rachel Anne. *Transgressive: A Trans Woman on Gender, Feminism and Politics*. London: Jessica Kingsley, 2019.

Williamson, Terrion L. *Scandalize My Name: Black Feminist Practice and the Making of Black Social Life*. New York: Fordham University Press, 2017.

Williamson, Terrion, and Kate Derickson. "Scandalize My Name: Terrion Williamson, Interviewed by Kate Derickson." Society and Space, 2018. https://www.societyandspace.org/articles/scandalize-my-name-black -feminist-practice-and-the-making-of-black-social-life-terrion-williamson -interviewed-by-kate-derickson.

Workneh, Lilly. "Angela Davis and Gloria Steinem on the Power of Revolutionary Movements." *Huffington Post*, June 3, 2016. https://www.huffingtonpost.com /entry/angela-davis-gloria-steinem-power-of-revolutionary-movements_us _57511492e4b0eb20fa0d900c.

Wright, Michelle M. *Physics of Blackness: Beyond the Middle Passage Epistemology.* Minneapolis: University of Minnesota Press, 2015.

Wynter, Sylvia. "The Ceremony Must Be Found: After Humanism." *Boundary 2* nos. 12–13 (1984): 19–70, https://doi.org/10.2307/302808.

Wynter, Sylvia. "Creole Criticism: A Critique." *New World Quarterly* 4 (1973): 12–36.

Wynter, Sylvia. "Ethno or Socio Poetics." *Alcheringa: Ethnopoetics* 2 (1976): 78–94.

Wynter, Sylvia, and David Scott. "The Re-enchantment of Humanism: An Interview with Sylvia Wynter." *Small Axe* 8 (2000): 119–207.

Zeisler, Andi. *We Were Feminists Once: From Riot Grrrl to CoverGirl®, the Buying and Selling of a Political Movement.* New York: PublicAffairs, 2016.

Index

ontology, 130; power's subjectivating qualities, 106; pronouns, 235n4; the subversive,
38–39; thinking in alliance, 7

Carastathis, Anna, 230n6
cárdenas, micha, 32
Carter, J. Kameron: blackness, 18, 88, 91, 212; flesh,
42, 246n11; parahuman life, 224; queer gen-
erativity, 223; sociality without exclusion, 41
Carter, Julian, 84
Cervenak, Sarah Jane: blackness, 88, 91; gather-
ing, 137; parahuman life, 224; queer generativ-
ity, 223; sociality, 41, 207
Chandler, Nahum, 7, 150–51, 218, 242n13
Christian, Barbara, 184
Chu, Andrea Long, 70, 153
circumscripts, 207
cis genders as normative endeavor, 38
Clarke, Cheryl, 144, 249n15
Clifton, Lucille, 209
clothing, 18–21
coalition, 207–8, 257n20
Cohen, Cathy, 7, 28, 37, 184, 249n15
Colebrook, Claire, 71, 78, 242n13
Collado, Morgan Robyn, 199
Collins, Patricia Hill, 21, 55, 239n39
Combahee River Collective, 49, 58–59, 128,
180, 192
Commander, Michelle D., 209
"cosmetics" (Selenite), 183–85, 255n15
counterintuitiveness, 111
Crawley, Ashon, 184, 210, 246n6
Crenshaw, Kimberlé, 186
cross-dressing, 20
crossing, 133
Cunningham, Nijah, 101

da Silva, Denise Ferreira: black feminism, 1, 48,
78, 227, 238n22; blackness, 90–91, 152, 186,
226, 247n5; Enlightenment rationality, 64;
imagining the world otherwise, 109–11; the
"other"-wise, 40; subjectivity, 152; the world
post-abolition, 140
Davis, Angela, 37, 218
death: blackness, 212, 223–26; black trans
women, 186, 213, 216; "Death Reality"
(McDonald), 214–16; narratives of blackness,
217; refusing, 224; transitioning as quiet killing,
164–65. See also violence
"Death Reality" (McDonald), 214–17
Deleuze, Gilles, 75–78, 80, 244n26, 245n35
"deliverance haiku" (Selenite), 187

demonic grounds, 95, 148, 247n16
de-personhood, 94–95
Derrida, Jacques, 210
desire's creative power, 5–6
Devereaux, Shaadi, 209
Diamond, Shea, 220
Diaz, Junot, 203
dodd, jayy: "Ask Two Different Niggas 'What
Is the Black Condition?,'" 152–53; "Babylon
After Ajanae Dawkins," 171–73; becoming-
black-woman, 151; being-but-not-being, 33;
The Black Condition ft. Narcissus, 166–73;
blackness, 152–53, 155, 164; black trans resilience, 214; blxckness, 149–53, 155–56; boundaries disinterest, 173; fear, 149–50; feminism,
162–66; femmeness, 154; futurity, 161–62, 167,
172; gender, 155–62, 168; gender radicality,
148–49, 160, 173–74, 253n6; joy, 205; "know I
been changed," 160; masculinity, 161; ouevre,
31; pronouns, 149, 252n5; subjectivity, 147–48,
152, 163, 165, 174; traniflesh, 151, 158, 160; transness, 151–53, 156–62, 164–66, 168; "We Cannot
Grieve What Doesn't Leave Us or I'll Be at
Every Function," 167–71
D'Oleo, Dixa Ramírez, 221
Douglass, Frederick, 98, 237n19
Dub: Finding Ceremony (Gumbs): overviews, 30,
116; abolition, 140–41; blackness, 141, 143–44;
black trans feminism, 133; experimental
aspects, 117; futurity, 143–44; gathering,
138–39; inclusivity, 136; letting go, 137, 143;
origin stories rejection, 136–37; ownership
critiques, 142–43; racial purity, 140–41; skin
color, 139–40; taxonomy rejection, 136–38;
transness, 138
Du Bois, W. E. B., 140, 146, 237n21
duCille, Ann, 86
Durban-Albrecht, Erin, 217

Edidi, Dane Figueroa: abolitionism, 193; "All Beginnings Have a Before," 197; black feminism,
31, 192; blackness, 192–94; For Black Trans
Girls Who Gotta Cuss a Mother Fucker Out
[...], 176; black trans womanness, 176, 194,
198; bodies, 195; fleshy emotionality, 196–97;
as goddess, 190–91, 197; identities, 191; "Life
Turns," 194–95; "Mythos: a Play in One Act,"
197–98; origins critiques, 197–98; "The Other
Four Women," 193; "Peaches," 194; "the rivers
of my flesh," 196–97; skin, 193–94; structural
critiques, 194; traniflesh, 196; transness,
191–93; transness vs. transgender, 191

Halberstam, Jack: black fugitivity, 26; on Butler, Judith, 235n4; identity terms, 13; revolution, 211; rightness, 85; trans feminism, 58; transgender and feminism, 2

Hammonds, Evelyn, 133–34

Harney, Stefano, 18

Hartman, Saidiya, 4, 73, 220

Hayden, Robert, 69, 242n6

Hayward, Eva, 226

Hedva, Johanna, 94–95, 247n14

Heilbrun, Carolyn, 49

Hinkle, Kenyatta A. C., 118

Hogan, Eboni, 115

homes, 84–86, 123–24

Hong, Grace, 184

hooks, bell, 15, 20

hope: black trans feminism, 31; challenges to, 199–202; definition, 202; fleeting escapes, 209–10; fugitive, 203–13, 215–17, 223–26; reasons for, 202–3; various thinkers on, 218–23. *See also* abolition

hopelessness, 200–1, 256n2

Horak, Laura, 1

Horton-Stallings, LaMonda, 128, 153–54, 161, 254n28

Howard, Zora, 223–25

Howie, Cary, 92–93

Hurston, Zora Neale, 11, 213, 238n11

Huxtable, Juliana, 248n39

identity: abolition, 64, 74–75; biocentric ordering problematics, 250n25; black and trans disrupting, 46–47; categories, 4–5, 13–14, 71–75, 95; as constant practice, 130–31; discourses, 6–7; dominant logics, 95; exteriority, 64; historically contingent, 90; limiting effects, 43; limits, 46–47; as normative ideal, 37; political, 40–41, 236n7; as practice, 130–31; putting-together of the self, 214; and subjectivity, 160; traniflesh reconfiguring, 71

identity theory (by author): Halberstam, Jack, 13; McDonald, CeCe, 215–16; McKittrick, Katherine, 250n25; Moten, Fred, 131; Wyeth, Geo, 37, 52; Wynter, Sylvia, 46

illusive flesh, 29, 69–70, 242n6

interpellation, 127

intersectionality: black feminism, 58, 239n47; blackness, 59, 178; black trans feminism, 7–8, 230n6; black women, 58, 239n47; Carastathis, Anna, 230n6; Nash, Jennifer, 58, 239n47, 241n4; Rifkin, Mark, 230n6; trans feminism, 58–59

Jardine, Alice, 244n22

Jordan, June, 249n15

joy, 205–13

Khan-Cullors, Patrisse, 203

Kincaid, Adrienne, 221

King, Tiffany Lethabo, 257n13

Kline, David L., 210

"know I been changed" (dodd), 160

Kokumo, 219

Koyama, Emi, 55–56, 239n40

Lamble, Sarah, 22, 229n1

Lang, Aaryn, 222

Lauretis, Teresa de, 7

Laurie, Timothy, 244n22

lesbianism, 249n15

Lewis, AJ, 53

life: abolition's commitment to different, 210; black, 210; blackness, 43, 100–1; as black trans feminism's aim, 201; endlessness, 225–26; fugitive hope, 203–13, 215–17, 223–26; parahuman, 224; possibility of, 224–25; social, 225–26; underlife, the, 98–100; various thinkers on, 218–23; "Won't Die Things (Howard)," 223–27

"Life Turns" (Edidi), 194–95

lived experience, 73, 243n17

living as resistance, 212–13

Lorde, Audre, 37, 50, 104, 178, 190

"loud haiku" (Selenite), 190

Lowe, Lisa, 104

Macharia, Keguro, 218–19

Mackey, Nathaniel, 83, 244n26

Malcolm X, 33

M *Archive: After the End of the World* (Gumbs): overviews, 30, 116; becoming-black-woman, 132; black feminist metaphysics, 129–31, 135; black trans feminism, 133; black women, 133–35, 144; experimental aspects, 117; gendered subjectivity, 126; gender radicality, 131–32; identity as practice, 130–31; paraontological aspects, 134–36; traniflesh, 132; the trans, 132–33; "you beyond you," 126, 130

marked woman, the, 121–22, 249n14

maroonage, 96–98

Martel, James, 97

masculinity, 161, 164–65, 168

Massumi, Brian, 236n34

McDonald, CeCe, 48, 208, 214–17, 238n22

McKittrick, Katherine, 100–1, 204, 247n16, 250n25, 257n13

183–85, 255n15; "deliverance haiku," 187; on
Edidi, Dane Figueroa, 190; failure, 181; *The
Fire Been Here,* 176; "loud haiku," 190; queerness, 177, 255n5; "rebellion haiku," 184–85;
"survival haiku," 190; "trigger," 187–90; trigger
overviews, 176, 182–83; violence shaping
life choices, 177; "water as substitution for
merlot," 256n16; on whiteness, 179–80
self-determination: blackness, 43; black trans
feminism, 14; gender, 24–25; legibilizing
frameworks limiting, 106; self-defense, 215;
trans feminism, 55–56; trans/figurative
blackness, 93; "trigger" (Selenite), 187–88;
unanticipation, 106
self-interrogation, 57
selflessness, 209
Serano, Julia, 229n1
sex as political category, 56
Sexton, Jared, 183
sexual orientation locations, 230n8
Shakur, Assata, 218
Sharpe, Christina, 125, 157, 202
silence, 190
skin, 134, 139–40, 193–94. *See also* flesh
Smith, Barbara, 249n15
Snorton, C. Riley: appositional flesh, 29; black
feminism, 52; blackness-transness relationship, 155, 196; enslaved people and gender,
20; epigraph quotations, 60, 62; "On Crisis
and Abolition," 199; queer emergence, 104–5;
subjectivities, 95; transfiguration, 91–92;
transness, 84
sociality: anti-social, 216; black feminism,
213; blackness, 91, 213; black social life, 99,
101, 212–13; black trans feminism, 211–12;
coalition, 207–8, 257n20; queerness, 179;
radical, 95, 112; traniflesh, 84; trans/figurative
blackness, 94–95, 101, 112; waywardness, 124;
without exclusion, 41
sociality-in-differentiation, 41
Spillers, Hortense: beginnings, 197; black
feminism, 2, 51, 249n6, 257n20; blackness,
29, 67, 180, 206–7, 240n2; black women, 128;
common ground-making, 257n20; femininity,
71, 242n13; flesh, 27, 68, 84; gender, 74; hope,
223; intramural critique, 32; marked women,
121–22; monstrosity, 71; names, 125; skin, 134;
ungendering, 67–68; the world's mess, 213.
*See also Spill: Scenes of Black Feminist Fugitiv-
ity* (Gumbs)
Spill: Scenes of Black Feminist Fugitivity
(Gumbs): overviews, 30, 116; becoming-

black-woman, 121–22; blackness, 127; black
trans feminism, 133; black women, 119–22;
cover image, 118–19; experimental aspects,
117; fugitivity, 118–20, 127, 144; gender, 125–27,
144; hell-no-subjectivity, 127–28; mirrors,
124–26; names, 125; narrative breakages, 117,
120; unpaginated section, 122–23; waywardness, 120, 123–24; women walking out, 123–25
Stallings, L. H., 29, 69–70, 242n6
Stanley, Eric A., 52
Stark, Hannah, 244n22
Steinbock, Eliza, 27, 236n34
Steven Universe (cartoon), 255n5
Stone, Sandy, 194
Stone Butch Blues (Feinberg), 145–47
Stryker, Susan, 58, 87, 102
subjectivity: overview, 3; after abolition, 130,
140; dodd, jayy, 147–48, 152, 163, 165, 174;
gender questions creating, 147–48; and
identity, 160; *M Archive* (Gumbs), 126;
power producing, 106; recognizability, 159;
Snorton, C. Riley, 95; *Spill* (Gumbs), 127–28;
traniflesh, 75, 86–87; trans, 105–8, 146, 159,
194; transed, 159; trans/figurative blackness,
95–96, 103–4; transsubjectivity, 194–95;
unanticipatable, 106
subversion and normativity, 38–39
"survival haiku" (Selenite), 190

Tate, Claudia, 5
taxonomies as constructions, 142
thinking multitudinously, 214
Tinsley, Omise'eke Natasha, 161, 198, 254n28
tranifest theory, 28, 68
traniflesh: overviews, 28–29, 68–69; black
radical tradition, 81; cutting sociality, 84;
dodd, jayy, 151, 158, 160; emergent force,
71, 86; gender, 70–71; home, 86; identity
reconfiguration, 71; and illusive flesh, 69–70;
M Archive (Gumbs), 132; opaque excesses,
82–83; subjectivity, 75, 86–87
trans: and blackness, 41–47; and the crossing,
133; and feminism, 53–60; homing desires,
84–86; living unapologetically, 159; radicality,
13; running from gender, 83–86; self-
effacement, 83; term meanings, 229n1
transblacking, 153–54
trans feminism: overview, 53–54; abolitionism,
3, 56–57; and black feminism, 58, 81; blackness, 59–60; gender disruption and radicality,
54, 56–57, 59–60; inclusivity, 55, 58–59; influ-
ences, 54; intersectionality, 58–59; politics